Phonological Templates in Development

OXFORD STUDIES IN PHONOLOGY AND PHONETICS

General editors
Andrew Nevins, *University College London*
Keren Rice, *University of Toronto*

Advisory editors
Stuart Davis, Indiana University, Heather Goad, McGill University, Carlos Gussenhoven, Radboud University, Haruo Kubozono, National Institute for Japanese Language and Linguistics, Sun-Ah Jun, University of California, Los Angeles, Maria-Rosa Lloret, Universitat de Barcelona, Douglas Pulleyblank, University of British Columbia, Rachid Ridouane, Laboratoire de Phonétique et Phonologie, Paris, Rachel Walker, University of Southern California

Phonological Templates in Development

MARILYN MAY VIHMAN

OXFORD
UNIVERSITY PRESS

OXFORD
UNIVERSITY PRESS

Great Clarendon Street, Oxford, OX2 6DP,
United Kingdom

Oxford University Press is a department of the University of Oxford.
It furthers the University's objective of excellence in research, scholarship,
and education by publishing worldwide. Oxford is a registered trade mark of
Oxford University Press in the UK and in certain other countries

First Edition published in 2019

Impression: 1

Published in the United States of America by Oxford University Press
198 Madison Avenue, New York, NY 10016, United States of America

British Library Cataloguing in Publication Data

Data available

Library of Congress Control Number: 2019938268

ISBN 978-0-19-879356-4

Printed and bound in Great Britain by
Clays Ltd, Elcograf S.p.A.

In memory of my parents,

Janine Nathan May
(1906–1963)
and
René Abraham May
(1895–1958)

Contents

Series preface

Oxford Studies in Phonology and Phonetics provides a platform for original research on sound structure in natural language within contemporary phonological theory and related areas of inquiry such as phonetic theory, morphological theory, the architecture of the grammar, and cognitive science. Contributors are encouraged to present their work in the context of contemporary theoretical issues in a manner accessible to a range of people, including phonologists, phoneticians, morphologists, psycholinguists, and cognitive scientists. Manuscripts should include a wealth of empirical examples, where relevant, and make full use of the possibilities for digital media that can be leveraged on a companion website with access to materials such as sound files, videos, extended databases, and software.

This is a companion series to *Oxford Surveys in Phonology and Phonetics*, which provides critical overviews of the major approaches to research topics of current interest, a discussion of their relative value, and an assessment of what degree of consensus exists about any one of them. The *Studies* series will equally seek to combine empirical phenomena with theoretical frameworks, but its authors will propose an original line of argumentation, often as the inception or culmination of an ongoing original research program.

How do children form generalizations over the shape of words in their developing lexicon in order for systems to emerge? Building on a lifetime of research, Marilyn Vihman demonstrates through case studies of nineteen children learning eight diverse languages that templatic shapes including foot type guide the structuring of whole-word forms, and that particular places of articulation are favoured to 'fill' these templates. The resulting model, accounting for cross-linguistic as well as ontogenetic variation, shows how prosodic and segmental strategies including coda omission, initial consonant omission, reduplication, and harmony are employed to achieve particular word-like targets. Grounding her work in exemplar theory and usage-based phonology, Vihman weaves together quantitative and theoretical analyses to shed light on the patterns of ambient language structures and individual child differences, as well providing far-reaching insight into the function of templates in child and adult phonological grammars.

Andrew Nevins
Keren Rice

Acknowledgements

I would like to begin by expressing my appreciation to the Series Editors, Andrew Nevins and Keren Rice, for inviting me to write for the series. This has given me the opportunity to pull together work I have been doing since the 1980s. It has allowed me to systematize and articulate my procedures, in the hope of tempting other investigators to test hypotheses I have developed over the years, using comparable analyses to address data from a more diverse range of languages. Beyond that, because my reviewers were enthusiastic about my tentative proposal to look into the role of templates in adult language—although I had given little serious thought to this proposition at the time—I have had the exhilarating further opportunity to expand my knowledge of Prosodic Morphology and to analyse intriguing short forms in both Estonian and French. To this I was also able to add a collection of English rhyming compounds that I began compiling over 15 years ago, inspired by Sharon Inkelas' (2003) study of her child's rhyming game. The search for more examples, and further analysis, led to fascinating reading and many helpful insights into the history and formation of rhyming compounds. I also thank Sharon for hosting me during a sabbatical term spent at the University of California, Berkeley, in 2016. And I am grateful to my reviewers, who read with attention and suggested many useful changes and clarifications both large and small. The revisions made with their advice in mind should make the book that much more accessible to my readers.

My investigation has been deepened and illuminated by discussion with many colleagues with similar interests, including Farrell Ackerman, Réka Benczes, Olivier Bonami, Wolfgang Dressler, Larry Hyman, Sharon Inkelas, Margaret Kehoe, Tobias Scheer, and Márton Sóskuthy. In addition, I am grateful to the colleagues who read chapters and provided invaluable feedback; these include Shelley Velleman, who collaborated with me on the very first paper I wrote on templates, as well as Dunstan Brown, Tamar Keren-Portnoy, and Peter Sells. But I must reserve my warmest thanks for my daughter, Virve-Anneli Vihman, who was the first to notice and begin collecting examples of the Estonian short forms analysed in Chapter 8; she is a collaborator on every aspect of that part of the book, for which she also hunted up sources and discussed analyses and interpretations. She and I also initiated the French short-form collection together in the summer of 2017, and she and her brother Raivo brain stormed up, in the past year, the first of the collection of English phonesthemes that I mention in a footnote in that chapter. Finally, Virve read through many of the chapters; I am grateful for her critical eye and constructive suggestions.

List of abbreviations

4wp	4-word point
25wp	25-word point
adess	adessive
AusE	Australian English
BEF	bisyllabic experimental form
BT	baby talk
C	consonant
CDI	Communicative Developmental Inventory
CH	consonant harmony
com	comitative
di	disyllabic
DST	Dynamic Systems Theory
ELC	early-learned consonants
Eng	English
FST	fixed shape templates
gem	geminate
gen	genitive
i	imitated word form
IDS	infant-directed speech
illat	illative
iness	inessive
K-S&D	Kilani-Schoch & Dressler
L1	first language
L2	second language
LLC	late-learned consonants
LT	late talker
MEF	monosyllabic experimental form
MLU	mean length of utterance
mono	monosyllabic
N	nasal
nom	nominative
ORF	ordinary replacement form
PCC	percent consonants correct
pl	plural
prop	proportion
prt	partititve
REDUP, RED	reduplication
sg	singular
TD	typically developing

TLT	transitional late talker
V	vowel
var	variant
VMS	vocal motor schemes
VOT	voice onset time
VST	variable shape templates
V&V	Vihman and Vihman (2011)
WILD	Workshop on Infant Language Development
WRAPSA	Word Recognition and Phonetic Structure Acquisition

The straight vertical line '|' in IPA transcription expresses 'a slight pause' in a child's production (see Bush et al., 1973).

1
Perspectives on phonological development

1.1 Phonological system

A theme running through linguistic research from its outset over 100 years ago has been the characterization of language *as a system*, conceptualized as something above and beyond individual acts of speaking or understanding speech. Saussure (1915/1959) famously distinguished *langue*, or the system of sound-meaning links that constitute the shared knowledge of a community of users, from *parole*, or particular instances of speech. Chomsky (1984, and in many other books and papers) specified a parallel but differently delineated distinction between *competence*, or the native speaker's knowledge of the grammar of his language, and *performance*, or what he saw as random deviations from that abstract, idealized grammar.

More specifically, phonologists have sought, at least since Baudouin de Courtenay (1871/1972), to establish the principles that distinguish a phonological system from the seemingly boundless variability of phonetics. Discussion and debate regarding the phonetics/phonology divide has been lively and highly productive in recent years. American structuralists of the mid-century maintained as axiomatic that 'once a phoneme, always a phoneme' (so that, for example, a speaker was not expected to waver, from one occasion to another, between American English /ɑ/ and /ɔ/ for the same words); in contrast, present-day usage-based phonologists recognize the well-established omnipresence of variation in speech and its relevance for the linguistic study of both perception and production, but also acknowledge the importance of phonological structure or system, which enables fluent and effective communication in the face of the dynamics of ongoing variation and change (e.g., Bybee, 2001; Pierrehumbert, 2016).

For some of us trained in mid-century a long-standing interest has been to demonstrate the force or active effects on usage (phonetics) of a constraining linguistic system (phonology). One place to look for such evidence is data bearing on the emergence of system in the child. This book is the culmination of nearly forty years of research into lexical and phonological development, motivated in part by the question, *how does the child create a system out of no system?* We ask what resources the child brings to the enterprise and what the mechanisms of system creation may be. As should be evident, these questions can only arise

Phonological Templates in Development. First edition. Marilyn May Vihman.
© Marilyn May Vihman 2019. First published 2019 by Oxford University Press.

consequent on a rejection of the nativist view that the most basic principles of language are a human genetic inheritance, known to the infant in advance of experience, since such a position would tend to undermine a developmentally oriented investigation into the mechanisms of lexical and phonological advance (for discussion, see Vihman, 2014, ch. 1; contrast Chomsky, 1964, who argues strongly that developmental data based on observation is irrelevant to linguistic theory).

This book is intended to explore the concept of templates in both child and adult phonology and to consider the pertinence of child data for understanding the origins and effects of linguistic system. This chapter will touch on a number of background issues in order to set the stage for thinking about them as, over the course of the book, we delve into data analyses bearing on both child and adult pattern-formation in the production of words and phrases. To anchor the account we first provide here our working definition of a template:

> A template is a *fixed pattern or schema* to which output must conform—regardless of the prosodic or segmental make-up of the input or of the processes that derive output from input.

Much of the burden of this book will be to elaborate on and illustrate this use of the term, as applied to adult as well as child phonology. For now, however, we turn more specifically to developmental issues.

1.1.1 Two paradoxes in early lexical and phonological development

Two seemingly paradoxical aspects of early child word production have long attracted the interest of researchers concerned with the child's transition into language in the first years of life. The first, which Ferguson and Farwell (1975) reported as a 'surprise' identified through close longitudinal analysis of the early words of three girls acquiring English, is the relative *accuracy of children's first word forms*. To show what this means, Table 1.1 presents the first recorded forms of *baby* as produced by three American girls at about 10 months of age[1] (this is a preview of data analysed in Chapter 3, where the data sources are also given; ample additional illustration of Ferguson and Farwell's finding will be provided in Chapter 4, which presents comparable data from children learning six more languages).

---

[1] Note that although neither the length of the target word nor the voicing of the stops is consistently matched in these early child attempts at the word, consonantal manner of articulation matches in all of them and place in all but one; similarly, the vowels are roughly equivalent to that of the stressed syllable of the target, if not the unstressed syllable. (We generally do not mark stress on child forms, which often give the impression of double-stress or spondaic rhythm: see Vihman, DePaolis, & Davis, 1998; Vihman & Velleman, 2000; Payne, Post, Astruc, Prieto & Vanrell, 2012.)

Table 1.1 Accuracy of early word forms: Three girls'
productions of American English *baby* /ˈbeɪbi/ at
about 10 months of age

Name	Child form
Alice	[pɛpɛ:], [tɛɪti:]
Deborah	[be], [pipe], [bebe]
Molly	[bæpæ]

The second paradox is that following the earliest word period most longitudinal studies uncover a *regression in accuracy*—a backwards step that can be ascribed to the emergence, in many if not all children, of more systematic, relatively stable phonological patterns that are 'idiosyncratic', or individual by child, and that may bear little or no resemblance to the patterns or processes familiar from adult phonology. Table 1.2 illustrates this regression by presenting two words from each of these girls following a few months of lexical and phonological development. We discuss these forms further in Chapter 3; for now, it can readily be seen that each girl's forms are more similar to one another than they are to their targets—and also that the pattern or template that underlies that similarity is different for each child. We encapsulate the three patterns in a tentative formulation of each child's apparent template.

This book will provide cross-linguistic data and analysis to demonstrate the extent of first-word accuracy and to discuss its origins. However, it will focus primarily on the emergent systematicity that underlies the child's temporary retreat from accuracy. This can first be observed in the organization of early words into a small number of preferred *prosodic structures* (CVCV, in the case of all of the word forms presented in Table 1.2); this is followed, for some but not all children, by the deployment of the more specific phonological patterns known as *templates* (which manifest the CVCV structure differently in Table 1.2 for each of the children).

We will begin with a brief account of the linguistic sources of the theoretical concept and term 'template' (1.2 Origins of 'templates' in phonological theory and child phonology). In order to more fully establish our theoretical and developmental orientation, we will then summarize (1.3 Dynamic systems and

Table 1.2 Regression in accuracy: Templates in three American children.
C consonant, V vowel, N nasal

Name	Age	Template	Target	Adult form	Child form
Alice	16 mos.	CVCi	*clean*	/klin/	[tiːni]
			flowers	/ˈflawərz/	[pʰɑːji, pʰadʲi, faːdi]
Deborah	17 mos.	C₁VC₁V	*bagel* (i)	/ˈbeɪgəl/	[bʌbu]
			pickle (i)	/ˈpɪkəl/	[baba]
Molly	16 mos.	CVN:ə	*bang*	/bæŋ/	[pɑnːə]
			down	/daʊn/	[tʰɑnːə]

the non-linearity of development) key tenets of Dynamic Systems Theory (DST: Thelen & Smith, 1994), which has informed our thinking for many years (see Vihman, DePaolis, & Keren-Portnoy, 2009, 2016). The overarching approach of DST, rooted in studies of motoric development, also serves remarkably well as a framework for understanding early lexical and phonological development.

In relation to language development more specifically our views draw on exemplar theory and usage-based phonology. In this chapter we provide a brief account of these approaches (1.4 Holistic approaches to phonology) and then present a sketch of phonological development research over the past forty years, with its heavy emphasis on infant speech perception, segmentation, and distributional learning and its relative neglect of production (1.5 Infant speech perception research, distributional learning, and the role of production). To this we add a production-oriented account of the transition from babbling to word use, based on observational data, theory, and experimental work (1.6 Phonological production and 'selectivity').

Finally, we consider evidence as to the process of lexical systematization, based on recent experimental studies of both adults and children (1.7 Lexical system-building). In closing the chapter we set out our goals and basic research questions and outline the plan for the book.

1.2 Origins of 'templates' in phonological theory and child phonology

Soon after the long promised publication of Chomsky and Halle's *Sound Pattern of English* in 1968 the field began to experience a shift in focus, away from segmental and rule-based phonology and toward prosodic structure and output forms. Although the shift took over twenty years to unfold in full, one of the first papers to mark the change in perspective was Kisseberth (1970). This paper proposed that some rules, although structurally distinct, share the common function of assuring *favoured output forms* (these are 'rule conspiracies').

Templates are a way of delineating output patterns. The adoption of templates into contemporary phonological theory originated in McCarthy's 1979 thesis, which drew on both the traditional concept of template in Semitic studies and emergent formal phonological ideas about autosegmental representation and planar segregation (see Goldsmith, 1990). McCarthy's prosodic analyses inspired the first use of the term 'template' with reference to child phonology (Menn, 1983), but the concept of 'whole-word' or 'holistic' child phonological patterns was introduced by Waterson (1971), who had been trained in Firthian linguistics (see Chapter 2). Nevertheless, for many years the dominant work in the field of phonological development was Smith's segment-and-rule-oriented diary study of his son Amahl (1973).

In the mid-1990s the fields of both adult and child phonology underwent further shifts. On the one hand, Optimality Theory began to be widely adopted as the preferred framework for phonological studies (see Kager, 1999; Scheer, 2011). On the other hand, ideas about exemplars, which had developed in psychology, began to figure in studies of phonological development (Jusczyk, 1992). And around the same time, experimental studies carried out with infants and children as well as adults demonstrated the power of distributional or statistical learning (Saffran, Aslin, & Newport, 1996; Saffran, Newport, Aslin, Tunick, & Barrueco, 1997; see the commentary by Bates & Elman, 1996). Both the exemplar approach and the experimental evidence of distributional learning added considerably to our understanding of the sources of infant knowledge about structure, as we discuss below.

Macken's overview chapter on 'Phonological acquisition' (1995), which appeared before the effect of these later dramatic changes in perspective could begin to be felt, marks a watershed in thinking in this area. As a way of framing the perspectives that we develop in this chapter we will consider some of Macken's arguments and constructs. Our views diverge from hers in many respects, but her formulation is sufficiently strong and clear to provide a useful point of departure.

Macken begins by highlighting the unfortunate polarization of the field of phonological acquisition into two camps: 'empiricists', who tend to be phoneticians or connectionists, and 'rationalists', who tend to be phonologists. The field remains divided today, but as we indicate in Chapter 9, formalists are no longer necessarily nativists (see Fikkert & Levelt, 2008; McAllister Byun, Inkelas, & Rose, 2016) and prosodic structure now plays a far larger role in adult phonology, while the notions of 'underlying representation' and the rules required to convert them to surface forms have largely disappeared from contemporary phonological discourse. It remains the case, however, that 'much of the acquisition field is [involved in] ... a vigorous debate over what the child knows and in what format the knowledge is represented' (Macken, 1995, p. 672).

Macken identifies as the central question for acquisition the difficult problem of how phonological learning is possible at all, given 'incomplete and contradictory input' (1995, p. 672). The question now appears out-dated, given ever-increasing evidence of the extent and significance of distributional learning, which demonstrates that infants are able to extract general patterns from ongoing exposure to speech. Many issues remain unresolved, but combining implicit statistical learning with the item learning that Macken discusses seems to put to rest the claim that learning alone could never be sufficiently powerful to deliver the complex linguistic knowledge that the child eventually attains (see Vihman, 2014, ch. 2, for further discussion). Macken herself is persuaded by Chomsky's claims that learning (from input speech) must be supplemented by 'a priori structures that determine the speed of acquisition, constraints on variation, and the independence from limiting factors like intelligence', but she concedes that 'empirical evidence showing the significant role of learning includes individual variation and cross-language differences' (1995, p. 672).

Macken notes that most children go through a stage in which their production is limited to one or two syllables—perhaps due to the universality of the CV syllable, the disyllabic foot, and the prosodic word. She argues against the view that these constraints might be due to memory limitations, but in the end, while arguing that 'memory capacity does not change much over the course of development' (1995, p. 684), she concludes that it is lack of lexical experience that prevents the child from successfully deploying memory in the earliest period. Indeed, research has shown that phonological memory both builds on and supports word learning (Keren-Portnoy, Vihman, DePaolis, Whitaker, & Williams, 2010). The issue of the role of memory in child phonological patterning, variability, and production errors will recur in the chapters that follow.

Macken discusses a type of child error that is the product of 'the child actively forming generalizations over classes of segments and subsets of the lexicon, in effect constructing interim, relatively abstract, autonomous phonological rule systems'; she sees this as supporting her contention that 'some aspects of acquisition fall outside the explanatory range of phonetic (segment-centered) theories' (1995, p. 687). These rules have their origin in 'isolated accuracy' (or item-learning), followed by a period of experimentation, rule construction, and overgeneralization, which eventually yields to construction of a more general and more accurate rule. A straightforward example is Hildegard Leopold's 'progressive idiom', *pretty* [prɪ̥ti̥], which is later assimilated into her system as [bidi] (Leopold, 1939): The early, more accurate production clearly shows that it is not articulatory limitations per se that lead to the later simplification; instead, the child's preferred word-production patterns are overgeneralized to assimilate this word, a templatic effect that nicely illustrates the kind of regression discussed above.

Macken asks, 'What is the purpose of creating generalizations only to discard them at the next stage?' (1995, p. 689)—but the question cannot be answered in this form, as it seems to ascribe intentionality to the child's behaviour, which should instead be considered an implicit expression of lexical systematization. (While avoiding the implication of intention or 'purpose', we will return repeatedly to the question of the function of both adult and child templates.) However, Macken makes the valid point that most adult assimilatory rules affect sequential segments (are 'string-adjacent'), whereas child templates, such as the commonly occurring consonant harmony pattern (seen in Deborah's form for *bagel* in Table 1.2), are based on the word as a whole. This is a major typological difference that stems, as Macken notes, from the 'predominance [in children] of highly rigid, simple prosodic structure' (1995, p. 693), which is rare in adult languages.

Macken begins her chapter by aptly stating that 'a theory of language acquisition is incomplete without a theory of cognition and learning that is compatible with what we know about the mind and human development' (1995, p. 671). This indeed is the underlying reason why much of her argument is no longer relevant: Besides the theoretical shifts in the study of both adult and child phonology mentioned above, a new approach to understanding development itself began to be widely disseminated with the publication, in 1994, of Thelen and Smith's monograph, *A Dynamic Systems Approach to the Development of Cognition and Action*. In section 1.3 we summarize some of the principal ideas of this influential work. Despite the fact that the model was in no way specifically designed to account for phonological development, we see it as the single most relevant framework available.

1.3 Dynamic systems and the non-linearity of development

Dynamic Systems Theory (Thelen & Smith, 1994 [DST]) derives its principles from chaos theory (e.g., Prigogine & Stengers, 1984) and is centrally concerned with accounting for developmental process in terms of a general theory of change in complex systems (see also Gottlieb, Wahlsten, & Lickliter, 2006 and Gottlieb, 2014, for the closely related psychobiological systems perspective). DST rejects linearity, in which the end is prefigured in the beginning state, in favour of

> a science for systems with a history, systems that change over time, where novelty can be created, where the end-state is not coded anywhere, and where behavior at the macrolevel can, in principle, be reconciled with behavior at the microlevel.
>
> (Thelen & Smith, 1994, p. 49)

With its close longitudinal studies of infant motoric development DST also provides a useful counterweight to the overwhelming emphasis in contemporary infancy research on group studies of perception and speech processing, in disregard of production. The theoretical ideas gain additional force and plausibility as an account of human development through their grounding in the theoretical framework developed by Edelman (1987, 1988, 1989, 1992) and related empirical evidence from neuroscience.

Thelen and Smith provide an extended critique of the entrenched Cognitive Science distinction between competence, or 'abstract-symbolic knowledge', and performance. In that conceptualization competence is 'independently determined by distinct biological constraints on human language; its structure is not determined by the vagaries of real-time language use, memory, attention, or other "performance" factors' (1994, p. 27). In sharp contrast, Thelen and Smith emphasize instead the *embodiment* of knowledge, which emerges from the constant interaction between the fundamental systems of action and perception, memory and attention. Thelen and Smith see 'knowledge and meaning' as 'distributed across units—in patterns of activation' (p. 39) and relate their view to connectionist approaches, in which 'knowledge is assembled in real time, in context, from units that do not in and of themselves look like or contain the resultant knowledge' (p. 39; for related views, see Varela, Thompson, & Rosch, 1991; Elman et al., 1996; Mareschal et al., 2007).

Throughout their 1994 monograph Thelen and Smith elaborate on the critical interaction of perception and action, both in general and in specific relation to the development of walking and reaching. Several key ideas, such as the essential non-linearity of development, the importance of past experience in system advances, and the role of variability, are strikingly pertinent to phonological development as well. The central DST tenet is that the interaction of perception and action is foundational for cognitive development. Thelen and Smith see infants as developing not so much through the *construction* of knowledge (as in Piagetian views, as well as related ideas about phonological development that were current in the 1980s: see Menn, 1983; Macken & Ferguson, 1983) as by *selecting* 'from all the possible multimodal associations those that represent persistent real-life correlates of perception and action in the world' (1994, p. 191).

Thelen and Smith assert paradoxically that '*movement must itself be considered a perceptual system*' (1994, p. 193, their italics) or a 'perceptual category' (p. 277). This follows from their finding that self-produced movement is critical, and that 'dynamic category formation – the infant's basic organization of the world – must be paced and constrained by the ability to produce and control that movement' (pp. 194f.). They propose further that 'the onset of a new motor skill...shakes up the stable system, it provides the needed variability, the quasi-stability that allows the system to explore new ways of grouping the components' (p. 204). In summary:

> categories – the foundations of knowledge – emerge from the infants' ongoing activities and encounters with the world...Their categories are informed by their experiences, which are naturally variable, and thus provide the messy, rich, redundant information from which neural selection can act...Movement is not incidental to learning, but part of the perceptual package that is the basis of categorization and recategorization...Knowledge is limited not primarily by deficits in storage but in the ability to adequately sample and thus categorize the world. (p. 211)

Thus, in sharp contrast with the emphasis in generative approaches on the 'poverty of the stimulus', or the absence of adequate information about linguistic structure in the data to which a child is exposed, Thelen and Smith emphasize the child's creation of an internal model of the world through their actions and experience of perceiving those actions in relation to the effects that follow. This extends quite naturally to vocal actions and the percepts they create as well as any social responses that they may trigger. The child's vocal production is highly instable or variable, but repeated deployment of vocal forms, accompanied by the perception of their time-locked auditory effects, builds an internal model that will serve to highlight broadly similar patterns in the input and to provide a schema onto which such patterns can be mapped. We see this as a critical first step in word-form learning; we further discuss this model, the 'articulatory filter' (Vihman, 1993, 1996), in a later section.

In an extended illustration of DST as an approach to the study of motor development Thelen and Smith offer an account of the process of learning to reach for and grasp objects, based on a longitudinal study of four infants observed weekly for a period of several months each. Thelen and Smith elaborate their general principles in this eloquent passage:

> Each act ... [has] within it nested scales of activity: the actions in the here and now that are inextricably tied to the immediate dynamic context, the history of actions in the past that built the attractor landscape, and the molding of the future landscape in the repeated acts of the here and now ... From the messy details of real time – from the variability and context sensitivity of each act – global order can emerge ... Knowledge ... is not a thing, but a continuous process; not a structure, but an action, embedded in, and derived from, a history of actions.   (1994, p. 247)

Thelen and Smith find that the achievement of effective reaching (like phonological development) shows both remarkable individuality *and* global convergence of solutions. They insist that 'reaching is neither prefigured nor constructed by the progressive mapping of the hand and the eye' (p. 249), as previous studies had suggested; instead of looking for *essential or innate components* or a single cause of visual-motor mapping to discover where the new behaviour comes from, Thelen and Smith focus on reach as an *emergent perceptual-motor pattern*, arguing that 'reaching is acquired through the soft assembly of mutually interacting, equivalent, multiple-component structures and processes within a context' (p. 249). For any given child, according to their analysis, one of these components acts as a 'control parameter' or gateway to further advance, depending on the particularities of that child's skills and experiences.

To draw a parallel to which we will refer later, among the components that enter into word production as potential control parameters we can mention such internal factors as advances in articulatory skill, the corresponding advances in phonological memory, the social or communicative impulse to 'join in' with interactional episodes, and the maturation of a capacity for focused attention, which may strengthen the infant's experience of selected input patterns as matches for internal schemas; in addition, the social context must, at a minimum, provide sufficient exposure to vocal forms in the input.

As is clear here as well as in Thelen and Smith's accounts of learning to walk and to reach, detailed longitudinal observations of a small number of infants provide a kind of understanding and insight into the nature of development that large group studies, which necessarily gloss over individual differences, cannot begin to offer. In this book we will pursue a similar approach in our investigation of first word production and template formation in groups of two to eight children, each learning one of eight languages.

1.4 Holistic approaches to phonology

Generative phonology has consistently emphasized the abstract nature of linguistic structure, characterized in terms of minimal units such as distinctive features (Chomsky & Halle, 1968), and its proponents have argued that phonological knowledge (taken to be unlearnable from mere exposure to speech, given the absence of surface evidence of structure) must derive from innately provided universal principles, or Universal Grammar. In contrast, cognitive linguistics has, since the 1980s, provided an approach to the analysis of language that sees representations as emergent from concrete episodes of use, whether receptive or expressive, and that relies on constructions and schemas, or units that go beyond the segment (Bybee, 1985, 2001, 2010; Langacker, 1987; Croft, 2001; see also Benczes, 2019). More broadly, over the past twenty to thirty years a number of important theoretical moves occurring outside the dominant generative paradigm have brought to phonology concepts of category formation long since proposed and widely accepted in psychology. Such psychological concepts include *exemplar theory*, with its rejection of the normalization of heard forms in the perceptual processing of speech (e.g., Goldinger, 1996, 1998; Johnson, 1997, 2006, 2007) and the related acceptance of redundant and non-essential information in representations (e.g., Goldsmith, 1990; Wade & Möbius, 2010; Pufahl & Samuel, 2014; Pierrehumbert, 2016), and *distributional learning*, a basic mechanism for deriving knowledge of structure from limited sampling (McClelland, McNaughton, & O'Reilly, 1995; Saffran et al., 1996, 1997; Ellis, 2002, 2005).

The move from atomic, stripped-down units of analysis to more holistic, informationally rich words, patterns, or schemas has been widespread within the fields of phonetics, phonology, and morphology (Pierrehumbert, 2016). For example, Redford (2015) proposes, from a speech production perspective, that the basis of on-line planning is 'schemas: temporally structured sequences of remembered actions and their sensory outcomes' (p. 141); these are activated by the associated communicative goals that link form and meaning. Similarly, Hall, Hume, Jaeger, and Wedel (2018) introduce a new model that emphasizes the role of word predictability in shaping phonology and treats as basic meaning-bearing units rather than sublexical units such as segments. Both of these approaches have grown out of usage-based models (Barlow & Kemmer, 2000; Bybee, 2001, 2006, 2010; see also Bybee & Hopper, 2001), which trace aspects of sound change to the dynamics of language use and also point the way to understanding language development as emerging from use.

In a related field Blevins (2006, 2016) has argued for 'word-based morphology', which receives strong support from current psycholinguistic studies (see Hay & Baayen, 2005, for an overview of relevant experimental work). Similarly, Ackerman and Malouf (2017) provide a lucid account of insights from the system-oriented word-and-paradigm approach into the 'paradigm cell filling problem' (Ackerman, Blevins, & Malouf, 2009), or the question of how speakers of languages with extensive inflectional morphology draw on their experience of a subset of forms to fill in elements that they have not yet heard. This approach also addresses the issue of learnability.

In what follows we briefly consider exemplar models and relate them to our central concern with phonological development and particularly production. We then discuss how holistic approaches to phonology relate to our use of *prosodic structure* as a starting point for template analysis.

1.4.1 Exemplar models in phonological development

Jusczyk (1992) was the first to bring to the attention of researchers concerned with child language long-standing ideas about exemplar representations that had developed through studies of categorization. Jusczyk (1992) provides a clear account of the distinction between prototypes (which serve as a basis for inter-preting experimental results with infants in Grieser & Kuhl, 1989, and Kuhl, 1991, for example) and exemplars, which he incorporated into his WRAPSA model (1992, 1993, 1997) and later tested in some of his experimental work (Houston & Jusczyk, 2000, 2003). Accordingly, we quote here at length from Jusczyk's account, which also provides his justification for preferring these more direct products of sensorimotor processing as a basis for understanding category formation over the more abstract conceptualization afforded by prototypes.

> Viewing lexical representations as prototypes implicitly assumes the existence of some sort of generic memory system wherein representations of categories are stored...Thus, the description of the sound structure of the lexical item in memory is a general one, as opposed to a particular one, that corresponds to an utterance that the child had actually encountered. Most cognitive models make this assumption that unitary, abstract representations of categories are stored in mem-ory and matched to incoming signals during recognition. However, recently an alternative conceptualization of this process has been put forth. Accounts based on the storage of individual exemplars may provide a more accurate view of the way that category information is recognized and remembered...The notion behind such models is that 'only traces of individual episodes are stored and...aggregates of traces acting in concert at the time of retrieval represent the category as a whole' (Hintzman 1986, p. 411). Jacoby and Brooks (1984) argue that if the available representations are of specific episodes, then generality would come from treating similar situations analogously...'A word could be identified by reference to a previous occurrence...in a similar context, from a similar source, and in a similar format, rather than by reference to a generalized representation...' (Jacoby and Brooks, 1984, p. 3). (Jusczyk, 1992, p. 45)

Among the points that Jusczyk makes in support of 'multiple-trace models', the demonstration, in Logan (1988), that 'an instance-based model can provide an account of automaticity in skill learning' (Jusczyk, 1992, p. 46) is particularly pertinent to the account of first word production that we propose below. Jusczyk notes that fluent speech recognition conforms to Logan's definition of automatic processing as 'fast, effortless, autonomous, and unavailable to conscious aware-ness' (p. 46). Jusczyk did not have production skills in mind here, but these ideas fit nicely with the suggestion that frequent exposure to a particular vocal pattern, particularly one that is self-produced, can result in the automatic, 'off-the-shelf' availability of a (sensorimotor) routine that may then be activated by hearing broadly similar phonological sequences in input speech.

Jusczyk (1992) further suggests that 'not every utterance that an infant hears will be recorded as an episodic trace...In general, storage of sound patterns requires that *some extra effort* be given to processing the speech' (p. 46, our italics). This is an aspect of exemplar learning or exemplar memory that has received very little attention. Jusczyk proposes *efforts after meaning* as one likely basis for infant memory for an utterance. It is equally likely that 'resonance' (Johnson, 1997, 2006), or global similarity with a vocal pattern that the child herself has been producing, would be important in marking utterances for reten-tion, especially as regards word learning in the first year, before an expressive lexicon has begun to develop (for experimental evidence, see Renner, 2017; Majorano, Bastianello, Morelli, Lavelli, & Vihman, 2019).

Jusczyk further elaborates his understanding of an exemplar model as follows:

> The role of experience is not to modify previously stored traces; rather, new traces are added to those already in secondary (i.e., long-term) memory. The addition of a new trace modifies the way that the whole memory system behaves. The more a new trace differs from preceding ones, the greater is the change in the behaviour of the memory system during subsequent efforts at identification of new items. Recognition in a system such as this occurs when a new input, or probe, is broadcast simultaneously to all traces in secondary memory. Each trace is activated according to its similarity to the probe...All traces in secondary memory contribute to this echo. If several traces are strongly activated, then the content of the echo primarily will reflect their common properties.
>
> (Jusczyk, 1992, p. 47)

(The idea is succinctly expressed in Goldinger's [1996] title, 'Echoes of echoes? An episodic theory of lexical access'.) Jusczyk goes on to suggest that children's early lexical representations are likely to be minimally specified, given a lack of any pre-existing lexicon, or a very small one; he assumes that random-like variability will gradually give way to greater stability with further development. He comments that only the stress pattern and 'a few of its key phonetic features' might survive in the memory trace of a word (Jusczyk, 1992, p. 47; cf. also Jusczyk, 1986).

Jusczyk's 1992 chapter is based on a talk presented at the 1989 conference that officially closed the Child Phonology project that Ferguson initiated in 1967 (see Ferguson, Menn, & Stoel-Gammon, 1992). It gives us the 'state of the art' in Jusczyk's thinking before he embarked on experimental work designed to discover the granularity, or level of detail, that children's early word representations might involve. Based on the very first of those studies (Jusczyk & Aslin, 1995) Jusczyk altered his earlier view of an initially global representation. Instead, he came to conclude that children were registering in their early lexical representations what he (and others after him) came to refer to as 'fine phonetic differences'.[2]

The limitations of these carefully structured experimental findings were not discussed at the time. These include at least the following:

(1) Jusczyk and Aslin tested for children's recognition of newly trained English monosyllabic words after a change to the onset consonant, which is highly salient, and found that the change blocked word-form recognition; they did not consider the difference that *position in the word* might make to a child's response to such a change.

(2) This and later studies along the same line—focusing on infants' ability to segment newly trained words from passages—gave no attention to children's long-term memory for word forms *familiar from frequent use in everyday life*. That line of research was initiated by Hallé and Boysson-Bardies (1994, 1996), who found that untrained, common French disyllabic words (e.g., *bonjour* 'hello', *lapin* 'rabbit'), when pitted against rarely occurring but phonologically similar words (e.g., *cobaye* 'guinea pig'), held infant attention by 11 months; this was also the case when the onset consonant was replaced (giving *vonjour, napin*, neither of them real words). This finding suggested 'global' rather than segmentally analysed representations; that is, it went against the characterization of infant lexical representations as being specified in 'fine phonetic' detail.

(3) Similarly, the trained-word segmentation studies did not address the representations that might underlie children's early lexical *output forms*.

(4) And, finally, those studies did not explore child responses to changes in other parts of words, such as the onset consonant of an unstressed syllable, or a coda consonant, or vowels in different positions, let alone possible interactions between these elements. (Hallé & Boysson-Bardies, 1996, explored the effects of changes to the onset of both first and second syllable of French disyllabic words, noting in passing that accentuation might be a factor affecting salience for infant learners.)

Several investigators working with different languages have since taken up the untrained word-form recognition experiments that began with consideration of French disyllables. These studies have generally replicated the finding of

---

[2] Pierrehumbert (2003) made the cogent objection that 'a phonologically minimal categorical distinction in the adult system' (such as the segmental categories targeted in Jusczyk and Aslin's experiment: /b/ vs. /d/, /b/ vs. /g/, or /t/ vs. /k/) cannot fairly be termed a 'fine phonetic difference' (p. 120).

reliable child representation, by 11 months, of the stressed syllable (e.g., in English: Vihman, Nakai, DePaolis, & Hallé, 2004; Welsh: Vihman, Thierry, Lum, Keren-Portnoy, & Martin, 2007; Dutch: Swingley, 2005; Italian: Vihman & Majorano, 2017; Hebrew: Segal, Keren-Portnoy, & Vihman, under review), while at the same time revealing children's tendency to *disregard* changes that occur in unaccented syllables or codas or at the onset of words with medial geminates. This series of studies thus provides useful insight into the way that the exemplars laid down by children in the early stages of word learning might be different from those of adults, as described by Bybee (2010, p. 14):

> Exemplar representations are rich memory representations; they contain, at least potentially, all the information a language user can perceive in a linguistic experience.

The extent to which the child's previous experience—with the flow of input speech, the repeated occurrence of high-frequency items in daily verbal interactions, and, in due course, her own adult-like vocal forms—informs the laying down of exemplar traces remains to be seriously investigated. Bybee (2010) comments further that 'for a child or language learner, each new token of experience can have a much larger impact on representation than it can for an adult' (p. 22)—but we note again that the granularity of those representations remains an open issue.

1.4.2 Prosodic structures and phonological templates

We use the term 'prosodic structures' here to identify the CV-skeletons basic to a child's early word forms. The point is to be able to characterize a child's favoured word production patterns in terms of *overall word shapes*, which differ from child to child within a single language group as well as from language to language. In contrast, in the analysis of children's patterns we reserve the term 'template' primarily for prosodic structures that are used to assimilate challenging adult forms through 'adaptation', as in the much cited case of Priestly's son Christopher, whose CVjVC template mediated production of disyllabic word targets with coda, such as *chocolate* [kajak], *candle* [kajal], *blanket* [bajak] (see Chapter 6 and Appendix II). In some cases, without going so far as to modify challenging forms to fit a preferred pattern or routine, a child may reveal template use through 'overuse' or 'over-selection' of a particular word shape ('selection' rather than 'adaptation'); this is an alternative response to the phonological challenges of the adult language. We will provide ample illustration of both prosodic structure and template use in later chapters. Here we briefly trace uses of the term 'prosodic structure' in the phonological literature, to clarify our own use and prevent misunderstanding.

The expression can be used in a number of different ways (see Prieto & Esteve-Gilbert, 2018). For example, it may refer to (i) the *accentual pattern of words* (trochaic, or strong-weak, vs. iambic, or weak-strong stress on disyllables: e.g., Jusczyk, Cutler, & Redanz, 1993), (ii) the *overall rhythmic pattern of a language*, rooted in the alternation of consonantal and vocalic intervals in the segmental stream (e.g., Mehler et al., 1988; Mehler, Dupoux, Nazzi, & Dehaene-Lambertz, 1996; Ramus, Nespor, & Mehler, 1999), or, more formally, (iii) the *units of the prosodic hierarchy* proposed by Selkirk (1980; see also Nespor & Vogel, 1986). Prosodic structure may also refer to units below the phonological or prosodic word level, the lowest level in the original hierarchy—namely, the *onsets and rimes* or *moras* that structure syllables (Fikkert, 1994; Kehoe, 2013).

The fundamental insight behind the edited volume *Signal to Syntax* (Morgan & Demuth, 1996) is Gleitman and Wanner's (1982) suggestion that the prosodic structure of the speech infants hear might help them to make a start on learning grammatical structure. The kind of infant sensitivity to the rhythms of their language on which this hypothesis was based received good experimental support in the decade following their proposal (e.g., Mehler et al., 1988), particularly from the studies initiated by Jusczyk and his colleagues (see Jusczyk, 1997). The expectation that infants build on an early attraction to what is prosodically salient is embodied in Jusczyk's WRAPSA model, which sees the grouping of prominent acoustic features (syllables with higher or more dynamic pitch pattern, or longer duration, for example) as basic to the child's ability to extract patterns from running speech.

The prosodic structures that Jusczyk sees as the outcome of that grouping process are akin to those that will constitute the first step in our analyses here: *whole-word forms made up of syllable sequences of different lengths and organization*, such as the universally occurring CV, disyllabic CVCV, onsetless VCV or the final-consonant-bearing structures CVC and CVCVC. In this usage 'prosodic structure' is roughly equivalent to the skeleton of autosegmental phonology (Goldsmith, 1990).

To account for children's knowledge of prosodic structure Selkirk (1996) refers to 'innate knowledge of the universal constraints' (p. 210). We take the position that instead of positing innate knowledge it is possible to trace the origins of children's initial representations of prosodic structure to sensorimotor or cognitive sources. These sources include not only (i) the *perceptual experience* of salient elements of the input speech stream that Jusczyk and others have emphasized but also, as described below, (ii) the *neurophysiology of vocal production* and (iii) the *memory processes* that relate heard patterns to existing knowledge based on production. An emphasis on the child's personal multimodal experiences with the perception and production of speech forms, and the construction of representations in memory based on those experiences, is fundamental to our approach to phonological and lexical development.

1.5 Infant speech perception research, distributional learning, and the role of production

From the first experimental study (Eimas, Siqueland, Jusczyk, & Vigorito, 1971) infant speech perception attracted strong scholarly attention. These studies quickly established that, like adult English speakers, infants as young as four months of age discriminate the voicing contrast /ba/ vs. /pa/ in a 'categorical' way. That is, infants showed (by increasing their sucking rate) that they were responsive to a change in the synthesized stimuli they were hearing (which differed systematically, in 20 ms increments, in the size of the voice onset time [VOT] lag between stop release and vowel onset)—but only when the change *crossed* the VOT category boundary between short lag and long lag, the boundary observed for obstruent voicing in English and many other (though by no means all) languages; the infants were unresponsive to changes occurring between equally distinct pairs of stimuli that fell *within* either of the two categories. The authors took this to be evidence that 'speech is special', another way of demonstrating innate infant preparedness for language use. This was in line with Chomsky's then current proposal (1965) that only an innate 'Language Acquisition Device' could account for infants' remarkable ability to learn a linguistic system successfully—and with surprising speed, compared to adult second-language learners—at an age when infants seem relatively incompetent with regard to most other skills. Chomsky had argued that, given the complexity of language (particularly its syntactic structure), it is hard to conceive of a way that language could be learned by 'an organism initially uninformed as to its general character' (1965, p. 58).

The Eimas et al. study was subsequently replicated with many other pairs of segmental contrasts. At the same time, however, studies with chinchillas (Kuhl & Miller, 1975, 1978) and other animals (Kuhl & Padden, 1982) demonstrated that infant sensitivity to the category boundary between short and long lag VOT is not special to humans; it must instead be due to a 'sweet spot' in the auditory mechanism that humans share with many other mammals and that thus has a long evolutionary history. As a result, the initial interpretation—that the infants' response demonstrated that 'speech is special'—was replaced by the less radical conclusion that speech contrasts are readily perceived in early infancy because language evolved to be efficiently processed by the long-standing auditory mechanisms of the mammalian brain (Kuhl, 1986; Hauser, 1996). This is not to deny that speech *is* 'special' to infants: It must be so because speech is the natural auditory accompaniment to the adult care and attention that is essential to infant physical and emotional survival.

By the 1990s Peter Jusczyk, who had co-authored the Eimas study while still an undergraduate, had become the most prolific researcher in the field of infant speech perception (see Gerken & Aslin, 2005). He laid out a blueprint for tackling what he saw as the next challenge for understanding how infants 'discover language' (Jusczyk, 1986, 1992, 1993, 1997; Jusczyk & Kemler Nelson, 1996). The highly successful research programme that Jusczyk initiated, and that has continued to unfold despite his untimely death in 2001, includes numerous experimental studies demonstrating infant advances over the first year as they gain familiarity with various aspects of the native language, including prosodic patterns affecting clauses, phrases, and words (Kemler Nelson, Hirsh-Pasek, Jusczyk, & Wright Cassidy, 1989; Jusczyk, Hirsh-Pasek, Kemler Nelson, Woodward, & Piwoz, 1992, Jusczyk, Cutler, & Redanz, 1993; Myers et al., 1996), segmental sequences or phonotactics (Jusczyk, Friederici, Wessels, Svenkerud, & Juscyzk, 1993; Jusczyk, Luce, & Charles-Luce, 1994), and allophonic or coarticulatory regularities (Jusczyk, Hohne, & Bauman, 1999).

In the mid-1990s Jusczyk and his colleagues and students began to publish reports that, from as early as 7.5 months, infants successfully segment or 'find' words in short passages of speech immediately after being briefly 'trained with' (i.e., repeatedly exposed to) those words in the lab (Jusczyk & Aslin, 1995; Jusczyk, Houston, & Newsome, 1999; Mattys, Jusczyk, Luce, & Morgan, 1999; Mattys & Jusczyk, 2001a, 2001b), or vice versa (exposure to passage, testing with words in isolation). Although Polka and Sundara (2012) replicated these findings with infants acquiring Canadian French, experimental work in Europe was less successful: Under the conditions used in the original Jusczyk and Aslin study Dutch infants showed an ability to segment only by 9 months (Houston, Jusczyk, Kuijpers, Coolen, & Cutler, 2000) and French infants only at 16 months (Nazzi, Iakimova, Bertoncini, Frédonie, & Alcantara, 2006; Mersad, Goyet, & Nazzi, 2010; Nazzi, Mersad, Sundara, Iakimova, & Polka, 2014; see also Bosch, Figueras, Teixidó, & Ramon-Casas, 2013, for segmentation results in Spanish and Catalan). Most surprising is that two baby labs in England were unable to replicate the findings at any age tested without using what to British ears is highly exaggerated 'birthday-party speech' (Floccia et al., 2016), and even with such stimuli, only at 10.5 months. The difference between North American and European results remains to be satisfactorily explained.

Two related lines of research did not initially enter into the account of infant speech perception and segmentation. The first, which has since become one of the dominant paradigms in current use with infants, children, and adults alike, is the study of *distributional (or statistical) learning*, a kind of implicit or procedural learning based on sheer tallying of probabilities of co-occurrence, as tested through experimental exposure to artificial language strings (Aslin & Newport, 2014; Saffran, 2014). This mechanism, which decades earlier had been shown to be used by adults (Reber, 1967, 1993), proved to be available to the infant by 8 months (Saffran et al., 1996) as well as to older children; relative age, experience, or maturity did not appear relevant in this regard (Saffran et al., 1997). Despite the reservations of Jusczyk and his student Elizabeth Johnson (Johnson & Jusczyk,

2001), who demonstrated preferential infant attention to stress cues over prob-abilistic distributional differences (see also the reply by Thiessen & Saffran, 2003, and further perspectives on segmentation in Seidl & Johnson, 2006; Johnson, 2016), the new line of research on distributional learning in infants has proven as productive as the study of the discrimination of contrasts.

Most importantly, perhaps, implicit distributional learning has been taken to account for the formation of native-language categories in the second half of the first year of life, providing a possible explanation for the well-established finding that already in that age-range infants lose their early capacity to discriminate virtually any contrast with which they are presented, retaining adult-like discrim-ination only of native-language contrasts (Maye, Werker, & Gerken, 2002). Although Werker and Curtin (2005) proposed PRIMIR, a model of infant speech perception and word learning, to incorporate these findings, solid understanding of how the early discrimination of contrasts and sound category learning come to be integrated with word learning has yet to be achieved (Swingley, 2009, 2017; Vihman, 2017).

The second line of research, at the centre of our concerns here, is a focus on *vocal production*, a critical component of word learning that cannot be disregarded if our goal is to understand how children learn to talk. Remarkably, none of the various chapters in Morgan and Demuth (1996) mentions production as a poten-tial source of knowledge to support segmentation of the speech stream. However, a number of theoretical and experimental studies conducted since then do address the question of how infants' own vocal production might affect the way that they listen to or process speech (DePaolis, Vihman, & Keren-Portnoy, 2011; Lewkowicz & Hansen-Tift, 2012; DePaolis, Vihman, & Nakai, 2013; Yeung & Werker, 2013; Guellaï, Streri, & Yeung, 2014; Majorano, Vihman, & DePaolis, 2014; Altvater-Mackensen & Grossmann, 2015; Bruderer, Danielson, Kandhadai, & Werker, 2015; Masapollo, Polka, & Ménard, 2016; cf. also Imada et al., 2006, a longitudinal study, using magnetoencephalography, of the connections between perceptual and production responses to speech vs. non-speech as they evolve and change over the first year of life). Most recently, DePaolis, Keren-Portnoy, and Vihman (2016) demonstrated, for 59 infants, that 10-month-olds with stable control of two different supraglottal consonants process familiar words (based on long-term memory, without training in the lab) in a different, more advanced way than infants who have not yet gained such control, providing direct support for a role for production in the long-term retention of word forms in memory. (For a review of evidence of the role of production in speech processing and word learning, see Vihman, DePaolis, & Keren-Portnoy, 2014.)

The highly dynamic period of research into the mechanisms and processes of infant speech perception that began in the 1970s led to numerous now well-established findings. This was paralleled by methodological and technological advances that the research also helped in part to fuel and that have resulted in the diverse and dynamic environment we see today. (See, for example, *Language Learning*, 2014, Supplement 2, a selection of papers from the first Workshop on Infant Language Development [WILD], held in San Sebastian in 2013; these papers give a fair representation of the wide range of interests and methods that currently characterize the field.) From the perspective of language learning the role of production in development has received considerably less attention than segmentation and distributional learning, however, despite its evident importance for full understanding of the dramatic changes that occur over the first two years of an infant's life. In section 1.6 we present evidence and arguments to support the view that production plays an increasingly important role in infant processing of the speech stream as their own production capacities mature and change, shaped by experience with the ambient language.

1.6 Phonological production and 'selectivity'

How might 'usage' help to explain the beginnings of lexical development? As Stoel-Gammon (2011) shows in a useful overview of the interaction of lexicon and phonology in the first years of life, phonetic skills and the vocal practice afforded by babbling are foundational for first word learning. This is apparent, among other things, from the role played by *selection* in first word use. Both the simplicity of the first words children attempt and their relative accuracy testify to 'phonological selectivity' in children's early word use (Ferguson, Peizer, & Weeks, 1973; Ferguson & Farwell, 1975; see Chapters 3 and 4, in this volume, for extensive illustration and discussion). A third critical reason to posit such selectivity is the finding that a given child's early words are closely related to the vocal forms which that child has been using in babble: see Stoel-Gammon and Cooper (1984) (3 children) and Vihman, Macken, Miller, Simmons, and Miller (1985) (9 children, six of whose early words are analysed here in Chapter 3). In other words, children first attempt to produce word forms for which they already have a vocal routine in repertoire. This idea seemed radical when Ferguson and his colleagues first proposed it in the 1970s. It was validated experimentally in the 1980s (Leonard, Schwartz, Morris, & Chapman, 1981; Schwartz & Leonard, 1982; see Schwartz, 1988, for a review, and Kay-Raining Bird & Chapman, 1998, for a more recent experimental study) and is no longer controversial today.

This is not to suggest that children's first words are chosen purely on phonological grounds: Given the large number of words used repeatedly in the course of the everyday routines that are typical of an infant's life, many possible words will suggest themselves for expressive use on the basis of their inherent interest for the child as well as their familiarity due to frequency and salience (Vihman, 2018). These include 'social' words such as greetings and interjections of various kinds, words that refer to the child himself, to family members, body parts (hands, feet, nose, eyes), pets and other animals whose activities attract the child's attention (e.g., birds, squirrels[3]), words associated with daily routines such as eating, bathing and also more culturally variable practices (e.g., words associated with Christmas in many Western countries, or with the use of a prayer rug in Muslim homes), and words for the child's own actions, such as *sit/walk, get up/fall down, eat/drink*, and so on. The frequency of occurrence of words in the input and their prosodic salience play a role in highlighting them for future recall; first word uses are likely supported by some combination of these factors (see Laing, Vihman, & Keren-Portnoy, 2017, on the sources of the salience in input speech of onomatopoeia, which are common in early vocabularies). However, the particular (unconscious) choices made by any one child necessarily also depend on his articulatory skills and, crucially, on his ability to *retain* word forms in relation to their situations of use.

The memory requirement is surely one reason for children's success at producing early words that *resemble their targets*, i.e., that are surprisingly accurate. A child's repeated production, over a period of several recording sessions, of what (based on transcription) is more or less the same articulatory gesture and resultant sound provides that child with cross-modal familiarity with the sound, leading to an ability to relate the proprioceptive and auditory effects of their own vocal production to the auditory and, in the case of labials at least, visual effects of others' vocalizations (for a recent review of the conflicting evidence and interpretations of perception–production links in infancy see Guellaï et al., 2014). Once a child has such a sound in repertoire it will be that much easier to bring to mind words that prominently feature the sound (especially if it is the only consonant type in the word: cf. /b/ in *baby* [as illustrated in Table 1.1] or *bye-bye*) in situations in which the word has repeatedly been used (Elbers, 1997). This accounts for the strong predictive effect of stable consonant use in babble for the onset of word use (Majorano et al., 2014; McGillion et al., 2017a).

If the child's articulatory skills have advanced sufficiently to permit identifiable production of the remembered form in such a priming context, his first words will be recognized as such (and reported or recorded, in the case of participants in a diary or observational study) and may well serve as the basis for parental responses as well (Veneziano, 1981; Messum & Howard, 2015). This is the likely basis for most of the first words, which are typically 'context-limited', or produced only in contexts strongly associated with use of that word (Vihman & McCune, 1994; McCune & Vihman, 2001). Properly 'symbolic' or referential word use involves the production of words that refer to *categories* of objects and events rather than referring, like proper names, to individual cases; referential words, which can be deployed even

---

[3] The word *squirrel* is unlikely to occur early in English because of the challenges posed by its phonological shape—the initial /skw/ cluster and two liquids; when the form is simpler—e.g., *orav* in Estonian—it is sometimes produced early on.

when their referent is not physically present at the moment of use, are definitional for language. However, such word use typically begins only some time after the child has begun producing situationally primed 'precursor' words that are memorable due to their familiar vocal form as well as their close connection with an often experienced setting or routine (Bates, Benigni, Bretherton, Camaioni, & Volterra, 1979; Menyuk, Menn, & Silber, 1986; Vihman & McCune, 1994; McCune & Vihman, 2001; Vihman, 2014, 2017, 2018).

The relevance of babbling practice for later word production has not always been accepted or acknowledged. In fact, Jakobson (1941/1968, 1949) famously proposed, based on the diary studies available to him at the time, that babble is entirely unrelated to speech. Jakobson formulated his 'general laws of irreversible solidarity that govern the languages of the world synchronically' (Jakobson, 1949, p. 370 [our translation]) based on programmatic ideas that grew out of the Prague School. According to this view, children's acquisition of 'phonemes' follows a strict order of emergent oppositions. In fact, Jakobson sees 'simple, clear, stable phonic oppositions, suitable to be engraved in memory and realized at will' (Jakobson, 1949, p. 369) as the critical hallmark of first words, as distinct from babble, which he believed to be phonetically far more diverse and unconstrained, given the lack of any communicative goal. His outline of the phonemic oppositions to be expected fits the data of the first words well enough, especially as regards consonants, with labials and coronals, stops and nasals predominating (see Chapters 3 and 4); his predicted systematic ('universal') sequential unfolding of oppositions was adopted as a model to be tested in numerous subsequent studies and received general confirmation. However, some linguists received Jakobson's views critically from early on (Olmsted, 1966; Ferguson & Garnica, 1975; Kiparsky & Menn, 1977). These critics pointed out, among other things, that establishing 'phonemes' in a child's early words is difficult if not impossible, given the small sample sizes, and that word-position is unjustifiably neglected in Jakobson's account of consonantal development, particularly in view of the important differences in order of acquisition between onsets and codas. Indeed, Jakobson focuses on *segmental inventory*, with a special emphasis on the emergence of contrast; prosodic structure, or the syntagmatic aspect of phonological system, is disregarded.

Brown (1958) took the opposite position to Jakobson's, seeing babbling as a period in which the child's vocalizations gradually 'drift' toward the ambient language. In other words, he expected children to show the influence of listening experience with a particular language even before their memory for particular word forms—in association with context of occurrence or meaning—becomes reliable enough to permit identifiable word use. This view has been hotly debated ever since, with inconclusive studies of adult listener judgements of linguistic influence on babble that sometimes do but often do not succeed in distinguishing between infants exposed to the listener's own as compared with other languages (e.g., Atkinson, MacWhinney, & Stoel, 1970; Boysson-Bardies, Sagart, & Durand, 1984;

Thevenin, Eilers, Oller, & Lavoie, 1985; Engstrand, Williams, & Lacerda, 2003; Lee, Jhang, Chen, Relyea, & Oller, 2017).

However, through acoustic analysis of vowels or simple tallying of consonants based on transcripts it has been possible to show clear differences, within the prelinguistic or single-word period, in children's use of vowel space (Boysson-Bardies, Hallé, Sagart, & Durand, 1989: Arabic, British English, Cantonese, French), place and manner of consonants (Boysson-Bardies & Vihman, 1991: American English, French, Japanese, Swedish), and pitch or tone and duration patterns (Hallé, Boysson-Bardies, & Vihman, 1991: French, Japanese; Engstrand, Williams, & Strømqvist, 1991: American English, Swedish) or tones (Lou, Vihman, & Keren-Portnoy, 2018: British English, Mandarin). This specifically applies to the sounds that have become stable elements in children's production in that period (such as low and front or central vowels, labials and coronals, stops and nasals, falling and level tones). Other aspects of early phonology, such as prosodic structure or word length in syllables, for example, show cross-linguistic differences only once a child is producing some thirty or more different identifiable words and has made some advances in the diversity of forms produced (Hallé et al., 1991; Vihman, 1993; Vihman & Boysson-Bardies, 1994). Thus the evidence generally supports Brown's proposal of 'babbling drift' insofar as infants do show, within the limits of their production capacities, increasing accommodation to the segmental patterns of the ambient language over the period of transition to word use, with identifiable words emerging out of this 'pre-shadowing' in babble.

1.6.1 Babbling and its relation to word production

The first supraglottal consonant use can be identified quite reliably between about 6 and 8 months, as it emerges in 'canonical babbling', a rhythmically repeated syllabic frame ([bababa], [dadada], or even [ŋaŋaŋa]: Oller, 1980; Stark, 1980). Oller (2000) establishes the great consistency of this maturational landmark, reviewing studies of infants with various handicaps—deafness, Down Syndrome, prematurity, low socio-economic status and extreme poverty—that might be expected to delay or block the emergence of typical babbling. Like other types of motor development, such adult-like production emerges on what appears to be a universal schedule and with a rhythmic base (Thelen, 1981, 1991). Dramatic postnatal changes in vocal tract shape and in neurophysiological control are required to enable such production. Accordingly, canonical syllables are normally observed only after a period of use of the reflexive or 'vegetative sounds', cooing and vocal play or exploration of vocal effects that are reported in convergent studies of children learning different languages (English, Dutch, Swedish: see Lindblom & Zetterström, 1986). Little if any cross-linguistic variation has been reported in the phonetics of the first adult-like syllables, which appear to be largely maturationally based, given typical auditory and vocal capacities.

Canonical babbling is the most significant vocal production landmark in the first year, as it brings adult-like syllables into the child's repertoire, creating the beginnings of an internally known database onto which to map the speech sounds heard in the input. Davis and MacNeilage refer to these vocal patterns as 'mandibular oscillation' (Davis & MacNeilage, 1990, 1995, 2000; MacNeilage & Davis, 1990), or cyclic jaw movement, which they take to be the chief motor for these first adult-like syllable productions, with the tongue riding rather passively on the jaw. They have tested the hypothesis by analysing babbling in a variety of languages and have found a strong tendency for the syllables to show C-V associations in this period. That is, they find that slight forward movement of the tongue, giving the auditory effect of a coronal consonant, is most often followed by a similarly fronted vowel; the less often produced velar consonants tend similarly to be followed by a back vowel. Labials involve no tongue movement and are accordingly neutral and typically followed by more or less central vowels (these are 'pure frames').

Consistent identifiable consonant use emerges only very gradually over the period of transition from babbling to words (Vihman & Miller, 1988; Stoel-Gammon, 1992). Based on evidence that babbling is closely related to the word forms produced in parallel (e.g., Stoel-Gammon & Cooper, 1984; Elbers & Ton, 1985; Vihman et al., 1985; Vihman, Ferguson, & Elbert, 1986), Vihman (1993, 1996) proposed that, contrary to Jakobson's views, babbling serves as valuable, if 'incidental' or unconscious, practice for word production: Babbling cannot be *intended* as practice for word production since the preverbal child can have no notion of the communicative value of word or language use—even if such a notion could guide them in discovering how to develop it. And indeed intentional communication, first seen in gestural expression, is emergent in parallel with these vocal advances (Bates et al., 1979; Woodward, 2009). It is worth noting that the relative order of emergence of stable vocal production patterns and intentional use of gestures to communicate meanings is variable, not fixed; it is one of many separate strands of precursor behaviour relevant to later language use (see McCune, 1992, 2008; Vihman, 2014, ch. 2). Instead of being a voluntary, goal-directed activity, babbling, like hand banging and kicking, for example, is produced as part of infants' spontaneous exploration of their emerging motoric mastery and skills, apparently without conscious goals (Thelen, 1991; Thelen & Smith, 1994).

Babble serves as a critical resource for the child, creating the raw material out of which words can be formed and triggering, in many cultures, a sympathetic response from caregivers, who are more likely to produce conversation-continuers in response to infant production of canonical syllables than of pre-canonical forms (Gros-Louis, West, Goldstein, & King, 2006; Goldstein & Schwade, 2008). Such adult responses may facilitate word learning through the timely provision of useful models. As Goldstein, King, and West (2003) observe, drawing on their parallel studies of vocal learning in birds:

early vocalizations become a channel of communication only after young birds or babies come to realize the instrumental value of sounds. The parallels in vocal development between birds and babies are in the synergy between adult responsiveness and the capacities of young organisms to use social information to refine their repertoires.   (p. 8034; see also Locke, 1993)

Finally, two kinds of evidence further support the value of babbling as practice for word formation. First, some premature ('aphonic') infants are blocked for several months from any attempt at vocalization by the presence of a cannula that has been inserted into their vocal tract to support breathing. These infants are reported to produce canonical babbling from one to several weeks before their first identifiably word-like vocalizations, no matter at what age the cannula is removed (Bohm, Nelson, Driver, & Green, 2010); in contrast, cooing and other pre-canonical types of vocal production have not been observed in these older infants.

Secondly, children who begin to talk later than is usual (i.e., after about 24–30 months), in the absence of any known physical or cognitive impediments, are almost invariably low vocalizers, who have thus been unable to profit from babbling practice to the extent that most children do (Stoel-Gammon, 1989; Paul & Jennings, 1992; Rescorla & Ratner, 1996; Baird-Pharr, Ratner, & Rescorla, 2000; Vihman, Keren-Portnoy, Whitaker, Bidgood, & McGillion, 2013). Both of these cases are consistent with the now generally held view that babbling constitutes a necessary (although not sufficient) prerequisite for word use.

1.6.2 'Articulatory filter' and the origins of the first words

Accepting that babbling is a key factor in early word production, and returning to the assumption that children are to some extent 'selecting' their first words, we can ask how they do this. How could they know, as is sometimes implied, what they do *not* know? To account for the accuracy and individual-babble-like characteristics of the first words Vihman (1991, 1993, 1996) proposed that something like an 'articulatory filter' might be at work:[4]

> The child may be seen as experiencing the flow of adult speech through an 'articulatory filter' which selectively enhances motoric recall of phonetically accessible words.   (Vihman, 1996, p. 142)

Instead of imputing precocious metalinguistic knowledge to the children, this suggests that children *experience as particularly salient and memorable word forms*

---

[4] A similar idea can be found in Locke (1986): 'There is evidence to suggest that infants...attend to particular patterns, and consult their store of available articulations in search of the closest matches' (p. 241).

in the input that are close enough to their experience of their own vocal practice to provide an approximate match.

A parallel in adult experience is the salience of a hyper-familiar word—a person's own name or that of his or her intimates, home town or profession, for example—when overheard as part of an otherwise unattended conversation (at a nearby table in a restaurant, for example). This 'cocktail party phenomenon' (Cherry, 1953; Wood & Cowan, 1995) has attracted several experimental studies in recent years. Most notably for our purposes, Newman (2005) found that 13-month-olds, unlike 5- and 9-month-olds, respond selectively to their own names as produced by an unknown female against a blend of female voices, even when the name is no more than 5DB louder than the multitalker background. (As Newman notes, infants' increased lexical knowledge at this age is likely to be one factor in their improved ability to listen selectively.) This is not the same effect that the articulatory filter proposes—hearing a familiar word in noise is not the same as picking out a familiar vocal form from fluent speech—but it presumably draws on similar resources of memory and attention.

In exemplar theory terms, similarity of form (between heard word form and existing child vocal pattern) creates an 'echo' or resonance with known forms, adding salience to the input signal. The idea that experience with one's own production facilitates processing of related patterns heard in the input is in line with the neuroscience literature. Broadly speaking, 'action' (here, production) supports 'perception' because they are automatically coordinated in real time, strengthening the network of connections between them; when any part of such a network is activated, it activates the connections to the others as well (Edelman, 1989; Thelen & Smith, 1994, ch. 5; see also Hickok & Poeppel, 2004, 2007).

1.6.3 Experimental evidence for an articulatory filter

As a way to test the articulatory filter hypothesis several recent studies have experimentally demonstrated an effect of production on the way infants process speech (DePaolis et al., 2011, 2013; Majorano et al., 2014). In each of these studies children were recorded several times in their homes, with a count made of each supraglottal consonant produced. Consonants consistently used with high frequency are taken to have been 'mastered', in the sense that production of the consonant has been practised sufficiently to be well represented, solidly established in the child's repertoire and thus ready to be used at will. By analogy with the mastery of other early motor routines (such as reaching: Thelen, Corbetta, & Spencer, 1996), we have termed these well-practised consonants 'vocal motor schemes' (VMS: McCune & Vihman, 1987, 2001; see also McCune, 2008).

To assess their response to hearing VMS in the speech signal, in each of these studies children were tested in the lab on nonwords that did or did not include the consonants that had been identified, on the basis of the recordings, as VMS for the particular child. In DePaolis et al. (2013) 53 children (27 English, 26 Welsh) were recorded every two weeks from 10.5 to 12 months and then tested two weeks later on short lists of highly similar nonwords. As stimuli DePaolis et al. developed two sets of nonwords for use with all of the English-learning infants, one set including one or more occurrences of /t/, a consonant likely to be used early by most infants, the other featuring /s/, a consonant unlikely to be produced often by any of the infants but of roughly equivalent input frequency in English. The English infants in this study showed the expected difference in use of /t/ vs. /s/ (ranging from an average, per infant per session, of about 30–50 for /t/, 0–5 for /s/). On the other hand, the infants' response to the stimuli unexpectedly showed a novelty effect, with those who produced /t/ the most often looking significantly longer in response to /s/ than to /t/.[5]

In the other two studies infants were recorded at home from one to four times per month and tested in the lab as soon as a VMS was identified (by which time the child sometimes had more than one stably used consonant); the stimuli were a list of isolated words in Majorano et al. (2014), a short passage incorporating the nonwords in different sentential positions in DePaolis et al. (2011). In these studies stop pairs were used (i.e., both voiced and voiceless exponents of each place of articulation; this was done simply to vary the stimuli, since voicing is not well controlled in the early word-use period [Macken, 1980] and is not expected to affect perceptual processing). Each infant was tested on one set of VMS and one set of stimuli that are VMS for other infants but not for that child, based on transcription of the infant's recorded sessions; nonwords featuring a third pair, /f/v/, not a VMS for any infant, were included as well to control for purely auditory effects. The results for the two VMS pairs tested in DePaolis et al. (2011) and Majorano et al. (2014) are shown in Figure 1.1.

In each of these studies the infants fell into two groups, those for whom only a single VMS could be identified and those for whom more than one was identified. As shown in Figure 1.1, infants with a single VMS (9 in the English, 12 in the Italian study) responded with longer looking to 'own' as compared with 'other' in both studies, although the difference between own and other was significant only in the Italian study. On the other hand, in both of these studies infants with multiple VMS showed a novelty response, as did the high-producers of [t] in DePaolis et al. (2013). Although this was not the result initially anticipated, it is in accord with the articulatory hypothesis, inasmuch as mastery of a single VMS can be seen to highlight that sound, attracting the infant's attention. Continued experience with the sound (as in DePaolis et al., 2013) or mastery of one or

---

[5] The monolingual Welsh-learning infants were tested on a pair of consonants (/b/ vs. /g/) that proved not to be used significantly differently in their vocalizations; as could be expected, then, there was no significant difference in the Welsh infants' responses to the contrasting sets of stimuli.

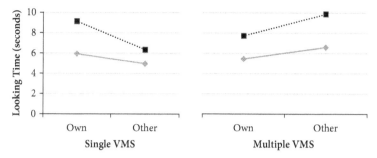

Figure 1.1 Experimental results of DePaolis et al., 2011 (solid grey line), and Majorano et al., 2014 (dotted black line): Looking time (in seconds) in response to own- vs. other-VMS in two groups of infants, defined on the basis of the number of VMS identified in their transcribed sessions.

From Vihman et al. (2014), reprinted by permission of John Wiley and Sons.

more additional consonants (as in the other two studies) then increases the infant's interest in sounds that he is not yet producing. This would have an evident advantage for lexical advance, in that the infant would not then become 'stuck' on the first consonant in repertoire.

As Figure 1.1 shows, the Italian infants looked longer under all conditions than did the English infants—presumably because the isolated word list provided a context in which the VMS was more salient than in the passages in which non-words were embedded in the English experiment. Indeed, when words familiar from everyday life are embedded in passages (i.e., in sentence-strings), untrained recognition emerges only at 12 months, about a month later than the point when children recognize untrained words presented in isolation (Vihman et al., 2004; DePaolis, Vihman, & Keren-Portnoy, 2014). It is likely that the VMS of interest is rapidly overwritten by oncoming speech in the passage but not in the isolated-word condition.

The findings of the three studies are consistent with one another, despite their methodological differences; considered together, they give strong support to the articulatory filter proposal. The findings suggest that mastery of one or more consonants provides the infant with an initial entry-point to the rapidly changing speech stream, although the mapping of word forms onto the child's emergent production patterns takes time. As will be seen in Chapter 3, about half of the infants represented in our analyses produced their first words before 12 months, in roughly the period covered by these experimental studies.

It is worth noting, however, that despite the novelty effect seen in these studies for infants with more than one VMS, as in the English and Italian studies just described, or with considerable experience using the consonant tested, as in DePaolis et al. (2013), children nevertheless show a preference, in their early word selection, for what is *familiar*, not what is unknown. As discussed in Vihman et al. (2014), the paradoxical difference between *novelty* in the experimental task and *familiarity* in word selection is probably best accounted for by reference to the differences in the tasks, (a) passive listening to auditory stimuli in the lab and (b) accessing for production a remembered word form associated with a situation of interest (with or without situational priming):

> Purely passive experimental perception tasks elicit novelty responses to the extent that the competing patterns are highly familiar and thus no longer interesting to the infant. Spontaneous word form production... on the other hand, makes quite different and more challenging demands, requiring that the infant recall a pattern... and marshal his or her resources to reproduce it.   (p. 127)

Thus it is not unreasonable to assume that having one- to two-syllable vocalizations in repertoire will support infant attention to and memory for some elements in input speech, as originally hypothesized (Vihman, 1993). Such matching is further facilitated by accentual prominence, as seen by the fact that infants recognize word forms despite changes to an *unaccented syllable*, which may be incompletely represented, but do not recognize words in which changes have been made to the *accented syllable* (Vihman et al., 2004; see also Swingley, 2017; Vihman, 2017; Segal et al., under review), for which representation is likely to be more complete and more accurate. Isolated words, which are relatively infrequent but more easily remembered than words embedded in sentences or passages (Brent & Siskind, 2001; Keren-Portnoy, Vihman, & Lindop Fisher, 2019), must also support such matching. As noted above, infant responses to their own preferred sounds (VMS) is less robust when tested with the use of short passages requiring segmentation than with a list of isolated word forms.

For prelinguistic infants, then, vocal production creates a sample of known patterns to which novel word forms can be mapped, which in turn leads to more robust or stable representations. A recent experiment demonstrated this effect for the first time in a word-learning task (Majorano et al., 2019). Thirty Italian infants, aged about 11 months, were briefly recorded in their homes, to establish extent of consonant use; a second recording was made before testing to establish stability of use over two sessions. Following the initial home recording the infants were trained through book-reading, over five sessions at nursery, on two nonwords featuring early-learned consonants (ELC: labial stops and nasals, which dominate early vocabulary in Italian) and two nonwords featuring late-learned consonants (LLC: labial fricatives and velar stops); the referents were fantasy animals. The infants were then tested, through a preferential-looking procedure, on pairs of trained images and foils, in combination with an auditory presentation of the trained nonwords (either ELC or LLC).

The children fell into two groups based on the home recordings: 12 had at least one VMS while 18 had none. At test, the only evidence of learning after this brief period of training came from the VMS group: When an *ELC nonword* was heard in association with the *matching image*, children with one or more VMS looked significantly longer—but only when the *contrasting image* was an *LLC nonword* (not when it was a foil). There was thus evidence that the children with the stronger start on consonant production (and only those children) had begun to learn the form–meaning association over the five training sessions, but the learning was not robust (see also DePaolis et al., 2014). When the paired *image* was completely novel (i.e., the foil), it apparently attracted infants' interest, drawing attention away from the trained form–meaning match. And when the nonword featured a late-learned consonant with which the child could not be expected to have production experience, there was no evidence of learning at all.

These findings provide additional support for the hypothesis that production boosts early word learning. We can tentatively conclude that an incipient capacity to map forms that are heard in input speech onto one's own production patterns facilitates the emergence of phonological memory, or the ability to retain phono-logical strings (Keren-Portnoy et al., 2010). And we can further infer that the slow process of constructing memory for speech is likely to be one reason for the evident delay between first adult-like syllable production, almost always observed in the middle of the first year, and first identifiable word use, typically identified toward the end of the first year at the earliest.

We suggest, then, that the targets for the first words produced are (implicitly) selected based on a combination of (i) their inherent interest and (ii) frequency of occurrence in the input, (iii) prosodic enhancement in the speech stream, (iv) occurrence in isolation, and (v) matching to familiar vocal patterns in the child's repertoire. The first points are perhaps uncontroversial and have been amply discussed elsewhere (see Vihman, 2018). The last point, the role of matching to own patterns that we have just discussed, is further evidenced by the relative accuracy of first words (see Chapters 3 and 4).

Words heard in isolation, without the need for segmentation, also play a disproportionate role in first word production: This is apparent from the large percentage of 'non-syntactic' words to be found in the listed sets of 4–6 first words from 17 monolingual children acquiring English in Menn and Vihman's (2011) Appendix I: Every one of these sets includes at least one such word (*boo, bye-bye* [2 children], *hello, hi(ya)* [5], *night-night, patty(-cake), rock-rock, thanks* [2], *uh-oh* [3]) or onomatopoeic form (*baa* [2], *bang* [2], *bow-wow* [2], *moo, quack-quack, tick, woof-woof*). Together these forms account for 28 (33%) of the 84 first-recorded words. Each of these words, none of which are likely to be the product of segmentation of longer strings (see Laing et al., 2017, for direct evidence regarding mothers' uses of onomatopoeia), reflects attention to and retention of word forms repeatedly heard in isolation in the course of everyday routines in the home.

1.7 Lexical system-building

Recent word-learning studies with adults have focused on the integration of novel word forms into an existing lexicon. Because these studies provide a critical new perspective on the key issue of system-building in lexical development we will review their main findings here, before going on to lay out the goals, research questions, and overall plan for this book.

1.7.1 Lexical configuration and lexical engagement

Gaskell and his colleagues have for some time pursued a line of research on the nature of memory consolidation in word learning (e.g., Gaskell & Dumay, 2003; Dumay & Gaskell, 2012; Lindsay & Gaskell, 2013; Tamminen & Gaskell, 2013; Brown & Gaskell, 2014), teaching participants words that are similar to but different from existing lexical items (e.g., *cathedruke* or *lirmucktoze*; cf. *cathedral, muck*) and then testing for *inhibitory effects* on lexical access to the familiar word as the novel form becomes established. The idea is that the newly taught word will not delay access to the known word as soon as the new word has been heard or briefly remembered shortly after training but only once it has been integrated into the lexicon. This then draws a critical line between encountering, being trained on and 'learning' a word form ('phonological learning'), on the one hand, and consolidating that knowledge ('lexicalization'), such that the new word begins to affect access to existing lexical forms, on the other.

Leach and Samuel (2007) follow up on this idea, presenting several experiments designed to systematically explore the distinction between what they term 'lexical configuration', or the 'factual knowledge' that comes with new word learning, and the contrasting phenomenon of 'lexical engagement', or the effects of new words on an individual's network of connections between known words (Gaskell & Dumay's 'lexicalization'). As Leach and Samuel elaborate:

> Lexical configuration is the set of factual knowledge associated with a word (e.g., the word's sound, spelling, meaning, or syntactic role). Almost all previous research on word learning has focused on this aspect. However, it is also critical to understand the process by which a word becomes capable of lexical engage-ment – the ways in which a lexical entry dynamically interacts with other lexical entries, and with sublexical representations. For example, lexical entries compete with each other during word recognition (inhibition within the lexical level), and they also support the activation of their constituents (top-down lexical-phonemic facilitation, and lexically-based perceptual learning).   (2007, p. 306)

The distinction between lexical 'configuration' and 'engagement' seems to be important, even foundational, but it is nevertheless a subtle point that can be experimentally established only by indirect means. Note that the experiments conducted by both teams address adults, who necessarily have large vocabularies already in place. However, Henderson, Gaskell, and their colleagues have run related experiments with school-age children (Henderson, Weighall, Brown, & Gaskell, 2012, 2013; Henderson, Weighall, & Gaskell, 2013; Henderson, Devine, Weighall, & Gaskell, 2015). These studies demonstrate that word learning in older children as well as adults involves not only the creation of new representations ('configuration') but also consolidation and integration into the existing lexical network ('engagement'). The distinction should be just as relevant to word learning in very young children, particularly at the outset, the period of interest here, when we can observe the very first word learning and subsequent consolidation of word knowledge. However, obtaining evidence of lexical engagement in infants just embarking on the process of network building will be challenging. As we shall see, evidence from templatic patterning in production provides some insight into this aspect of early word learning.

Leach and Samuel lay out their procedures at some length, trying out two methods each for detecting *what* has been learned (testing for successful learning of the lexical configuration of the new word) and the *effect* of the learning on the lexical network ('engagement'). First, following Gaskell and Dumay, they trained adult participants, over five days, on 12 three- or four-syllable novel word forms (e.g., *galasod, naronesay, marfashick, benemshalow*: six each with *s* and *sh*), using a phoneme-monitoring task to provide implicit exposure to the new words. That is, the participants were required to judge, for each word, whether or not it included a particular sound; no direct *memory training* was involved. Note that this way of training new words focuses on the *form alone*, making no link with meaning.

Two procedures were then chosen as the most discriminative for evaluating initial word learning. To test for lexical configuration Leach and Samuel settled on a 'threshold discrimination' (or 'word in noise') task, in which the newly learned word is repeatedly presented against a background of white noise, with successively lower levels, until the participant signals that he can identify the form. Real (well-established) words are more readily identified in noise than unfamiliar word forms, so the relative speed and accuracy of word recognition in noise can be taken as a reliable measure of the extent to which the new word form has become a lexical unit for the participant.

To test for lexical engagement, in contrast, 'lexically driven perceptual learning', a procedure introduced by Norris, McQueen, and Cutler (2003), was used. An ambiguous sound is created by splicing into the stimulus a mix of two consonants—in Leach and Samuel's study, /s/ and /ʃ/; for the test phase this replaces the relevant sound in the trained word, creating something between, say, *galasod* and *galashod*. The rationale for the task is as follows: Participants who hear the ambiguous sound in a lexical context, where a particular sound is expected, are biased to hear the sound that fits their expectations; thus, for example, their /s/ category expands to accommodate the percept of words with the modified, ambiguous /s/. No such effect is seen with nonwords. In short:

> Lexical items can cause substantial changes in the definition of sublexical categories, a clear case of lexical engagement... Thus, we can use the ability of our trained words to produce perceptual learning as an index of the development of lexical engagement.   (Leach & Samuel, 2007, pp. 312f.)

In Baese-Berk and Samuel (2016) the more transparent term 'perceptual recalibration' is used for this same effect, together with this account of its function in everyday life:

> Perceptual recalibration is necessary for optimal comprehension because speakers vary in how they produce speech sounds – one person's version of a particular vowel or consonant can be rather different than another person's. Listeners must adjust to the idiosyncracies of each speaker, and recent evidence shows that native speakers use their detailed knowledge of sounds and words to do so.   (p. 25)

Leach and Samuel used an old-new recognition task to expose their participants to either the *s*- or the *sh*-words, modified to create the ambiguous sounds. First, each participant heard a list including, along with several fillers, half of the novel trained words, either those with /s/, balanced by an equal number of untrained (real) words with /ʃ/, or the reverse. The critical words were all ambiguous-sound versions of the trained words; this was followed by an old-new recognition test, which provided additional exposures to the ambiguous sounds.

After 18 exposures to the modified-sound words participants took the critical perceptual recalibration test: They listened to a seven-step synthesized continuum of the sequence /asa-aʃa/ and were asked to categorize the medial sibilant as either /s/ or /ʃ/. If the novel-word training had successfully resulted in lexical engagement, those participants exposed, through the old-new test, to trained words with an /s/ modified to include more of the /ʃ/ sound were expected to shift their categorical boundary to include more of the stimuli as /s/ (and vice versa for those exposed to modified /ʃ/-words).

In their first experiment the threshold (word-in-noise) task provided good evidence of lexical configuration. On the other hand, the recalibration task showed consistent but quite weak effects, suggesting that the training had not led to lexical engagement strong enough to induce perceptual learning or recalibration. Note that the same type of initial training (through phoneme monitoring) resulted in lexical engagement in Gaskell and Dumay's study, but in that case the evidence of such engagement was lexical competition or, more specifically, the effect of the implicit training on word access when making a lexical decision. Given the difference in the types of new-word stimuli used in the two studies, Leach and

Samuel conclude that 'it may be easier to grow an offshoot of an existing lexical representation than to establish a fully functional one with no such links. That is, it is possible that "cathedruke" inherited some of its lexical functioning by virtue of its obvious ties to "cathedral"' (2007, p. 320).

In several further experiments Leach and Samuel used the same tasks to test for the two types of lexical learning with which they were concerned, exploring the effects of training methods and raising a number of additional questions. It will suffice for our purposes here to describe Experiment 2, which provided results that contrasted clearly with those of Experiment 1. In Experiment 2 the words were trained through association with pictures of highly distinct and unusual novel objects. Participants were presented auditorily with each word form together with a pair of pictures, required to guess as to the correct referent and given immediate feedback. In subsequent testing lexical configuration showed steady improvement over the course of the five days, much as was seen in Experiment 1. However, the perceptual learning effects were much stronger than those of Experiment 1, with clear evidence of learning over the course of the five days and a remarkable 30% shift in the category boundary by the last day. This suggests that, with the addition of referents (in other words, with a *link to meaning* of some kind), the training successfully promoted lexical engagement, as defined in this study. Importantly, the two experiments taken together demonstrate that word learning may result in *lexical configuration without lexical engagement* (as in Exp. 1), which confirms the value of making the distinction.

1.7.2 Developmental implications of the configuration/engagement distinction

What are the implications of these findings for our understanding of shifts in the course of infant word learning? By 11 months, as indicated earlier, infants respond differently to high-frequency word forms familiar from their everyday experience as compared with rare, unfamiliar word forms (e.g., Hallé & Boysson-Bardies, 1994; Vihman et al., 2004); furthermore, children with more advanced vocal skills give evidence of word-form recognition at 10 months, a month earlier than the age at which the group effect is reliably observed (DePaolis et al., 2016). We suggest that word-form recognition reflects *lexical configuration*, or the first step in word learning, as described above. The link with vocal preparedness (skill in producing at least two supraglottal consonants) suggests some potential for mapping input forms to vocal schemes. Meaning is not implicated in this early word learning (see also Swingley, 2007) and there is no reason to think that lexical engagement—or indeed a lexical system of any kind (Vihman, 2002)—is involved at this stage.

At about this point, or within a few weeks, most children begin to produce highly familiar word forms in situational contexts that serve as strong reminders of the uses of those words—i.e., in priming contexts (Vihman & McCune, 1994; McCune & Vihman, 2001). Evidence suggests that vocal production supports access to memory for these familiar forms, while contextual priming strengthens a still fragile meaning association; this too is consistent with the construct of lexical configuration but not, as yet, with systematization or lexical engagement.

As the infant's lexical experience grows, stronger semantic links are forged, leading to referential word use (i.e., word use that generalizes across referents, reflecting category- rather than individual item-based word knowledge: Vihman & McCune, 1994; McCune & Vihman, 2001; Vihman, 2017, 2018); this marks the onset of *lexical engagement* or *system-building*. That evidence of meanings being generalized to encompass cross-situational uses is also reflected in emergent changes to word forms. A child's use of a phonological template, with many new words produced in accord with a single schema, strongly implies the existence of *inter-word connections, or incipient lexical organization* (Vihman & Velleman, 1989, 2000). In other words, whereas there is little evidence of systematicity in the first word forms produced (Menn & Vihman, 2011), emergent templatic patterning, drawing on and adding to similarities across the child's word shapes, reveals the first steps in establishing a lexical system; this in turn should, by hypothesis, be related to the internalization of word meanings that previously depended on contextual priming. Such a relationship between referential word use and phonological templates has not so far been tested experimentally, however.

1.8 Summary, goals, research questions, and overall plan

We began by speaking of the nature of language as a system of links or associations (oppositions but also relationships of similarity and contiguity), and of the goal of studies of lexical and phonological development like this one of gaining an understanding of the origins of systematicity in the child. We stated the paradox of early accuracy followed by later regression as a concomitant of emergent, idiosyncratic system-building, reflecting children's sensitivity, as their knowledge of the lexicon grows, to the patterns and rhythms of word forms in input speech. We followed this with an account of the theoretical advances that led to the concept of templates, first in adult, then in child phonology, and we placed our thinking about development within the framework of Dynamic Systems Theory and, more specifically, of holistic approaches to phonology, including the now widely accepted idea of exemplar representations. We complemented our broad chronological account of research into infant speech processing with a brief review of production studies and the articulatory filter hypothesis, designed to shed light on the first word forms, and the experimental work that has supported it in recent years. Finally, we reviewed studies of adult word learning which, by distinguishing between lexical configuration and lexical engagement, bring new insights to the construct of emergent systematicity.

The primary objective of this book is to carry out a thoroughgoing investigation of the concept of child phonological templates; our intention is to test their reality, scope, and time span of occurrence on a cross-linguistic database. Because the concept is not widely accepted in developmental research and has a somewhat ill-defined role in current phonological theory, we will devote a great deal of space to presenting the empirical evidence that justifies positing such a phenomenon for early lexical and phonological development.

Our second objective is to reconnect the findings of child phonology studies with research carried out, especially since the 1990s, on prosodic patterns and prosodic morphology in adult systems. In that regard the book offers an exploration of the creation of lexical and phonological systematicity, broadly understood. Looking at children simplifies the picture but also amplifies the problem, given children's paucity of resources: a short attention span, an immature or undersupplied memory mechanism, and limitations in both perceptual processing experience and articulatory skills. In demonstrating ways in which systematicity can develop from existing piecemeal knowledge we provide a model against which to test some of the areas in which adult word formation has evolved; this will make it possible to consider the mechanisms of and limitations on creative lexical expansion.

Accordingly, over the course of the book we will seek to address two distinct sets of questions:

1. To what extent do child patterns reflect (a) biological or neurophysiological constraints on child production, (b) ambient language structure, or (c) 'idiosyncratic' or individual preferences or proclivities?

2. How, if at all, are child patterns related to what is understood by 'template' in adult languages or linguistic theory? And what insight into the mechanisms that motivate adult structure can we gain from child patterns based on emergent production skills and growing perceptual experience of the adult language?

In Chapter 2 we provide a brief history, from its first manifestations in the 1970s to recent theoretical discussion, of 'whole-word phonology', out of which the concept of phonological templates in development has emerged. In Chapter 3 we launch our first empirical demonstration and detail our analytic procedures. Drawing on American English data from six children, we define and characterize templates, observe how they fit into the children's developmental progression, and note the ways in which they may differ by child within a single language group. In the next two chapters we provide analyses of child data from several languages as a basis for evaluating the typological characteristics of prosodic structures (Chapter 4) and consider the differences between prosodic structures and templates, elaborating the notion of emergent systematicity as a critical aspect of the development of linguistic knowledge (Chapter 5). In Chapter 6 we introduce data from two more languages before considering unresolved issues regarding the generality, timing, emergence and fading, quantification, and function of templates.

In Chapter 7 we move to adult language to consider how the notion of template has been applied in phonological theory and description, while in Chapter 8 we explore 'language at play', or linguistic usage that is outside the grammatical core (shortenings, hypocoristics, and rhyming compounds) and thus more open to creative extension and innovation. This allows us to consider deeper relationships between pattern creation and pattern use in adult and child systems. Chapter 9 concludes the book with a summary of our main themes, some consideration of an alternative model of phonological development, and an overview of our findings.

2
Whole-word phonology
Historical and theoretical overview

2.1 Prosodic analysis

The idea of analysing a child's word forms as whole units rather than focusing on the acquisition of potentially contrasting phonemes (as did Jakobson, 1941/1968) was first raised at least indirectly in the 1960s. Francescato (1968) critiqued Jakobson's approach, remarking that:

> Children do not learn a phonemic system as such ... They do not, therefore, learn the sound following a paradigmatic scheme ... [but instead] in syntagmatic occurrences ... In fact children never learn sounds: they only learn words, and the sounds are learned through words.   (p. 148)

These proposals echo the highly original ideas set forth by J. R. Firth in 1948 in his landmark paper, 'Sounds and prosodies' (reprinted, along with several more accessible papers by Firth's followers, in Palmer, 1970; see especially Robins, 1957/1970). Firth begins by proposing:

> principles for a technique of statement which assumes first of all that the primary linguistic data are pieces, phrases, clauses, and sentences within which the word must be delimited and identified, and secondly that the facts of the phonological structure of ... various languages ... are economically and completely stated on a polysystemic basis ... For the purpose of distinguishing prosodic systems from phonematic systems, words will be my principal isolates.   (Firth, 1970, pp. 1f.)

By 'polysystemic' Firth is referring to the idea of multiple systems of contrast within a single language; the expression 'prosodic systems' here refers to the 'syntagmatic' approach, 'phonematic systems' to paradigmatic contrasts within a specific word position.

The radical theoretical position adopted by Firth and his followers explicitly rejects the almost exclusive focus on the individual segment or phoneme that characterized the practice of both the Prague School (e.g., Jakobson, 1949; Trubetzkoy, 1949) and American structuralism and the generative model that grew out of it (cf. Bloomfield, 1933, the papers collected in Joos, 1957, and Chomsky & Halle, 1968). Anderson (1985) provides a useful overview of the Firthian position, which was little remarked by mainstream American linguistics in the

Phonological Templates in Development. First edition. Marilyn May Vihman.
© Marilyn May Vihman 2019. First published 2019 by Oxford University Press.

period when Firth was most influential in Britain, and its relation to the American structuralists working in parallel. As Anderson points out, Firth's ideas, presented in writings that Anderson terms 'nearly Delphic in character' (1985, p. 179), had come to seem more familiar and relevant by the mid-1980s. That familiarity and relevance is all the stronger now, when representational phonology, with its focus on output constraints rather than on rules and rule ordering, has become dominant.

Two theoretical differences between Firthian 'prosodic analysis' and the American structuralist approach are particularly worth noting. The most important point for 'whole-word phonology' or the templatic approach to child phonological development is the core idea of a 'prosody', similar in some ways to the 'long component' introduced by Zelig Harris (1944). A prosody is a feature typically expressed 'syntagmatically' over a stretch of speech (a sequence of multiple segments) rather than being limited in expression to any one segment—although a prosody such as aspiration, for example, may be characteristic of certain word positions, where it can serve a demarcative function (unlike Harris' long components, which are more closely tied to phonemic contrast);[1] the extent of influence of a prosody may or may not be limited by independently identified morphological or lexical boundaries.

Firth speaks of the 'convenience of stating word structure and its musical attributes as distinct orders of abstractions from the total phonological complex... [i.e. as] prosodies' (1948/1970, p. 5). Under 'musical attributes' Firth is referring to word length in syllables, quantity, stress, and 'tone', including voice quality (breathiness, creakiness) and nasality, palatality, labiovelarity, retroflexion, etc. Anticipating McCarthy's 1981 analysis of Arabic phonology by thirty years, Firth notes that the 'syntagmatic study of the word complex' provides a better analysis of Arabic than does the study of the individual segments or phonemes (Firth, 1948/1970, p. 20); he suggests that the same may be true of the role of tone and voice quality in Sino-Tibetan languages, pitch in West African languages, and the syllable-based glottal feature (i.e., stød) in Danish.

Secondly, the principle of 'polysystematicity' refers to the positing of mini-contrast systems within particular word positions (initial, medial, final). Ferguson's (1963) later emphasis on the value of comparing child and adult target sounds separately in each word position is in accord with this principle (cf. also Ferguson & Garnica, 1975), as is Pierrehumbert's (2003) proposal of contextual phonemes, which she illustrates with consonantal contrasts. Vihman and Croft's (2007) 'radical templatic phonology' takes the same position, insisting on the differences so often found between the vowel inventories of stressed vs. unstressed syllables, for example.

---

[1] Anderson (1985) gives as an example the contrastive function of aspiration in cases where it obtains for syllable-onset consonants only. However, aspiration may also be a prosodic feature in the sense of stretching over a longer segmental sequence (cf. Blevins, 2004, p. 150: 'In many languages, *Vh* or *hV* sequences are produced with ambient aspiration or breathiness.').

2.2 Waterson (1971) and whole-word phonology

Natalie Waterson (1971), who was trained in the Firthian tradition, was the first to propose in some detail the concept of whole-word patterns in early phonology, with extensive illustration from a case study of her son P, at a point (18 months) when he was producing about 150 words, monosyllables and to a lesser extent open disyllables, but also combinations of up to three or four words. In this classic and highly original paper Waterson makes a striking intuitive leap from the general practice of prosodic analysis as applied to the synchronic or diachronic study of adult languages to the small corpus of words produced by a child relatively early in his development. Waterson notes the distance between her approach and the dominant perspective in the phonological literature of the time, disclaiming any relation of the 'articulatory features' she draws on to the distinctive features of generative phonology and pointedly denying any universal status for the features and structures she identifies.

Waterson's primary goals in this paper are to show, first, that there is patterning or systematicity in the child's forms. This is a point that had been previously made—although without reference to actual child data—by Fry (1966, p. 194):

> the [child's] system must be thought of as being at each stage complete in itself . . . The . . . child does not start with a set of . . . pigeonholes of which the majority remain to be occupied during the development of his speech; he is actively constructing the framework and, as each pigeonhole [i.e., phoneme] is added, the shape of the whole structure and particularly the interrelations of the units are changing.

At the same time Neil Smith (1973) explicitly rejected the idea that the child's forms might constitute a system of their own, independent of their mapping to the adults' forms. His book-length account of his own son's phonological development adheres closely to Chomsky and Halle's 1968 model, with ordered rules relating presumed adult input forms, taken to be 'underlying representations', to child forms at age two to four years. Note that Smith's analysis begins when his child was not only seven months older than the subject of P's study but was also at a more advanced point in terms of word use, having a recorded list of over 200 words.[2]

Secondly, Waterson wished to demonstrate that the words were related holistically to their targets, not segment-by-segment. As she rightly points out, the application of a 'nonsegmental analysis' frees her 'to express various correlations between child and adult structures' (Waterson, 1971/2013, p. 61). This make it possible to answer such a question as 'Why does the child "drop" certain sounds of the adult form or "substitute" for them when he is already capable of making such sounds and is in fact using them in some other contexts?' (e.g., the words with

---

[2] Unlike Waterson, Smith was also willing to claim 'universality' for characteristics he identified in his son's phonology, such as heavy reliance on consonant harmony.

Table 2.1 Waterson's P (1971): Word forms at 18 months

Adult target	Child form
(i) Reduplicated structure: Nasal	
another /əˈnʌðə/	[ɲaɲa]
finger /ˈfɪŋgə/	[ɲẽːɲẽ], [ɲiːɲɪ]
Randall /ˈrændəl/	[ɲaɲø]
window /ˈwɪndəʊ/	[ɲeːɲeː]
(ii) Reduplicated structure: Stop	
biscuit /ˈbɪskɪt/	[beːbeː]
Bobby /ˈbɔbɪ/	[bæbuː]
bucket /ˈbʌkɪt/	[bæbuː]
dirty /ˈdətɪ/	[d̪ə̩ːtɪ]
kitty /ˈkɪtɪ/	[tɪtɪ]
pudding /ˈpʊdɪŋ/	[pʊpʊ]
(iii) C₀VC$_{SIBILANT}$	
brush /brʌʃ/	[byʃ]
dish /dɪʃ/	[dɪʃ]
fetch /fɛtʃ/	[ɪʃ]
fish /fɪʃ/	[ɪʃ], [ʊʃ]
vest /vɛst/	[ʊʃ]
(iv) CV(wV)	
barrow /ˈbærəʊ/	[bʌwʊ][1]
flower /fla, ˈflawə/[2]	[væ], [væwæ]
fly /flaɪ/	[βæ], [væ], [bβæ]

Notes:
[1] At 17 months the child produced this form as a reduplicated structure, [wæwæ]; at that age he also produced [wæ] for *fly*, alongside [bβæ], and three variant forms for *hymn* or *angel* (referring to a hymn-book with angels on the cover), [aʜɔ], [æhə], [aʜõ], using a structure which also accommodates a variant of *Rooney*, [ẽʜẽ], which P produced at 18 months along with the reduplicated nasal form.
[2] Waterson (1971) provides these two adult variants.

initial fricatives in Table 2.1). More generally, Waterson's prosodic approach allows her to find the systematicity in the child's production in the absence of any evident sound-by-sound alignment of child to adult form (and thus without positing rules mapping target to child forms).

Table 2.1 provides the forms that Waterson reports for P at 1;6 (one year, six months), on which most of her analysis is based; the forms have been grouped here into four patterns, according to their prosodic structure. The child's range, in the sample Waterson provides, is limited to structures involving one or two open syllables and the closed monosyllable C₀VC$_{SIBILANT}$; the only words with more than a single supraglottal consonant are the latter, with the final limited to the voiceless palatal sibilant. With regard to the 'reduplicated structures', note that reliable vowel transcription, particularly for infant production, is notoriously difficult. As these are diary data, not based on recordings subject to repeated listening (let alone instrumental analysis), we use the term 'reduplicated' loosely here to cover both exact and less exact repetition of syllables, extending to consonant harmony, as in *Bobby, bucket*, and (disregarding the difference in voicing) *dirty*. The child has a reduplication pattern, then, that he extends to quite complex target words with nasals; he fills the C slots with the consonant that is most accessible to him, based on his current production practice.

The CV(wV) forms must also be viewed as selected, as are the C_{STOP}VC forms. The child's treatment of onset fricatives in these two patterns is paradoxical, but seems to reflect difficulty with a sequence of two similar yet distinct supraglottal consonants within a single word form—i.e., two fricatives (*fish, vest*) or a fricative and an affricate (*fetch*). In the case of *flower* and *fly*, no second supraglottal consonant is present to complicate access to the onset fricative. Thus the paradox of the differential treatment of fricative-initial targets is resolvable within a whole-word analysis.

It is unclear from study of the data Waterson provides—and of early child word forms more generally—whether the challenges posed by the words that are less accurately produced (or more radically adapted to a template of the child's own) derive from difficulties with articulation, planning, or memory. What is indisputable is that the difficulty is not only or primarily in the production of the individual sounds (although that is an issue in the case of some sounds that the child is not yet producing, such as the interdental fricatives or /r/) but in the representation, planning, or production of those sounds in a particular context.

Waterson's third goal with this paper was to defend the idea of a perceptual source for the whole-word patterns that she identified in P's word forms. She argues, based on close analysis of the phonetic features of, first, the child forms, and then of the corresponding target forms, that the child retains the 'strongly articulated features' of the adult form but not others; this accounts for the words falling into the distinct structures she identifies, which she classifies in terms of their 'dominant feature': Labial (Table 2.1, iv), Sibilant (iii) and Stop and Nasal (i, ii). In addition, Waterson identifies a Continuant structure—not used at 1;6 but produced as <VhV> at 1;5 and 1;8—for *hymn/angel* and *Rooney* (see Note 1 of Table 2.1).

The identification of what the child perceives in the input forms on the basis of what he produces cannot escape the charge of circularity. It seems unnecessary to elaborate this point, but we should bear in mind that the first experimental work in infant speech perception dates from the year in which this paper appeared. This can explain why Waterson felt able to make claims regarding infant perception of adult speech in the absence of experimental evidence of the kind we would now require (but see Waterson, 1987, a collection of her papers on child language; see also Queller's 1988 critique).

Waterson's broader insight, supported by the Firthian insistence on syntagmatic analysis, is that 'the child perceives some sort of schema in words or utterances through the recognition of a particular selection of phonetic features... which go into the composition of the forms of the words...' (1971/2013, p. 87). Importantly, Waterson further suggested that, in addition to the 'strongly articulated features', the second factor affecting what the child retains from the adult form is 'features that are already established' in the child's repertoire (Waterson, 1971/2013, p. 79), i.e., their experience with a vocal schema of a similar or somehow related shape through previous use. Experimental support for the perspicacious suggestion that the production repertoire developed by the child can affect their perception or representation of adult speech has been reported only within the past few years (see Chapter 1).

2.3 Ferguson and Farwell (1975) and lexical primacy

Charles A. Ferguson, best known for his work in the areas of sociolinguistics and applied linguistics, founded the Child Phonology Project at Stanford University soon after becoming the first linguist to be appointed there in 1967. He had a long-standing interest in child language (see Ferguson & Slobin, 1973; Snow & Ferguson, 1977; Yeni-Komshian, Kavanagh, & Ferguson, 1980; Ferguson, Menn, & Stoel-Gammon, 1992) and an analytic principle that extended to all of his work: *Let the data speak for themselves.* As Huebner (1999) puts it in his fine appreciation of Ferguson as scholar and mentor, 'he characteristically investigated phenomena in some limited, manageable, but potentially revealing domain, often something considered peripheral to legitimate inquiry by many linguists' (p. 431).

One of the most cited papers in the field of phonological development is Ferguson and Farwell (1975). The paper is in clear continuity with Waterson's case study and is also an excellent illustration of Huebner's description. It comprises a close analysis of the initial consonants of the words produced by three girls in their first months of language use; the analysis is detailed and highly specific, yet it draws broad conclusions that continue to be important today (see, for example, Beckman & Edwards, 2000b; Stoel-Gammon, 2011). Given that Ferguson began his academic life as a student of Zelig Harris, moreover, the emphasis he and Farwell place on the 'primacy of the lexical item' as opposed to the individual segment as a unit of contrast may in some sense have evolved from Harris' earlier identification of 'long components' in adult phonology.

Whereas Waterson focused on a particular moment in P's phonological and lexical development, Ferguson and Farwell trace the emergence of phonological knowledge in three girls over time. In order to maintain as open an approach to the data as possible they adopt from comparative linguistics the use of 'sound correspondences' to relate cognate lexical items; this is operationalized here as a set of 'phone trees' for each child, tracking the phones used in variants of each lexical item over the several months of the study. The method is complex and has only rarely been applied since, but the lessons that these investigators draw from the procedure are clear.

Ferguson and Farwell begin by reporting three surprises that their method uncovered. First, the children's word forms proved to be remarkably *variable*. In particular, in a single child's data a given consonant might show a different range of variants from one word to the next. This variation by lexical item is problematic if the goal is to establish either a general order of acquisition of contrasts (Jakobson, 1941/1968), or 'unique underlying forms and systematic rules' (Smith, 1973). As the authors point out (1975/2013, p. 103), the theoretical tension, for phonological development, between a focus on variability based on 'lexical primacy' and the mainstream insistence on universal principles underlying phonological structure is strongly reminiscent of the parallel but incompatible views in historical and comparative linguistics that coexisted for decades: For the European dialect geographer, *chaque mot a son histoire* 'every word has its own history', whereas for the neogrammarian, the 'laws' of sound change operate without exception (Bloomfield, 1933, pp. 328, 354; for discussion, see Malkiel, 1967; Labov, 1981).

Secondly, these early words were generally produced *more accurately than expected*, which relates closely to the third surprise, that the *target words themselves* fitted phonological constraints that corresponded rather closely to those of the child, as though they had been *pre-selected for production* (see our discussion in Chapters 1 and 3, which illustrate and elaborate these ideas). Furthermore, the later forms of some child words were less accurate but more similar to the child's other forms, reflecting in phonology the kind of non-linear advances then being reported in other domains (see the 'cognitive model' outlined in Macken & Ferguson, 1983). Ferguson and Farwell relate all three surprises to the single principle that phonological development, like historical sound change, involves not only phonetics or phonology but also the lexical parameter.

Note that the phenomenon of lexical exception to general phonological rules or mappings to the adult target is also one of the puzzles which Waterson's 1971 prosodic analysis was designed to address. In that case the phonological context proved to be sufficient to account for the difference in the child's treatment of onset /f/ and /v/ in various words, as described above. Ferguson and Farwell cite several examples in which seemingly simple words (e.g., *ball*, for Hildegard Leopold) are more variably produced than words that might seem more complex in structure (e.g., Hildegard's *Carolyn*). Some of these are instances of purely lexical exceptions, which demonstrate the difficulty of establishing contrast in the early stages of phonological development.

To illustrate variability and apparent regression in terms of target-like production or accuracy Ferguson and Farwell offer a striking phonological account of Hildegard's precocious use of the lateral in *hello* and later German *alle* 'all', between ages 1;5 and 1;7, followed by a period of use of yod as a substitute for /l/ in each of these words. Ferguson and Farwell conclude that over this period of instability in the treatment of /l/ a rule of 'liquid reduction' (or gliding) is competing with 'the acquisition of *l*, or the combining of features for liquids' (1975/2013, p. 107; see Menn & Matthei, 1992, and Menn, Schmidt, & Nicolas, 2009, 2013, for discussion of rule competition).

Here and throughout the paper the authors are explicitly engaging with Jakobson's theoretical ideas and also with the generative rule-ordering approach. However, the puzzle of early accuracy followed by a period of systematization, well illustrated in the microanalysis of Hildegard's acquisition of /l/, is also a challenge for a purely phonetic model in which the child could be expected to begin with faulty approximation to adult models and gradually improve (e.g., Davis & MacNeilage, 1990; Davis, MacNeilage, & Matyear, 2002). The final surprise, the child's apparent pre-selection of words to say, further challenges Jakobson's assumptions of a strict separation between phonetic and phonological development; the close analysis of the data from three children at the onset of phonological and lexical development casts some doubt on universalist claims while pointing up the importance of individual differences.

However, the real strength of the paper is brought out in the final section, in which child data are shown to have lessons for phonological theory. Ferguson and Farwell here make plain their disagreement with the mainstream views that were current at the time:

> The data and analysis of this study suggest a model of phonological development and hence of phonology which is very different from those in vogue among linguists. The model would de-emphasize the separation of phonetic and phonemic development, but would maintain in some way the notion of 'contrast', i.e., the distinctive use of sound differences. It would emphasize individual variation in phonological development, but incorporate the notion of 'universal phonetic tendencies' which result from the physiology of the human vocal tract and central nervous system... It would emphasize the primacy of lexical items in phonological development, but provide for a complex array of phonological elements and relations...   (1975/2013, p. 112)

Most radically, Ferguson and Farwell propose that 'a phonic core of remembered lexical items and articulations which produce them is the foundation of an individual's phonology, and remains so throughout his entire linguistic lifetime' (1975/2013, p. 112). They specify further that they see the 'primacy of lexical learning in phonological development' as implying phonetic storage of some kind that is not at first organized in terms of phonological categories or contrasts. This line of thinking readily lends itself to interpretation in exemplar terms. It allows for initial phonological representations that might be overspecified for some words or parts of words, sketchily specified for others. Ideas of this kind have only recently begun to be discussed in relation to child phonology (Menn et al., 2009, 2013; Munson, Edwards, & Beckman, 2012; Vihman & Keren-Portnoy, 2013a, pp. 5f.; Vihman, 2014).

2.4 Macken (1979) and developmental reorganization

The third foundational paper for whole-word phonology and templates in phono-logical development, Macken (1979), builds on the two studies just discussed, tracing one child's construction of a phonological system over a ten-month period. Macken begins with the child's earliest words (at age 1;7), with their lexically based organization, and concludes with the child producing multiword combinations (at 2;5), when the evidence for word-based systematicity has largely faded away and description of the consonant system in terms of phonemic contrasts and regular substitution rules has become more straightforward. As Macken points out, however, the nature of the transition from one kind of system to the other is difficult to ascertain, as the two kinds of organization actually co-occurred ('overlapped considerably': 1979/2013, p. 140) for some period of time.

This is a case study based on weekly recordings of 'Si', one of several children acquiring Mexican Spanish in Northern California who were followed as part of the Stanford Child Phonology Project. Macken begins by picking out several unique characteristics of her child subject; her study is designed not to argue for 'prosodic analysis' in general (as does Waterson), nor to indicate the importance of the word for both child and adult phonological description (as do Ferguson and Farwell), but to persuade the reader that, for some children, only a word-based phonological account will do adequate justice to the data at hand, at least for the earlier period of word use. In other words, Macken presents word-based organ-ization as a characteristic of this particular child—an individual difference in the acquisition of phonology.

Si is a voluble child who imitates roughly as many words as she produces spontaneously (though only spontaneous productions are analysed for the paper). She regularly precedes her word forms with a dummy vowel or syllable and in the earlier sessions she is also prone to embedding words in longer strings of syllables similar to those of the word form itself—a kind of advanced babble or 'jargon'. She begins combining words into longer utterances at a point when her articulatory or planning capacities are not quite ready for this advance, collapsing the intended longer utterance into two syllables in lieu of the four or more syllables that full production of each combination would require. And she frequently repeats adult words incorrectly, producing 'slips of the ear' or misperceptions based on a holistic match of target and replica (*Fernando* [a brother's name] for *Armando*, *caballo* 'horse' for *gallo* 'rooster' and so on). For the first six months of the study Si appeared to represent words as having 'a general prosodic shape (perhaps as yet unanalysed segmentally) and which can be prosodically similar in a loose way to other words' (1979/2013, p. 137).

Macken focuses on the acquisition of consonants. Of central interest are the word patterns Si produced in the early months of the study and the transformations that these patterns underwent up to the time (at around 2;1) when the system began to settle into more regular sound-based correspondences of adult to child form. Macken describes the patterns in terms of constraints on output forms, as regards both length in syllables and permissible consonantal sequences within a single form.

Macken tracks the loosening of constraints on the co-occurrence of different supraglottal consonants over the seven 'stages' she identifies; glides co-occur from the beginning with other consonants and so are excluded from the discussion, as are any words that include only a single consonant (V_0CV). The stages Macken lays out are distinguished by additions or changes to the consonants that can occur as C_1 or C_2 in two- or three-syllable word forms. In the first stage the child produces only forms with consonants that agree in place (including p...m..., with change in manner) and words with the sequence m...n.... The latter pattern is then extended to more consonants, stage by stage, but the preference for the LABIAL – DENTAL melody (and occasionally LABIAL – VELAR) persists for several months, to nearly age 2. At that point the labial-first pattern is supplemented by a velar-first option, with dentals retaining their preferred C_2 slot. As Macken shows, Si gradually filled in new consonants in each position, stage by stage, while retaining the overall constraint on possible combinations. This growth in consonant inventory occurred most strikingly at around age 2;0, when Si added several new C_1 labial and C_2 dental options and also, for a two-week period, the velar nasal, which does not occur in the Spanish system, as an option at syllable onset (e.g., *rana* 'frog' ['waŋa, 'gaŋǝ, 'ŋana] [Macken, 1979/2013, p. 144]).

The centrality of lexical learning that Ferguson and Farwell highlighted is also well in evidence here, with a variety of phonological processes being apparent as Si fits adult words into her preferred output patterns. Metathesis, for example, is used to fit *sopa* 'soap' into her most frequent pattern p/b – t/d as [pwæta]. Many more words are adapted to the pattern through truncation, beginning at 1;7 with *manzana* 'apple' [mǝn:a] and at 1;8 with her brother's name, *Fernando* [man:ǝ, wan:o]. When the labial she preferred to place word-initially came later in the target word, the initial syllable of a long word might be deleted: at 1;8 *zapato* 'shoe' [pwat:o]; at 1;9 *elefante* 'elephant' [bat:e]. Macken notes that only words with both a labial and a dental somewhere in the word were adapted to this pattern; other C_1 / C_2 combinations were realized with harmony. Furthermore, consonant substitutions differed from one word to the next, depending on the target structure and the potential for fitting into one of Si's patterns. For example, /f/ is realized as [m] in *Fernando* but as [b] in *elefante*. There are also examples of words changing patterns over time, sometimes under the apparent influence of words of similar prosodic structure, as filtered by Si's patterns, and again we sometimes see competition between different processes available to adapt adult words to an existing pattern.

As indicated, Si's consonant inventory was increasing over the period of sway of the word patterns. Furthermore, as Macken points out, Si could be seen to be learning the system of consonantal contrasts of the adult system as she added words to one pattern or another, always respecting the potential of the particular make-up of the adult word. Macken traces the construction of a phonemic inventory over this period, noting the sounds that gave Si more difficulty (e.g., the liquids) and the nature of the variability in production that ensued. In the period after 2;1 Si was producing correctly most of the words she knew. (One form, [bəˈdʌɹ] for *tenedor* 'fork', persisted in the LABIAL – DENTAL pattern that had developed at an earlier stage, a 'regressive idiom' out of step with the rest of Si's phonology.)

Macken concludes by defending the idea of the word as a basic organizational unit in Si's early phonology, based on her ample illustration of the force of Si's word patterns; the fact that this is no longer the case in the later period, when an analysis in terms of contrasts and sequencing constraints can be satisfactorily expressed in terms of phonemes, suggests to Macken that words and phonemes (and possibly features) can be taken to be part of a developmental hierarchy.

2.5 Menn (1983) and 'template matching'

Menn's influential 1983 state-of-the-art overview, the most insightful account then available of the changes in perspective in child phonology over the preceding decade, constitutes an attempt to build a new model of phonological development (itself reconsidered and thoroughly revised in Menn & Matthei, 1992, and again in Menn et al., 2009, 2013, discussed below). Menn proposes to treat the child as an active problem-solver, trying to learn how to 'sound like her companions when communicating with them' (1983/2013, p. 168). This is in agreement with Macken, who emphasized not only individual differences but the role of the child as a hypothesis-tester (cf. also Macken & Ferguson, 1983), but it contrasts with previous models—such as Jakobson's 'unfolding' of phonemic oppositions— that saw development as entirely passive (like 'the development of an embryo').

Menn begins by extending the data of interest to the prelinguistic period dismissed as irrelevant by Jakobson, providing a thoughtful account of the some-times months-long co-existence of 'sound-play' or babbling and protowords. Under 'protowords' she includes both forms 'invented' by the child—babble vocalizations used in consistent situational contexts—and forms based on input targets but used in a more limited or idiosyncratic way (see also Menyuk & Menn, 1979; Menyuk, Menn, & Silber, 1986; Vihman & Miller, 1988, in their account of the gradual shift from protoword to symbolic word use, restrict the term to forms that lack any identifiable adult model and use the expression 'context-limited words' for Menn's 'protowords' with adult models). By Menn's definition protowords are typically the first recurrent uses of a vocal form in consistent contextual settings; in line with her focus on the child's meaningful communicative efforts Menn sees them as the place where phonological learning begins.

Menn gives special attention to the nature of 'underlying representations' for child words. Despite the strong evidence of early infant ability to discriminate contrasting sounds, whether the contrast occurs in the ambient language or not, it had become clear by 1983 that for word production the child's registering of input forms was greatly influenced by their existing repertoire of vocal patterns and lexical items (as suggested by both Waterson and Macken; see also Barton, 1980). That is, from at least 8 or 10 months children filter what they hear through their increasingly rich knowledge of both the ambient language and their own vocal production (see Chapter 1). At the same time, as Menn emphasizes, the discrimination of sounds that are not in the speaker's repertoire remains wider (for adults as well as for children) than the contrasts the speaker can readily produce, suggesting a difference between an 'input' and an 'output' lexicon—hence a 'two-lexicon model'.[3]

Pinpointing the difficulty of making a sharp distinction, as much for adults as for children, between phonetics and phonology, Menn extends Ferguson and Farwell's ideas and anticipates later studies by Bybee (2001) and others that demonstrate the lexical as well as contextual basis for phonetic variability (the most striking examples, provided in Menn et al., 2013, p. 466, are the wide situationally-based variation in production of the auxiliary *can* or isolated refusal form *no* in contrast with their putative homophones, the noun *can* and the main verb *know* or adjectival *no*). As Menn also indicates, a child may be sensitive to a phonological contrast before being able to make the distinction in their production; conversely, they may be able to produce some sounds correctly, showing adequate phonetic control, without those sounds as yet participating in any contrast.

Menn's cognitive model focuses on the various 'strategies' children deploy to deal with the word forms that go beyond their current resources. Her discussion of 'avoidance' and 'exploitation of favourite sounds' are both subsumed in later templatic models under the ideas of selection (the complement to 'avoidance') and adaptation, in which well-practised sounds are overused or overgeneralized (Vihman & Velleman, 2000). However, Menn here draws the overly strong conclusion that 'avoidance is a stunning phenomenon because it implies considerable metalinguistic awareness... Avoidance must be the result of a kind of decision' (1983/2013, p. 178). This inference is no longer tenable in the light of

---

[3] Menn provides the example of the front vowels /e, ɛ, æ/ that many American dialects merge before /r/ (as in *Mary, merry, marry,* resp.). For those of us who do not have the contrast in our dialect, the forms are distinguishable only with difficulty or by reference to the context of use. Furthermore, although it is possible to learn to *produce* the sounds in a second language, it is difficult to retain such a distinction in memory (e.g., for the author as an L2 learner, the vowel-quality difference between the stressed syllable of Estonian *veri* /'veri/ 'blood' and *värv* /værv/ 'colour'). This suggests that L2 representations, even after 50 years of L2 use, may continue to be filtered through the system of contrasts initially established in the L1.

our current understanding of the impact of the implicit sense of familiarity—as well as the evidence of production affecting perception and the exemplar models Menn herself espouses in her later work.

Much of the paper is couched in terms of rule use, part of Menn's expressed intention to achieve 'a compromise model' that admits of both whole-word-based patterning, where that seems to be required, and wholly regular or predictable changes to input forms, described using the rules and rule ordering that still prevailed in mainstream adult phonology at that time. However, Menn tempers her account of 'rule use' by insisting that

> rules are always to be regarded as the analyst's tentative hypotheses about the child's mental operations. And it is also important to remember that a rule is no more than a description of a hypothesized regularity of behaviour...not an explanation.   (1983/2013, p. 179)

In discussing consonant harmony, so much more prevalent in child than adult phonology, Menn asks in what sense distance assimilation might be considered 'easier' or 'more natural' than producing a sequence of differing target consonants. She explains this in terms of the relative motoric advantage of repeating an action as compared with performing a sequence of different actions, but argues that repetition will make production easier only if it can be *planned or known in advance*; this leads her to conclude that there must be a stage in which the child plans ('programs or assembles') a word before producing it.

This understanding of the value of a known routine leads Menn to consider the then still relatively unexplored notions of 'output constraints' and 'conspiracies', or the joint functioning of several different rules or processes to create common surface forms such as permissible clusters or vowel harmony, for example (Kisseberth, 1970). Menn concludes that '*the child has to learn sound patterns, not just sounds*' (1983/2013, p. 184, her italics). She encapsulates this idea with the term 'template matching', intended to refer only to cases in which no simple alignment of child with adult form (even in combination with the relevant phonological rules or processes) will account for the child's apparently unsystematic changes to targets.

The psycholinguistic account that Menn provides for harmony readily extends to the alternative 'strategy' for dealing with the challenge of producing multiple consonants, namely, the adoption of a fixed pattern or sequence (e.g., Si's LABIAL – DENTAL pattern, discussed above; Christopher Priestly's CVjVC: see Chapter 6 and Appendix II). Here the advantage afforded by the template is not that of simple repetition but inheres in the pre-set status of the routine as a whole: It is clearly easier to redeploy a frequently used motoric routine than to plan and produce any one of a variety of different sequences, some of which may be unfamiliar to the child. However, the advantage of a fixed routine, whether it includes repetition or not, goes beyond the planning of a motoric routine. It is to be expected, as indicated above, that the child's knowledge—including their existing repertoire of motoric routines—provides critical support for the *retention* (or *representation*) of new forms. A 'schema', fixed routine, or 'template' affords a memory structure onto which a new form can be mapped, even if some aspects of the new form are lost or changed in the process. This important insight—that the child's existing knowledge must serve as one kind of filter on the wide diversity of input patterns to which he is exposed—was expressed already by Waterson (1971), as noted above.

Menn's 'two-lexicon model' is designed to capture the important point that the child's gradually increasing experience of producing particular output forms plays an active role in their processing of speech, which is taken to include the following steps: (i) perceive the input more or less correctly (*'collection of percepts/ understandings'* in the box-and-arrow flow charts Menn uses to illustrate her model), (ii) develop input representations (*input lexicon*), (iii) relate the forms heard and remembered to motor routines that the child has mastered (apply the relevant *rules*), and (iv) create an *'output lexicon'*, a parallel set of representations of known word forms embodied in ready-to-go programs which may or may not include variable slots (e.g., CVjVC, where only the <j> is set, vs. 'phonological idioms', where the word is represented as a whole program or motoric routine). This then serves as the input to the final step, articulation of the programmed vocal sequence (*'articulatory instructions'*). Menn refers to the 'programs' for individual lexical entries in the output lexicon as 'canonical forms' (following Ingram's [1974b] use of 'underlying canonical forms' to describe the commonalities— expressed as CV(S), where (S) means 'syllable'—between the words *blanket* [ba] or [babi], *by[e]-by[e]* [ba] or [baba], *daddy* [da] or [dada] and *mommy* [ma], [mami], or [mama] in the speech of one child at 1;3). Menn's usage, although not Ingram's, corresponds fairly closely to the template as we understand it here.[4]

2.6 Thelen and Smith (1994): Dynamic Systems Theory

Thelen and Smith's highly influential monograph is a theoretical account of development rooted in empirical research in the motor and cognitive domains, in no way specifically designed to speak to phonological development. Instead, it is an attempt to broadly model the *developmental interaction and integration of perception and action*. Thelen and Smith 'argue for the critical role of movement in

---

[4] Ingram (1974b) emphasized the importance of considering not only paradigmatic substitution relations between child and adult forms but also the syntagmatic relations due to both constraints on the child's word forms and the accentual patterning of the adult forms, which may in turn affect the overall shape of *what the child perceives well enough to reproduce*—resulting in an 'underlying canonical form' that is not necessarily the same as the adult form. This again is a position similar to Waterson's and directly opposed to that of Smith (1973, 2010).

the formation of dynamic representations ... [and] show how this perception-action unity is revealed in both real and developmental time in studies of infant learning and memory' (1994, p. xxii).

To get a better idea of the relevance of this approach to phonological development, consider these remarks, which apply without modification to the emergence of canonical babbling and its association with similar sound patterns in input speech:

> Correlated movement is important and perhaps critical in establishing dynamic categories ... It is movement that provides the dynamic sampling of the stimulus attributes ... [Self-initiated movement] may well be the dynamic control parameter in the emergence of many early skills ... (p. 194; on the dramatic social and cognitive effects of self-produced movement see Campos et al., 2000, who focus on the emergence of crawling)

In other words, for our purposes, the universal, maturationally paced emergence of adult-like syllable production in the middle of the first year enables a critical 'dynamic sampling' of the rapidly changing input speech stream. This sampling (as suggested in Chapter 1) results in familiar 'schemas'—word-like vocal units that provide a representational framework onto which new word forms can be mapped. This is the fundamental idea behind whole-word phonology.

Vihman, DePaolis, and Keren-Portnoy (2016) draw out some of the parallels between phonological development and DST. They see as critical elements of the theory (a) the role of variability in development advances (variability being an essential element in the selection process), (b) the cumulative effect of changes among several related skills in catalysing 'phase shifts' (stage-like changes, but with each contributory element advancing at its own rate, in parallel, in different ways in different children, with the phase shifts occurring whenever the requisite skills have all been mastered), and (c) the interaction of action and perception as the key mechanism underlying the dynamics of development. Like Studdert-Kennedy (1983, 1986), Locke and Pearson (1992) and other biologically informed approaches, Thelen and Smith characterize variability as 'the stuff of development', with individual paths or transitions reflecting 'exploration, the opportunistic seizing of possibilities, momentary choices and their exploitation in the service of function or use' (Vihman et al., 2016, p. 209). Vihman et al. provide an account of the transformation of babble into early words through this exploratory and opportunistic process (see also Chapter 1).

Thelen and Smith emphasize the importance of even small-scale longitudinal studies of infants, since, as they say:

> Groups do not change; individuals do ... While cross-sectional studies may be necessary to map the boundaries of behavioral change and to assess the stability of behavioral attractors, long sampling at an appropriately dense time scale is essential to understand the dynamics of this change. (p. 99)

This emphasis provides a welcome theoretical validation of production studies in phonological development, since so much of the literature is based on studies of small numbers of children followed fairly intensively over a period of time. More importantly, in Thelen and Smith's terms again, the 'history of actions' is critical to understanding the nature of an individual's behavioural advances. This is the kind of observation that can provide insight into phonological advance as we trace a child's forms from the first relatively accurate word production to later regression and concomitant systematization. (See, for example, Macken, 1978, 1979; Vihman & Velleman, 1989; Vihman, Velleman, & McCune, 1994; Vihman & Vihman, 2011; Khattab & Al-Tamimi, 2013; Oliveira-Guimarães, 2013: Each of these studies traces the individual paths of one to three children from the vocal production preferences observable in first word use to the beginnings of lexical organization apparent from later word forms and templates.)

Furthermore, the non-linearity we have identified as part of the process of template formation and use is entirely characteristic of developmental pathways as Thelen and Smith characterize them (as summarized in Vihman et al., 2016, p. 210):

> The notion of a predictable succession of categorically distinct 'stages' is generally revealed, on closer analysis, to be a false lead. Rather than progressive, step-by-step advances we find temporary regressions as an effect of overgeneralization or reorganization.

Finally, the concept of a developmental 'attractor' is a way of describing 'comfort zones' for the individual child in any area of learning and change. The attractor is a stable state, though not necessarily a final or fully successful one. It is a plateau or 'landing point' in the process of development, which will give way to variability only under an accumulation of pressures from other areas of action or experience before the system settles into a new attractor state. For our purposes, *templates themselves can be seen as attractors*, accessible motoric routines that serve the child well for a while but that nevertheless have to be overcome as the child continues to monitor and modify his own vocal production in the interest of matching that of his interlocutors—i.e., to achieve 'accuracy'.

2.7 Vihman and Croft (2007): Radical templatic phonology

Vihman and Croft (2007) pull together evidence for templatic structures from diary studies of children learning several languages and relate it not only to the ideas about whole-word phonology proposed by the 'classic' papers reviewed above but also to the theoretical position of Croft's *Radical Construction Grammar* (2001). In that perspective, the word, as a meaning-bearing phonological form that is also a possible 'usage event' (Bybee, 2001; Pierrehumbert, 2003), is the simplest construction or symbolic unit. This adheres to the spirit of Ferguson and

Farwell but more concretely begins to formulate a template-based phonological model for adult as well as early child phonology. This model

> proposes that a limited number of specific, actual word shapes are the first steps in phonological learning. The child gradually develops first one or a small number of phonological templates, then a wider variety of them, while at the same time inducing a range of other phonological categories and structures from the known word shapes. The result of differentiating and generalizing knowledge of the phonological structure of words in the course of language acquisition is an adult template-based model of phonological representation, with neither discontinuity [which would require eventual replacement of the child's system by the adult system, organized along different lines] nor an assumption of pre-specified adult competence.   (2007/2013, p. 19)

This is a strong stance even from the developmental point of view, making the assumption not only that all children begin with templates but also that templates (along with other 'categories and structures') continue to characterize a child's phonology as well as that of adults as the system evolves and changes—a sharp departure from Macken (1979), for example, with her emphasis on the idiosyncrasy of pattern use and her demonstration that Si's melodies fade as she masters the adult system. It also directly contradicts the evidence from studies like Macken (1979), which demonstrate the replacement of templates over the course of early development.

A broadly similar psycholinguistic model has been proposed by Redford (2015), who conceptualizes the basic planning unit for speech production as a holistic motor 'schema' like those postulated for other goal-oriented, routine, and highly automatized motoric skills (Norman & Shallice, 1986; Cooper & Shallice, 2000). Schemas are defined as 'temporally structured sequences of remembered action and their sensory outcomes' (Redford, 2015, p. 148); crucially, schemas are also associated with goals. To help with the daunting problem of identifying the goals and schemas that serve as units in adult speech production planning Redford turns to development, which she sees as 'a process of schema formation triggered by the identification and repeated implementation of communicative goals' (Redford, 2015, p. 4). Accordingly, she sees the prelinguistic occurrence of protowords, whole-word-like units with either global or highly specific, context-limited meanings, as a plausible starting point for schema formation. Thereafter the child proceeds to learn word forms linked to referential meanings but more broadly usable across situations. Typical length of utterance and the complexity of the articulatory action sequences of the word forms themselves are initially limited by working memory and the child's lack of practice. 'These schemas are proposed as initially equivalent to the "word templates" of very early child language... but are assumed to become elaborated and differentiated... over developmental time' (Redford, 2015, p. 148).

Thus both of these adult-oriented models make farther-reaching, bolder proposals than are generally seen in the developmental literature. However, the two models are complementary: Redford does not concern herself with sublexical phonological elements or structure but with the representation and implementation of articulatory action-plans and their combination into larger schemas (in other words, the emergence of automatized collocations or formulas), while Vihman and Croft do not address issues of phonetic implementation or the build-up of constructions beyond the word.

One critical aspect of whole-word phonology, mentioned above primarily in connection with Waterson's Firthian approach, is the greater attention paid to syntagmatic than to the paradigmatic substitutions that were the main focus, for example, of the earlier large-scale studies undertaken to determine at what age most children could accurately produce each of the sounds of English (see Ingram, 1974b; Vihman, 2003). Vihman and Croft point out that recent research, facilitated by technological advances in creating corpora that make frequency counts straightforward, has demonstrated the effects of phonotactic familiarity, or frequency, on the processing of both nonwords (which is facilitated by such familiarity at the sublexical level) and real words (which is made somewhat more difficult, due to lexical competition: Vitevich, Luce, Charles-Luce, & Kemmerer, 1997; Vitevich & Luce, 1998, 1999). In several studies Beckman and her colleagues have used nonword repetition to test these ideas with three- to four-year-old children (e.g., Beckman & Edwards, 2000a; Edwards, Beckman, & Munson, 2004; Beckman, Munson, & Edwards, 2007). These studies show that child familiarity with whole-word sequences leads to more accurate production (see also Storkel, 2001, 2004; Keren-Portnoy, Vihman, DePaolis, Whitaker, & Williams, 2010). This then is evidence of the continuing importance of whole-word patterns or schemas (in Redford's sense, not Waterson's, in the case of three- to four-year-olds), well past the single-word period.

In their section on development Vihman and Croft (2007) focus on early phonological learning, however. Four diary studies of the first fifty-word period (featuring children acquiring English, Estonian, or German) are presented in some detail, including the words selected or adapted to each child's templates. In addition, a brief account of the VCV pattern in a few children each learning English, Estonian, Finnish, French, or Welsh demonstrates the role of the accentual or rhythmic patterns of the ambient language on template formation. French words are accented on the second syllable (when phrase-final); the remaining languages are trochaic (strong-weak stress), but have phonetically (Welsh) or phonologically (Estonian, Finnish) long or geminate consonants; only English, with its strong initial-syllable stress, rarely shows onset consonant omission in children's adapted forms. Thus child experience of the accentual patterning of the ambient language interacts with the articulatory, planning, or representational challenges of adult word forms:

> In most cases ... omission of the initial consonant appears to be a way to arrive at a pronounceable form despite the difficulty posed by a word-internal noncontiguous consonant sequence. This is a striking demonstration of the effect of the

whole-word (disyllabic) pattern on learning, since it is the lengthening of a medial consonant or final vowel, or both, which appears to draw the child's attention away from the initial segment, typically considered critical to word learning in English. (Vihman & Croft, 2007/2013, p. 38. For experimental evidence of the effect of medial geminates in drawing child attention away from the onset consonant in Italian children's word-form recognition as well as production, see Vihman & Majorano, 2017.)

Vihman and Croft conclude that the templates are the result of 'implicit inductive generalizations from the lexicon':

> We take them to be the emergent product of three sources of phonological knowledge for the child: (1) familiarity with the segmental patterns typical of the adult language, which advances steadily over the last few months of the first year [i.e., implicit knowledge gained in the prelinguistic period] . . . ; (2) developing motoric control and familiarity with a subset of adult-like phonological patterns due to production practice (babbling); and (3) increasing familiarity with the structure implicit in the children's own first lexicon.
>
> (Vihman & Croft, 2007/2013, p. 40)

They see phonological organization as being expressed in the templates each child develops, with other phonological categories expected to emerge only later.

In the final section of the paper Vihman and Croft provide reasons to adopt a templatic model of adult phonology, drawing on exemplar and usage-based approaches. The primary argument is that neither phonemes nor distinctive features, the key abstract elements of phonological theory, are usefully defined either 'universally' or in the absence of context or reference to the particular word forms in which they occur. In other words, the variability of speech production as well as the typological variability manifested in the world's languages makes such definitions problematic. First, high variability characterizes 'individual usage events' in adult as well as child speech production. Secondly, feature assignment to vowels, for example, is highly variable in cross-linguistic perspective, as features must be defined very differently from one language to the next. Finally, the variability between vowel inventories in stressed vs. unstressed syllables, for example, or in the phonetic manifestation of consonants in onset vs. coda position constitutes good reason to define phonemes positionally rather than in absolute terms for any given language.

Vihman and Croft note the similarity of the position they advocate to that of both Bybee (2001) and Pierrehumbert (2003):

> The word template must be the primary unit of phonological representation, and the individual segment category is derived from it. . . . Although Pierrehumbert does not take this position explicitly, she does assume that the lexicon is a central part of the cognitive architecture that is the target of phonological acquisition (Pierrehumbert 2003a: 116) and she recognizes that the ability to perceive what

she calls 'prosodic structure', which is basically our notion of template, must be (and is) acquired very early (Pierrehumbert 2003a: 140). Bybee explicitly takes the position that the word is the basic unit of phonological representation (Bybee 2001: 29–31) and that segment categories are 'emergent' (Bybee 2001: 85; 89–95).

(Vihman & Croft, 2007/2013, pp. 46f.)

Vihman and Croft conclude that 'the adult templates are both more general and more varied than those of the child, but this is a difference in degree, not kind' (Vihman & Croft, 2007/2013, p. 47).

2.8 Menn et al. (2013): Usage-based models and exemplar theory

In a recent overview Menn and her co-authors have proposed a new model that takes account of the major changes that have occurred over the period since Menn (1983), not only in child phonology but also in phonological theory itself, which has begun to take on board insights from psychology, establishing a far more fertile ground on which to develop a deeper understanding of the learning process. As Menn et al. (2013) put it, usage-based models

> permit us to consider the representation of a word's form as something that develops continuously over time in strength, precision and accessibility – a reconceptualization of 'representation' which has long been psycholinguistically necessary for really understanding language development. And these models allow us to bring frequency data to bear on development without ignoring the equally important contributions of linguistic structure. (p. 460)

These introductory words make it clear that Menn's goals in developing a model of child phonology have not changed: She is still addressing the same challenge, to combine psychological approaches to learning (which she previously referred to as 'cognitive') with the understanding of the role of linguistic structure that has accumulated over the years, an understanding that relates to the notion of 'pattern force' introduced by Macken (1979). The essential puzzle—the origins of linguistic system in the child—remains a challenge. However, the advances afforded by usage-based models (in which each vocal production affects all subsequent processing, in both production and perception) and exemplar theory (according to which each perceived utterance takes its place in a 'cloud' of experienced speech, providing a model of representation that accounts for the effects on subsequent processing) now give us a far richer platform on which to build.

Menn et al. see their linked-attractor model as elaborating on Vihman and Croft's radical templatic phonology, addressing such missing elements as the relation of the child forms to the adult input and the way in which that gap is gradually filled. Specifically, it is meant to extend the radical templatic approach 'beyond its focus on the child's developing sensory-motor output representations ... [to] handle three other basic aspects of phonological representation: the child's developing input representation of the adult model word, the web of relationships among the input representations, and the child's auditory representation of her own productions' (p. 461; for a related approach Menn et al. recommend Munson et al., 2012).

Menn et al. emphasize that they are attempting to develop 'a psycholinguistic model, not a purely linguistic theory' (p. 474), and accordingly feel free to include theoretical elements that developed independently as part of earlier competing approaches to child phonology and that to some extent overlap (or do the same work): TEMPLATES, not only for output forms but also for the perception (or misperception) of unfamiliar input forms as more familiar ones (e.g., the name *Menn* heard as *mend*, *Chafe* as *Chase*, or more radically, over the telephone, *Marilyn* /ˈmɛɹələn/ as *Ryan* /ˈrajən/, in which the stressed initial syllable apparently failed to register with the listener); OUTPUT CONSTRAINTS, which limit the forms a child can produce; STORED OUTPUT FORMS, which account for the persistence of earlier 'entrenched' forms even after the child's phonetic skills and phonological systematizing have moved on (i.e., 'regressive idioms'), and RULES, which serve the purpose of mapping adult to child forms when these are recurrent and regular or systematic, as is the case for the phonological processes that came to be so widely used in the 1970s (Ingram, 1976; Grunwell, 1982) and that continue to play an important role in clinical phonology (Preston & Edwards, 2010; Macrae, 2017). Menn and her colleagues are very conscious of the changing fashions in linguistic description (e.g., the move to rely on constraints instead of rules) but maintain that 'a rule is a way of directly describing input-output mapping, and if children behave as if they have directly accessible maps from "how I hear it" to "how I say it," then it's useful to be able to describe this behavior formally' (p. 474.).

These constructs all form a part of the linked-attractor model-in-progress, which adopts as basic the chaos-theory notion of 'attractors', or ways of perceiving or producing linguistic forms that range in strength from minimal to strongly entrenched, depending on the speaker/listener's experience—a welcome escape from the unrealistic categorical distinction between 'having' or 'not having' a representation that characterized earlier models. This means that the emergence of representations, for both input forms and the child's own output forms, can be traced over development, beginning in the prelinguistic babbling period and involving both situational meanings and their lexical and affective associations—the foundation for linguistic meaning—and auditory-articulatory matches, which may be supported and strengthened by social responses.

2.8.1 Development in representation

Menn and her colleagues account for the well-established finding of strong continuity between babble and early words and the relative accuracy of those words in terms of their attractor metaphor:

> Many of a child's early attempts to say words are likely to "fall into" the late babble articulatory attractors, so late babble attractors typically become the articulatory routines for early words...Each attempt to say a word also builds or strengthens links between the child's representation of that word's articulation and what the child means by saying it, as well as between those representations and the adult responses to it, etc.   (p. 476)

Menn et al. add the general principle (prefigured in Menn, 1983), 'everything that we do becomes engrained with repetition, regardless of whether this involves links within modalities (like purely auditory templates) or across auditory and motor modalities (like babble routines/patterns or lexical entries)' (p. 477). A novel proposal in this model, which further illustrates this principle, is that, once well established, an input-output mapping—i.e., a child's 'rule' or link between an adult form and their own production—may itself become an 'attractor', or the source of further 'adaptations' (in templatic terms) of an analogous kind.

Thus babble practice and the typical infant experience of hearing some of the same speech forms over and over in the course of daily routines, along with early attempts at word use, lead to the output and input lexicons and the increasingly dense *network of connections* between child word forms and adult targets, between those phonological forms and other, similar sounding words, and between the meanings (situational contexts or occasions of use) associated with those word forms. This, in other words, is the foundation, in child exposure and learning, for the systems that constitute adult knowledge of language, a constant work in progress from the perspective of usage-based theories that see 'performance', or language in action, as continually being transformed into 'competence' (see Thelen & Smith, 1994, ch. 1; Bybee, 2001, pp. 5f.).

2.8.2 The problem of variability

Variability has generally been seen as an obstacle to linguistic analysis of child speech and has often been simply disregarded, with single child variants chosen to represent each word type produced (e.g., Ingram, 2002). Yet variability, long since recognized in sociolinguistics as a critical element in adult languages, is an even more unavoidable characteristic of child language, as mentioned repeatedly in this chapter (see Sosa & Stoel-Gammon, 2006); recognition of this fact is critical to understanding the nature of development. Menn and her colleagues outline four 'levels of pervasive variation in child phonology' (p. 480), two of them internal to the individual child, two of them external.

(i) *Tokens of the same word may vary from one moment to the next.* This may reflect lapses of memory or attention, neuromotor or articulatory instability, competition between emergent templatic models, or transient priming effects from recently heard word forms, among many possible sources.

(ii) *Variation in sound substitutions*, or phonological rule or constraint applications, *may vary lexically*, as discussed above in connection with Ferguson and Farwell (1975). The 'phonological idiom' (Moskowitz, 1970) is one kind of lexical exception; wholesale adaptation of word forms to templates, as seen in Waterson's P and Macken's Si, for example, is another. Menn et al. note that, 'given the relatively coarse grain of most child phonology data, it may even be the case that all rule changes will turn out to be word-by-word when we have enough data to examine them closely' (p. 482) and, like Ferguson and Farwell, Menn and her colleagues note the similarity of this problem to the problem of the spread of historical sound change: Does change occur across the board, affecting all words with the relevant phonological patterns at once, as the neogrammarians insisted (see also McAllister Byun, Inkelas, & Rose, 2016; Rose, 2018)? Or do they diffuse gradually across parts of the lexicon?

(iii) *External variability—individual differences across children—is the rule, not the exception*, as Macken and many others have convincingly shown. Despite a chronic expectation on the part of linguists and psychologists not involved in research with children, differences in input cannot be the source of most of these individual differences: Adults speaking the same language are remarkably similar in all the ways that we can easily quantify (e.g., frequency of use of different segmental features, length in syllables and use of open vs. closed syllables: Vihman, Kay, Boysson-Bardies, Durand, & Sundberg, 1994; DePaolis, Vihman, & Keren-Portnoy, 2011; Majorano, Vihman, & DePaolis, 2014), while their children differ sharply in these respects in their babbling and first words.

(iv) *Cross-linguistic variability plays a substantial role in phonological data*; we document and discuss cross-linguistic effects in Chapter 4.

2.8.3 Linked-attractor model

In the last part of their chapter Menn et al. outline their own model in greater detail, fleshing out the concept of the strengthening of links through repeated experiences of perception, production, or the mappings between them by working through some specific examples. Generally speaking, the model emphasizes the process, neural activation, by which the representations of input and output forms become more solid and more readily accessible. This is the process that culminates in the phonological and lexical networks of the adult system. Finally, the 'attractors' in terms of which the model is conceptualized are multimodal, reflecting the many distinct aspects of speech perception and production and language use that can affect the form a word takes—i.e., the many sensorimotor effects, proprioceptive and visual as well as auditory, and also elements outside of phonetics and phonology including syntax, meaning, and discourse context.

The model is ambitious and admittedly a work in progress. Menn and her colleagues conclude with problems and challenges for the model but also note its advantages over other, less broadly conceived approaches. The insights gained from drawing on a range of distinct theoretical models are balanced by a realistic assessment of the difficulty of the task: As the authors point out, regardless of what can be learned from the conceptual approach they recommend, which proposes rules, constraints, and attractors as ways to model the child's advances in systematicity, all of these 'are just schematic compared to the real level of explanation ... [that] of patterns of neural activity' (p. 495), and that level remains far beyond our reach for the foreseeable future.

2.9 Concluding remarks

The notion of whole-word phonology, as it evolved from Waterson's Firthian-based analyses of her son's data to Vihman and Croft's explicit attempt to characterize adult phonology within a 'radical templatic' framework, is rooted in the phenomena of word production in the single-word period. As we will see in later chapters, reliance on these holistic patterns is driven by the challenges peculiar to the developmental period when a child's cognitive capacities and understanding of communication outpace articulatory advances. Linguists who have not themselves carried out observational studies of development in this period, such as Jakobson, for example, or Chomsky and Halle—or even Smith, who began observing his son Amahl at a considerably later point in terms of lexical knowledge, have failed to take into account the nature of word learning and phonological development at a time when a phonological system has yet to be established (Vihman, 2002).

Within a generative theoretical framework Rose (2018) takes issue with what he calls 'models [that] limit formalism to readily identifiable units such as words, syllables and phones. These latter, *more holistic approaches to phonology* generally consider sub-segmental units (features) and sub-syllabic constituents (e.g. onsets, codas) to be irrelevant to the functioning of human languages' (p. 1; our italics). Rose himself, in contrast, 'support[s] the view that *abstract categories are fundamental to our characterization of phonological systems*' (p. 46, our italics). Formally, he 'embrace[s] the emergentist position that abstract categories are not innately available to the child but gradually emerge within his/her lexicon through learning' (p. 46). He goes on to observe correctly that 'most of the arguments brought in favour of templates come from studies documenting the earliest (and most idiosyncratic) period of phonological productions' (p. 50); however, he mischaracterizes these arguments as being 'based on babbles and early words from children with vocabulary sizes often restricted to 25 or 50 words' (p. 50).

As we will illustrate at some length, the arguments for templatic organization are based not on babble or the first words but on the period that follows, when the child has begun to accumulate a small database of her own word forms. The emphasis on 'own output' is critical and runs as a unifying thread throughout the literature we have reviewed in this chapter. The initial matching of familiar articulatory routines to comparable input forms can be understood as 'kick-starting' word production, while the emergent lexical base of output structures, together with the cognitive and communicative advances that underlie an expanding representational network of related forms, support the generalization and initial systematization that template use reflects.

3

Building the evidence

From item learning to templates

The evidence for templates as a phenomenon in phonological development comes from the study and analysis of forms used in the early stages of word production, from first words to the period of first word combinations or a little later. In this chapter we present data from six children acquiring American English as a way of illustrating the progression from early, relatively accurate forms to later, more holistic (and less accurate) matches to the input. In the process we also outline procedures for identifying prosodic structures and templates in child data.

3.1 First word use

Children's first identifiable words, regardless of the ambient language or languages, share a number of characteristics: They are limited both segmentally and in terms of prosodic structure (that is, length in syllables and syllable structure), yet they are nevertheless relatively accurate. Menn and Vihman (2011) demonstrate this by providing the first four to six recorded words of 49 children learning 10 languages.[1]

As a starting point for discussion consider the sample of first recorded words of six monolingual American English learners included in Menn and Vihman's Appendix I (Table 3.1). These data derive from two observational studies (Vihman & McCune, 1994; McCune & Vihman, 2001) in which twenty children were recorded weekly or monthly in the home, by one or two familiar investigators, while engaged in a half-hour of largely unstructured play with a caregiver, usually the mother. The data from these children give some idea of the range of child ages at first words (from 9 to 13 months) and preferred first word forms; in the larger set of first words from sixteen children learning American English provided in Menn and Vihman's Appendix I, the oldest observed age for first identifiable word use is 20 months.

We see from Table 3.1 that the 29 target words are themselves 'child-like' in form: Six (counting as separate instances the same word targets used by different children) are onomatopoeia, or conventional adult words representing non-verbal

---

[1] To illustrate the range of variability present in early word forms, if recorded and transcribed on multiple re-listenings (as opposed to diary records, which are typically written 'on the fly'), Menn and Vihman also provide data from nine children recorded from 9 to 18 months in Yorkshire, England (App. II); some of these data are included in Chapter 4.

Phonological Templates in Development. First edition. Marilyn May Vihman.
© Marilyn May Vihman 2019. First published 2019 by Oxford University Press.

Table 3.1 First word forms: American English (adapted from Menn & Vihman, 2011); a published source is indicated for each child. The data sets are ordered by child age; textual references to individual children retain that ordering

Child name, age	Target word	Adult form	Child form
1. Alice (Vihman, Velleman, & McCune, 1994); 9–10 mos.			
	baby	/ˈbeɪbi/	[pɛpɛ:], [tɛɪti:]
	daddy	/ˈdædi/	[dæ]
	hi, hiya	/haɪ/, /ˈhaɪjʌ/	[haːi:], [ʔaːjɛ], [haɪje] [haɪjʌ] …
	mommy	/ˈmɑmi/	[m̩ːɑnːə]
	no	/noʊ/	[njæ]
2. Deborah (Vihman, 2014); 10 mos.			
	baa	/bæ:/	[bæː]
	baby	/ˈbeɪbi/	[be], [pipe], [bebe]
	hi, hiya	/haɪ/, /ˈhaɪjʌ/	[hai], [ai], [haie], [aie], [eː], [aː]
	monkey	/ˈmʌŋki/	[mamːɛ]
	uh-oh	/ˈʌʔːoʊ/	[ʌʔːɛ]
3. Molly (Vihman & Velleman, 1989); 10–11 mos.			
	baby	/ˈbeɪbi/	[bæpæ]
	cracker	/ˈkɹækər/	[pakæ], [kwɑ], [wæʰk], [pækwɑ], [kʌk]
	moo	/muːː/	[meʔje]
	night-night	/ˈnaɪtnaɪt/	[hʌnːʌ], [noʊnæ]
4. Timmy (Vihman et al., 1994); 11 mos.			
	ball	/bɔl/	[pæ], [bæ], [ʔəpæ], [abːa]
	block	/blɑk/	[əpʰə], [ʔʌβæ], [pæ]
	car	/kɑr/	[kɑə], [akːɑʰ]
	kitty	/ˈkɪti/	[kʰə̣], [kʰɑ̣], [kɑkɑ], [ʔukɑ] …
	quack-quack	/ˈkʰwækwæk/	[kʰə̣], [kʰɑ], [kʰɑʰkɑʰ], [gaga] …
5. Sean (Vihman & Kunnari, 2006); 12 mos.			
	all gone	/ˈɔlgɔn/	[ʔɔdæː]
	boo	/buː/	[pʊ]
	dog	/dɑg/	[tak]
	tick	/tɪk/	[tɛh], [tɪʔ], [tɪ̣], [tʊ̣t]
	woof	/wʊf/	[wʊ], [ʔʊʔ], [ʔoʊ]
6. Emily (Vihman, 2010); 13 mos.			
	baa, bow-wow	/ˈbæː/, /ˈbaʊwaʊ/	[pæpæ], [bæbæ], [ʔapɪæ], [pæː]
	beads	/biːdz/	[bi], [pʰi]
	daddy	/ˈdædi/	[tæ], [hadatɛ]
	up	/ʌp/	[ʌp], [ʌpə], [ʌpije], [æb]

sounds (*baa* [*2], *bowwow, moo, quack-quack, woof*), a part of the 'baby talk' repertoire that is particularly salient in the input (due to special sound effects, use in isolation and often repeatedly within a turn, and so on: see Laing, Vihman, & Keren-Portnoy, 2017).

The target words include no more than two syllables, with mono- and disyllabic forms about equally represented. Most feature open syllables, with few word-final consonants; clusters are rare, except across the occasional morpheme boundary (three word-initial clusters, *block, cracker, quack-quack*; two medial, *all gone* and *night-night*, and one final, *beads*). Disregarding these clusters, which the children generally do not produce and show little evidence of representing at all, most of the target words include only a single consonant type (19 words, or 66%).

Consider now the word shapes the children produce: All are monosyllables or disyllables, or vary between the two. The children differ in their preferred forms, however, with some consistently producing all or mainly monosyllables (e.g., Sean) and others mainly disyllables (Molly), while the remaining children produce monosyllables for some targets, disyllables for others, or vary between the two for the same adult target. Of the variable forms some include 'dummy' syllables unrelated to the target (i.e., non-target syllables preceding or following the more target-like portion: cf. Timmy's forms for *ball* and *block* or Emily's forms for *up*). The children's forms largely consist of open syllables. Codas occur in one or more of the first words of just three of the six children (Molly *cracker*, Sean *dog, tick*, Emily *up*).

The segments that the children produce are variable by child. Four of the 29 words produced lack a 'true' supraglottal consonant (we group glides and glottals together as not fitting that category, as these are the only consonants produced in the pre-canonical period of vocal production: see Vihman, 2014, ch. 4, for an overview). These are based on two target words with /h/ or glottal stop in the adult form (*hi(ya), uh-oh*) and *woof*. All of the children produce stops, primarily labial or coronal, but Timmy produces onset velars in three words (matching the initial consonant of the targets) and Molly in just one, showing by the range of variants recorded that the production was exploratory and perhaps in some sense effortful; Sean has a single word-final velar, a match to target. Two children produce words with nasals in the stressed syllable, for the word targets *monkey, moo*, and *night-night*. Only two child words include more than one supraglottal consonant type within the same word: Molly produces [pɑkæ], [pækwɑ] among her several variants of *cracker*, the onset labial perhaps reflecting the child's response to the lip-rounding that accompanies English [ɹ]; Sean succeeds in producing *dog* quite accurately.

Finally, the vowels, which are notoriously difficult to transcribe reliably (see Davis & MacNeilage, 1995), are largely drawn from the lower and front portions of the vowel triangle, as transcribed. High front [i]—more common in words than in babbling (Davis & MacNeilage, 1990)—occurs both as the final syllable of disyllables (Alice *baby*) and in monosyllables (Emily *beads*). Non-low back vowels, like velar consonants, are more rarely produced. Finally, one child produces the front rising diphthongs [ei] and [ai] in her first words, matching the target (Alice *baby, hi*).

These English-learning children's very first words can be termed relatively accurate in the sense of being close to their targets, with 'errors' or failures to achieve a match being due more often to omission than to substitution or other more radical changes. We disregard voicing, for two reasons: Voicing contrasts are not mastered in production until a year or more after the first words are produced (Macken, 1980) and the accurate transcription of voicing is particularly challenging, especially in the absence of acoustic analysis, which has not been carried out for most of the data we draw on here.

The word forms are limited in many ways by the children's emergent vocal resources and are thus broadly similar, although individual differences are also evident. Similarity to the targets can be understood to reflect an unconscious selection process on the child's part, as discussed in Chapter 1; this provides a plausible account for the simplicity of the targets themselves as well as for their relative accuracy. We will return to the characterization of first words in Chapter 4, when we look at children acquiring British English and five other languages.

3.2 Prosodic structures and templates

We now skip ahead to look at the word forms to be observed a few months later, when the children are producing some 30–50 different word types in a half-hour recorded session.[2] We turn to that lexical point because it is difficult to identify patterns in a sample much smaller than that.

To provide a solid basis for discussion we stay with data from the six children included in Table 3.1. We begin by focusing on the *prosodic structures* used by each child, which will make it possible to compare both across children, looking at individual differences, and over time, looking at changes with development. We will again find notable similarities across the children with respect to developmental path. At the same time, the extent of individual differences will now be more apparent as well, as each child settles into one or more preferred prosodic structures or production patterns. Consideration of the full set of readily defined prosodic structures used by each of the children will then provide a basis for considering how templates may be identified.

Templates can generally be observed only some time after a child's first 20–50 words have been produced but before the child has achieved an expressive lexicon of as much as 200 words (Renner, 2017; see discussion in Chapter 6). Here we analyse for each child data from the first session in which she produces about 30 or more distinct word types. A comparison of parental reports with recorded and transcribed sessions occurring in parallel suggests that the word types produced in a half-hour recording session in the home, with familiar investigators and a relaxed atmosphere (Vihman & McCune, 1994), may represent close to half of the child's vocabulary in this developmental period (Vihman & Miller, 1988). Thus the data provided here can be taken to reflect a total cumulative vocabulary of about 60 to 80 or 100 words.

---

[2] In previous studies we have identified a 'twenty-five-word point' (25wp), based on spontaneous word use only; here we have selected sessions with closer to 30 or more words, including imitations.

The children's ages at the lexical point that we are considering here fall within a narrower range than did age at first word production—from about 15 months for Molly to 17 months for Deborah and Timmy. This is not a random sample, however, and the mean age is lower than is typical. These data are drawn from two studies that transcribed child word production only up to the age of 16 or 17 months; the children included here are the only ones, out of ten children each seen by McCune and Vihman in separate studies in New Jersey and California, respectively, who reached the '25wp' criterion (spontaneously attempting to produce 25 or more different words in a single session by that age: Vihman & McCune, 1994; McCune & Vihman, 2001). The data are thus biased towards children who made relatively rapid lexical progress. The time lapse between first recorded words and the data reported here ranges from three (Emily) to six months (Alice, Timmy: see Vihman et al., 1994, which tracks Alice's and Timmy's progress over this period).

3.2.1 Identification of prosodic structures and distinct word variants

The principles that underlie the establishment of prosodic structures and distinct word variants are described here. We distinguish prosodic structures only when they account for *at least 10% of the total identifiable variants* in the session (see Vihman, 2016). Distinct forms that share the same prosodic structure while differing in voicing, for example, or in the quality of a low vowel (front or non-front) or in the presence or absence of a dummy vowel, are listed together and treated as a single variant; however, *no more than a single variant of any word is included in a given prosodic structure*. This means that an initial exploratory analysis must be made to determine the total 'identifiable variants' before a final categorization is possible.

Where the child has produced *variants of a single target form that fit differing prosodic structures*, we count the variants separately (e.g., Alice, *clean*: CVC [tʰind], CVCV [tiːni]). That is, word targets are counted more than once if and only if they are produced with variants that fit different structures, out of those found to account for over 10% of the child's variants. This necessarily requires an iterative process: Once the child's variant productions have been sorted into the generic categories of CV and CVCV—i.e., into structures differing by length in syllables—they are analysed more finely, to identify the proportion of forms with diphthong (VV) or coda, for example, or with and without harmony. The total number of variants in distinct structures is used to assess the 10% criterion; this must be done again each time that new structures are identified by reanalysing the more generic categories.

However, to keep a clear account of the extent of use of prosodic structures, special attention is required in cases in which two structures posited in an initial categorization are later combined because one or both is found to account for fewer than 10% of the potential total variants. In any such case variants of a given word that differ only by the difference between these two structures are combined as free variants within the structure and the total variants are reduced accordingly. We exemplify this here with two concrete cases; see Table 3.2b for a fuller account of each child's word production and prosodic structures in the relevant half-hour recording session (at 16 months).

(1) Emily, who produced 29 different words spontaneously—and a potential total of 44 variant forms—has 20 CV forms (45% of all variants in distinct structures) and 4 CVV forms (9%). As CVV is not sufficiently well represented to be included as a separate structure, the variants are combined as CVV_0. In this case the differences in the structures of variant forms of both the letter name A—[eː] and [ʔeɪ]—and *more*—[mʌ, me] but also [mɔə]—are overlooked, to avoid including more than one variant of the same word in the one structure. The resulting CVV_0 structure then accounts for 22 (or 52%) of the variants Emily produced in the session, which now number only 42.

(2) Molly, who produced 31 different words spontaneously, 14 imitations, and a potential total of 48 structurally distinct variants, has 12 CVV_0C forms (34% of all variants in distinct structures) and 3 monosyllabic harmony forms (C_1VC_1: 7%). Here again, as monosyllabic harmony is not sufficiently well represented to be included as a separate structure, the variants are combined in the generic CVV_0C structure, disregarding the differences in the two variant forms of *glasses*, [tˈak] and [kak]. The resulting structure then accounts for 32% of the variants Molly produced in the session, which now number 47.

Aside from harmony and reduplication, which are particularly common in this period of word production, none of the structures are specified as to segmental content for any slot; analysis involving pre-established segment classes, segmental sequences, or specific fixed segments will be discussed below, when we take up the question of defining templates.

The key steps in the procedure for distinguishing variants and prosodic structures are as follows.

1. All of the variants produced in a session are broadly categorized by prosodic structure (with regard to segmental specification in the case of harmony or reduplication only) and counted to establish the total number of prosodic variants. Variants with differences in voicing, minor differences in vowel quality, consonant substitution, etc. are not counted separately.

2. Variants that differ in length in syllables, syllable shape (with or without coda, with single-vowel or diphthongal nucleus) and presence or absence of harmony, for example, are distinguished to create prosodic structures (e.g., CV, CVV, CVC, for monosyllables, CVCV, VCV, CVCVC, C_1VC_1V and Reduplicated for disyllables) for all occurring variants. These variants

are then tallied by structure to arrive at the number of distinguishable variants.

3. Each structure is treated as separate if and only if it accounts for 10% or more of the total variants. Structures with and without harmony are combined if there are fewer than 10% in either structure (as is the case with Molly's monosyllabic harmony structure, given as an example above).

Note again that the procedure must be iterative: Variants are distinguished if there are at least 10% such forms in a given structure; the proportions change as variants are separated out from the more general category. The inclusion of differing variants, according to the criteria given for identifying such differences, is meant to be as exhaustive as possible. However, where there is no more general structure under which to subsume variants that account for fewer than 10% of the total, those 'left-over' variants are included in the overall variant total but are not taken to constitute a structure in their own right. For example, Emily has a single monosyllabic harmony variant, *truck* [kæk]; as she has no other CVC variants, this is treated as a 'stray' variant or 'one-off' production, a likely indication of later advances but not yet a systematic element in her own production. It is not included in Table 3.2.

Table 3.2(a, b) shows, for the six American children, the prosodic structures that account for at least 10% of the word-form variants each of them produced in the session analysed. For each structure the table indicates the proportion of all variant forms produced in the session that conform to it. The variants within a given structure generally adhere to that structure, but with a certain amount of variability, including the frequent presence of non-target-like vowels or even CV syllables preceding the target-related form (dummy syllables). Note that, for English, glottal stop is treated as a possible coda consonant, as glottal stop may be the manifestation of a coda consonant in input speech. However, forms with and without final glottal stop may be included in the (open) CV or CVCV structures, depending on their status (i.e., their relative frequency) in the child's production. Similarly, variants with and without other codas are included in the open-syllable structure if the structures do not reach 10% separately. We begin by presenting one child, Alice, in Table 3.2a, followed by some discussion of what the table shows; the remaining children are presented in Table 3.2b.

To provide a basis for later discussion of prosodic structures and templates, Table 3.2a distinguishes SELECTED and ADAPTED variants within each structure. This involves a comparison of each child word variant with its adult target form in relation to the prosodic structure to which it conforms: Where the *target form* already fits one of the child's preferred structures, without need for child modification, we call the child variant 'selected'. In other words, we take it that the word was (implicitly) selected for production in part because it takes the form of a

Table 3.2a Later words: American English. Proportions refer to variants in structure over total variants. i = imitated. 'Selected' and 'adapted' are defined in the text following the table. Note that here and elsewhere we follow the original child transcription conventions established in Bush et al. (1973) in distinguishing clear aspiration of voiceless stops (^{h}) from slight aspiration, indicated with '; this symbol is also used for the strong release of final voiceless stops

Selected words		Adapted words	
Target	*Child form*	*Target*	*Child form*
1. Alice (Vihman et al., 1994): 16 mos.; 34 target words, 39 variants in distinct structures			
A. CV 9 (.23)			
(grand)pa /pɑ:/	p'ɑ (2), fa	*hat* /hæt/	ʔa (2)
key /ki:/	çi	*man* /hæt/	mæ̃:
no /noʊ/	næ^h	*milk* /mɪlk/	m̥mæ̃^{h}
shoe /ʃu:/	çi	*nose* /noʊz/	n:æ̃
tea /ti:/	t^{j}i:		
B. CVV 8 (.21)			
bye /baɪ/	baɪ	*bang* /bæŋ/	pãi
eye /aɪ/	ʔaɪ	*belly* /'bɛli/	vei
h(e)llo (i) /'h(ɛ)loʊ/	loʊ	*down* /daʊn/	dãʊ̃
		egg /ɛg/	ʔeɪ
		plate /pleɪt/	p'ɛɪ, faɪ
C. CVC 8 (.21)			
clean /kli:n/	t^{h}ind	*apple* /æpəl/	ʔæʔ, ʔaʔ
duck /dʌk/	tæʔ	*blanket* /'blæŋkət/	k'ɛt
meat /mi:t/	miʔ	*iron* /'aɪjərn/	ʔaɪŋ:
up /ʌp/	ʔɑ:p	*Oscar* /'askər/	ʔaʔ, ʔap:
D. C₁VC₁V 4 (.10)			
baby /'beɪbi/	beɪbi	*lady* /'leɪdi/	jɛ:ji
daddy /'dædi/	da:di		
mommy /'mami/	əma:mi^h		
E. C₁VC₂VC₀ 10 (.26)			
bottle, botty /'batəl, 'bati/	baɖɪ (4), pa:di (2), badiç	*clean* /kli:n/	ti:ni
bunny /'bʌni/	bʊɲ:ɪ (2), beɪŋji	*elephant* /'ɛləfənt/	ʔeĩjĩ, ʔãĩ:jʌ, ʔai:njə
		flowers /'flawrəz/	p'ɑ:ji, p'ad^{j}i, fa:di
		iron /'aɪjərn/	ãĩji

Table 3.2a *Continued*

Selected words		Adapted words	
(*lady* /ˈleɪdi/	l̥ɑːti)	*lady* /ˈleɪdi/	lɛji
		mommy /ˈmɑmi/	maːɲi, nɑːɲi
		plate /pleɪt/	p'ɑɪjɪʒ
		shiny /ˈʃɑɪni/	tɑːji, daji, hetʰɑɪɲ

structure familiar to the child from motoric experience—that is, a structure that the child has already mastered in production.

The choice of the term always relates to the individual child's existing phonological knowledge, based on the evidence available from their production in the session. That is, we identify as 'selected' those words that are close enough to the target form to count as roughly accurate, *within the resources available to the particular child*. Thus words with reduced onset clusters may nevertheless be treated as selected for any child, since no child is as yet consistently producing such clusters. Similarly, words with a missing sibilant coda count as 'selected' in the case of a child like Alice, who produces stop but not sibilant codas (see *nose*), or Deborah, who produces no codas at all, but not in the case of Molly or Sean, who do produce them (see Table 3.2b).

Where the target does not fit the structure, we term the variant 'adapted'. More specifically, we list as 'adapted' words that are modified *in ways that fit them to a particular prosodic structure*. Thus, for example, words may be truncated (Alice, CVC: *apple, Oscar*) or lengthened by epenthesis (Molly, C_1VC_2V: *bang, down, green*); the consonants may be harmonized (Deborah, C_1VC_1V: *bagel, spaghetti*) or the monophthongal vowels turned into diphthongs (Alice, CVV: *bang, egg*). We consider selection and adaptation at greater length below, in relation to each of the children. (Note that while Alice's *lady* variant with medial yod is adapted, her other variant is not; as the two variants count as part of the same structure, we have simply placed the 'selected' variant in parentheses in Table 3.2a.)

It is worth noting that 'adaptation', as we use the term here, bears an evident relation to Piaget's (1951) concept of 'assimilation', as briefly stated in Vihman (1976):

'Assimilation' means the *reduction of complex stimuli to the dimensions of an existing mental schema*, while 'accommodation' is the expansion of an existing schema to encompass more complex stimuli.   (p. 233, italics added)

On the other hand, 'selecting', unlike 'accommodation', does not imply *expansion* but merely child identification of a match to an existing schema.

A few general tendencies can be observed. First, voiced and voiceless obstruents are sometimes accurately produced but they are not well distinguished, as is typical at this age (Macken, 1980). Transcribers generally hear onset obstruents in English child word forms as voiced, or unaspirated, while codas are heard as voiceless or aspirated. The aspiration required for onset obstruents in stressed syllables in English is seldom produced consistently in the single-word period; in final position it is not required. Accordingly, we group voiced and voiceless obstruents together in identifying patterns.

Second, we note that, in line with earlier findings (Boysson-Bardies & Vihman, 1991), all of the children produce a high proportion of labials in this period. If we count only those variants whose *only non-glottal consonant type in one or more*

Table 3.2b Later words: American English. Proportions refer to variants in structure over total variants. i = imitated. A vertical line indicates a brief hiatus in child production. The children are listed alphabetically by name

Selected words		Adapted words	
Target	*Child form*	*Target*	*Child form*
2. Deborah (Vihman, 2014): 17 mos.; 37 target words, 41 variants			
A. CV (and CV?)[1] 16 (.39)			
baa /bɑː/	bɑː		
ball /bɔl/	ba, əbɔː, aba		
book /bʊk/	bʌʔ		
bus /bʌs/	mbʌʔ		
car /kɑːr/	ka		
cheese /tʃiːz/	tʃi (i), ki		
cow (i) /kaʊ/	kə̰		
good (i) /gʊd/	gʊ, kʊ		
hello /h(ə)ˈloʊ/	hwo		
hot /hɑt/	ḁ̊		
(o)kay /(oʊ)ˈkeɪ/	gɛ		
more /mɔːr/	əmɔː		
see /siː/	ṣi		
soup /suːp/	su		
teeth /tiːθ/	ti, sθi (i)		
two /tuː/	tʰu		
B. CVV 7 (.17)			
A (i) /eɪ/	ei	*car* /kɑːr/	kwaɪ
bye /baɪ/	baɪ	*one* (i) /wʌn/	waɪ
eye /aɪ/	eɪ		

Continued

Table 3.2b *Continued*

Selected words		Adapted words	
Target	*Child form*	*Target*	*Child form*
hi /haɪ/	haɪ, aɪ		
my, mine /maɪ(n)/	maɪ		
C. C₁VC₁V 9 (.22)			
around & around (i) /ˈraʊndənəˈraʊnd/	waʊwʌ	*bagel* (i) /ˈbeɪgəl/	bʌbu
baby /ˈbeɪbi/	bebi	*cracker* (i) /ˈkrækər/	w̥æ̃w̥ə̃
[cock-a-]doodle-do /kɑkədudəlˈduː/	dʌʔdu	*giraffe* (i) /ˈdʒəræf/	dɪdæ
kit[ty]cat (i) /ˈkɪtikæt/	kɪkæ	*spaghetti* (i) /spəˈgɛti/	kɪgw̥ɛ̃
mommy, mama /ˈmɑmi, ˈmamə/	mɑmi, mʌmɑ		
D. Reduplication N = 4 (.10)			
round & around (i) /ˈraʊndənəˈraʊnd/	waʊwaʊ	*bus* /bʌs/	bʌbʌ
		pickle (i) /ˈpɪkəl/	baba
		water (i) /ˈwɑtər/	bawawa
3. Emily (Vihman, 2010): 16 mos.; 36 target words, 43 variants			
A. CVVₒ 22 (.51)			
A (letter) /eɪ/	eː, ʔeɪ	*all gone* (i) /ˈɔlgɔn/	kɑ̃ː
B (letter) /biː/	piː	*apple* /ˈæpəl/	biː (i)
beads /bidz/	piː, ʔɪbɪ, ʔʊβi	*button* /ˈbʌtən/	bɑː
bib /bɪb/	bɪ, pɪː		
box /bɑks/	pʰɑː		
Burt /bərt/	pœ		
C (letter) (i) /siː/	sɪ		
car /kɑr/	kʰa		
I (letter) /aɪ/	aɪ		
mail /meɪl/	mɛʰ		
man /mæn/	kwæ̃		
more /mɔːr/	mʌ, mœ, me, mɔə		
nine /naɪn/	ŋ̩ːːnaːː		

no /noʊ/	no, nʌ, nɔ, nɑː, n̩ːnʌ		
nose /noʊz/	nʌʰ		
ten /tɛn/	tʰĩː		
toes (i) /toʊz/	tʰɪ		
two (i) /tuː/	tʰːœ̨		
up /ʌp/	aʊ		

B. C₁VC₁V (and Reduplication)   7 (.16)

Bambi /ˈbæmbi/	papi	*water* /ˈwɑtər/	wɑːwi
Big Bird /ˈbɪgbərd/	bʊːpːɛ, pepːɪ		
choochoo /ˈtʃuːtʃu/	tʰʊtʰœ		
Cookie (Monster) /ˈkʊki/	kɛkɛ (i)		
no /noʊ/	nõno, næṇʌ, nə(nə)no, nʌnʌ		
tick-tock /ˈtɪktɑk/	tʰɪtʰɪ		

C. VCV   6 (.14)

all gone (i) /ˈɔlgɔn/	ɑːkˈɪ	*overalls* (i) /ˈoʊvəralz/	oːji, oːwɪtɪ
apple /ˈæpəl/	api		
Ernie /ˈərni/	aɪnʔːə, ʌɪntɛ (i), hœʌnjʌ		
open (i) /ˈopən/	oːʔ	pĩ		
Oscar /ˈɑskər/	ʔake		

D. C₁VC₂V   7 (.16)

button /ˈbʌtən/	pʌte	*car* /kɑr/	kɑːʔɑ
Cookie (Monster) /ˈkʊki/	həkʰi	*P* (letter) /piː/	pʰɪhɪ
tickle-tickle /ˈtɪkəltɪkəl/	kɪtikʰə	*water* /ˈwɑtər/	wɑːmɪ
walking /ˈwakɪŋ/	wɔki		

4. Molly (Vihman & Velleman, 1989): 16 mos.; 45 target words, 47 variants

A. CVVₒ   12 (.26)

baa /baː/	pˈæː	*bead(s)* /biːdz/	pi
ear /iːr/	heː	*click* /klɪk/	kˈi
hi /haɪ/	ʔaɪ	*piano* /ˈpjænoʊ/	pˈau
moo /muː/	muː	*tail* (i) /ˈteɪl/	tʰeʊ

Continued

Table 3.2b *Continued*

Selected words		Adapted words	
Target	*Child form*	*Target*	*Child form*
nose /nouz/	no:		
three /θriː/	wiː		
two /tuː/	tʰʊ		
woof /wʊf/	wu		
B. C₀VC 15 (.32)			
block /blɑk/	pʻɑk		
book (i) /bʊk/	pʊk		
Brett /brɛt/	pʻɑt		
click /klɪk/	kʻɪkʻ		
glasses /ˈglæsəz/	tʻɑk, kʻɑk		
house (i) /haʊs/	haʊt		
oink (i) /ɔɪŋk/	hoː | kʰ		
peek(-a-boo) /piːk/	pikʻ		
pig (i) /pɪg/	pʰɪkʻ		
red (i) /rɛd/	wɑːːtʻ		
rug (i) /rʌg/	wɑːk		
Ruth /ruθ/	hwʊtʻ		
stuck² /stʌk/	kʻɑkʻ		
that (i) /ðæt/	tɑtʻ		
work (i) /wərk/	hʌkʻ		
C. C₁VC₁V (and Reduplication) 8 (.17)			
baby /ˈbeɪbi/	pebi	*click* /klɪk/	kʰæ̥kʰi̥
choochoo /ˈtʃuːtʃu/	tʻutʻːu	*glasses* /ˈglæsəz/	kʻækʻæ, kʰæ̥kʰi̥
good girl (i) /ˈgʊdgərl/	gʊgəː	*picture* /ˈpɪktʃər/	pʻœpʻœ
mama /ˈmɑmə/	mɑmːɑ		
Nonny /ˈnɑni/	nɑnːi		
D. C₀VCV 12 (.26)			
camera /ˈkæm(ə)rʌ/	kɑmːə	*bang* /bæŋ/	pɑnːə
gran'ma /ˈgrænmɑ/	mɛᵘwʌ	*down* /daʊn/	tʻɑnːə
gran'pa /ˈgrænpɑ/	kʻæpʰɔ	*glasses* /ˈglæsəz/	tɑkʰɪ
open (i) /ˈoʊpən/	hɔpʻɔ	*green* (i) /griːn/	kɚːni

		in (i) /ɪn/	ɪnːi
		Nicky /ˈnɪki/	ɪnːi
		name (i) /neɪm/	nɛmːɪ
		walk(-walk) /ˈwɑkwɑk/	wɑkʰə̰, hɔkʰə̰

5. Sean (Vihman, 1996): 16 mos.; 27 target words, 45 variants

A. CV   12 (.27)

baa /bɑː/	bɑʰ	*blocks* /blɑks/	bɑ (2), ʔəbæʰ
blue /bluː/	bweː, bʊʰ	*book* /bʊk/	pɚː
ma(ma) /mɑː(m)ɑ/	mɑ(ː), mɔː	*dog* /dɑg/	tʰɑʰ
moo /muːː/	ʔõːʰ, mɔʰ, mœːː	*Ian* (i) /ˈijən/	nĩ
more /mɔːr/	mɔ(ː) , mɔʔ, mɑ	*mouse* /maʊs/	mɑ(ː), mæ (i)
oh /oʊ/	ʔɔ(ː)	*quack* /kwæk/	ʔɑːː

B. CVV   5 (.11)

mouse /maʊs/	maʊ̥, mɑːɨ	*bug* /bʌg/	βaɪ
oh /oʊ/	əoː (i)	*dog* /dɑg/	daʊ, taʊ̥
woof, wow-wow /wʊf, ˈwaʊwaʊ/	waʊ		

C. CVC   N = 16 (.36)

bird(s) /bɚdz/	pəʃ (2), pɚç, byːʃ, bɚːsʲ, b(w)iɭ, (bwɪːts, pwɚːts)	*berries* (i) /ˈbɛriz/	bɛːts, bɛʃː
block /blɑk/	pɑk (2), pʌk, pat, aʰk, jɑk, kwɑk	*cracker* /ˈkrækər/	dʒɑk, ʔœɑkʰ
book /bʊk/	bɨk, jɛk	*rabbit* /ˈræbɪt/	pʰæts, bɑːp, pl̥ɛ̥ʰp
bug /bʌg/	m̩bʌkl̩		
duck /dʌk/	tʌk (3), tʰæk		
fish /fɪʃ/	vəf, føːtʃ		
horse /hɔrs/	ʔɪʃ(ː), ʔɯʃ, tɯʃ, hɪːʃ		
look /lʊk/	jɛkʰ, ljʊk		
mom /mɑm/	ɑmam		
mouse /maʊs/	mɑːs		
quack /kwæk/	ʔaʔ		
stuck (i) /stʌk/	nɑkʰ		
this /ðɪs/	dɪs, dʌɪs		

Continued

Table 3.2b *Continued*

Selected words		Adapted words	
Target	**Child form**	**Target**	**Child form**
D. $C_1VC_1VC_0$ (and Reduplication) N = 6 (.13)			
mama /mɑ:mə/	mɔmɔ	*baa* /bɑ:/	pɑbɑ
		berries (i) /ˈbɛriz/	bɛbiʃ
		bird /bərd/	pɚbwɚ
		snowman /ˈsnoʊmæn/	mɪmɪ:
		this /ðɪs/	dʒɨdʒiʃ (i)
E. $C_1VC_2VC_0$ N = 6 (.13)			
blue /blu:/	bᵃ́lʊ	*block* /blɑk/	tɛnpʊ̃k
		book /bʊk/	tebyk
		butterfly /ˈbʌtərflaɪ/	bɑ:ijaɪ, pʌjʌɪ
		cock-a-doodle-do /kɑkədudəlˈdu:/	dəludəlu::
		moo /mu:/	nomɔ
6. Timmy (Vihman et al., 1994): 17 mos., 34 target words, 43 variants			
A. CVV_0 17 (.40)			
ball /bal/	pæ::, bɛ::	*balloon* /beˈlu:n/	bɛ::, bɛi:, bɛ:ʊ
bee (i) /bi:/	bi	*flower* /ˈflawər/	əv:æ
car /kɑr/	kɑ	*sun* /sʌn/	nɑ (i), inæ, ijæ̃:(i)
Drew /dru:/	du	*toot-toot* /ˈtu:tut/	du
hi /haɪ/	ʔai:		
juice /dʒu:s/	du, ɖu, ədu, əd:u (i)		
key /ki:/	gɪ		
knee /ni:/	ni , ən:i, əni:		
moo /mu:/	mʊ::, mɛʊ		
neck /nɛk/	ɪnæ		
peg /pɛg/	bæ		
plum /plʌm/	əv[:]æ::		
toe (i) /toʊ/	du		
B. CVC 6 (.14)			
hot (i) /hɑ:t/	ʔɑʔ (2)	*ball* /bal/	bæʔ
moon /mu:n/	mɛʊ:m	*boat* /boʊt/	bɛʔ

		bubble /ˈbʌbəl/	bæb:
		Nana (i) /ˈnænə/	nɑn::

C. C₁VC₁V (and Reduplication)   12 (.28)

bobby /ˈbabi/ (bottle, family term)	baˈbi, əbab:ʊ	balloon /beˈlu:n/	bɛbɛ
bubble /ˈbʌbəl/	bæˈby[:],³ ʔʌbæby:	bicycle (i) /ˈbaɪsɪkəl/	əgɛg:u
daddy (i) /ˈdædi/	dad:i:	coffee /ˈkɑfi/	ga:gi
quack-quack /ˈkwækwæk/	ʔakʰa:kʰa	computer (i) /kəmˈpju:tər/	kʼugɪ
toot-toot /ˈtu:tut/	dud:u	lizard /ˈlɪzərd/	jaɪjaʔ, i:jaɪjaɪ
owl sound 'hoo-hoo' /ˈhu:ˈhu:/	ʔʊʔ:u::	money ('coin') /ˈmʌni/	mam:i

Notes:
¹ Recall that, in the case of a child who is not yet producing other codas, we combine CVʔ with CV if the coda variants do not reach 10%.
² This form shows harmony, but as there is no more general harmony pattern among monosyllables, the word is included here.
³ There is reason to believe that the child intended the vowel of *bubble*, used only in this word (very frequent in this particular session, which included some bubble blowing), to contrast with the often-used word *bottle* or *bobby* (a family variant, perhaps derived from the child's form).

tokens is a labial, the proportion for the six children is 35%, ranging from 23% for Molly, who favours CVC structures and final velars, to 49% for Deborah.

For the purposes of cross-linguistic comparison (see Chapter 4) we apply a higher criterion—20% use—to the structures produced by each of the children in the language group. Thus Table 3.3 lists all and only the structures that account for *20% of the total variants for at least one child* in the American English group; only those children who made at least 20% use of the pattern are included in the mean incidence given for each structure. For each child we note the proportion of word types whose variants fall within a given structure out of the total identifiably distinct prosodic variants produced; the children are ordered by proportionate use within structures. We will refer to structures accounting for 20% or more of any one child's variants as 'meeting criterion' for that individual or language group.³

The range of prosodic structures observed in these later words is relatively restricted and not dissimilar to what we saw in the first words. None are more than two syllables long. CV, the simplest phonological structure, accounts for over 20% of the variants of all six children. Consonant harmony figures as a favoured

³ For the purposes of establishing structures that meet the 20% criterion we combine structures (with and without coda, for example) *only when at least one structure fails to reach criterion separately*.

Table 3.3 Prosodic structures accounting for 20% or more of the variant word forms produced by six American children in sessions with about 30 words. CH consonant harmony; RED reduplication

Structure	Child name	Proportion of all variants
CV Mean .34	Emily	.51 (22/43)
	Timmy	.40 (17/43)
	Deborah (and CV?)[1]	.39 (16/41)
	Sean	.27 (12/45)
	Molly	.26 (12/47)
	Alice	.23 (9/39)
CVV	Alice	.21 (8/39)
CVC Mean .30	Sean	.36 (16/45)
	Molly	.32 (15/47)
	Alice	.21 (8/39)
CH	Deborah	.22 (9/41)
Harmony (and reduplication)	Timmy	.28 (12/43)
C_1VC_2V Mean .26	Alice (and C_1VC_2VC)	.26 (10/39)
	Molly	.26 (12/47)

Note:
[1] In the case of a child who does not yet produce other codas, we combine CV? with CV if the structure does not reach 10%.

structure (in the sense of meeting or surpassing criterion) for two of the children and only in disyllables. (The few monosyllables with harmony do not add up to even 10% of any one child's variants, as we see in Table 3.2a, b.) These structures again recall the first words, which rarely included more than a single consonant type within a word form.

Two structures that meet criterion here are less typical of the earliest words and thus suggest developmental advance. First, three children (Alice, Molly, and Sean) make high use of *closed monosyllables*. Both Molly and Sean produce final codas with true consonants in most cases, whereas Alice produces a mix of matches and glottal stops for target obstruent codas. Timmy produces both codas that harmonize with the onset of the target word (*moon/sun, bubble, Nana*) and glottal stop, for *hot, ball, boat* (14% variants with coda). Deborah's two variants with glottal coda are included in the CV structure as she produces no other codas. These variable ways of handling codas are an indication of the challenge a common element of English phonological structure presents to children at this level of lexical production and phonological advance.

Secondly, one child, Alice, makes criterial use of *monosyllables with diphthongs*. Two other children produce two or three monosyllabic variants with diphthongs (fewer than 10%); these are included in the CV structure (hence CVV_0).

3.2.2 Template identification

Templates constitute a subset of a child's most often produced prosodic structures but are distinguishable from those structures in two ways (Vihman, 2016): First, whereas prosodic structures are identified on the basis of their sequencing of consonants and vowels alone, templates may be further specified segmentally, in that particular consonants or vowels, or consonant or vowel classes, or particular consonant or vowel melodies may be fixed in advance and apply to 20% of variants or more (see Kehoe, 2015). Second, templates can be identified by either (i) the child's overuse (or 'over-selection') of certain patterns in comparison with other children learning the same language or (ii) the child's adaptation of target forms to fit the constraints of the preferred pattern. Here we will focus on the occurrence of adapted alongside selected child word forms. The strongest evidence that a child is implicitly following a templatic pattern in attempting and producing new word targets is provided by a combination of pre-specification (of segments or segmental classes) that goes beyond the generic prosodic structural description and instances of adaptation. As we will see, not all children provide such evidence and the data from a single session is not always a sufficient basis for identifying template use.

3.3 Consonant inventories and templates in six American children

A key question to be addressed in the study of templates, which emerge and then fade within a few weeks or months in the period of early word production, is how the templates may be seen to serve the child (recall the question of 'purpose' posed by Macken, 1995, as discussed in Chapter 1; we reframe the question here): What role do they play in facilitating word learning? The limitation of early words to a small number of prosodic structures is inevitable, if only because the child necessarily begins with only a few words. A child's reliance, beyond that, on a particular segmentally specified pattern or template should relate in some way to the child's vocal preferences or skills. A hypothesis that we can test on the basis of the data presented here is that the *challenges of consonant production* and especially *consonant variegation across a word* are at the root of most template use. The hypothesis is based in part on the fact that children's output forms typically involve systematic changes to target consonants, not vowels.

In order to test the hypothesis and gain some perspective on how templates function for individual children we begin by presenting an overview of each child's consonant inventory in both onset and coda position in their full set of *word tokens* (i.e., all forms of the words identified in the recorded session). In Chapter 5 we will apply the same analyses—tracking onset and coda consonant inventories, with or without match to target—to data from two children each from the six remaining language groups to be considered in detail. To provide a full and comparable account of the consonants in the repertoire of each of the children, both here, in American English, and in Chapter 5, the following principles inform our counts and tables:

- We provide up to two child forms (from *different word targets*), in each of two positions (onset and coda), to illustrate use of each consonant: See, for example, Alice's productions of words with onset or coda /p/: *(grand)pa* [pʰa], *plate* [pʰɛɪ]; *up* [ʔʌːp], *Oscar* [ʔap:]. Where the child produces a sound accurately for only one target we include, if available, a non-match or substitution as the second instance (as in the case of coda [p] in the child form for *Oscar*).

- If *more than two uses* of a consonant occur for distinct target words in the corpus, for either word position, we indicate, in the column headed 'T[otal]', the total number of words in which the consonant is used (including the two shown; for example, Alice makes use of onset [p] in five different words). We count no more than one use of a given onset or coda consonant per target word but repeat the target word, as needed, for different consonant uses.

- Where a consonant is used *only* as a replacement for a target sound (i.e., with no matching use), we indicate this by bracketing the sound in the left-most column. Here too we provide up to two instances and also the total count if greater than two. For example, Alice uses [v] as an onset only as a substitute for the target consonant /b/ in *belly* [vei] and [j] as a substitute in six words, including *elephant* [ʔeɪ̃jɪ̃] and *flowers* [pʰaːji] (Table 3.4); there are no accurate (match-to-target) uses of either /v/ or /j/.

- Consonants used as substitutes for a target consonant are not always part of the adult language system at all. Alice produces several palatal consonants that do not occur in adult English: cf. [ç] (*key* [çi], *shoe* [çi]) and [ɲ] (*bunny* [bʊɲːɪ], *mommy* [maːɲi]), in Table 3.4. However, Alice systematically substitutes [ç] for /ʃ/; accordingly, we list /ʃ/ and its phonetic substitution in the left-most column.

- We do not list consonants *outside the inventory of the target language* if the consonant is produced only in *a variant form that occurs alongside a variant with a target-language consonant* in the same word. For example, Alice produces the palatal stop [ɟ], which is not part of the English phoneme inventory, in one of her forms for *bottle/botty* [ʌbaːɟi], alongside [badʲɪ] and other forms; we do not include [ɟ] in her inventory.

Table 3.4 Alice's consonant inventory at 16 months

Target C (N = 8)	Onset		T	Coda		T
p	(grand)pa [p‘a]	plate [p‘ɛɪ]	5	up [ʔʌːp]	Oscar [ʔap:]	
b	baby [beɪbi]	botty [baḍɪ]	4			
t	tea [tʰiː]	clean [tiːni]	5	blanket [k‘ɛt]		
d	daddy [dɑːdi]	down [dɑ̃ʊ̃]	4			
k	blanket [k‘ɛt]					
[v]	belly [vei]					
ʃ [ç]	key [çi]	shoe [çi]				
m	man [mǽː]	meat [miʔ]	4			
n	clean [tiːni]	nose [nːǽ]	5			
[ɲ]	bunny [bʊɲːɪ]	mommy [mɑːɲi]	3	shiny [hetʰaɪɲ]		
[ŋ]				iron [ʔaɪŋː]		
l	hello (i) [loʊ]	lady [lɛji]				
[j]	elephant [ʔeɪ̃jĩ]	flowers [p‘ɑːji]	6			

- Similarly, we do not include among the child's target-language consonants those that occur only as a *non-match* in either onset or coda position. For example, Alice produces [h] just once, in two of her several uses of *egg* [heːɪ], alongside six tokens of [ʔeɪ]; we do not list [h] as part of her inventory.

- N[umber] target consonants (Table 3.4) refers to consonants matched in at least two child forms, in either syllable position (**target C** marked in **bold face** in only those cases). Individual word forms that match the target for the consonant in question, in the relevant syllable position, are also in **bold face**. Here, exceptionally, we consider voicing in assessing a match.

We distinguish adapted from selected words in the prosodic structures we identify in order to highlight the major change between first words and later words, namely, the children's readiness to go beyond matching relatively simple target forms to attempt to produce more challenging words. This provides a first step in idiosyncratic template formation: The children extend one or more well-practised patterns (most-used structures) to words that would otherwise remain beyond their articulatory, planning, or representational resources. Because templates are, by definition, individual and idiosyncratic, here we consider consonantal inventories and uses of the prosodic structures shown in Table 3.2a, b for each of the children separately. We begin with the five children with the strongest evidence of template use, reserving discussion of Emily for last.

3.3.1 Alice

Alice's consonant inventory reveals a preference for producing palatal sounds: It includes the palatal consonants [ç] and [ɲ] that do not occur as English phonemes (Table 3.4); we treat [ç] as a 'lawful' substitute for /ʃ/, but not [ɲ], which Alice does not use as a consistent phonetic substitution. Note that although Alice's uses of [j] are never matches to target, she produces this consonant in more words than any other.

Alice has four structures that reach the 20% criterion (see Table 3.2a), but the one used most is $C_1VC_2VC_0$ (26%). Given that Alice is the only American child to produce non-harmonized disyllabic word structures to criterion at this developmental point, her variants merit close attention. This is Alice's structure with the highest proportion of adapted forms, and many of them are surprisingly dissimilar from their targets (e.g., *elephant, flowers, iron*). These variants are also notably similar to one another, many of them having medial yod or a palatal or palatalized consonant. This suggests template use.

Looking more closely at Alice's data, we can see a preference for monosyllables ending in a high front vowel as well as for palatalized consonants and word-final [i] (seen in all of her disyllabic word forms; see Table 3.5). This preference cuts across the prosodic structures identified in Table 3.2a. If we analyse these as potential templatic patterns, organizing structures or phonological whole-word categories based on Alice's tendency to adapt words to them, we find that together they account for fully 69% of her word variants, including all of her disyllables and most of the adapted monosyllabic variants. This pattern was described in Vihman et al. (1994) and traced back to the child's exceptional preference, in the babbling period, for yod, or a high-front tongue posture, at the onset of adult-like vocal production (see also Table 3.1, where four of Alice's first five recorded words have /i/ or /aɪ/ in the target form and three have a palatal gesture in the child form).

The palatal pattern that we identify for Alice thus actually includes two distinct but phonetically related patterns: (i) monosyllables, with or without a coda, with a high-front vowel or glide as their nucleus and (ii) disyllables ending in /i/, often with palatalization of the medial consonant. Note that Alice's exploratory attempts to produce *elephant*, the Jack-in-the-box regularly provided in the recording sessions, include two forms with a V + front-glide nucleus and a schwa-like second syllable that combine the monosyllabic pattern with diphthongal nucleus and the disyllables ending in [i] (the entire form is often nasalized). In general, the formulaic labels for the five structures given in Table 3.5 fail to capture the 'spirit' of the template, which is best characterized as a palatal or palatalized motor plan that extends across as much of the word as the child's articulatory ability to make a segmental match allows.

Table 3.5 Alice's palatal pattern

Prosodic structure	Selected words: target	Child form	Adapted words: target	Child form
Ci	key	çi	shoe	çi
	tea	t̪iː		
CVɪ	bye	baɪ	bang	pãi
	eye	ʔaɪ (2)	belly	vei
	plate	pʻɛɪ, faɪ	egg	ʔei (6)
CiC, CₒVɪC(V)	clean	tʰind	iron	ʔaɪŋː
	meat	miʔ	elephant	ʔãːjʌ, ʔaiːnjə
C₁VC₁i	baby	beɪbi	lady	jɛːji
	mommy	əmɑːmiʰ		
	daddy	daːdi		
C₁VC₂i, CVCVVɪC	bottle/botty	badʲɪ (4), pɑːdi (2), badiç	clean	tiːni
	bunny	bʊɲːɪ (2), beɪnji	elephant	ʔeĩjĩ
	lady	ḷḷaːti	flowers	pʻɑːji, pʻadʲi, faːdi
			iron	ãĩji
			lady	lɛji
			mommy	maːɲi, naːɲi
			plate	pʻaɪjɪʒ
			shiny	tɑːji, daji, hetʰaɪɲ

Alice's monosyllabic structures CV and CVC, which together account for 44% of her variants, all have either a low vowel or [i] (the latter variants being included in the palatal pattern); in the CVV structure we see a single variant with a back-glide diphthong (*down*). These non-palatal variants may be the first indicators of a new template in formation, one that addresses the challenge of words requiring a motoric plan very different from the one that Alice has mastered so successfully over her early months of word production.

3.3.2 Deborah

Deborah's consonant inventory at 17 months includes heavy use at word onset of the labial consonants [b, w] and also [k] and [s]. She produces no codas (Table 3.6).

Table 3.6 Deborah's consonant inventory at 17 months

Target C (N = 6)	Onset		T	Coda	T
b	baby [beːbi]	ball [bɑ]	11		
t	teeth [ti]	two [tʰu]			
d	cock-a-doodle-do [dʌʔdu]	giraffe [dɪdæ]			
tʃ	cheese (i) [tʃi]				
k	car [kɑ]	kittycat (i) [kɪkæ]	6		
g	good [gʊ]	okay [gɛ]			
ʔ	uh-oh [ʌʔoʊ]				
s	soup [su]	see [ʂi]	3		
h	hi [haɪ]				
m	mommy [mɑmi]	more [əmɔː]	3		
w	water [bɑwɑwɑ]	one [wɑɪ]	7		

Deborah's most used pattern is the CV(ʔ) structure (39%) (see Table 3.2b). We may consider all of the variants included in this structure to be selected, given that the adult forms for *hello* and *okay* can take the monosyllabic forms /hloʊ/ and /keɪ/. The variants are more phonetically varied than those produced in Alice's CV structure, with a wide range of different vowels, high and low, front, central and back. There are no onset consonant restrictions; Deborah matches the adult target for all but *cheese*, in which she succeeds in producing the onset correctly in imitation but substitutes onset [k] for the affricate in a spontaneous attempt at the word.

Since Deborah is not yet producing codas, many forms with target codas fall into the open-syllable CV structure. The rare variants with glottal stop in coda position (fewer than 10%) are also included in the structure. The glottal stops may reflect Deborah's sensitivity to syllable closure in the input along with an inability to correctly represent such words: The glottal stop is used where we might expect it (*book*) but also where we would not (*bus*). And it is missing where we might expect it (*soup, hat*) as well as where we would not (*ball, good*). Interestingly, Deborah also incorporates the typically late-learned coda of *teeth* in the onset-cluster to one (imitated) variant ([sθi]). Although Deborah's CV structure is of high frequency, it is implausible to suggest that she is 'over-selecting' it (which might suggest templatic activity), given that the same structure is used to criterion by all six children (Table 3.3).

Deborah's next most used pattern is disyllabic consonant harmony (22%). Although the proportion of variants accounted for is smaller for this structure than for CV, the evidence of templatic use—or child extension of a preferred or well-practised form to more challenging targets—is stronger in this case, as almost half of the word variants included are adapted. (Deborah also uses reduplication, which might be categorized together with harmony, but as her four reduplicated words—with *round & around* having a reduplicated as well as a harmonized variant—amount to 10% of all variants, we do not combine them.)

3.3.3 Molly

Molly makes use of a large number of consonants as matches to target. It is clear from her inventory that she has a preference for producing voiceless stops and codas (Table 3.7). Her consonant production is fairly stable, in that she tends to produce the same consonants repeatedly, although not always accurately; there is little experimental or exploratory sound production (see Vihman & Greenlee, 1987).

Molly's strongest pattern is the closed monosyllable (32%). This favoured structure primarily includes selected words, restricted to targets with final obstruents (all produced as voiceless stops). The only exception is *glasses*, which is not only truncated to a monosyllable but also shows metathesis of an initial velar and a final (stopped) coronal sibilant (cf. also *house* [haut']). Ten of the 15 words in the structure end in velars, reflecting an association of velar production with word-final position that has been commented on repeatedly but never satisfactorily explained (Ingram, 1974a; Menn, 1975; Vihman & Hochberg, 1986). Note, finally, that this structure includes four monosyllables with harmony (selected: *click, that*, adapted *glasses, stuck*); these are not categorized as a separate structure because they amount to only 9% of the total, as discussed above.

Table 3.7 Molly's consonant inventory at 15 months

Target C (N = 8)	Onset		T	Coda		T
p	peek(-a-boo) [pik]	piano [p'au]	13			
b	Brett [bat']	baby [pebi]				
t	tail [tʰeʊ]	two [tʰʊ]	6	Brett [p'at']	Ruth [hwʊt']	5
d	down [dɑn:ə]					
k	camera [kɑmə]	click [kʰækʰi̥]	7	block [p'ɑk]	book [pʊk]	9
g	good girl (i) [gʊgə:]	green (i) [gɚn:i]				
h	hi [haɪ]	house (i) [haut']	5			
m	grandma [mɛʊwʌ]	camera [kɑmə]	6	vroom (i) [brʌm]		
n	nose [no:]	bang [pan:ə]	5			
w	walk-walk [wɑkʰə]	woof [wu]	7			

Two more of Molly's patterns each account for 26% of her variants. Her non-harmonic disyllables are related to her attraction to final consonants, here expressed in adapted rather than selected words, with an epenthetic schwa or high front vowel (devoiced after [k]) applied to monosyllabic targets ending in a nasal or velar. Six nasal-final monosyllabic targets are produced in this way; we characterize *camera* as 'selected', based on the likely input form /kæmrʌ/; the word happens to fit into Molly's final-nasal production plan. *Nicky*, on the other hand, is metathesized, as Molly produces the onset nasal in her preferred word-final position (while omitting the medial /k/ of the target)—despite the fact that her forms [nɛmːi] for *name* and [nanːi] for *Nonny* show that onset-nasal production is not itself a problem for the child.

The other well-used pattern is the CV default, which includes a variety of vowels and also both front and back diphthongs (*hi, piano, tail*). Besides *piano* and *tail*, *beads* and *click* are adapted to this pattern, although *click* also occurs as a variant within Molly's consonant harmony structure, with a voiceless vowel following the voiceless velar in all cases. (Because disyllabic harmony forms account for 17% of her variants we separate out the structure, but *click* and *glasses* both conform to a CVK̥ template. Some of the other harmony forms—*choochoo, mama, glasses, picture*—are fully reduplicated, but these are not numerous enough to warrant positing a separate structure.)

Vihman and Velleman (1989) tracked Molly's preference for both final consonants and velars over several months. What we see in the data presented here are the two structures, CVC and non-harmonic C_1VC_2V, that represent, in her case, alternative ways of producing targets with word-final velar obstruents and nasals, or of assimilating other words to those patterns; both may be considered actively templatic.

3.3.4 Timmy

Timmy's consonant production is highly restricted (Table 3.8). Although he produces five different consonants in at least two words each, all in onset position (there is only a single token with a coda), what is remarkable is that he produces virtually no other consonants. The voiceless labial [p] does not occur, for example, nor do any attempts at sibilants, liquids, or even the glide [w].

Timmy makes use of only two high-frequency structures in his word production at this point, CV (40%) and disyllabic harmony (28%). As these are closely related as open-syllable structures with further specification of harmony in the disyllables, we can take them to constitute a single templatic pattern accounting for 68% of Timmy's variants. Although high, mid, and low vowels all occur in these structures, low vowels account for half of all the stressed syllables. Vihman et al. (1994) trace the development of these preferred patterns back to Timmy's

Table 3.8 Timmy's consonant inventory at 17 months

Target C (N = 5)	Onset		T	Coda	T
b	ball [bæːː]	bottle/bobby [əbabːi]	9		
d	daddy [dadːiː]	Drew [du]	6		
k	car [ka]	computer (i) [kʼugɪ]			
g	coffee [gaːgi]	good boy (i) [gɪbːiː]	6		
[v]	flower [əvːæ]	plum [əvæːː]	3		
m	money [mamːi]	moon [mɛuːm]	4	moon [mɛuːm]	
n	knee [ni]	neck [ɪnæ]	5	Nana (i) [nanːː]	
j	lizard [əjaːdʒu]				

babbling and indicate that his vocalizations were restricted to CV and redupli-cated open disyllables for several months after his first words appeared. For Timmy CV still appears to be an active template, as suggested by the metathesis of *sun* (/sʌn/ [na]) to achieve the structure.

Several word variants included in the CV structure include a dummy vowel preceding the CV syllable (cf. selected *neck, plum* as well as adapted *flower, sun*); this was characteristic of his production from the first words (see Table 3.1). These cases appear to be best categorized as belonging in the CV structure because the pre-syllabic vowel is a schwa (*flower, plum*) or a high-front vowel, which also occurs alongside other variants that lack the vowel (*neck, sun*). In contrast, Timmy produces disyllabic VCV forms with a low central vowel in the first syllable; as this is the vowel used in most of his word forms we hesitate to count it as a 'dummy vowel' and thus treat *bubble* [ʔæˈbyː], *Heidi* (i) [ʔadːiː], and the VCV variant of *balloon* [ʔæbæ] as constituting a separate VCV structure; along with the owl sound *hoo-hoo* [ʔʊːbʊːː]; these forms amount to only 9% of the 43 variants, however, and thus constitute a 'left-over' category, included in the total but not listed in Table 3.2b.

Some of Timmy's disyllabic harmony variants have full reduplication (*toot-toot, balloon, lizard*). Here again we see the support vowel in some variants (*bottle/ bobby, quack-quack, bicycle*). The assimilating consonant is a stop or nasal in all cases except *lizard*, where Timmy substitutes a glide onset for initial /l/ and assimilates the sibilant in the second-syllable to that glide. This is thus also an active template. In general, the combined one- and two-syllable template is a conservative pattern, favouring the simplest production routines.

Timmy's only other structure that accounts for over 10% of variants is the closed monosyllable, which occurs in two forms, CVʔ and $C_1VV_0C_1$. There are variants adapted to each of these, but the number of words involved is too small to posit established templatic activity.

One more structure, CVCV without harmony, is represented by only four words, accounting for just 9% of the total variants; accordingly this structure is not included in Table 3.2b. Nevertheless, two forms look as though they might be adapted: (i) *lizard* [əjɑːdʒu], with the medial affricate blending medial /z/ and coda /d/; (ii) *Simon* [ʔənːɪmːi], which suggests adaptation to a melodic pattern, <CVC$_{LABIAL}$V>—in other words, fixed labial C$_2$—given the metathesis of second-syllable onset [m] and coda [n]; the selected form *good boy* [ɡɪbːiː] is the only other exponent of the pattern observable in the recorded session, however. A template facilitating the production of different first- and second-syllable onsets may be emergent here, but there is insufficient data within the recorded session to permit a firm conclusion.[4]

3.3.5 Sean

With just six consonants that occur as match to target in at least two different words, Sean—in sharp contrast to Timmy—explores a wide variety of additional consonants (Table 3.9). His inventory is distinguished by the range of coda consonants produced, sometimes without corresponding use in onset position.

Like Molly, Sean makes the most use of the CVC structure (36%). The final consonants he produces are differently constrained from Molly's: Of the 16 variants in this structure seven end in [k] (recalling Molly's pattern) and seven in a sibilant (fricative or affricate); we also include in the structure a variant ending in glottal stop (*quack*, which may typically have a glottal coda in the input). Sean's adapted forms are disyllables truncated to arrive at the CVC shape. Two harmonized forms for *rabbit* [bɑːp, pl̥ɛ̆ʰp] occur alongside the sibilant cluster-final [pʰæts]; the harmonized forms show assimilation of the difficult onset /r/ to the medial labial, while the cluster-final form seems to reflect the second syllable of the target as well as pattern force deriving from the template. The one remaining variant has labial harmony ([ɑmɑm] for *mama* or *mom*). Thus CVC can be considered a template for Sean.

Sean's second most used structure is the basic CV (27%). Four of the obstruent-final targets adapted to CV by coda omission end in /k, g/ and one in /s/; Sean's production of these CV variants is best ascribed to the natural variability observed in this period, as he had long produced these or similar words with final consonants. The name, *Ian*, which shows metathesis, is the only other variant adapted to the CV structure. Evidence of template use here is weak.

One of the two remaining structures involves disyllabic harmony, with or without a coda. Although there are not enough words to designate a template, Sean may be beginning to develop such a pattern, given his attraction to coda production. (Use of harmony to achieve the challenging English CVCVC

---

[4] The one remaining form in this structure is *balloon* [bɛː[j]ʊ, bɛ[j]iː].

Table 3.9 Sean's consonant inventory at 16 months

Target C (N = 6)	Onset		T	Coda		T
[p]	birds [pɚç]	block [pɑk]	6	rabbit [bɑːp]		
b	berries (i) [bɑʰ]	blue [bweː]	9			
[t]	dog [taʊ]	duck [tʌkʼ]	4			
d	cock-a-doodle-do [dəludəluːː]	dog [daʊ]	3			
k	block [kwɑk]			block [pɑk]	stuck [nɑkʰ]	7
f	fish [føːtʃ]			fish [vəf]		
[v]	fish [vəf]					
s				this [dɪs]	mouse [mɑːs]	
[ʃ]				berries [bɛbiʃ]	birds [byːʃː]	5
h	horse [hɪːʃ]					
m	mama [mɔmɔ]	more [mɔː]	5			
n	stuck [nɑkʰ]	Ian [ni]	3			
l	look [ljʊk]	blue [bᵆlʊ]	3			
[j]	look [jɛkʰ]	butterfly [bɑːijaɪ]				
w	woof/wow-wow [waʊ]					

disyllables is a pattern sometimes seen in English-learning children with larger vocabularies: Vihman, Keren-Portnoy, Whitaker, Bidgood, & McGillion, 2013). In the light of Sean's exploratory variability in production, moreover, it would also be possible to consider the variants with coda (*berries, mama, this*) as falling within the sphere of the CVC template.

The remaining forms, all disyllabic non-harmonic variants except *cock-a-doodle-do*, scarcely constitute a structure; they are simply the forms that remain unaccounted for by the other structures.

3.3.6 Emily

Emily has a good foundation of consonants that match the target at word onset but she produces only a single variant with coda (Table 3.10).

The CV structure accounts for over half of Emily's word variants, as noted earlier; she adapts some words to the structure by truncation and produces a

Table 3.10 Emily's consonant inventory at 16 months

Target C (N = 7)	Onset		T	Coda	T
p	P [pʰɪhɪ]	apple [api]	11		
b	beads [ʔɪbɪ]	Big Bird [bʊːpːɛ]	6		
t	ten [tʰɪ̃ː]	tick-tock [tʰɪtʰɪ]	7		
k	car [kʰɑː]	Oscar [ɑːkːe]	7	truck [kæk]	
s	C (i) [si]				
m	mail [mɛʰ]	more [mɔə]	3		
n	nine [n̩ːnɑːː]	no [no]	4		
[j]	overalls [oːjɪ]				
w	walking [wɔki]	water [wɑːwi]	4		

diphthong in naming the letter *I* and a harmonized coda in *truck*. None of her other structures accounts for as much as 20% of all variants. The 21 remaining forms are roughly equally divided between disyllabic harmony, VCV—a structure seldom, if ever, seen as exerting templatic force in English—and non-harmonic CVCV. Twelve of these variants have final [i], with a few, such as *overalls* and *water*, suggesting possible adaptation to a CVCi pattern; however, there are too few forms to posit a template. It is worth noting that only one of these variants, *button* [pʌte], has more than a single supraglottal consonant type. Thus Emily's word production at this point looks quite cautious or conservative, with some heavy use of simple forms and little adaptation. We posit no template here.

3.4 Templates observed in the American children

Our close analysis of the word variants produced in a single recording session at the end of the one-word period has provided evidence for several likely templates, based both on use in a large proportion of the child's words and on adaptation, or application of the form to target words of different, less practised shapes. Table 3.11 presents the results of this analysis, ordered by extent of template use. One of the six children (Emily) failed to provide sufficient evidence to posit any template.

In summary, we see that a favoured child pattern or template may include more than one prosodic structure (cf. Alice's palatal template, Molly's targeting of final consonants, Timmy's limitation to open syllables in both mono- and disyllabic structures). The high-frequency occurrence of word-final /i/ in English, particularly in baby-talk words (*mommy, daddy, botty, bunny*, etc., and also names, like *Nonny*), influences at least two of the children (Alice, Emily), although in Emily's

Table 3.11 Templates identified for the American children (ordered by proportion of variants accounted for)

Child name	Templatic pattern	Structure	Proportion of variants accounted for
Timmy	open-syllable forms (mono- or disyllabic), with harmony across disyllables	CV, C_1VC_1V	.68
Alice	palatal pattern	Ci, $CVV_{\text{HIGH FRONT}}$, CiC, $CVV_{\text{HIGH FRONT}}C$, CVVCi...	.67
Molly	word-final consonants	CVt, CVk, $CVkV_{\text{voiceless}}$, CVnV (where final V = schwa or i)	.58
Sean	closed monosyllable	CVk, CVC_{sibilant}	.36
Deborah	consonant harmony	C_1VC_1V	.22

case template identification would be premature; the high occurrence of CVC words has affected two others (Molly, Sean). It is evident that some children rely on templates more than others, and in some cases, as with Timmy, the template appears to reflect limited production capacities—which are, however, effectively extended through adaptation to allow a greater diversity of word types to be produced. In other cases the template looks less like a constraint and more like active use of a preferred motoric routine—selection of final velars, for example, with adaptation of words with velars in other positions to achieve that output form (Vihman & Hochberg, 1986).

Returning to the hypothesis with which we opened our discussion of template identification, we can see the challenge of consonantal variegation across target words in the templatic patterns shown in Table 3.11. Both Timmy and Deborah restrict themselves to a single consonant type per word. The other children produce words with more than one consonant type but manage the challenge by constraining the second consonant, which must include a palatal gesture (Alice), a dental or coronal stop or /n/ (Molly), or a final velar or sibilant (Sean); this pre-setting of C_2 simplifies *planning for word production* and also, perhaps more basically, *representation*.

3.5 Developmental comparison

Having examined the word-form variants produced at a time when each of the children was targeting about 30 different words we can now look again briefly at their first words (Table 3.1), to see to what extent later patterning was fore-shadowed at that point and to consider what advances can be observed. A preference for palatal patterns is apparent in the first words that Alice attempted and to some extent in her production, even of *no*, the one word with no palatal element in the target. Deborah shows her contrasting preference for harmonizing forms in two of her five early words. Molly produces *cracker* with a closed monosyllable in two of five variants; Sean produces two words with closed monosyllables, both of them with target velars. Timmy's early words are highly variable but otherwise not unlike his most common structures at the later point. Emily produces a variety of different word forms; no later preferences are discernible at the earlier stage. Thus we see some continuity between earlier and later words, but with individual variability. (See Sosa & Stoel-Gammon, 2006, and Szreder-Ptasinska, 2012, for longitudinal analyses of word-form variability over the early developmental period.)

Some of these children are clearly making more rapid progress than others, despite the fact that we have attempted to roughly equate them by lexical level. The key difference between the first and later words of the six American children is the expansion of closed monosyllabic variants, which now account for more than 20% of the variants for three of the six children (Table 3.3). The production of diphthongs is also common, although these play a role in templatic adaptation only in the case of Alice and Deborah. On the other hand, clusters occur only sporadically; similarly, none of the children attempts more than a handful of targets of more than two syllables or produces longer forms more than once or twice. This detailed description provides a profile of phonological development in children acquiring American English that we can use for later comparison with the prosodic structures and templates of children learning British English and five other languages, following the same analytic procedures.

4

First words and prosodic structures

A cross-linguistic perspective

The primary goal of this chapter is to identify similarities and differences in the types of structures children learning different languages target and produce, both in their first words and later, toward the end of the single-word period, when word production and use are well established. Cross-linguistic analysis of the first words will provide a comparative perspective on the word shapes available to children at the onset of phonological development. In addition, it will address the question of (i) the extent to which *general or 'universal' resources* constrain the child's lexical choices and production patterns, regardless of the ambient language, and, conversely, (ii) the extent to which the *ambient language* shapes these choices and patterns. Finally, (iii) the analyses of several children exposed to each of the six languages will give an idea of the *range of individual differences* within the broader constraints that obtain at this time. The chapter will begin by focusing on analysis of the target forms of first words in two dialects of English and five other languages. We will then consider prosodic structures in the data sets from the same six groups of children at the point of reaching a cumulative lexicon of 50 to 100 words.

4.1 The phonology of the first words

To evaluate cross-linguistic similarities or differences and also gain an idea of the advances and changes we can see over the course of the single-word period we provide analyses of comparably complete data for each of 39 children in six language groups: British English (8), Estonian (5), Finnish (5), French (4), Italian (7), and Welsh (4), in addition to the American English group presented in Chapter 3 (6). The data have been chosen on the basis of what is available for analysis at *both* of the designated lexically defined points, early and late in the single-word period. In the case of diary data, we include for the second point of comparison all variants reported, whether as single words or in combination and whether spontaneous or imitated, in the period of the last 30 words produced out of the child's first 100 words of cumulative vocabulary (i.e., in the period in which new words 71–100 were recorded).

We restrict our analyses to data available for both data points, following the model of our analysis of American child data in Chapter 3, in order to be able to compare cross-linguistic similarities and differences in the same children's earliest

Phonological Templates in Development. First edition. Marilyn May Vihman.
© Marilyn May Vihman 2019. First published 2019 by Oxford University Press.

recorded words and in words they produce when word use is well established and word combination is just beginning. The inclusion of the same children at both ages is intended to limit the 'noise' that inevitably results from the high level of individual differences in lexical and phonological development in this early period and also the unavoidable differences due to the different transcribers across the language groups and sometimes within groups. Carrying out the cross-linguistic analysis of data from the same children both early and late in the single-word period gives us some control over that variability, although larger samples from each of the language groups would be desirable.

To the American English data presented in Chapter 3 we add British English data from two longitudinal observational studies.[1] For Estonian we draw on diary data, supplemented by data transcribed from recordings in the case of Madli, the only child in this group being raised as a monolingual in Estonia (Kõrgvee, 2001). Similarly, the earliest words of one Finnish child, Sini, were reported as a diary record, followed by seven sessions of audio-recording as her lexicon began to increase more rapidly over the period from 14–15 months (Savinainen-Makkonen, 2001). For both Madli and Sini we include all of the words produced in one recorded session (44 and 28 different words attempted, resp.). For the children in the other language groups we draw on video-recorded sessions made by outside observers.

For British English, French, Welsh, and the Finnish children other than Sini, much the same procedures were used as we reported for the American children. The Italian children were recorded for 20 minutes in the lab, with both parents present, at 1;3 and 1;9 (Vihman & Majorano, 2017); we include here the seven Italian children (of 30 included in the study) who produced 4–8 words in the earlier and 30–60 words in the later session. For all of the children we include imitations in the later data point analyses, to provide a sufficiently representative number of prosodic variants and structural diversity—and because imitated forms do not tend to be more complex or more accurate than spontaneous production in this period (Lewis, 1936).

Table 4.1 presents the first 4 to 8 words identified, whether in the form of diary notes or transcribed data, for all of the children included in each group. Within groups the children are listed by age at first words.

The data presented in Table 4.1 are meant to serve two purposes. First, they provide a basis, along with the first words of the American children shown in Table 3.1, for comparing children's first recorded words across different languages. This gives us an idea of the resources available to children at the onset of phonological development. Second, they make it possible to consider the

---

[1] The data derive from seven of the nine British children whose first words are given in Menn and Vihman (2011, App. II)—namely, from those who were producing 25 words or more by the final recording session at 1;6 (see also DePaolis, Keren-Portnoy, & Vihman, 2016). We also include an additional British child, Jude, from an earlier study (see Keren-Portnoy, Vihman, DePaolis, Whitaker, & Williams, 2010; Vihman, DePaolis, & Keren-Portnoy, 2016).

Table 4.1 First word forms in six languages (adapted and expanded from Menn & Vihman, 2011); a published source is indicated for each group or, where sources differ, for each child. Imitated word forms are not included here. BT = baby-talk form

ENGLISH (UK) (Menn & Vihman, 2011; DePaolis et al., 2016).
Stress is marked on target forms

Target word	Adult form	Child form
1. *Ella, 11 mos.*		
Amelia	/əˈmiljʌ/	[ɪdʒiːijaʰ], [ziːʔijaʰ], [iːʔɪjaʰ], [iːijaʰ]
Eva	/ˈiːvʌ/	[iːːjaʰ], [niːjæʰ], [iːːjæʰ]
hat	/hæt/	[aʔ]
hello	/hɛˈləʊ/	[əɹaʊ], [eʔaʊː], [eʔɬə], [ɪhəʊ]
hiya	/ˈhaɪjʌ/	[aɪjɛ], [aʔaɪː]
row row	/ɹəʊ ɹəʊ/	[mːɹəʉːuːwa], [ɪbuɹaʊːwaː], [əwaʊːevəva], [mβaʊʔvəʊ]
William	/ˈwɪljəm/	[iːːjɛ]
2. *Flora, 13 mos.*		
hello	/hɛˈləʊ/	[ɛjəʊ]
oh dear	/əʊˈdijə/	[ata], [ætæ], [ætʰaː], [ətɪː]
star	/staː/	[tæːʰ]
ta	/taː/	[həʔtæʰ], [tæʰ]
there	/ðeə/	[tæ]
uh-oh	/ˈʌʔəʊ/	[ʔaʔəʉː], [ʔæʔæːə]
3. *Jude, 14 mos.*		
ball	/bɒl/	[baba]
barnaby	/ˈbɑnəbi/	[babi]
caterpillar	/ˈkætəpilə/	[biɔ]
yeah	/jɛə/	[jə]
4. *Rachel, 14 mos.*		
hiya	/ˈhaɪjʌ/	[ʔəʔaːɪja], [heʒəːaʰ[, [ɑːjəʰ], [heːɪjəʰ]
juice	/dʒuːs/	[tsɜːdʒːː], [dɪdʊsːʊ], [tʰə̥sː], [dʊs], [təðʊs], [gʊsː], [dəʔɵːʃ]
sheep	/ʃiːp/	[ta], [dɛːɪ], [tθaː], [tʰə̥]
this	/ðɪs/	[dɪəʃ], [dʊɪθ], [iːhɪθ]
5. *Lewis, 15 mos.*		
all gone	/ɔlgɒn/	[ɔːːgʊ], [ɔːgə], [ɔːgʊkʰ], [ɔːkɟəː], [ɔːʔgə], [ɔʼɣɒə], [ɔgɒkʰ], [ɔgə], [əgɒːː], [əʊgɒːː]
clock	/klɒk/	[kʰɒːkʰ], [kʰɒːʔkʰ]
duck(s)	/dʌk(s)/	[dəs]
that	/ðæt/	[dɑːtʰ], [daʔətʰ]
this	/ðɪs/	[ndəːʃ], [dɪːʊʃː]
6. *Patrick, 16 mos.*		
baa	/bɑː/	[bɑ]
buck (chicken sound)	/bʌk/	[boʔ]
hello	/hɛˈləʊ/	[ɛlɔːʰ], [əɹəʊ]
hiya	/ˈhaɪjʌ/	[haɪ ji], [aɪ jəʔjɛ], [heɪʔjɛʰ]
two, three, four	/tuθɹifɔː/	[paː ʤeɪ fʷɑ]

Continued

Table 4.1 *Continued*

---

7. Tania, 17 mos.

book	/bʊk/	[vəʊ], [bʌː], [wəʊ]
bye (bye)	/baɪ(baɪ)/	[baɪː], [paiː], [pæiː], [bɛjʊɸbeɪ]
daddy	/dædi/	[tɛðɛ]
fish	/fɪʃ/	[tʉʃs]
meow (meow)	/miaʊ/	[ɪjʊ], [jaʊ]], [jʊ], [tɪjʊjʊ], [jæʊjæʊ], [ɛʊ æo]
mummy	/ˈmʌmi/	[ʔmʔəməmæh]
woof woof	/wʊfwʊf/	[ʔmbʊɸʔʊɸʔʊɸ]

8. Tobias, 17 mos.

baby	/ˈbeɪbi/	[bɛːbɪʰ], [beɪbiːʰ], [biːbiːʃ], [biːbiːʰ], [biːbiʰ],
		[bɹiːbɪʰ], [mbiːbɪç], [nːːbiːbiç], [biːbiç],
		[pɸbiː], [biːːbɪʰ], [bibiːç], [biːbiʃ], [bɪːːbɛʰ],
		[əbiːbɪʰ]
bear	/bɛə/	[nabɛː], [beɪ], [bijɪː], [bɛːʰ], [bɪʰ], [pɪʔə]
digger	/ˈdɪgə/	[gigɪjə], [di tʰɪʔɪ]
hiya	/ˈhaɪjʌ/	[aɪjɪ], [aɪjɪː], [əɪjɛːʰ]
neenaw (fire-engine sound)	/niːnɔː/	[ŋːæŋːəm], [nɒɪnə], [inaːnəʰ], [ndɒɪŋna]
there	/ðɛə/	[də], [dəʔɛ]
uh-oh	/ˈʔʌʔəʊ/	[ɛʔəː]
whee	/wiː/	[ʊʒiʰ], [h̥ʷwiː]

ESTONIAN (diary data)

Stress is on the initial syllables of target forms unless otherwise marked. English target words are in italics. (For discussion of the 'extra length' of Estonian Q3 syllables, marked with `, see Chapter 7.) sP = Partitive singular.

Target word	Gloss	Adult form	Child form
1. Virve, 10 mos. (Vihman, 1976; Vihman & Croft, 2007)			
aitäh	thanks	/aɪˈtæh/	[ta]
hi		/haɪ/	[aɪ]
isa	daddy	/isa/	[saʔ]
see	this	/ˋseːː/	[seʔ]
tere	hello	/tere/	[tete]
2. Kaia, 11–14 mos. (Vihman, 2016)			
aua	bowwow (BT)	/aua/	[wawawawa]
kiisu / *kitty*	kitty	/kiːsu/ / /kɪɾi/	[ki̥ːtʒ]
meow		/miaʊ/	[mæ]
nämma, nämmi	yum	/næmːæ/, /næmːi/	[mæmː]
3. Madli, 11–16 mos. (Kõrgvee, 2001)			
aiai	ow (hurting or being hurt)	/aiai/	[aiai]
auh	bowwow (BT)	/ˋauh/	[auh]
auto	car	/auto/	[auto]
kaka	caca	/kaka/	[kakːa]
kass	cat	/ˋkasʲː/	[asʲː]
kotti	bag (sP)	/ˋkotːi/	[kotʲi]
kuu	moon	/ˋkuː/	[kuː]
naba	bellybutton	/napa/	[aba]
nämm	food (BT)	/ˋnæmː/	[næmː]

4. *Maarja, 12–14 mos.* (Vihman & Vihman, 2011)

aitäh	thanks	/ɑɪˈtæh/	[aiˈtæʰ], [tæʰ]
auh-auh, aua	bowwow (BT)	/ɑuhˈɑuh/, /ɑuɑ/	[wɑwɑwɑ], [wʊwʊwʊ] (growly)
daddy		/dædi/	[dæ:], [dæ	i:]
kuku / *uh-oh*	peek-a-boo	/kuku/	[uʔu:], [ʌʔʌ:], [ʔo], [m̩ʔm̩:]
mõmm-mõmm,	teddy (BT)	/ˈmɤm: ˈmɤm:/,	[mɤm:mɤm:], [mɤm:i], [mɑm:i]
mõmmi		/ˈmɤm:i/	[ɑm:i]
pai	nice (petting, patting)	/ˈpɑɪ/	[ʔɑɪ], [dɑɪ]

5. *Raivo, 13–14 mos.* (Vihman, 1981, 2014, 2016)

aitäh	thanks	/ɑɪˈtæh/	[ta], [taʔ]
ei	no	/ˈeɪ/	[ei]
pall	ball	/ˈpalʲ/	[bæ], [pæ]
pömm	boom	/ˈpömm /	[bm̩]
shoe	(English)	/ʃu:/	[ʃ], [ç]
viska (& vesi)	throw (& water)	/viska/ (& /vɛsi/)	[is], [iɬ], [ɬ], [ʂ]

FINNISH
Stress is on the initial syllables of target forms.

1. *Sini, 10–13 mos.* (Savinainen-Makkonen, 2001)

kukka	flower	/kuk:ɑ/	[ʔka], [aˈka]
kiikkaa	swings, is swinging (BT)	/ki:k:ɑ:/	[ki:k:ɑ:]
kissa	cat	/kis:ɑ/	[ki]
vettä	water	/ʋet:æ/	[et:æ]
nappi	button	/nɑp:i/	[pi], [əp:i]

2. *Eliisa, 1–13 mos.* (Kunnari, 2000; Vihman & Kunnari, 2006; Vihman & Velleman, 2000)

hau	woof	/hɑu/	[hɑʊ], [hnari, 2000; V
katso	look	/kɑtso/	[tɑto]
kiikkuu	is swinging	/ki:k:u:/	[ki:k:ʊ̝], [ki:ko], [ki:], [ki:kao]
lamppu	lamp	/lɑmp:u/	[pɑpʊ]
pallo	ball	/pɑl:o/	[pɑpʊ̝], [pɑpɑu̯], [bɑpa], [pɑpʊ], [pɑp:ʊ], [pʌpɑ̝]
tyttö	girl	/tyt:ø/	[tito]

3. *Mira, 14 mos.* (Kunnari, 2000)

mammaa	milk (BT)	/mɑm:ɑ:/	[mɑm:ɑ:]
mamma	Muumi mama	/mɑm:ɑ/	[mɑm:ɑ]
tätä	this	/tætæ/	[tætæ]
pallo	ball	/pɑl:o/	[pɑpu]

4. *Atte, 17 mos.* (Kunnari, 2000; Vihman & Kunnari, 2006)

anna	give	/ɑn:ɑ/	[nɑ]
hauva	doggy	/hɑuʋɑ/	[vɑ], [hɑ/ i,
heppa	horse	/hep:ɑ/	[pɑ], [ɑp:ɑ]
mummo	grandmom	/mum:o/	[mo], [ɑm:o]
pappa	grandpa	/pɑp:ɑ/	[pɑ], [pɑp:ɑ]

5. *Eelis, 18–19 mos.* (Kunnari, 2000; Vihman, 2014)

äiti	mother	/æiti/	[æiti:]
anna	give	/ɑn:ɑ/	[ɑn:ɑ], [æn:æ]
ei	no	/ei/	[ei]
heppa	horsie	/hɛp:ɑ/	[bɑp:ɑ]

Continued

Table 4.1 *Continued*

| kiikkuu | is swinging | /kiːkːuː/ | [kikːu], [kɑːkːu] |
| kukka | flower | /kukːɑ/ | [kɑ], [kr ːi] |

FRENCH
Phrasal accent falls on the final syllable; there is no word stress.

1. *Laurent, 10 mos.* (Vihman, 1993; Vihman, 1996)

allo	hello	/alo/	[hailo], [ailo], [haljo], [aljo], [alo]
donne (le)	give (it)	/dʌn(lø)/	[dlə], [də], [ldɛ], [heldɔ]
l'eau-l'eau	bottle (BT)	/lolo/	[ljoljo]
non	no	/nõ/	[ne]
tiens	here, take it	/tjɛ̃/	[ta]

2. *Carole, 11 mos.* (Vihman & Kunnari, 2006)

balle	ball	/bal/	[ba], [baba]
bébé	baby	/bebe/	[bebe]
Mickey	Mickey Mouse	/mike/	[kə]
nounours	teddy bear	/nunuʀs/	[ne], [nene]
papa	papa	/papa/	[papa]

3. *Charles, 11 mos.* (Vihman, 1996; Vihman & Kunnari, 2006)

au-revoir	byebye	/ɔʀvwaʀ/, /ɔvwaʀ/	[awa, haɥa]
boum	boom	/bum/	[ba, bœm]
beau	beautiful, good	/bo/	[bo]
donne, tiens	give/here	/dʌn/, /tjɛ̃/	[dæ]
mama	mama	/mama/	[mama]
non	no	/nɔ̃/	[nɛ]

4. *Noël, 13 mos.* (Vihman, 2014)

coucou	peek-a-boo	/kuku/	[tətə]
miam	yum	/mjɑm/	[ʔam], [ʔʌm]
papa	papa	/papa/	[pæpæ]
poum	boom	/pum/	[põm]

ITALIAN (Vihman & Majorano, 2017)
Stress is on the initial syllables of target forms unless marked.

1. *A.P., 15 mos.*

basta	enough, stop!	/basta/	atːa
ecco	look, here it is	/ekːo/	ɛkːo
grazie	thank you	/grazie/	tatːe, gatːʃe
mamma	mama	/mamːa/	mamːa
pappa	food (BT)	/papːa/	papːa
qua	here	/kʷa/	kwa
scotta	hot	/skotːa/	kɔtːa
tutto	whole (m.)	/tutːo/	toto

2. *C.L., 15 mos.*

biberon	baby bottle	/bibeˈron/	biˈbeo, bibi
bimbo	baby (m.)	/bimbo/	bibo
cosa	what	/kosa/	kɔza
mamma	mama	/mamːa/	mamːa
nanna	sleep (BT)	/nanːa/	nanːa

qui	here	/kʷi/	kwi
tata	girl (BT)	/tata/	tata
via	all gone	/via/	bia, ia

3. G.A., 15 mos.

babbo	daddy	/bab:o/	bab:o
bimba	child (f.)	/bimba/	baba
mamma	mama	/mam:a/	mam:a
pappa	food (BT)	/pap:a/	pap:a
papà	papa	/paˈpa/	pa'pa

4. G.C., 15 mos.

ciao	hi, hello	/tʃao/	tʃao
mamma	mama	/mam:a/	mam:a
papà	papa	/paˈpa/	pa'pa
tutti	all, everyone	/tut:i/	tut:i

5. J.A., 15 mos.

acqua	water	/akʷa/	ak:a
mamma	mama	/mam:a/	mam:a
papà	papa	/paˈpa/	pa'pa
tetè	mother's milk (BT)	/te'te/	te'te

6. I.S., 15 mos.

bimba	baby (f.)	/bimba/	ib:a
ciccia	meat	/tʃitʃ:a/	tʃit:ʃa
mamma	mama	/mam:a/	mam:a
nanna	sleep (BT)	/nan:a/	na:na
pappa	food (BT)	/pap:a/	pap:a
prendo	I take	/prendo/	ep:o
questo	this (m.)	/kʷesto/	kwet:o

7. I.L., 15 mos.

apro	I open	/apro/	ap:o
grazie	thank you	/grazie/	ga:e
mamma	mama	/mam:a/	mam:a
mio	my, mine (m.)	/mio/	mio
pappa	food (BT)	/pap:a/	pap:a

WELSH (Vihman, 2000)
Stress is on the second syllables of target forms unless marked.

1. Carys, 12 mos.

Breian		/breian/	bɑːjɑõ, pɔpːɸõ
Dad			dadːtʃ, dadʰ, daːdʰ, də dad, daːdʰ
hiya			aɪjəʰ, ɑidɑõ, ʔejɑõ
lemon			nːɛneõ
mami		/mami/	mɔːme
Meira		/meɪra/	m̥aɪwə, meɪjə, meɪjaʰ, m̥ːeɪjəː
mochyn		/mɔxɪn/	buʃːa̰

2. Gwyn, 12 mos.

babi	*baby*	/babi/ [bab:i]	bab:i, baʰbiː, babi
ball/pêl		/peːl/	baːu, bauː
choochoo			ʔɔhːɔː, ʊʔɞːʊː, ʊeʔɔː
Guto		/gitɔ/	gitɑː, gitɑõ

Continued

Table 4.1 *Continued*

3. *Elen, 13–14 mos.*

choochoo			tʃʊtʃʊə, tʰʌtʰʌ, ɪtʃʊː, iʒus:
cwaccwac	*quack-quack*	/kwækkwæk/	gəgɒg, gˈgakˉx
gogalw	*bird* (family word)	/goˈgalu/	gak:u
sit (to dog)			sʰɪt, sːɪʰ, sɪːt
tân	*fire*	/tʰaːn/	dʰaː
tata	*bye-bye*	/tʰaˈtʰa/	dɪdə, dɛtɛ

4. *Fflur, 13 mos.* (/flɪr/)

agor	*open*	/agɑr/	gəga, gəgːaː, gɒgːa, gʌgːa
blodyn	*flower*	/blɒdɪn/	ʔɛbə, bəba, bəʊwa, bəbːə
ceg	*mouth*	/kɛg/	gag, gɛːg
golau	*lights*	/gɒla/	baʊwa, ʔʌwa
na	*no*	/na/	na, naː, ɲaː, ɭaːː, naʔ, næː
sannau	*socks*	/sana/	dənəʰ
sgidie	*shoes*	/sgidʒɛ/, /sgidijɛ/	gəga, dadæ, dada

differences, if any, in accuracy and in preferences for particular prosodic structures between the two data points to be discussed in this chapter; this will help us to identify and characterize the advances children make as they reach the point where they are producing words more frequently. We begin by comparing, in Table 4.2, the length in syllables of the early word targets and the extent to which the child forms match their targets in that respect. Words that vary in adult presentation, such as onomatopoeia like *woof-woof*, are excluded from the match count; child forms that include variants of differing length are counted as a match if at least one variant matches the target in length.

Table 4.2 Length in syllables of targets for first words and proportion of matches in first word forms (ordered by *proportion of disyllables*)

	Length in syllables						Child form	Total words
	one		two		three		proportion matching in length	
Finnish	2	0.08	24	0.92	0	0.00	1.00	24
Italian	3	0.07	37	0.90	1	0.02	1.00	41
Welsh	6	0.25	17	0.71	1	0.04	.96	24
Estonian	9	0.35	17	0.65	0	0.00	.81	26
French	9	0.45	11	0.55	0	0.00	.90	20
US English	14	0.48	15	0.52	0	0.00	.83	29
UK English	22	0.47	18	0.38	4	0.09	.88	47
mean		*0.31*		*0.69*		*0.01*	*.91*	

Extending the data to five more languages does not change the basic finding as regards word length: *The first words attempted are almost exclusively one or two syllables long.* The first words of the Finnish and Italian children are almost all disyllables, the Welsh and Estonian children use considerably more disyllables than monosyllables (excluding from the count the bilingual Estonian children's English target words), and the French and both groups of English-learners are fairly evenly divided between one- and two-syllable words.

For comparison, the mean proportional distribution of length in syllables in American English and French content words, based on five samples of mothers' speech to their infants at age 12–13 months (including the five American children from the Vihman et al. studies cited in Table 3.1 and the four French children included here), is reported in Vihman, Kay, Boysson-Bardies, Durand, and Sundberg (1994): for US English, 69% monosyllables, 23% disyllables and 8% longer words; for French, correspondingly, 56%, 39%, and 10%. However, the proportion of nouns in the input speech was more closely related than the overall distribution to the words attempted by the children in each group over the seven months of the longitudinal study. For English, the percentage of monosyllabic nouns in the input was a little lower than the overall input distribution (52%, with 30% disyllables), while French monosyllabic nouns were far fewer (23%) and disyllables (67%) more common.

Overall, both American and French children attempted far fewer long words than occur in the input, but also somewhat fewer monosyllables and more disyllables than might be expected from the input distribution. Furthermore, children's first words are not necessarily as short as possible; in many cases we find additional vowels preceding the onset of the adult form, for example, as noted in Chapter 3. The level of match between actual child forms and the target forms differs between groups but is generally high, with a mean of .91.

Table 4.3 provides a comparison of some additional aspects of target phonological structure across the language groups. The mean of (supraglottal) consonant variegation (C1–C2) within the adult words is 38%, with a low of 20% (Italian) to a high of 58% (Welsh); variegation in child forms is far lower, as could be expected.

Table 4.3 Total word types targeted, consonant changes (C1–C2) within targets and **child forms**, target word-final consonants and medial geminates (where C = supraglottal consonant)

	Total	Target C_1–C_2		Child C_1–C_2		Word-final C		Medial geminates	
US English	29	11	0.38	2	0.07	11	0.38	n/a	n/a
UK English	47	19	0.40	6	0.13	15	0.32	n/a	n/a
Estonian	26	10	0.38	3	0.12	5	0.19	10	0.38
Finnish	23	7	0.30	0	0.00	0	0.00	19	0.83
French	20	8	0.40	3	0.15	8	0.4	n/a	n/a
Italian	41	8	0.20	4	0.10	1	0.02	21	0.51
Welsh	24	14	0.58	4	0.17	11	0.46	n/a	n/a
mean			*0.38*		*0.10*		*0.26*		*.57*

Word-final consonants occur in almost half of the Welsh and about one-third of both English and French target words, despite the considerable difference in coda occurrence in input speech in English and French (with means of 66% and 25%, resp.: Vihman, Kay, et al., 1994); word-final consonants are rare in target words in the other three languages. Only Estonian, Finnish, and Italian have medial geminates; their proportionate occurrence (disregarding any English words for the bilingual Estonian-learning children) differs sharply by language.

4.1.1 Discussion

This analysis generally supports Ferguson and Farwell's (1975) suggestion that the relative accuracy of the first words may be due to children's (unconscious) pre-selection of word targets that are accessible to them, given their limited production skills and existing vocal patterns (as practised in babble). The targets are largely restricted to monosyllables and disyllables. Although child forms may be longer, with repeated syllables and dummy syllables or fillers occurring commonly enough in some of the data,[2] the length limitation on words *attempted* corresponds closely to the length of *well-controlled vocalizations* supported by babbling practice.

Word-final consonants are under-selected, in line with the strong preference for open syllables in babbling (Oller, Wieman, Doyle, & Ross, 1976; Vihman, Macken, Miller, Simmons, & Miller, 1985; Vihman, 1991; Kent, 1992). In contrast, geminates are over-selected in the languages that have them. This is likely due not only to their perceptual salience but also to the fact that medial consonants are perceptibly long in infants' first word production (given sluggish articulatory gestures) even in English and French, which lack geminates in the adult language (Vihman & Velleman, 2000): This suggests that children's perceived match of target medial geminates to their own vocal patterns may be a factor (Vihman & Majorano, 2017).

Finally, consonant change across the word is minimized: Although variegation is common in babbling, achieving the necessary neuromotor control for the articulation and planning of two consonants in a single word form is challenging for the inexperienced speaker, as discussed in Chapter 3, and memory for the sequence may be challenging as well. Here then we see the starting point of word production: Children are sensitive to target forms for which they may have a rough vocal match in repertoire and the first words they produce in a recognizable way are similarly constrained cross-linguistically.

Children's production skills advance only quite slowly; what changes with the onset of word production is child familiarity, through ongoing practice with production and the experience of hearing their own output, with a growing number of phonological forms. A key point regarding the formation of preferred

---

[2] Differences in the extent of variability in this regard may reflect differences in transcription in the different studies.

prosodic structures is that the timing of this development differs from one child to the next. However, persistent production of words of a particular prosodic structure is typically seen only *after* a period of early word use; an initial data sample, leading to a few well-developed word-production routines, usually develops first. This accounts for the typical lack of systematicity, or relatively rare reuse of particular word shapes, syllables, or features, in the first few recorded words (Menn & Vihman, 2011).

4.2 Prosodic structures at the end of the single-word period

We turn now to the period when each of the children can be observed to produce a small set of preferred prosodic structures, some of which may be serving or may come to serve as templates, or more fully specified attractors for new word forms. In Chapter 3 we presented the prosodic structures of six American children, as identified through iterative categorization of all of the variant forms produced in a session with about 30 words or more. We saw that although the categorization of variants into prosodic structures need not correspond directly with template formation, it allows one to lay out the data in such a way that templates are readily recognized. Here we will follow the procedure we described in Chapter 3 with a focus on cross-linguistic comparison, postponing discussion of templates in children learning these languages to Chapter 5.

Appendix I indicates, for each of the children whose data we are considering here, age at the point of producing at least 25–30 words spontaneously in a 20–30-minute session or, for the diary studies that do not include recorded sessions, age range at achieving a cumulative vocabulary of 70–100 words. As mentioned earlier, this developmental point is chosen for comparison across children and language groups because it is readily identifiable and typically corresponds to the end of the single-word period; first child word combinations are generally observed within the month at which this point is reached. It is typically the earliest point at which children show reliance on templatic patterns.

Imitations as well as spontaneous word forms and variant prosodic shapes that fit distinct structures are included in these analyses to assure sufficient material, at as early an age as possible, to identify favoured prosodic structures and allow for cross-linguistic comparative analysis. The Appendix indicates, for each child, the number of target words produced in the session, whether spontaneously or as imitations and the number of different prosodic variants recorded for each target word (or, for diary studies, the number of distinct word variants reported over the period of the last 30 words in a cumulative lexicon of 100). Note that four of the five Estonian children we include here were exposed to English as well as Estonian input; the number of English words that occurred between their 71st and 100th recorded word type is indicated. Discussion will focus primarily on the Estonian words of these children. Although the Welsh children are being raised in primarily monolingual Welsh-speaking homes, each of them also produces a few English words due to the fact that the community they live in is bilingual, with English as the dominant language. For example, one of the children uses the expression *oh God!* at this point, presumably learned from her older siblings. Since English words occur frequently in everyday adult Welsh speech (Deuchar, 2005), we do not distinguish English and Welsh in our analyses.

In the tables that follow these abbreviations are used: (i) imitation, CH consonant harmony, REDUP reduplication, gem geminate, var variant, * reduplicated form.

4.2.1 British English

Table 4.4 provides an overview of the structures used to criterion by any of the eight children acquiring British English. As in Table 3.3 we note for each child the proportion of variant forms that occurred in each distinct structure out of the total

Table 4.4 Prosodic structures in British English, ordered by proportionate use within structures

Structure	Child name	Proportion of all variants
CVV_0 Mean .28	Tania	.40 (18/45)
	Jude	.36 (18/50)
	Patrick	.25 (9/36)
	Lewis	.25 (8/32)
	Rachel	.21 (16/75)
	Flora	.20 (10/50)
CVC Mean .26	Lewis	.34 (11/32)
	Flora	.26 (13/50)
	Rachel	.24 (18/75)
	Ella	.24 (13/55)
	Tania	.22 (10/45)
Disyllabic harmony Mean .26	Jude	.38 (19/50)
	Patrick	.28 (10/36)
	Flora	.22 (11/50)
	Tobias	.20 (9/46)
	Tania	.20 (9/45)
CVCV Mean .24	Ella	.27 (15/55)
	Lewis	.25 (8/32)
	Tobias	.24 (11/46)
	Rachel	.24 (18/75)
	Flora	.22 (11/50)
	Jude	.20 (10/50)
CVCVC	Ella	.24 (13/54)

such variants produced (disregarding variants that fall *within* the same structure after completion of the iterative analysis procedure); the children are ordered within structures from most to least proportionate use.

All of the children make high use of one or both of the monosyllabic structures CVV_0 and CVC; disyllabic structures, with and without consonant harmony, account for a similar proportion of variants for a smaller number of children. Note that one child, Ella, has over 20% variants in the CVCVC structure as well as 27% non-harmonized disyllables without coda (noted as CVCV).

For comparison, we repeat as Table 4.5 the results of the corresponding analysis of six American children's data carried out in Chapter 3 (Table 3.3).

Table 4.5 Prosodic structures in American English, ordered by proportionate use within structures

Structure	*Child name*	*Proportion of all variants*
CVV_0 Mean .34	Emily	.51 (22/43)
	Timmy (and CVV)	.40 (17/43)
	Deborah (and CV?)[1]	.39 (16/41)
	Sean	.27 (12/45)
	Molly	.26 (12/47)
	Alice	.23 (9/39)
CVV	Alice	.21 (8/39)
CVC Mean .30	Sean	.36 (16/45)
	Molly	.32 (15/47)
	Alice	.21 (8/39)
CH	Deborah	.22 (9/41)
Harmony (and reduplication)	Timmy	.28 (12/43)
CVCV Mean .26	Alice (and CVCVC)	.26 (10/39)
	Molly	.26 (12/47)

Note: [1] In the case of a child who does not yet produce other codas, we combine CV? with CV if the structure does not reach 10%.

At the point of first producing 25 or more words in a half-hour session the eight British children are, on average, almost two months older than the six American children (18 vs. 16 mos.: see App. I); their mean number of targets (US 29, UK 39) and variants (US 43, UK 49) are also a little higher. The variants of the children in the two communities fall into much the same prosodic structures, but with small differences in the distribution:

- Proportionately more British children produce monosyllables with codas, but the mean use is higher in the American group.
- One American child produces 21% of her variants in the CVV (diphthongs only) substructure in addition to the 23% that fall into the CV structure.

- More British than American children make use of disyllabic harmony.
- The CVCVC structure is used to criterion by one British child.

Harmony is well established as the most widely used phonological process, one which persists sporadically even to age 3 or 4 (Grunwell, 1982; Vihman & Green-lee, 1987) and it occurs in 22–38% of the structures for the two English-learning groups. It is instructive to look at such commonly used structures to see to what extent they are due to children *adapting* target words to fit them. Accordingly, we present in Table 4.6 the number and proportion of adapted variants over all variants that fit the structure for the children who reached criterion for harmony in each of the English-learning groups. Table 4.6 also illustrates the kinds of adaptation that occur in each group. Recall that reduplication is combined with harmony when it fails to reach 20% of a child's variants on its own; examples of reduplicated adaptations (with or without additional elements) are starred in Table 4.6. Also, some of the harmony is partial (see Flora, for example).

From Table 4.6 we see that the mean proportion of variants adapted to har-mony (or reduplication) is higher for the American children than for the British children who make criterion use of it. As we saw in the discussion of templates in Chapter 3, adaptation is generally, though not always, associated with high use. It is worth noting that one British child, Flora, is using harmony as an aid to producing CVCVC structures. This is a mark of 'ambition' in children at this developmental point; it reflects attempts at the most challenging structure available, in the single-word period, for children learning English. Use of harmony to reduce the number of distinct consonants to retain, plan and produce such structures is common at this point (Vihman, Keren-Portnoy, Whitaker, Bidgood, & McGillion, 2013).

4.2.2 Estonian

In Estonian stress falls on the first syllable of most content words; some loanwords and a few colloquial forms (such as *aitäh* 'thanks') have stress on another syllable. Nine vowels occur in the stressed syllable, front unrounded *i, e, ä* (/i/, /e/, /æ/), front rounded *ü, ö* (/y/, /ø/), back rounded *u, o* (/u/, /o/), and back unrounded *õ* (/ɤ/), which is of very high frequency, and *a* (ɑ). Estonian lacks vowel harmony (unlike closely related Finnish) but only /i, e, ɑ, u/ occur in unstressed syllables. There is no unstressed vowel reduction. In stressed syllable vowels may also combine to create diphthongs with any of the four vowels that can occur unstressed.

It is important to mention that Estonian has a length contrast in both vowels and consonants, although long vowels occur only in stressed syllables. Segmental length is indicated orthographically by doubling the letters for vowels and for most consonants, word medially and finally; for stops, however, the voiced stop symbols (*b, d, g*) are used for the short, lax stops and the voiceless stop

Table 4.6 Adaptation to consonant harmony in English-learning children. Note that several variants include 'extra' (non-target) syllables preposed to or following the variant form; this is characteristic of child forms in this period

	Target word	Forms adapted to harmony structure (*reduplication)	N adapted forms	Total CH & REDUP	Proportion adapted
British children (mean: .41)					
Tania	Daisy	dædi	5	9	.56
	elbow	bɛːboː			
	Iggle-piggle	ɑgigɔ			
	nose	nəʔnʊ			
	there it is (i)	dædɪʔ			
Jude	ball	bɒbɔː	9	19	.47
	cake	*kɪkʰɪ			
	chocolate	tɕata, ɕɔtə			
	circle	*tʰʊtʰʊ, tɕtɕ, tɬutɬu, tʌtɬʌ			
	dinner	nɪnɛ, ɲɪnɪnːɛ			
	football	pʌbɔ, babɔ			
	in 'ere	nənaː, nɪnɪnɛː			
	Noddy	nɒnɪ			
	trousers (i)	tətɕɪ			
Patrick	bee	*bʷiːbʷiːː (i)	3	10	.33
	horsey	hɔʔhiːːː (i)			
	water	waʔwɔːː			
Flora	giraffe (i)	puwæɸ	3	11	.27
	rabbit	bæbɪtʰ			
	story	ʉmɔwɪ(ɕ)			
American children (mean: .56)					
Deborah[1]	round & around (im.)	waʊwʌ, waʊwaʊ	8	13	.62
	bagel (i)	bʌbu			
	bus	*bʌbʌ			
	cock-a-doodle-do	dʌʔdu			
	cracker	w̥æw̥ə (i)			
	pickle (i)	*baba			
	spaghetti (i)	kɪgw̥ɛ			
	water (i)	*bawawa			
Timmy	balloon	*bɛbɛ	6	12	.50
	bicycle (i)	əgɛgːu			
	coffee	gɑːgi, gagŋ̥			
	computer (i)	kʼugɪ			
	lizard ('caterpillar')	*iːjaɪjaɪ			
	money ('coin')	mɑmːi			

Note: [1] The total number of Deborah's harmony and reduplication variants differs from the proportion given in Table 4.5. That is because her reduplication variants (T = 4, including [waʊwaʊ] for *round & round*) account for 10% of her variants and thus constitute a separate prosodic structure but not one that reaches the 20% represented in the overview in Table 4.5.

symbols (*p, t, k*) for long, tense stops; doubling to *pp, tt, kk* is reserved for stops in extra-long syllables (Q3, discussed in Chapter 7.)

Table 4.7 presents the most-used prosodic structures for the five children learning Estonian, three of them in a bilingual environment. Vihman (2016) tested for differences by language in the distribution of prosodic structures for the first 100 words of these bilingual children. The difference proved to be significant for one of them (Maarja). Here, drawing on the period of the last 30 of those words, we indicate the distribution of structures accounting for 20% of variants both overall and for Estonian only; where criterion is not reached for Estonian only (Maarja, CVV_0), the structure is not listed.

Table 4.7 Prosodic structures in Estonian, ordered by proportionate use within structures

Structure	Child name	Proportion of all variants	Estonian words only
CV(:), CVV Mean .29	Kaia	.34 (20/59)	.28 (11/39)
	Maarja	.28 (14/50)	–
	Raivo	.24 (15/63)	.21 (10/48)
CVC Mean .25	Maarja	.30 (15/50)	.29 (8/28)
	Virve	.21 (8/39)	[n/a]
	Raivo	.29 (18/63)	.29 (14/48)
	Madli	.21 (10/48)	[n/a]
CH-mono	Raivo	.24 (15/63)	.21 (10/48)
VCV	Madli	.25 (12/48)	[n/a]
Harmony (and reduplication) Mean .24	Kaia	.27 (16/59)	.26 (10/39)
	Maarja	.22 (11/50)	.32 (9/28)
	Madli	.21 (10/48)	[n/a]
$C_1VC_2VC_0$ Mean: .27	Virve	.33 (13/39)	[n/a]
	Maarja	.20 (10/50)	.29 (8/28)
	Kaia	–	.21 (8/39)

As with the larger data set analysed in Vihman (2016), the three Estonian-learning children with substantial exposure to English do not differ greatly in the overall distribution as compared with Estonian words alone. The exceptions are the CVV_0 structure, which reaches criterion only in the combined count for Maarja, and the CVCV structure, which reaches criterion only in Estonian for Kaia.

Raivo is one of only two children in any group to produce over 20% closed monosyllables with harmony (his use of monosyllables across all structures reaches 76%). Here, all five English variants involve adaptation (e.g., *book* [bʊp], *fish* [sɪs], *moon* [muːm]), as do 8 of 10 Estonian variants (e.g., *jakk* 'jacket' [kakː], *konn* 'frog' [nʊnː], *part* 'duck' [pap], *piim* 'milk' [miːm]). Also, somewhat unusually, Raivo shortens open disyllables to CV monosyllables (*kana* 'chicken' [ka], *Marie (cookies)* [ma, mʷɨ]).

Virve, who produced Estonian almost exclusively in the period covered here, made heavy use of consonant harmony in her earlier word production but at this developmental point fails to reach criterion for harmony in either monosyllables or disyllables, though she has over 10% in both. She reaches criterion in both CVC and disyllables without harmony, five of them including a coda (13% of her variants).

Madli is the one child being raised as a monolingual in Estonia. Like the other children, she makes use of both CVC and disyllables with full or partial harmony. The structure that accounts for the highest proportion of her words is VCV, however, which is not used to criterion by any of the children also being exposed to English.

4.2.3 Finnish

Although Finnish is closely related to Estonian, the word structure is different in many ways, as is evident from our analysis of the target forms for the children's first words: (i) monosyllables account for nearly one-third of the targets in Estonian but are of negligible importance in Finnish; (ii) codas play a substantial role only in Estonian; (iii) (medial) geminate consonants are far more prominent in Finnish target words than in Estonian. Both languages make use of both long vowels and diphthongs, but in Finnish both long vowels and diphthongs may be found anywhere in the word. An additional difference is that Finnish has vowel harmony, requiring backness harmony across all of the morphemes of a word and also within the stem. Specifically, the front vowels ä /æ/, ö /ø/ and y /ü/ do not co-occur with the back vowels a /a/, o /o/ or u /u/; however, the vowels i and e are neutral and can co-occur with any vowel. The orthography is largely transparent; accordingly, adult forms will not be given in phonemic transcription.

Table 4.8 provides an overview of the most-used structures of the five Finnish children. The distribution of structures is strikingly different from that of either

Table 4.8 Prosodic structures in Finnish, ordered by proportionate use of each structure

Structure	Child name	Proportion of all variants
CVV	Eelis	.32 (12/37)
VCV	Atte	.61 (17/28)
Mean .38	Eelis	.38 (14/37)
	Sini	.33 (20/60)
	Eliisa	.23 (8/35)
Harmony (and reduplication)	Mira	.69 (22/32)
Mean .44	Eliisa	.57 (20/35)
	Atte	.36 (10/28)
	Sini	.35 (21/60)
	Eelis	.24 (9/37)

English or Estonian. Only one child makes over 20% use of a monosyllabic structure, CVV. Both reduplication and harmony affect all of the children's variants to some extent, but reduplication—identified only when the medial consonant is a singleton—never reaches 20% on its own. All of the children show over 20% use of consonant harmony, with one child, Mira, reaching 69% (including four reduplicated forms, only one of them selected: *jalka* 'foot' [lala], *kala* 'fish' [ʎaʎa], *napa* 'bellybutton' [papa], and *paapaa* 'sleeping (BT)' [pa:pa:]).

We saw in the first words attempted that monosyllabic words are far less common in Finnish than in English or French (only 2 [8%] of the 24 first Finnish target words: Table 4.2). At this later developmental point they make up 14% of the child variants. An important structural effect is the presence of long vowels in Finnish and the minimal-word constraint: Content words cannot take the mono-moraic structure CV. The structure C_0VV accounts for 10 of the 12 monosyllabic targets (e.g., *ei* 'no', *kuu* 'moon', *pää* 'head', *puu* 'tree', *suu* 'mouth', *tuo* 'that'); as noted above, one Finnish child makes criterial use of this structure.

Finnish has many long words, mostly due to the agglutinative morphology, which can lead to several morphemes being strung together at the end of a noun, for example (Savinainen-Makkonen, 2000a), but the basic uninflected content words are seldom longer than two syllables. The children attempted relatively few long words (16 different word targets, such as Eelis *aukasta* 'open' [ak:a], Eliisa and Sini *paperi* 'paper' [pape], Sini *kirahvi* 'giraffe' [ki:.a], *lusikka* 'spoon' [uk:a]), and produced even fewer.

For the Finnish children the VCV structure accounts for the next highest proportion of target words attempted (38%), after C_1VC_1V (44%). Nearly half of the word targets have word-medial geminates, counting uses of any given word target by any of the children (79 of 171, or 46%); thus high use of this pattern is plausibly related to the high incidence of geminate consonants in the words the children target (see also Savinainen-Makkonen, 2000b, and Savinainen-Makkonen, 2007, who reports that fully 21 of the first 50 words of one Finnish child fit the VCV structure, while 15 fit VCCV more specifically; of these, eight are adapted to fit the pattern through initial consonant omission and even, in one case, medial-consonant lengthening: *meni* 'went' [en:i]). As noted in relation to Table 4.3, these long consonants present a salient perceptual marker for infants and are also easy to match in production, given the slow articulation that characterizes early speech; these factors together help account for the fact that geminates are of higher frequency in words targeted than in input speech and of higher frequency in word forms produced than in words targeted (Vihman & Velleman, 2000; Vihman & Majorano, 2017).

Given the association between geminate occurrence and VCV structure in child word forms, Savinainen-Makkonen (2000a) proposed that the geminates may exert a perceptual pull in the words in which they occur, drawing attention away from the word-initial consonant. Experimental work with Italian 11-month-olds has now demonstrated such an effect on word-form recognition (Vihman & Majorano, 2017).

Table 4.9 Occurrence of VCV structures in Finnish: Target words with geminates, word forms produced with gem(inate)s and child forms adapted to fit the structure by C_1 omission

	Child VCV vars	Targets with gems/ child VCV vars	Child long C/VCV vars	Words adapted by C_1 omission	Adapted VCV with gems	Adapted VCV gems/all VCV adapted
Atte	16	0.53	0.65	6	5	0.83
Eelis	14	0.71	0.93	5	5	1.00
Eliisa	8	0.13	0.13	5	1	0.2
Sini	20	0.45	0.65	16	11	0.69
mean		*0.45*	*0.59*			*0.68*

To further test its plausibility we consider here the proportion of Finnish words adapted to fit the VCV structure by omission of the initial consonant in the forms produced by the four children who make use of the structure (Table 4.9).

As shown in Table 4.9, nearly half of the words produced in the VCV structure have target words with geminates and 61% of the child forms have long consonants. The additional child forms with long consonants are generally due to child substitutions for heterogeneous target clusters (e.g., Eelis: *istu* 'sit!' [it:u:], *itkee* '(s/he) cries' [ik:e:]). Furthermore, 68% of the words in which the VCV form is the result of the child omitting a word-initial consonant (e.g., Eelis *makkara* 'sausage' [ak:a], *nappi* 'button' [ap:i], *loppu* 'all gone' [ɔp:u]) have geminates in the target as well as long consonants in the child form. This supports the hypothesis that the geminates in target words are a factor contributing to the high use of VCV in Finnish.

4.2.4 French

Table 4.10 provides an overview of the structures most used by the four French children. There are a number of similarities with Finnish. The French too produce a considerably higher proportion of variants in disyllabic than monosyllabic structures, although the preference is less extreme than in Finnish. One French child, like one Estonian and several Finnish children, makes use of the VCV structure; three of the four use consonant harmony and one child makes 20% use of reduplication. On the other hand, CVV does not occur, as French has no diphthongs; one child produces over 20% of his variants in the CVC structure, which is not seen in Finnish.

The VCV structure, which was seen in most of the Finnish children, attracts more than 20% of the variants of only one French child, Charles, but at 47% this child's use of the structure is far higher than any other child's use of any structure. As in Finnish, the structure includes mainly cases of adaptation through omission of the initial consonant of the target. Whereas in English onset-consonant

Table 4.10 Prosodic structures in French, ordered by proportionate use within structures

Structure	Child name	Proportion of all variants
CVC$_0$ Mean: .27	Charles	.33 (12/36)
	Noël	.25 (11/44)
	Carole	.23 (10/44)
CVC	Noël	.23 (10/44)
VCV	Charles	.47 (17/36)
Reduplication	Carole	.20 (9/44)
Harmony (and reduplication) Mean: .26	Noël	.30 (13/44)
	Laurent	.28 (13/46)
	Carole	.20 (9/44)
CVCV (and longer) Mean: .35	Laurent	.48 (22/46)
	Noël	.23 (10/44)

omission is seen only in cases where the consonant presents a special challenge (e.g., the fricatives /f, v/: see the word forms of Waterson's son P, Table 2.1, C$_0$VC), here, as in Finnish, even early-learned consonants may be omitted—and even when the onsets to the two syllables are the same (e.g., Carole *tortue* 'turtle' [aty]). In this case a likely contributor to use of the structure is the effect of the lengthening of phrase-final syllables on the perception and retention of target sequences (Vihman & Croft, 2007).

Again, experimental evidence can be cited here. Studies with 11-month-old infants show that, in both English and French, the onset consonant of an accented syllable plays a more important role in (untrained) word-form recognition (and so, by implication, in retention in long-term memory, or representation) than does the onset of an unaccented syllable (Hallé & Boysson-Bardies, 1996; Vihman, Nakai, DePaolis, & Hallé, 2004). Accordingly, in French we see a tendency to omit the onset of the word-initial syllable, which is unaccented. The structure may also be influenced by the fact that French nouns, which dominate the production lexicon at this point, are typically presented with an article preceding them in everyday usage, often providing the children with disyllabic phrasal targets (Charles *les yeux* 'eyes' [aʒoː], Carole *la poire* 'the pear' [apa]; see Veneziano & Sinclair, 2000). This helps to account for the strong preference for disyllables in French child word production (Wauquier & Yamaguchi, 2013).

Two structures, harmony and reduplication, singly or combined, account for the largest proportion of variants for two children (Carole, Noël) and for almost 30% for a third child (Laurent). As a clue to the sources of these structures in French we can again look at adaptation. As Table 4.11 makes clear, French reduplicated forms fit the process of reduplication as it is understood in English, with a whole syllable being added or changed to create the structure—in contrast with Finnish, where

Table 4.11 Forms adapted to harmony or reduplication in French. Consonants or syllables affected in adapting forms to the structure are highlighted in **bold face**

	Target word	*Gloss*	*Variants adapted to harmony or *reduplicated*
Carole	*canard*	duck	*ka:**ka**
	chapeau	hat	**pa**po:
	cuillère	spoon	ko**ko**a
	encore	more, again	*kɔkɔ
	fromage	cheese	məmæ
	lapin	rabbit	***pa**:pa
	petite voiture	little car	tity
	sac	bag	kəka
Charles	*poupée/bébé*	doll/baby	*bapa
	chaussures	shoes	ʒaʒo
Laurent	chapeau	hat	***bo**bo
	chaussettes/chaussures	socks/shoes	ʃoʃy
	gateau	cake	**ta**to
	non	no	na:nɔ̃
Noël	canard	duck	tɛta, *tætæ
	chapeaux	hats	***pʌ**pʌ
	gateau	cake	**ta**to
	lapin	rabbit	**pa**pɛ̃
	(la) main	hand	**pæ**mã
	(le) paletot	overcoat	*papa, papapo
	peinture	picture	*papa[n]

the constraint on vowel use across target words means that change to a single consonant may suffice to yield a reduplicated form. Disregarding a few forms in which a syllable has been added or in which it is difficult to say which element has changed, we find that the initial consonant or syllable can be identified as adapted in half of the variants of French disyllabic targets (11/22 [in **bold face** in the table]). This suggests that, as in Finnish, relative disregard of the onset consonant in perception—in this case due to the accent falling on the final syllable—likely underlies much of the use of harmony and reduplication as well as of VCV.

4.2.5 Italian

Italian shares a number of characteristics with Finnish, as we saw from the analysis of first-word targets: Neither language presents many monosyllables in the core lexicon (although they are targeted more often in Finnish than Italian). More importantly, content words in both languages have mainly open syllables,

Table 4.12 Prosodic structures in Italian, ordered by proportionate use of each structure

Structure	Child name	Proportion of all variants
VCV Mean: .29	G.A.	.36 (12/33)
	L.L.	.22 (13/60)
Harmony and reduplication Mean: .27	G.C.	.36 (12/33)
	J.A.	.25 (9/36)
	A.P.	.24 (8/34)
	L.L.	.23 (14/60)
CVCCV Mean: .26	A.P.	.32 (11/34)
	C.L.	.26 (13/50)
	J. A.	.25 (9/36)
	G.C.	.24 (8/33)
	I.S.	.23 (11/47)
C1VC2V(CV) Mean: .24	J.A.	.28 (10/36)
	L.L.	.27 (16/60)
	I.S.	.26 (12/47)
	A.P.	.24 (8/34)
	C.L.	.22 (11/50)
	G.A.	.21 (7/33)
	G.C.	.21 (7/33)
Longer words	C.L.	.30 (15/50)

except for the frequent occurrence of geminates in word-medial position. And unlike English or French, there are no reduced vowels, regardless of stress.

Table 4.12 provides an overview of the most-used structures in Italian. As in Finnish, the minimal CVV_0 structure used so commonly in English and French occurs only rarely; no monosyllabic structure reaches 20% of all variants for any of the children. In fact, two of the children have only one monosyllabic variant each. In general, Italian content words are seldom monosyllabic; the only three mono-syllables produced by more than one child each are the deictics *qua* 'here', *qui* 'here', and the greeting *ciao* 'hi'.

The disyllabic structures are somewhat differently distributed in Italian as compared with Finnish. Whereas Finnish children made the most use of the VCV structure, often adapting words to it (54% of the VCV word forms are adapted), Italian children make less use of that structure and adapt just under half of their variants to fit the pattern (44%; see Table 4.13). In other words, the Italian children select for VCV more often than they adapt words to the structure, whereas the reverse is true for Finnish children. The percentage of geminates in the adapted forms (80%), is even higher than in Finnish.

Table 4.13 Italian children's adaptations to the VCV structure. Target words with geminates and child forms with long consonants are in **bold face**

Child	VCV variants	Proportion of total variants	Target word and gloss	Adult form	Child form
A.P.	6	.18	*grazie* 'thank you'	**/grat:sie/**	**[at:e]**
			quella 'that one (f.)'	**/kwel:a/**	**[ɛl:a]**
			questi 'these'	/kwesti/	**[et:i]**
C.L.	4	.08	*cosa* 'what?'	/koza/	[oza]
			questa 'this one (f.)'	/kwesta/	**[et:a]**
G.A.	12	.36	*grazie* 'thank you'	**/grat:sie/**	**[at:ʃe]**
			latte 'milk'	**/lat:e/**	**[at:e]**
			letto 'bed'	**/let:o/**	**[et:o]**
			quello 'that one (m.)'	**/kwel:o/**	**[ɛl:o]**
			questo 'this one (m.)'	/kwesto/	**[et:o]**
			rosso 'red (m.)'	**/ros:o/**	**[os:o]**
			rotto 'broken (m.)'	**/rott:o/**	**[ot:o]**
G.C.	5	.15	*forchetta* 'fork'	**/for'kɛt:a/**	**[et:a]**
			latte 'milk'	**/lat:e/**	**[at:e]**
I.S.	3	.06	*rotti* 'broken (pl.)'	**/rot:i/**	**[ot:i]**
J.A.	5	.14	*grande* 'big'	/grande/	[ande]
			succo 'juice'	**/suk:o/**	**[uk:o]**
			zitto 'silent'	**/tsit:o/**	**[it:o]**
L.L.	13	.22	*cane* 'dog'	/kane/	[ane]
			gallo 'rooster'	**/gal:o/**	**[al:o]**
			jeep (English)		**[ip:e]**
			luce 'light'	/lutʃe/	[utʃe]
			paura 'fear'	/paura/	[aula]
			rosso 'red (m.)'	**/ros:o/**	**[os:o]**
			rotto 'broken (m.)'	**/rot:o/**	**[ot:o]**

The Italian children also make considerably less use of both reduplication and consonant harmony than do Finnish children, and in particular, most of their variants in these structures are closely based on the target; there is very little adaptation. This is in contrast with both Finnish and French, where adaptation is more common than selection of targets in these structures. Furthermore, all of the Italian children produce more variants with reduplication than with harmony (i.e., partial reduplication), unlike the mix of preferred structures seen in Finnish. In short, Italian provides large numbers of 'reduplicated' target forms (disregarding the difference in syllable structure due to medial geminates); these make up a fair proportion of the children's prosodic variants (e.g., *mamma* 'mommy' and *pappa* 'food, BT': all 7 children; *tata* 'child': 6 children).

The most used Italian structure is disyllabic (or longer) CVCV(CV), without harmony (mean 24% use, all seven children). This is the case despite the fact that we separate out a disyllabic (or longer) structure with medial geminate, which accounts for a mean of 26% of the variants for five children. The non-harmonic disyllabic structure, with a within-word change of place of articulation in many cases, is rare in both English and French child forms. When it is used in those groups, a particular template (generally with specification of the second segment or segmental type) can often be identified, as discussed in Chapter 3 for American English. No such templatic specialization is seen in these cases in Italian. The surprising level of consonant variegation at this lexical level suggests that the simple sequence of CV-syllables found in much of the input may facilitate earlier mastery of within-word variegation than is seen in any of the other groups. (See Kehoe, 2015, who reports, for roughly the same lexical level as we are focusing on here, high use of variegation in children acquiring Spanish as compared with children acquiring German.) Furthermore, Italian is the only language group in which words of more than two syllables reach 20% for even a single child (C.L.). The long words this child targets range from 3 to 5 syllables; C.L. reduces just under half of them by one syllable (e.g., *animaletti* 'animals' [amalet:i], *motoci-cletta* 'motorcycle' [patet:a, ka'pet:a]). Here we can compare Italian with Japanese, where one of the 7 children recorded produced words of up to five syllables at a comparable lexical level (e.g., targets bearing the honorific ending -*chan*, produced as /tan/ in infant-directed speech (IDS): *bebichan* 'Miss Baby' [bebetan], *oningyochan* 'Miss dolly' [ɔnitjã:n], *omachan* 'Mr. Horsie' [omatamata]; see Vihman, 1991).

4.2.6 Welsh

Table 4.14 presents the prosodic structures most used by the four Welsh children.[3] Here it is immediately evident that the use of structures in Welsh resembles that of English more than that of any of the other languages. There is relatively little use of harmony and high use of structures with coda. Consideration of the actual patterns used will make this clearer.

First, it is important to mention that although four of the 24 first words targeted by the Welsh children were English, at this point two of the children use no English words, one uses two and one (Elen) uses as much as one-third English words—although these include words such as *dad, hello, ball, teddy* and *uh-oh*, which are fully integrated into everyday Welsh speech.

As in English, diphthongal structures are included among the monosyllables these children produce. Gwyn just reaches criterion with CVV words alone; he also uses five CV variants, three of them onomatopoeic. The balance is the reverse

---

[3] For a brief account of relevant aspects of Welsh phonetics and phonology, see Chapter 5 (5.1.6).

Table 4.14 Prosodic structures in Welsh, ordered
by proportionate use within structures

Structure	Child name	Proportion of all variants
CVV$_0$ Mean: .27	Gwyn	.30 (16/53)
	Fflur	.23 (11/48)
CVC Mean: .26	Carys	.31 (11/35)
	Elen	.21 (8/39)
CH-mono	Fflur	.21 (10/48)
VC & VCVC	Fflur	.31 (15/48)
CVCV & longer	Elen	.38 (15/39)

for Fflur, who produces just two diphthongal and nine CV variants, reaching .23
only when the structures are combined.

Two children produce closed monosyllables to criterion and one child, Fflur,
reaches criterion in C$_1$VC$_1$ (10 variants, or 21%). Her non-harmonic CVC words
are mainly of the shape [ʔVC] (e.g., *boch* 'cheek' /bɔx/ [ʔɒx], *diod* 'drink' [ʔɒd],
gwallt 'hair' /gwaɬt/ [ʔax]), but these reach only 19%, even when all non-harmonic
variants are combined. Similarly, the fourth child, Gwyn, has more harmonic than
non-harmonic closed monosyllables, but they reach only 19% when combined.

This is the only language group not to make criterial use of disyllabic harmony.
Instead, close analysis of the large number of different prosodic structures reveals one
case in which only combination of mono- and disyllabic structures provides a satis-
factory account of the child's preferences. Fflur has a large number of forms in which
the onset is replaced by glottal stop, as noted above for monosyllables. Combining one-
and two-syllable word forms clearly reveals her bias, which affects 31% of her variants.

All four children use non-harmonic longer word structures, making roughly
even use of VCV, CVCV, CVCVC. Elen also uses the open CVCV structure
for seven 'long-word' variants, some based on multiword routines (*dau, tri,
pedwar* /daɪtriˈpɛdwar/ 'two, three, four' [daɪ: | tʃi | dida]; *seesaw (Marjorie-
Daw)* [mʌsɪsɪjɔ]) or word combinations most likely learned as whole units
(*baba fyna* 'baby here' /babaˈvina/ [baba:əʊa]); these reach criterion if combined
with the disyllabic open-syllable structure, accounting for 38% of her variants.

4.3 Overview of findings

Table 4.15 provides an overview of the distribution of prosodic structures in the
six languages, with numbers of children making criterial use of each structure
indicated for each language group. (We include in the more narrowly defined
structures—CVV, Reduplication, CVCVC—only cases that reach criterion on
their own. Thus Harmony is counted for children who use harmony, whether or

Table 4.15 Number of children producing over 20% of all variants in each structure. Shading highlights use by half or more of the children in a group. For the bilingual children only the Estonian words are included here. *Italics mark structures logically included under the broader structure indicated in the row above (see text).* Mono = monosyllabic, di = disyllabic, longer = structures including more than two syllables

Language group	US English	UK English	Estonian	Finnish	French	Italian	Welsh
N children	6	8	5	5	4	7	4
CVV_0	6	6	3	0	3	0	2
CVV	1	0	0	1	n/a	0	0
CVC	3	5	4	0	1	0	2
CH-mono	0	0	1	0	0	0	1
VCV_0	0	0	1	4	1	2	1
CH-di	2	5	3	5	3	4	0
REDUP	0	0	0	0	1	0	0
CVCCV	n/a	n/a	0	0	n/a	5	n/a
$C_1VC_2VC_0$	2	6	3	0	2	7	1
CVCVC	0	1	0	0	0	0	0
longer	0	0	0	0	0	1	0

not some of those structures may be considered reduplicated, whereas Reduplication does not include harmony.)

There are a number of cross-linguistic similarities. One- and two-syllable forms account for all the often-used prosodic structures except for those of one Italian child; CV, the simplest structure, is found in at least two children in five of the seven groups. Disyllabic harmony is used to criterion by some children in all but one group.

The table also brings out a sharp difference between the English, Estonian, and Welsh groups, with their common uses of monosyllabic structures and of coda, and the other three language groups. Beyond that, each group has its own profile. The VCV structure is used to criterion by at least one child in all but the two English groups, but it is used by half or more of the group only in Finnish; reduplication occurs as a high-use structure on its own for one French child only. Harmony in monosyllables occurs to criterion only in one Estonian and one Welsh child. Finally, (i) disyllabic variants with both onset and word-final consonant and (ii) variants more than two syllables long occur to criterion in only one British and one Italian child, respectively.

It is clear that, as suggested in Chapter 3, variegation, or producing words with two different supraglottal consonants across the form, is the major challenge for most children at this developmental point. Ways around the difficulty include shortening the word to eliminate a syllable (adaptation to CVV_0), coda omission, initial consonant omission (adaptation to VCV), reduplication and harmony. In every group except Finnish some children succeed in producing 20% or more of their variants in the $C_1VC_2VC_0$ structure (sometimes including longer words).

Table 4.16 Variegation in child variants and adult targets

	Total variants	Child variants with supraglottal C1 & C2	Proportion C1–C2 over all variants	Targets with supraglottal C1 & C2
US English	258	44	0.17	.56
UK English	388	81	0.21	.50
Estonian [Est. forms only]	222	75	0.34	.64
Finnish	192	10	0.05	.42
French	170	34	0.20	.51
Italian	293	144	0.49	.61
Welsh	175	49	0.28	.51
Total and mean	1698	437	0.26	.54

However, in this analysis we have not separated out glottals and glides from 'true consonants', as none of the children make criterial use of structures with medial glottals or glides independently of the overall C_1VC_2V structure. We take up this distinction in Chapter 5.

Table 4.16 provides the raw numbers and proportions of all variants with more than one supraglottal consonant, including monosyllables (CVC), disyllables and the relatively few longer forms. Note that we include as variegation child forms with C_1–C_2 sequences that correspond to a non-contiguous supraglottal consonant sequence in the target, regardless of whether or not the target is itself variegated and regardless of the accuracy of the child's consonants. We exclude from this count variants that are variegated only by virtue of stray consonants, not warranted by the target. See, for example, Ella *byebye* [baːbaɪx], with a stray coda, or Sean *moo* [nomɔ], where the first syllable is unwarranted (a filler). In contrast, we consider Alice's *mommy* [maːɲi] to be variegated despite the lack of variegation in the target, as it does include a target-related consonantal sequence. We also exclude heterogeneous clusters here, as the challenge in producing such sequences cannot be considered to be at the whole-word or prosodic level. Finally, as in most of our analyses, voicing is disregarded within child forms, as a change in voicing only (e.g., Maarja *saapad* 'boots' [bop]) is not taken to constitute consonantal variegation.

Table 4.16 shows that structures with two different 'true consonants' account for about one quarter of all child variants, or half the level of variegation in the words they target. The exceptionally high proportion in Italian child forms follows from the fact that in that language alone all of the children make criterial use of the CVC(C)V structures and, furthermore, virtually all of the disyllables with geminates show within-form variegation (whereas many disyllables with singletons have medial glides; glides do not occur as geminates in Italian). This distribution is in sharp contrast with Finnish, which has geminates but also an unusually small consonant inventory and a correspondingly low proportion of target words with variegation.

4.3.1 Developmental changes

In the analysis of prosodic structures toward the end of the single-word period we noted the main similarities and differences across the language groups; we also supplemented the distributional analysis with some consideration of the extent to which children make active use of their preferred structures, extending them, through adaptation, to words that do not fit the pattern in their adult form. Returning now to the target word analysis with which we began the chapter we can ask what changed for these children as they gained greater familiarity with the lexicon of the language(s) they were learning while also gaining greater mastery in production. The most striking finding is the considerable increase in variegation in the target words (from a mean of 38% to 54%) by the later lexical level. This is consistent with the claim that children are *selecting* words to attempt, based on matches to their own relatively simple existing vocal repertoire, which necessarily becomes more complex over this intensive word-learning period. The increase is seen in all but the Welsh group. In fact, there is a negative correlation (−.21) between the two mean levels of variegation; this is due to the fact that a *decrease*, from 58% to 51%, is seen in Welsh, which has the highest proportion of variega-tion at the 4wp, while the biggest increase is seen in Italian, from lowest ranked, at 20%, to highest, at 61%. It is unclear whether these findings relate in some way to ambient languages differences in structure or are simply artefacts of the relatively small sample sizes.

The overview of child use of prosodic structures in Table 4.15 shows how far the children diverge by language group by the time they reach the later lexical level; it also shows how far they have come from the restrictions reflected in the narrow range of words they attempted at the onset of word production. The cross-linguistic differences in length in syllables identified in analyses of *input speech* (but less evident in the children's *targets*) have now begun to be apparent in the children's *own word forms*, from the monosyllables that clearly dominate English and Welsh to the high use of longer words by at least one Italian child. And the low level of consonant variegation seen in the words targeted at the onset of word production (38%) is now reflected in children's *production* of prosodic struc-tures with no more than a single consonant type despite generally *targeting* more words with consonant variegation; This is largely achieved through adaptation to harmony, reduplication, or initial consonant omission, based on the analyses presented so far. However, variegation in the children's own forms has also more than doubled, from 10% in the first words to 26% by the end of the single-word period. In Chapter 5 we will consider, on a cross-linguistic basis, how at least some children concentrate much of their production on one or more *segmentally specified* templates, which allows them to increase their vocabulary within the limits of their capacities for retaining or representing, planning, and articulating word forms.

4.4 Concluding remarks

We now return briefly to the questions we invoked at the beginning of this chapter, concerning the relative effects on lexical choices and production patterns of (i) the resources generally available to the infant just beginning to speak, (ii) the power of differing adult structures to shape early words, and (iii) the extent of individual differences between children's profiles in this early period of lexical and phonological development.

As already noted, the first words—in all six language groups—are almost exclusively one or two syllables in length, as are most of the target forms, and most include only open syllables and only a single consonant type. By the end of the single-word period, however, the children have begun to target more challenging prosodic structures, including longer words, words with final consonants and words with more than one consonant type; the frequency of input occurrence of those challenging elements is likely a key determinant of the typological differences between the language groups that we begin to see at this point.

At the same time, within language groups some children quickly begin to accommodate to the adult language challenges, regardless of their own articulatory or memory-based limitations, by adapting target forms to their existing word patterns; other children advance more cautiously, with selection and production more closely aligned. We have not yet considered the effect of the child's segmental inventory on such advances; in Chapter 5 we will see how differences in inventory size interact with selection and adaptation of adult targets to fit child patterns or templates.

5

Phonological templates in development

In Chapter 3, after presenting the first words and later prosodic structures of six American children, we provided each child's consonant inventory and then considered whether the child's data gave evidence of template use; in several cases we were able to refer to evidence from previous longitudinal studies of these same children. In this chapter, in order to obtain a cross-linguistic picture of templatic patterning, we will draw on some of the children whose prosodic structures were detailed in Chapter 4 but will add, as needed, data from other children learning those same languages but for whom the earliest word forms are not available; this will enlarge the range of templates that we can use for discussion and illustration—since not all children produce identifiable templates over the period of data collection—while nevertheless allowing us to draw on the background information provided by the language-group profiling in Chapter 4. The data for most of these additional children have been published previously, based on longitudinal recordings. This will sometimes make it possible to supplement evidence from the single session or the subset of diary data we analyse here.[1] Our goal throughout will be to consider the favoured segments and structures and individual patterning of each child we discuss, reflecting the particular challenges they were dealing with; we will identify templates where the evidence warrants it.

5.1 Cross-linguistic identification, description, and evaluation of templates

As indicated in the conclusion of Chapter 4, templates can serve as facilitators of word-form learning by providing ways around the difficulties infants face, given limited articulatory and representational skills, especially in the face of target word forms with consonant variegation. While templates typically involve some regression in accuracy, they also support advances toward more systematic and eventually more target-like production and they increase a child's ability to retain segmental sequences by providing a supporting framework or schema onto which

---

[1] Full prosodic structure analyses were carried out for each of these children, following the procedures laid out in Chapter 3. We will sometimes refer to and illustrate the relevant structures but we will not show the full analyses here.

new words can be mapped. We will discuss those effects in Chapter 6; here, we focus on (i) establishing, for each language group, cases where a template appears to be active and (ii) considering the contributing factors, from ambient language structures and from the individual child.

5.1.1 British English: Jude, Jack

Vihman, DePaolis, and Keren-Portnoy (2016) present data from one British child, Jude, to illustrate variability in early word use, and from another, Jack, to illustrate the use of templates in phonological development. Here we present the data from Jude and Jack in greater detail and with some reanalysis, to exemplify two different pathways to lexical advance in this language group. (Of these two only Jude was included in Chapter 4, as Jack's early words were not recorded.)

Jude. Jude was one of twelve children followed monthly in North Wales from 11 months until they had produced about 25 words spontaneously (Keren-Portnoy, Vihman, DePaolis, Whitaker, & Williams, 2010). All but one of these children later served as the typically developing control group in a study of late-talking toddlers (Vihman, Keren-Portnoy, Whitaker, Bidgood, & McGillion, 2013). At 15 months Jude produced 42 word types in a recording session, making him one of the youngest children to reach that lexical level (see Appendix I). He was also one of three children whose development Szreder-Ptasinska (2012) followed in her thesis, starting with the session we detail here. Szreder-Ptasinska notes that in the preceding session Jude had produced only six words (see Table 4.1); two of those were onomatopoeia with unclear or variable adult models, which we exclude from the analysis. Thus this 15-month session marks a lexical leap forward for the child, with several instances of phonetically exploratory word productions that Szreder-Ptasinska ranks high on a scale of 'boldness'.

Before looking at Jude's word structures we present his inventory of consonants (Table 5.1). We follow the principles for listing consonants and counting matches to target outlined in Chapter 3. Word forms that match the target for the consonant in question are in **bold face**, as are target consonants matched in at least two child forms.

Jude produces eight onset consonants as match to target in more than one word type: the stops [p, b, t, d, k], the nasals [m, n], and the glide [j]. He produces codas in only two variants in the session but nevertheless targets numerous words with codas; similarly, he produces as a match to target only one liquid (/l/) and one fricative (coda /ʃ/, produced as [ç]), but he targets all of these sounds and produces them with a remarkably variable set of phonetic forms. He also makes use of the affricate [tç], not only for target /tʃ/ but also for /st/ and even /kl/.

Jude produced a total of 50 distinct prosodic variants, including one produced as a single syllabic consonant (*fish* [ç:], alongside the more conventional attempt,

Table 5.1 Jude's consonant inventory at 15 months

Target C (N = 8)	Onset		T	Coda	T
p	apple /ˈæpəl/ [apʰɪ]	caterpillar /ˈkætəˈpilə/ [pia]	4		
b	baba /ˈbaba/ 'baby (Welsh)' [baba]	ball [bɔ]	8		
t	star /stɑ:/ [ta]	teeth /tiθ/ [tʰiː]	8		
d	dada /ˈdɑdɑ/ [dadʒa]	daddy /ˈdædi/ [datʰi]	5		
tʃ [tç]	chocolate /ˈtʃɔklət/ [tçata]	stuck /stʌk/ [tçʌ]	5		
k	cake /keɪk/ [kɪkʰɪ]	circle /ˈsɜkəl/ [tʰkʰɪ]	5		
ʃ [ç]				fish /fɪʃ/ [ɪç]	
[x]				book /bʊk/ [bʊx]	
h	hiya /ˈhɑɪjʌ/ [haɪə]				
m	Emma /ˈɛmʌ/ [æmæ]	mummy /ˈmʌmi/ [mʌmi]	3		
n	night-night /ˈnaɪtnaɪt/ [nənə]	Noddy /ˈnɑdi/ [nɒnɪ]	4		
l	flower /ˈflɑwə/ [la]				
j	hiya /ˈhɑɪjʌ/ [jaija]	yay /jeɪ/ [jɛə]	3		
w	square /skwɛ:/ [wɛ]				
ʔ	uh-oh /ˈʔʌʔəʊ/ [ʔʌʔʌʔ, ʌʔɔ:]				

[ɪç]). He also produced one extra-long word, an attempt at *caterpillar*, transcribed as [pʰɪtʰɪpʰʌpʰkʰkʰæ . . .], a rendition that reveals (i) Jude's response to the variegated stop consonants in the target word as well as its exceptional length and (ii) his boldness or willingness to 'take a risk', tackling a word form that is far beyond his phonetic and planning skills.[2]

To further illustrate this, consider Jude's numerous attempts to produce the disyllabic words *chocolate* and *circle*, including, for *chocolate*, [tçata, çɔtə], and for *circle*, [tʰʊtʰʊ, tçtç, ɬʊtɬu, tʌtɬʌ]. The forms for *circle*, in particular, appear to reflect the child's exploration of possible ways of conveying the combination of word-initial /s/ and the sequence /k/ + syllabic /l/. In fact, these are the only sibilant-initial target words attempted in the session, aside from *stuck*, in which /st/ is rendered as [tç], and the sC-cluster words, *sky* [ca], *star* [tɑ:], *square* [wɛ], in which the /s/ is disregarded, as is common in the early stages of English cluster acquisition (Smith, 1973; Vihman & Greenlee, 1987). As with *caterpillar*, we see in these variants the child's high 'tolerance for variability' or willingness to venture beyond the limits of his actual phonetic skills.

---

[2] Recall that this word was attempted, surprisingly, already in the previous month as one of Jude's first four recorded words (see Table 4.1). At that point the word took the form [biɔ], suggesting that at first only the final portion, -*pillar*, had been retained.

Table 5.2 Jude's use of C_0VGLIDEV

Selected target word	Child form	Adapted target word	Child form
hello	aijɔ	baba	bawa
hiya	aija, jaija	caterpillar	pi[j]a
orange	ɒwi	in 'ere (there)	ıjɛ
		yeah	wəjɛ

Unlike most of the other British children, Jude produced only two words with coda.[3] Most of his variants fit into three prosodic structures, CVV_0 (18, or 36%), disyllabic harmony (19, or 38%) and 10 variants with VCV or CVCV (20%). However, a non-harmonic pattern to which a few words are adapted, in what may be an emergent template, is C_0VGLIDEV, which accounts for seven of the ten C_0VCV variants: See Table 5.2.

We consider *orange* to be selected because the target form is disyllabic, as required by the template; the use of [w] for /r/, which the child is not yet producing, is a regular phonetic replacement; the vowels are not specified by the template. In contrast, consider the adapted forms: The child elsewhere produces *baba* with both stops and *in 'ere* with medial nasal; *caterpillar* is truncated to fit the pattern (as in the earlier session),[4] while *yeah* is extended with a non-target syllable.

Jude's CVV_0 words are largely selected; see the variants for words with initial /sC-/, noted above.[5] The exception is *flower*, shortened to [la]. Since CV, used by virtually all of the children acquiring English, may be considered a default, we do not see this as the kind of 'overuse' that suggests templatic action.

The use of harmony is evenly distributed between selected and adapted forms (Table 5.3). Here we see adaptations of various kinds. *Ball, cake,* and *football* are reduplicated. The words *dinner* and *Noddy* and the frozen expression *in 'ere* are produced with nasal harmony. *Chocolate, circle,* and *trousers* present particular challenges, as noted above; the child forms are phonetically adventurous but prosodically constrained by the harmony pattern.

Thus in contrast to Jude's boldness in *phonetic exploration*, his word forms at this developmental point are shaped by just two or three prosodic structures, one of them a default largely based on selection, the other two including a good deal of adaptation. Szreder-Ptasinska argues that it is this very restrictedness in prosodic structure that frees the child to boldly explore the articulatory gestures needed for word forms outside his existing repertoire.

---

[3] A stray final consonant also occurs in a single variant of *baba* 'baby', transcribed as [baβaχ].

[4] More plausibly, [pia] may be taken to reflect an incomplete representation of the target, as proposed in fn. 3, rather than 'truncation' at the point of production. That would mean that a new child representation, underlying the long variant with alternating voiceless stops, was emergent in this session in competition with the earlier, less complete one.

[5] Only two CVV variants occur: *yay* [jɛə] and a variant of *ball* [boʊ].

Table 5.3 Jude's uses of consonant harmony

Selected target word	Child form	Adapted target word	Child form
baba	baba, bɔbɑ, bʌba, bafa	ball	bɒbɔː
Barnaby	babʷi	cake	kɪkʰɪ
bubble(s)	babo	chocolate	tɕata, çɔtə
dada	dadʑa	circle	tʰʊtʰʊ, tɕtç, tɬʊtɬu, tʌtɬʌ
daddy	datʰi̯	dinner	nɪnɛ
mummy	mʌmi	football	pʌbɔ, babɔ
night-night	nənə	in 'ere	nənaː, nɪnɪnɛː
ticktock	tʰʊtʰaː	Noddy	nɒnɪ
uh-oh	ʌʔɔː, ʔʌʔʌʔ	trousers (i)	tətçɪ

Jack. At 26 months Jack is the oldest of the children we consider here. He was originally included as a late talker in the study reported in Vihman et al. (2013), based on his having only a small vocabulary at age two years and no word combinations. However, his productive vocabulary advanced rapidly in the next few months and when formally tested on the Reynell-III Scales for expressive language (Edwards et al., 1997) at 2;6 he was found to be within four months of the normal range. Accordingly, he was designated a 'transitional late talker' within the study. As explained in Vihman et al. (2016):

> Children who, like Jack, make a later start than is typical differ from the younger children whose templates have been described previously in the literature by virtue of their far larger (age-appropriate) receptive lexicon in relation to their expressive word use. Their lexical targets are accordingly more advanced than those of typically developing children at the same level of phonological develop-ment, which means that the 'adaptations' observed are sometimes more radical than those reported for younger children. At the same time, their word forms reflect phonological categorization and template formation in a way that closely resembles that of younger children.   (p. 220)

During the session Jack was primarily engaged in naming pictures with his mother and produced 57 identifiable words. His production is highly variable and features several unusual adaptations, resulting in 70 variants. He engaged in little phonetic experimentation; instead, and in contrast with Jude, he dealt with his phonetic limitations by attempting—seemingly somewhat haphazardly—numerous alternative ways of fitting a target word into one of the relatively small number of prosodic structures that he was using in word production.

Jack's segmental inventory is less advanced than Jude's, despite his age advantage, with only five matches to target (see Table 5.4). Jack produces no fricatives except [h], which he uses only rarely, and indeed he attempts only two words with

Table 5.4 Jack's consonant inventory at 26 months

Target C (N = 5)	Onset		T	Coda		T
p	pizza /ˈpitsʌ/ [pisi]			Jacob /ˈdʒeɪkəb/ [deidʌp]		
b	balloon /bəˈluːn/ [bɔːʊ]	bubbles /ˈbʌbəlz/ [bɔːwʊːə]	24	Jacob /ˈdʒeɪkəb/ [ɡɪdʌb, deiɡʌb]	up /ʌp/ [ʌbˈ]	
t				plate /pleɪt/ [bɛɪtʰ]	cake /keɪk/ [nədeɪtʰ]	
d	down /daʊn/ [daʔhaʊ]	cat /kæt/ [dæʔ]	18			
k				bike /baɪk/ [maɪʔkʰ]	grapes /ɡreɪps/ [ɡeɪk]	
g	green /ɡriːn/ [ɡɪːn]	guitar /ɡɪˈtɑː/ [ɡɪːaː]	8			
h	Harriet /ˈhɛɹɪət/ [hɛɪjɛː]	crane /kɹeɪn/ [hɛɪːːn]				
m	mummy /ˈmʌmɪ/ [mʌmɪʰ]		4	worm /wɜːm/ [bɛʊm]	bump /bʌm/ [bəm]	7
n	no /nəʊ/ [nəʊː]			clown /klaʊn/ [daʊn]	plane /pleɪn/ [deɪːɪn]	9
[ŋ]	ski /skiː/ [ŋɪːa]	hammer /ˈhæmə/ [m̩ːbaŋɒn]				
l	clown /klaʊn/ [laʊː]	ladybird /ˈleɪdɪbɜːd/ [laːbwaʊm]				
j	yeah /jɛə/ [jɛɪː]					
w	hoover 'vacuum clean' /ˈhuːvə/ [əwʊːwæʔ]	strawberries /ˈstrɔbɛriz/ [daʊwi]	3			
[ʔ]	scooter /ˈskutə/ [m̩ːdjuʔæʔ]	Harriet /ˈhɛɹɪət/ [haɪjaʔɛːja]		cat /kæt/ [dæʔ]	socks /sɒks/ [ndaʔ]	10

singleton initial fricatives, *sun* and *shark*, both produced with [d]; he produces the liquid /l/ in just two forms. Only three consonants occur as match to target at onset in more than a single word: /b/, by far the most frequently occurring consonant, /ɡ/ and, surprisingly, /l/; there are matches to the nasals /m/ and /n/ in coda position and one match for /k/. There is no production of [k] in onset position, whereas the velar nasal occurs only at onset. Many consonants are produced accurately in only a single word.

Jack generally produces the voiceless stops and /sC/ clusters with what are transcribed as the corresponding voiced stops, as is typical for children in the early stages of word production in English (Macken, 1980). Most of Jack's substitutions

Table 5.5 Jack's uses of [m] for /b/ and of [b] for targets with other onsets. Two instances of each type are shown if available, as in consonant inventory tables

Target onset C	target word (1)	child form	target word (2)	child form
/b/: [m]	bike	maɪʔkʰ	boat	məʊ, bəʊ:
/ pC, sp/	plate	bɛɪtʰ	spoon	m̩buːm, bʊ:::::n
/m/	moon	bʊ:, bʊ:ən	mushroom	m̩bʊːm
/w/	worm	bɛʊm	wee (adj.)[1]	biːə
other	rabbits	bɛːgɪʔ		
	robot	maʔ, mbaʔ		
	hammer	m̩:baŋɒn[2]		

Notes:
[1] This form was mistakenly given as *whee* in Vihman et al. (2016).
[2] This form may reflect a situational association with *bang*.

are less expected and less consistent, however. The voiced labial [b] tends to be produced (sometimes in alternation with [m] or [mb]) in words with the labials /p/, /m/ or /w/ as well as in words with target /b/ (Table 5.5).[6]

The alveolar voiced stop /d/ similarly substitutes for a range of coronal target consonants, including the sibilants /s/ and /ʃ/, the affricates /tʃ/ and /dʒ/ and some /sC/, /Cl/ and /Cr/ clusters (Table 5.6).

As indicated in Tables 5.4 and 5.6, only eight words with /t/ or /d/ are actually produced with [d]; most uses of the alveolar stop replace a target velar stop or a

Table 5.6 Jack's uses of [d] for targets with other onsets. Two instances of each type are shown if available, as in consonant inventory tables

Target onset C	Target word (1)	Child form	Target word (2)	Child form
/t/	two	du:	toast	dəʊ::a
/(s)tr/	train	dəɪn	strawberries	daʊ:wɪ
/k/	cat	dæʔ	cake	nədɛɪtʰ, hɪdeɪʔ
/sk/	scooter	m̩djʊʔæʔ		
/Cl/	planɛ	dɛɪ:[j]ɪn	clown	daʊn
/s/	sun	dʌm	socks	n̩daʔ
/ʃ/	shark	da:		
/tʃ/	chocolate	daʔdaʔ		
/dʒ/	jacob	dɪdʌb, deɪdʌpʰ, deɪdʌb		
/sn/	snow	dəʊ:		

[6] Note that as much as 16% (11/70) of Jack's word forms are preceded by a syllabic nasal or short vowel, which may constitute a simple motoric aid to production; accordingly, we disregard these elements in categorizing variants into prosodic structures.

sibilant or affricate. The liquid clusters are inconsistently produced with [d] or with the velar stop [g] (*train* [gɛɪ:]), or /h/ (*crane* [hɛɪ::n]). In one instance the lateral element of the cluster is produced (*clown* [laʊ:]).

Jack produces many words with coda, but his range of possible codas is even more limited than his onsets and the match to target even less consistent. The nasals /m/ and /n/ and glottal stop account for the majority of closed-syllable variants (Table 5.4). Nevertheless, several variants occur as CV(V) where a coda nasal would be required (*clown, down, green, moon, train*).

It is reasonable to assume that difficulty in making a stable match of perceived form to corresponding motor plan was a factor holding Jack back in his expressive lexical development, as the session in which he first produces 25 words shows an explosion of word forms but with exceptionally inconsistent uses of the consonants in repertoire. Some patterns, such as [bɛʊm] or [bu:m], recur for distinct word targets, evidence that despite the large number of words produced in this session Jack is still representing words holistically. (See also the variants used for *ladybird* [la:bwaʊm] and *worm* [bɛʊm], in which the second syllables appear to be somehow conflated.)

Jack's most used prosodic structures are the ones generally expected for English, CV(V), CVC, disyllables with consonant harmony or full reduplication (including reduplicated CVC), and non-harmonic disyllables. By the procedures of Chapters 3 and 4 three structures meet the criterion of 20% (+) use: CV(V) 17 (24%), CV(V)C 20 (29%), and CVGLIDEV 16 (23%). However, taking into account the use or overuse of particular segment-to-word-position frames requires some restructuring of this picture.

Jack produces the default open monosyllable with a single vowel or a diphthong equally often (Table 5.7). Although a few variants are selected, Jack adapts to the pattern both disyllables (which he truncates) and closed monosyllables, despite

Table 5.7 Jack's use of default CV(V)

Selected target word	Child form	Adapted target word	Child form
CV(V)			
baa	ba::	balloon	bʊ::, bɔ:ʊ
no	nəʊ:	bananas	baʊ
skɪ	gɪ, gɪ::	bed	bæ
snow	dəʊ:	boat	məʊ, bəʊ:
tree	əgɪ:	clown	laʊ:
		green	gi::::
		moon	bʊ:
		page	m̩bɛɪ
		shark	da:
		train	gɛɪ:

the fact that he regularly produces both stops and nasals in coda position in other instances. As Vihman et al. (2016) comment:

> Despite its high frequency...this is not a stable or consistently used template, given the high variability of coda production. Instead, it may be a 'fall-back' pattern for Jack, produced in alternation with his competing templatic structures, reflecting instable or rapidly evolving representations and inconsistent access to them.   (pp. 221f.)

It is worth noting the frequent use of the diphthongs [aʊ] and [əʊ] in these variants, whether selected (*no, snow, toast*) or adapted (*bananas, boat, clown*; see also *down* and *strawberries* [Table 5.4], *hammer* [Table 5.8] and *ladybird*, mentioned above). In fact, back-rising diphthongs occur in variants of 10 of the 57 words in this session (18%), suggesting a templatic pattern in itself, a back-rising [Vʊ] counterpart to that of Alice, with her templatic reliance on front-rising [Vi] (Chapter 3). Vihman et al. note that 'for Jack, the diphthong itself, though not a whole-word pattern, may be considered "templatic", or an attractor for vowel nuclei' (2016, p. 222).

The most accurately used structures—those with the highest proportion of selected variants—are closed monosyllables. All but one of the variants of the structure CVSTOP may be considered selected, although the choices of both onset and coda consonant are somewhat unpredictable: *bike* [maɪʔkʰ], *cake* [hɪdeɪʔ], *cat* [dæʔ], *grapes* [ɡeɪk], *plate* [beɪtʰ], *robot* [maʔ, mbaʔ], *socks* [n̩daʔ], and *up* [ʌbʻ]. *Robot* shows selection of the (unstressed) second syllable only and is thus adapted to the monosyllabic structure (recall Jude's productions of [biɔ] and [pia] for *caterpillar*; in both cases the unusual selection of the unstressed syllable can be related to the fact that this provides a better match than the stressed syllable to the child's existing word shapes). The eight variants constitute just 11% of the total in

Table 5.8 Jack's monosyllables and disyllables with nasal coda

Selected target word	Child form	Adapted target word	Child form
(CV)CVN			
bump	bəm	boat	bɛɪn (x3)
clown	daʊn	hammer	m̩ːbaŋɒn, baʊm | bæʔ
crane	hɛɪːːn	ladybird	laːbwaʊm
green	ɡɪːn	moon	buːən
paint	bɛɪn (x2)	mushroom	m̩buːm
pink	bɪn		
plane	dɛɪːɪn		
spoon	m̩buːm, ʊːːːːːn		
sun	dʌm		
train	dəɪn		
worm	bɛʊm		

the session and are almost all selected; the frequency is well within the range of typical English child usage for this structure.

Variants in the heavily used structure (CV)CVN cross the word-length division between monosyllables and disyllables. Combining Jack's various forms with nasal coda in either syllable gives 16 variants (23% of the total for the session), most of them selected (considering the limits and inconsistencies of Jack's segmental substitutions). Three of the adapted forms have a nasal in the target; the nasal can be considered the 'hook' in these forms that attracts production to this particular templatic structure.

Two disyllabic patterns remain to be described. All but one of the disyllables with medial glide are adapted (Table 5.9; a glide is assumed to intervene, in phonetic forms like [bɪːa] or [duːə], between high or higher-mid vowel and the lower back or central vowel that follows, whether it was so transcribed or not.)

This template is reminiscent of Molly's and Alice's disyllabic templatic patterns with final [i] or schwa (see Chapter 3): There is a certain rhythmicity to the pattern that appears to exert a pull for Jack as it does for those American children (despite the differences in their emergent systems), even when the word he targets would fit better into one of his other patterns (cf. *bee*, for example); indeed some have variants in other structures (such as *no, pizza, two* and *twit twoo*). *Harriet* can be considered to be selected as Jack's form shows the expected substitution of a glide for the medial liquid and omission of the coda.

Finally, a few variants show full reduplication while others show consonant harmony (Table 5.10). The identification of *chocolate* as 'selected' for reduplication is speculative, suggesting that Jack has retained it as such, but this seems plausible, given the variability of the child's substitutions: The target (/tʃɑklɪt/) is disyllabic and

Table 5.9 Jack's use of CVGLIDEV

Selected target word	Child form	Adapted target word	Child form
CVGLIDEV			
harrɪet	hɛɪjeː	*bananas*	bɛːːaʊ
		bee	bɪːa
		bubbles	bɔːwʊːə
		guitar	gɪːaː
		no	nəʊːːə
		paint	bɛɪːəⁿ
		pizza	mbɪa, bɪə
		skɪ	ɲɪːa
		toast	dəʊːːa
		twit twoo	duːə, duːaʔ
		two	duːə
		wee	bɪːə

Table 5.10 Jack's use of reduplication and harmony

Reduplication			
Selected target word	*Child form*	*Adapted target word*	*Child form*
chocolate	dɑʔdɑʔ	*bear*	m̩baːbaː
		bike	m̩baɪʔbaɪʔ
		pasta	m̩bæʔbæ
		twit twoo	du duːː
Harmony			
mummy	mʌmɪʰ	*dinner*	ŋjɪnja
teddy	dæʔdɪʰ	*hoover*	əwʊːwæʔ
		jacob	dɪdʌb, deɪdʌpʰ (x3), deɪdʌb

includes consonants that Jack is not yet producing. The selected harmony variants are standard, as are the adapted variants in that structure. The proportion of total variants for the two structures taken together amounts to 14%, but it is unclear, without longitudinal data, whether this represents the remaining traces of a structure that Jack may have been using for some time or a template still actively in use.

The account we provide here of Jack's complex treatment of English words in his variable and often idiosyncratic production differs somewhat from that provided in Vihman et al. (2016). The changes are not substantial, however, but relate to details as to which words are included in which patterns. (For example, in the earlier account several words with two-vowel sequences are included in the CVGLIDEV pattern: *bee* [biː[j]a], *moon* [bʊː[w]ən], *no* [nəuːː[w]ə], *worm* [bɛ[j]ʊm]; most of these have monosyllabic variants in the same session: CVV$_0$: *no* [nəuː], *ski* [gi], *two* [duə].) Here we have isolated the single pattern to which the most words conform, as this represents a more identifiable templatic attractor than do the more loosely related forms included in Table 10.3 of Vihman et al., 2016.) We repeat here the conclusions of that account, which apply equally well to the revised account offered here:

> The patterns we see in Jack's word forms reflect, as do the patterns of younger children, his reliance on a small core consonant inventory, one that consists primarily of stops, nasals and glides. Recall that, unlike younger children at this level of expressive vocabulary, Jack has good comprehension of a much larger number of words and, given his later start, more experience of the world of possible referents: This is evidenced by the words he produces, which would be surprising in children of 16 or 18 months, for example (e.g., *robot, shark, hoover* [British English for American 'vacuum [cleaner]']). Beyond that, the many 'adapted' forms, or forms that fail to match the target (even in cases where the child clearly has the necessary articulatory or phonetic resources to make a more accurate match, e.g., *boat, toast*), provide evidence that Jack is inducing generalized patterns from his own output.   (Vihman et al., 2016, p. 224)

5.1.2 Estonian: Maarja, Kaia

The Estonian child data available for the developmental period of interest, pre-sented in Chapter 4, include a student bachelor's thesis on her child Madli's first 50 words (Kõrgvee, 2001) and diary studies of the author's children and grand-children. Diary studies have both advantages and disadvantages (see also Deuchar & Quay, 2000): A family member has access to the child's word knowledge, both receptive and expressive, in a variety of situations that an observational study would be unlikely to catch; the diarist is able to observe the child in interaction with a number of different interlocutors, generally in unforced situations with minimal pressure on either adult or child. This permits access to the child's most natural output and is particularly useful from the point of view of pursuing the child's development over time, as even 'dense sampling' (Lieven & Behrens, 2012) can miss important moments in a child's phonological and lexical advance.

On the other hand, diary data not supplemented by recordings has the disadvan-tage, especially for phonetic/phonological analysis, that data are captured 'on the fly', in real time; there is no opportunity to listen repeatedly to individual vocalizations while transcribing nor to subject the transcription to reliability checks, let alone acoustic analysis. However, diary data have long constituted basic data for gaining knowledge of the course of language acquisition, including phonological develop-ment (such as, for example, the highly influential contributions of Leopold, 1939; Waterson, 1971; and Smith, 1973). The limitations should be kept in mind, then, but there is no reason for the data not to be taken seriously, to the extent that it derives from the reports of an observer professionally trained in a relevant discipline.

Before going on to describe the use of templates by two of the children whose data we analysed in Chapter 4 a brief account of the Estonian consonant inventory is in order, to supplement the information given in Chapter 4 about stress and consonant, vowel and syllable length ('third degree of length' or Q3, marked with a grave accent before the word: See Chapter 7) and the inventory of vowels and diphthongs. The consonant inventory includes a voiceless unaspirated (lax) stop series and a longer, tense series (p, t, k); when lengthened to Q3 in stressed syllables, (tense) stops are represented with double letters (pp, tt, kk). The core vocabulary also includes the fricatives /s/, /h/, and /v/, the nasals /m/ and /n/, the liquids /l/ and /r/, and the glide /j/. In addition there is a full set of palatalized coronal consonants that contrast with the plain coronal consonants word-finally and also medially in certain diminutive forms (e.g., /kutʲsu/ 'doggy', /notʲsu/ 'piggy'). All of the consonants except /v/ and /j/ may occur short, long or extra-long (long /j/ becomes /i/, as in *maja* /maja/ 'house', *maia* /`maia/ 'into the house'). The orthography, aside from the conventions regarding length in stops, is largely phonemic, although palatalization is not marked. The /r/ is a tap when short, a trill when long or extra-long. A few consonants (/f/, /ʃ/, /z/) occur only in loanwords, which are seldom learned early. Onset clusters are relatively rare;

medial and final clusters generally involve sonorant + stop and in stressed syllable the sonorant of a cluster participates in syllable lengthening under Q3 (Chapter 7).

Maarja. Two previous studies have traced the phonological development of Maarja, a child raised bilingually in Tartu, Estonia, by her American linguist mother, V.-A. Vihman, who collected the data, and her Estonian father. Vihman and Vihman (2011; hereafter, V&V) focused on evidence for the whole word as a functional unit in the child's initial phonological system and on the transition to more segmentally oriented phonology thereafter; Vihman (2016) included Maarja as one of five bilingual children whose development is analysed in terms of prosodic structures and templates, focusing on the question of whether a bilingual child develops two separate systems 'from the start' or whether she draws on whatever resources are available, in either language. Although, as noted earlier, some children—and Maarja was the one clear example—make significantly different use of prosodic structures in their two languages, all of the children applied their templatic patterns to words in both languages, suggesting ongoing interaction of the lexical and phonological representations.

Appendix I indicates that Maarja had the highest proportion of English words of the three bilingual Estonian-English-learning children (47% in the period analysed, beginning when her 71st word was recorded, at just under 17 months). That was the age at which Maarja began to attend a full-time nursery school. Whereas her mother had been her primary caretaker to that point, addressing the child in American English while her father and others spoke to her primarily in Estonian, she now began to hear substantially more Estonian than English and gradually stopped using English even in response to her mother, who persisted in using English.[7]

V&V considered the child's development over her first 500 recorded words, covering age 12 to 22 months; Vihman (2016) covered only the first 100 words (to 17 months). V&V note that the first word combinations were observed at 15 months but that they reached a total of over five new combinations per month only at 18 months. Thus the period sampled in Chapter 4 above corresponds to the period of the first relatively infrequent word combinations; this aligns the data nicely with those of individual 25wp sessions in the other language groups. Following V&V, who referred to the child's data in relation to 50-word bins, we will analyse Maarja's template use here in relation to her 50th to 100th word (at 16 to 17 months).

In the previous section we described the phonological patterning of two British children, of different ages, both with a limited capacity to accurately match their targets. The child Maarja shows quite a different developmental course, with a rich set of consonants in both onset and coda, in her Estonian words taken alone as well as in her combined word forms, and a fair range of different structures. Her phonetic inventory is charted sample by sample in V&V, including sounds from both languages. Here we draw on Estonian words only (Table 5.11).

---

[7] The resistance to English continued until, at age 2;6, Maarja spent a few weeks in California; she quickly resumed productive use of English at that point and has remained a fluent bilingual ever since.

Table 5.11 Maarja's consonant inventory at 51–100 words, in Estonian only (age 16–17 months). Stress is word-initial unless otherwise indicated

Target C (N=7)	Onset		T	Coda		T
p				saapad 'boots' /saːpɑt/ [bop], **[bɑp]**	ampsti 'bite, BT' /ampːsti/ **['ɑmpti]**	
[b]	saapad 'boots' /saːpːɑt/ [bop], [bɑp]					
t	aidaa, tadaa 'byebye' /aiˈta, taˈtaː/ **[taita]**, **[tata]**	tool 'chair' /toːl/ **[toːn]**	13	kott 'bag' /kotʲː/ **[kot]**, [kət]	lind 'bird' /lind/ [nʌnt]	
[d]	tadaa 'byebye' /tataː/ [dada]	tudu 'sleep, BT' /tutu/ [dudu]		lind 'bird' /lint/ [nʌnd]		
k	kott 'bag' /kotʲː/ **[kot]**, **[kət]**	kala 'fish' /kala/ **[ka]**, **[kalə]**, **[kaja]**	9			
[g]	kuku 'fall' /kukːu/ [guku], [gugu], [goku]					
s		kiisu 'kitty' /kiːsu/ [kəˈsu]	4			
s:	suss 'slipper' /susʲː/ **[susː]**			suss 'slipper' /susʲː/ **[susː]**, [ʃusː]		
[ʃ]	kiisu 'kitty' /kiːsu/ [ʃiu]	suss 'slipper' /susʲː/ [ʃusː]				
h	tahan 'I want' /tahan/ **[tahan]**					
m	Meelo (name) /meːlo/ **[melo]**			ampsti 'bite, BT' /ampːsti/ **['ɑmpti]**		
n	anna siia 'give (it) here' /anːa siːa/ **[anəˈsiː]**	notsu 'piggy' /notʂu/ **[nunu]**	5	konn 'frog' /konː/ **[konː]**, [kunː]	lind 'bird' /lind/ **[nɪn]**, [nʌnd], [nʌnt]	6
l	Meelo (name) /meːlo/ **[melo]**	kala 'fish' /kala/ **[kalə]**		hallo 'hello (telephone)' /halːoː/ **['aljo]**		
j	hallo 'hello (telephone)' /halːoː/ ['eɪjoː], ['aioː], ['ajo]	küünal 'candle' /küːnal/ **['kajə]**	4			

We can see from Table 5.11 that Maarja does not favour labial production but makes ample use of all the coronal consonants except /l/, which occurs only three times. There is only a single target word with onset /m/ and none with /p/; no words with /v/ (or /r/) are attempted. The codas Maarja produces are all coronals, with the exception of *saapad* and *ampsti*, both produced with coda labials.

Maarja's major prosodic structures were presented in Table 4.7, where only the last 30 of her first spontaneously produced 100 words were taken into account. In the Estonian part of her vocabulary she used three structures, CVC (.29), disyllabic harmony or reduplication (.32), and CVCV (.29). Here, we add in 20 more words but include only Estonian words in the analysis; this gives us a database of 26 words altogether, with 34 variants.

The distribution of words over prosodic structures does not greatly change with the addition of the 12 earlier-learned words. There are 24% CVC variants, but these divide equally into harmony and non-harmony sets. Of the harmony set (4/34, or 15%: Table 5.12), two are actively harmonized (*nina* is merely truncated); we can consider CVC with harmony to be a template of limited scope at this point.

Seven variants have disyllabic harmony (21%: Table 5.13) and another four are reduplicated, for a total of 11 variants in the combined structure (32%, the same proportion as in the more lexically advanced sample of Chapter 4).

However, Maarja's most-used structure is (non-harmonic) $CVCV(CV)C_0$, with 14 variants (41%), including one with coda (*tahan* 'I want' [tahan]) and two produced with three syllables (*anna siia* 'give it to-here [i.e., to me]' [anə'siː], *notsu* 'piggy' /notsʲu/ [nononos], [nənosu], [nonotsu][8]). Maarja produces consonant variegation in half of her variants (36% of her monosyllables, 57% of her disyllables).

Table 5.12 Maarja's use of monosyllabic harmony

Selected target word	Child form	Adapted target word	Child form
suss 'slipper'	sus:	lind 'bird'	nɪn, nʌnd, nʌnt
		nina 'nose'	næn:
		saapad 'boots'	bop, bɑp

Table 5.13 Maarja's use of disyllabic harmony

Selected target word	Child form	Adapted target word	Child form
aidaa, tadaa 'bye-bye'	tɑidɑ, tɑtɑ, dɑdɑ	linnu	ninə
nina 'nose'	ninɑ	notsu	nənos
sussi 'slipper, sP'	ʃusu	saapad	pɑpɑt, pɑput
tɑntsi 'dance'	tɑtsi		

[8] The large number of variants of *notsu* indicates the challenge that this baby-talk form poses for the child. All of the sounds are within her repertoire, but she seems to find it difficult to produce the whole word without simplifying the structure through reduplication of the first syllable, while only then adding some version of the second syllable of the target.

Taking our cue from V&V, who outline the rise and subsequent fading from use of the palatal pattern that dominated Maarja's production in the early months of word use, we find traces of it here: Ten words can be said to show one or more elements of the pattern, which includes the front-rising diphthong [ɑɪ], unstressed [i] and medial yod (e.g., *hallo* 'hello [on telephone]' [ɑio:], *kala* 'fish' [kɑjɑ], *küünal* 'candle' [kɑjə]). However, most of these variants can be considered selected, as the substitution of yod for /l/ is still a regular process for the child, in alternation with [l]; in contrast, *küünal* 'candle' is adapted: Maarja produces medial /n/ in many other forms, so the inclusion of medial yod here must be ascribed to the pull of the template.

In V&V it is largely English words that show the kind of otherwise unpredictable adaptation that persuasively suggests template use (*banana* [bɑɪ], [bɑiə], *apple* [bʁi:], [əˈbʁi], [bʁiə], *bath* [bɑɪ], [bɑɪs], all within the first 50 words, the period preceding our sample). A few similar adaptations affect English words within our sample (*button* [bʁi], *book* [bɑɪ], *mitten* [mɑɪ]). The fact that the words are largely *selected* in Estonian but *adapted* in English suggests that at this point this bilingual child may be producing her English words through a perceptual filter that is more closely tuned to Estonian, the language of her community. In general, with her large repertoire of consonants Maarja has little need to rely on the favourite pattern that supported her early word production. In short, for Estonian words, at least, she appears to have outgrown the template.

Kaia. Maarja's younger sister Kaia is another of the bilingual children whose first 100 words were included in Vihman (2016). Like Maarja, she began attending full-time nursery, where she heard only Estonian, from 17 months. The age range of the sample we drew on in Chapter 4 is 19–20 months, well into the period in which she was attending nursery, which could account for the higher proportion of Estonian words recorded for her in comparison with Maarja, who was younger at the same lexical point. Kaia began producing combinations in this period, at 20 months, and produced several in quick succession, reaching 11 by the end of the period, about two weeks later. Here we again expand the sample to include the words from 51 to 100, covering age 18 to 20 months. This means adding 11 words, for a total of 55 Estonian words and 51 variants. Table 5.14 illustrates Kaia's consonant use in this period.

Kaia's output is less variable than Maarja's. However, as she produces more of her words in Estonian, there is a larger database of segmentally variant word forms. We see from Table 5.14 that Kaia produces, in at least two words each, most of the core consonants that occur at onset in Estonian; the exceptions include /h/, /v/, and /r/, none of which she has yet attempted. Kaia does not show the bias toward production of coronals evident in her sister's early lexicon. Both /k/ and the coronals /t, n, l, r, j/ are common at word-onset in Estonian, but whereas both girls produce /k/ frequently at onset (Maarja in 21%, Kaia in 23% of their variants), Maarja produces 41% of her forms with coronals at onset (14/34)

Table 5.14 Kaia's consonant inventory at 51–100 words, in Estonian only (age 18–20 months). Stress is word-initial unless otherwise indicated

Target C (N = 7)	Onset		T	Coda		T
p	*padi* 'pillow' /pɑti/ [pɑ, pɑbi]	*pai* 'nice (patting kitty)' /pɑi/ [pɑi:]	8	*tipa-tapa* 'step-step (BT)' /tip:ɑtɑp:ɑ/ **[tɑp tɑp tɑp]**		
b	*Bupa* (name) /bupɑ/ [**bupɑ**]	*saba* 'tail' /sɑpɑ/ [bɑbɑ]				
t	*tere* 'hi, hello' /tere/ [**tede**]	*tiiger* 'tiger' /tiːker/ [**tiː**]	9	*lutt* 'pacifier' /lutʲ:/ [otː, utː]		
d	*adaa* 'byebye' /ɑˈtɑː/ [ɑdɑː]	*tere* 'hi, hello' /tere/ [tede]	3			
k	*ka* 'too' /kɑː/ [**kɑ**]	*kiigu* 'swing' /kiːku/ [**kigu**]	13			
g	*kiigakaaga* 'swing-swing (BT)' /kiːkɑkɑːkɑ/ [kigɑkɑgɑ]	*Kribu* (name) /kripu/ [kigu]	3			
s	*see* 'this' /seː/ [**seː**]	*siin* 'here' /siːn/ [**siː**]				
m	*minu* 'my' /minu/ [**minu**]	*pime* 'dark' /pime/ [**pimːe**]	5			
n	*Nana* 'grandmother (BT)' /nɑnɑ/ [**nɑnɑ**]	*kinni* 'closed' /kinːi/ [**kinːi**]	5	*õun* 'apple' /ɤʊn/ [ɑnː]	*pane kinni* 'close [lit., put closed]' /pɑne kinːi/ [**pɑnː kinːi**]	3
ŋ				*kuu* 'moon' /kuː/ [kʊŋ]	*minu* 'me (too)' /minɑ (kɑ)/ [məŋ (kɑ)]	
l	*tuli* 'came' /tuli/ [**tuli**]	*tooli* 'chair, sP' /ˈtoːli/ [**toli**]				
j	*jaajaa* 'yes-yes' /jɑːjɑː/ [**jɑːjɑː**]	*Meelo* (name) /meːlo/ [miju]				

against Kaia's 26% (14/53). Most noticeably, Kaia produces far fewer coda consonants (15%, against Maarja's 29%).

Kaia's preference for open syllable production is necessarily reflected in her most used prosodic structures. She produces 26% of her variants as CVV_0 (14/53, four with CVV). Reduplication and consonant harmony each account for over 10% of Kaia's variants, but reduplication is used more (9/53 [17%]); together they account for 28% of her variants. Kaia's reduplicated forms match the input, however, with just two adapted forms: *saba* 'tail' [baba] and *tipatapa* 'step-step (BT)' [taptaptap]. In contrast, half of the harmony forms are adapted (Table 5.15).

Table 5.15 Kaia's use of consonant harmony

Selected target word	Child form	Adapted target word	Child form
Bupa (name)	bupa	Kribu (Scribble, cat's name)	kigu, kiku
kiigukaagu (onomat. for swinging)	kigɑkagɑ	lumi 'snow'	numi
kiigu 'swing!'	kigu	Meelo (name)	meːno, ninːo, ninːu

Kaia's profile contrasts with Maarja's here again, in that reduplication and harmony play a slightly greater role in this larger sample than they do in the (later-word-based) sample analysed for Chapter 4. Also, whereas Maarja largely selects disyllabic Estonian words with full or partial harmony, Kaia adapts more words to these structures and makes more use of reduplication, although mainly through over-selection. Both harmony and reduplication may be considered actively templatic in Kaia's lexicon at this point.

Over a third of Maarja's variants are in the CVCV structure, sometimes with coda or additional syllables. In contrast, Kaia's only long forms are reduplicated (her form for *kukk* 'rooster' [kukukuku]—possibly influenced by the onomatopoeic form used to designate the rooster's crowing, *kikerikii*—and *tipatapa* 'step-step' [taptaptap]) and Kaia produces only 17% of her variants in the CVCV structure, all of them selected.

Here again, as with Maarja, our findings, based on the latter half of the first 100 words, contrast with those of Vihman (2016). In that study two templates were identified for Kaia, both of them affecting words in both languages. The more striking of the two was the VCCV pattern (seen in 29 of Kaia's words), which reflects Estonian rather than English, given the medial geminate produced in most of the variants. However, 13 of the 14 forms adapted to this template were produced between 16 and 18 months, among the first 50 words, so before our sample begins; the one later form adapted to the template was English. In our Estonian-word sample there are just five VC(C)V variants, with initial consonant omission in the case of *juua* 'to drink' [uːa] and *lutti* 'pacifier, sP' [ɑdi]. The other template identified for Kaia in Vihman (2016) was reduplication, which comprised 20 reduplicated child word forms; however, the five adapted forms were all recorded prior to the period covered here. Accordingly, we can see that Kaia, like Maarja, made more use of templates within the period of her first 50 words and had begun to outgrow them by the time of the second 50-word sample.

5.1.3 Finnish: Eelis, Eliisa

In Chapter 4 we presented data from five Finnish children; they shared a small set of prosodic structures, most of which have not played a role as separate structures or templates in the English or Estonian data considered here so far. These include CVV, the only monosyllabic structure used by any Finnish child, the VCV structure used to a limited extent by Kaia, and reduplication as a structure in its own right. To consider possible template use we will look more closely at two of the Finnish children, Eelis and Eliisa.

Recall that Finnish has both front and back rounded and unrounded vowels, with their co-occurrence restricted by vowel harmony (see Chapter 4). Stress occurs consistently on the first syllable, but with alternating weak and strong syllables thereafter (Suomi & Ylitalo, 2004). All vowels may occur short or long (shown by doubling of the letter in the orthography), in any syllable, as is also true of the many possible diphthongs.

The consonant inventory is small: There are three voiceless stops, labial, alveolar and velar, two fricatives, /s/ and /h/, the nasals /m/ and /n/, the liquids /l/ and /r/, and the approximants /j/ and labiodental /v/ [ʋ], which the children tend to produce as [w]. The stops, sibilant, nasals, and liquids occur as geminates medially. Only coronals can occur as codas. Clusters are restricted to word-medial position in the core vocabulary (some loanwords may have initial clusters); nasals assimilate to a following stop. Under certain morphosyntactic conditions consonants undergo 'gradation', the geminates becoming singletons, nasal + consonant clusters becoming geminate nasals (creating the contrastive geminate nasal velar /ŋ:/ from /ŋk/) and singleton stops changing from /p/ to /v/, /t/ to /d/ (which occurs only under these limited conditions, like the velar nasal, and is accordingly acquired late) and /k/ to /j/.

Eelis. Eelis produced his first words at 18–19 months and reached the 25wp at 22 months. Table 5.16 displays Eelis' inventory of consonants. Note that the medial consonants he targets are almost all long (83%, in 20/24 disyllabic target words); in his output forms, 96% of all disyllables have long medial consonants.

Eelis has mastered few consonants, even considering that the Finnish core vocabulary includes only 11. The child produces only five as match to target

Table 5.16 Eelis' consonant inventory at 22 months

Target C (N = 5)	Onset		T	Coda	T
p	*pää* 'head' [pæ:]	*omppu* 'apple' [ɔp:u]	12		
[b]	*pappa* 'grandpa' [bap:a]	*pois* 'away' [boi]	3		
t	*tuo* 'that' [tu:]	*istuu* 'sits' [it:u:]	4		
k	*kukka* 'flower' [kak:a]	*kiinni* 'closed' [ki:]	9		
[g]	*kiitos* 'thank you' [gi:]	*kiinni* 'closed' [gi:]			
m	*mamma* 'milk (BT)' [mam:a]	*mamma* 'grandma' [mum:u]			
n	*anna* 'give' [an:a]	*noin* 'this way' [noi]		*noin* 'this way' [noin]	

and only two of those, /p/ and /k/, are used more than five times. He produces only a single coda consonant and no consonant variegation across any word.

Eelis has three often-used prosodic structures, CVV (32% of all variants; both long vowels and diphthongs are included as VV), VCV (38%), and reduplication (24%, including two words with partial reduplication or harmony). Half of the 12 CVV forms are selected; most of the adapted variants (*kiikkaa* 'is swinging', *kiinni, kiitos, suu, tuo*) are realized with a long vowel instead of a diphthong. *Suu* 'mouth' is produced as [u:], with omission of the onset sibilant, which Eelis is not yet producing.

The two harmony forms and five of the reduplicated variants are selected while the vowels of the remaining two—*kukka* and *poppa* 'hot' [popo]—are changed to create the reduplicated form. Although the CVV structure does seem to be actively attracting more difficult word targets, then, the high use of harmony and reduplication looks like accommodation to the shape of Finnish word forms; this is not convincingly templatic behaviour.

Eelis' single most-used structure is VCV. Here more words are adapted than selected (Table 5.17). Based on the *high proportion of adapted words* it is reasonable to posit VCV as an active templatic pattern, although no segmental specification is involved. Some of the consonants omitted are beyond Eelis' current articulatory skills (the words listed are the only ones attempted with either of the liquid consonants, for example), but the omission of the nasal onsets of *makkara* and *nappi* appears to be a response to the challenge of consonant variegation.

Eliisa. Eliisa, at 15 months, is the youngest Finnish child to reach the 25wp. Her consonant inventory (Table 5.18) has only one more match-to-target consonant than Eelis and only three stops are used over five times. But the inventory is different, as Eliisa produces three attempts at onset /s/ and two at /h/; she does not produce /n/, instead applying consonant harmony to the two /n/-initial words that she attempts. The only codas are variants of *juusto* with [s] and [h].

Eliisa's most used prosodic structures resemble those of Eelis, but her preferences are ordered differently and her limitations on consonants within a word are

Table 5.17 Eelis' use of VCV

Selected target word	Child form	Adapted target word	Child form
ankka 'duck'	ak:a (*6)	*aukasta* 'open'	ak:a
anna 'give'	an:a	*heppa* 'horse'	ep:a
Eetu (name)	e:tu	*Hippi* (name)	ip:i:
istuu 'is sitting'	it:u:	*loppu* 'finish, all gone'	ɔp:u
itkee 'is crying'	ik:e:	*makkara* 'sausage'	ak:a
omppu 'apple'	ɔp:u	*nappi* 'button'	ap:i
		räppää 'is scratching'	æp:æ:
		rikki 'broken'	ik:i

Table 5.18 Eliisa's consonant inventory at 15 months

Target C (N=6)	Onset		T	Coda	T
p	*pallo* 'ball' [pap:u]	*paperi* 'paper' [papa]	7		
t	*istu* 'sit!' [it:u]	*lintu* 'bird' [titu]	6		
k	*kirja* 'book' [ki:a]	*nukke* 'doll' [kuk:e]	9		
s [ç]	*isi* 'father' [içi]	*kissa* 'cat' [iç:a]		*juusto* 'cheese' [u:sto]	
h	*hauva* 'woof' [haʊ]	*oho* 'oops' [oho]		*juusto* 'cheese' [u:hto]	
m	*mammu* 'grandma' [mum:u]	*Muummi* (child book character) [mu:i]			

less strict. Her most used structure is consonant harmony (37%), but she also has several reduplicated variants (20%). Out of the 13 variants with harmony, six are adapted (Table 5.19); similarly, of seven reduplicated variants four are adapted. Both may be considered templatic.

Eliisa also makes use of VCV (8 variants, or 23%), and again several forms are adapted: Eliisa omits initial /p, k, h, j/—and in each case there is a consonant contrasting in both place and manner later in the word (*juusto, kissa, piiloon* '[go] into hiding'). The remaining variants fall into two structures, CVV (14%), with three words truncated to fit the pattern, and CVCV (6%), with all three variants having as the medial consonant approximant [ʊ] or a glide-like transition between

Table 5.19 Eliisa's use of consonant harmony and reduplication. s singular, p plural, P partitive

Consonant harmony			
Selected target word	**Child form**	**Adapted target word**	**Child form**
kakku 'cake' (i)	kak:o	*li(n)tu* 'bird'	titu, tito
kiikkuu 'is swinging'	ki:k:u	*nuke* 'doll'	kuk:e
kukka 'flower'	kuk:a	*pallo* 'ball'	pap:u
kukkia 'flower, pP'	kuk:ia	*paperi* 'paper'	pape
pomppi 'jump!'	pop:i	*tippu(u)* 'drop(s)' (verb)	pip:u
pupu 'bunny'	pupo, pop:i:	*vettä* 'water, sP'	tit:ɔ
tyttö 'girl'	tyt:ö		
Reduplication			
kaka(lla) 'sitting on potty/making caca'	kaka	*hauva* 'doggie'	hauvau
mummu /muumuu 'grandma'	mum:u /muumu	*nukkuu* 'is sleeping'	kuk:u:
pappa 'grandpa'	pap:a	*paperi* 'paper'	papa
		rikki 'broken'	kik:i

two vowels: *kirja* [kiːa] and *muumi* [muːi], and *hauva*, with repetition of the stressed syllable rime: [hauʋau].

Forty-seven per cent of Eliisa's variants have long medial consonants, in comparison to Eelis' 96%. Like Eelis, Eliisa produces no distinct supraglottal consonants across a word (disregarding the medial cluster in Eliisa's *juusto*). In comparison with English- or Estonian-learning children the Finnish children are notably slow to attempt C1–C2 sequences.

Recall that children learning Italian and Finnish target the fewest first-word forms with C1–C2 contrast within the word (20% and 27%, resp.: Table 4.4). The low level of lexical demand for supraglottal variegation has an apparent effect on later child structures in Finnish (although Italian differs sharply, as we indicated in Chapter 4). We can infer that the presence in Finnish of sequences of open syllables, long medial consonants and repeated vowels, with a good deal of reduplication in baby-talk register, is sufficient to permit children to increase their word production while remaining safely within the bounds of a few manageable structures and with a similarly restricted set of distinct consonant types.

Neither vowel nor consonant length is fully accurate as yet (see Vihman & Velleman, 2000), although the high use of closely similar word forms, a natural result of the children's small consonant inventories and repeated uses of a small set of structures, should support relatively early learning of the system of long and short contrasts. There is some experimental evidence of older children's earlier mastery of the geminate/singleton nasal contrast in Finnish as compared with Japanese (Aoyama, 2001, 2002), but longitudinal study of the emergence of contrastive use of gemination is needed to gain more insight into the process. In summary, heavy use of a small number of structures, with adaptation as needed, seems to provide sufficient templatic support for the Finnish child at this point; no further specification of fixed consonantal anchors or melodies is in evidence.

5.1.4 French: Béryl, Laurent

Here we first look more closely at Laurent, one of the four French children included in Chapter 4, and then consider data from Béryl, a child whose lexical and phonological development was followed from about the 25wp on, for a year of monthly recordings (Wauquier & Yamaguchi, 2013).

We saw in Table 4.2 that French children's first words were as likely to have monosyllabic targets as those of children learning English. In our overview of the later prosodic structures, most of the French children made considerable use of CV and one child used CVC to criterion. Otherwise, the disyllabic structures most often observed in Finnish dominated the French children's output as well, although harmony and reduplication played less of a role than in Finnish. Looking more closely now at French target words and the child output we will see stronger templatic effects than have been in evidence for the children discussed here so far.

A brief summary of French phonological structure will be useful. There are a large number of vowels, front unrounded (high /i/, mid-high /e/, and mid-low /ɛ/) and rounded (/y, ø, œ/) and back high /u/, mid-high /o/, mid-low rounded /ɔ/, and low unrounded /a/; in addition there are four nasal vowels (/ɛ̃, ã, õ, ʌ̃/). There is also a rich consonant repertoire: voiced and voiceless labial, alveolar and velar stops (/p, b, t, d, k, g/); voiced and voiceless labiodental, alveolar and palatal fricatives (/f, v, s, z, ʃ, ʒ/); labial, alveolar, and palatal nasals (m, n, ɲ); an alveolar lateral (/l/), a uvular trill /ʁ/ (alternatively produced as a voiced uvular fricative [χ]) and two glides, palatal /j/ and front-rounded /ɥ/. Thus French presents a considerable segmental challenge to the child but, as noted in Vihman, Nakai, and DePaolis (2006), the rhythmic pattern is relatively homogeneous across words and phrases, with phrase-final lengthening and no word stress (for discussion, see Wauquier & Yamaguchi, 2013). This has the effect, at the lexical level we are considering here, of creating prosodic structures that are more adult-like than comparable child forms in English or Welsh (Vihman et al., 2006).

Laurent. Laurent, followed bimonthly from 9 months to the 25wp (Boysson-Bardies & Vihman, 1991), first used 25 words spontaneously at 18 months. His word list from the recording session includes only 29 words and 32 variants, and no word combinations. However, Laurent's word use in this session is sufficient to provide a window on his templatic approach to gaining mastery of French phonology (see also Vihman, 1993). Laurent's consonant use is shown in Table 5.20.

As we saw in Chapter 4, one prosodic structure accounts for well over half of Laurent's variants, namely, non-harmonic CVCV and longer forms (48%). Looking more closely at the disyllabic and longer words included in the forms *selected* for this structure we find that most of them have [l] in the final (accented) syllable (Table 5.21); this is also true of the child's forms, which extend the pattern to several adapted words, sometimes including several syllables with no clear basis in the target. The variants are divided more or less evenly between selected and adapted forms, but in this case the selection is itself clearly guided by Laurent's template. The mean incidence of content-word-initial liquids in five French mothers' IDS (including Laurent's mother) is .13 (vs. .11 for five American English mothers and .8 for five Swedish mothers: Vihman, Kay, Boysson-Bardies, Durand, & Sundberg, 1994), with the considerably higher mean of .21 in French running speech (vs. .16 for English, .15 for Swedish). This is presumably due to the high frequency of French determiners with initial /l/ (e.g., the articles *le, la, les,* pronouns *la, le, lui*).

In addition to this striking template Laurent also makes use of reduplication and consonant harmony (28% in combination). Most of Laurent's forms in this combined structure are selected, but there are exceptions: *chapeau* [bobo, bəbɔbo], *chaussures* [ʃoʃy], *gateau* [tato, totot], *non* [na:nɔ]. Thus Laurent can be credited with using two templates in parallel.

Table 5.20 Laurent's consonant inventory at 18 months

Target C (N = 8)	Onset		T	Coda
p	*papa* 'papa' /papa/ [**papa**]	*chapeau* 'hat' /ʃapo/ [**pobo**]	5	
b	*bébé* 'baby' /bebe/ [**bəbə**]	*(la) brosse* 'brush' /bʁɔs/ [**bəla**]	7	
t	*tiens* 'here, take it' /tjɛ̃/ [**ta**]	*gateau* 'cake' /gato/ [**toto**]	4	
d	*de l'eau* 'some water' /dəlo/ [**dəlo**]	*dodo* 'sleep (BT)' /dodo/ [**dodo**]	4	
k	*coucou* 'peek-a-boo' /kuku/ [**kuku**]	*Kola* (name) /kola/ [**kɔla**]	7	
ʃ	*chaussettes / chaussures* /ʃosɛt, ʃosyʁ/ [**ʃoʃy**]			
ʒ	*chaussettes / chaussures* /ʃosɛt, ʃosyʁ/ [ʒəʃa:tizə, bɛ̃ʒiʒeʒəje]			
m	*maman* 'mother' /mamã/ [**mamã**]	*moi (là)* 'me (there)' [ma:, pɔmaɥa]		
n	*nano* 'blanket (BT)' /nano/ [**nano**]	*non* 'no' /nɔ̃/ [**nɔ̃, nã, na:nɔ̃**]		
l	*allo* 'hello (telephone)' /alo/ [**alo**]	*coucou là* 'peek-a-boo there' /kukula/ [**kukula**]	14	*ballon* 'big ball' /balɔ̃/ [**bəl**]
j	*aï* 'ow' /ai/ [a::jœ]	*moi (là)* 'me (there)' [jemo]		
w	*voilà* /vwala/ [wal:a]			

Table 5.21 Laurent's (CV)ₙCVlV template

Selected target word	Child form	Adapted target word	Child form
ballon /balɔ̃/ 'big ball'	palɔ̃	allo /alo/ 'hello (on telephone)'	alo
coucou là /kukula/ 'peek-a-boo there'	kukula	(la) brosse /bʁɔs/ 'brush'	bəla
de l'eau /dəlo/ 'some water'	dəlo	(la) cuillère /kɥijɛʁ/ 'spoon'	kola, koləkola
Kola /kola/ (name)	kɔla	canard/ coincoin /kanaʁ/, /kwɛ̃ kwɛ̃/ 'duck/quack-quack'	kɔla, kwalakwala
la dame là /ladamla/ 'that lady'	lələdala	(canard) dans l'eau /dãlo/ '(duck) in the water'	balad:alo
voilà /vwala/ 'here it is'	wal:a	chapeau /ʃapo/ 'hat'	bolo
		maman 'mommy'	məmʌʒəla

Béryl. Béryl is one of seven French children followed in another longitudinal study (Wauquier & Yamaguchi, 2013). At 18 months she produced 56 different words, including imitations; she experimented freely with challenging words and produced 79 variant forms. However, Béryl produced just a single word combination in the session, which suggests that her level of linguistic advance corresponds closely enough to what we have been observing in the other children. Table 5.22 presents her consonant inventory.

It can readily be seen that Béryl has a strong preference for a particular prosodic structure, VCV, and that she produces far more of her consonants in medial position than at word onset. Word-initial consonants occur only rarely (voiceless [p] as a substitute for /b/ in *bracelet* 'bracelet' [paʒe], [t] in one variant of *micro* 'microphone' [taχo], [k] as a substitute for /t/ in *tétine* 'dummy' [keti] (twice) and in several reduplicated or harmony forms, the voiced stops [b] and [d] in *ballon* 'ball' [babo], *hibou* 'owl' [bobo] , *dodo* 'sleep (BT)' [dodo], *dans l'eau* 'in the water' [dɔlo], [z] in *crapaud* 'toad' [zoʒo] (im.), apparently as a substitute for the /kʁ/ cluster, [n] in *non-non-non* 'no-no' [nɔ̃ nɔ̃] (twice), one instance of [l] in *la main* 'hand' [lama] and one of yod in *la lune* 'moon' [ja du]). The only word-final consonants are [p] in *hippopotame* 'hippopotamus' [taptap], two instances of what is transcribed as syllabic [n̩]: *sardine* 'sardine', imitated as [an̩], and *le nez* 'nose' [an̩], and the voiced uvular fricative that renders syllabic [ʁ] in *arbre* 'tree' [abəχ].

Most of the consonants occur as match to target in at least some variants; others occur only as substitutes, such as some of the voiced and voiceless sibilants (although [ç] is a phonetic variant of /s/, close enough to be counted as a match). As an additional mark of Béryl's phonetic adventurousness we note variants with medial [χ] (for *les flaques* 'puddles'), voiceless [ʎ] in an imitation of *lézard* 'lizard' [aʎa] (im.), and fricative [ɬ] in two variants of *musique* 'music' [aɬə], [aɬi]. As Wauquier and Yamaguchi observe in their description of this child's forms, Béryl actually produced the word *micro*, a salient object in a recording session, 26 times in the half-hour observation, with 13 repetitions of [aχo], two each of [əχo] and [oχo], variants with medial [x], [k], [kʰ] or [χk], and one attempt each with a CV [χo], reduplicated [koko] and C_1VC_2V [taχo]. On the other hand, there are at least three French consonants that Béryl does not produce at all: /v/, /ɲ/ and the glides /w/ and /ɥ/. The palatal nasal is replaced by /l/ in *agneaux* 'lambs' /aɲo/ [alo]; neither /v/ nor word-initial /ʁ/ are attempted, although Cʁ clusters occur in several of Béryl's words and are expressed in a variety of ways.

In short, Béryl has a profile somewhat reminiscent of the British child Jude, with a tightly constrained set of prosodic shapes but a good deal of phonetic exploration. In fact, VCV, which accounts for 63% of Béryl's variants, is the only structure to occur in more than 20%; of the remaining structures only reduplication and harmony (17% when combined) surpass 10%.

Béryl's VCV structure can safely be considered templatic. But the more fully specified structure <aCV> accounts for 39 of her variants (55%); the remaining six

Table 5.22 Béryl's consonant inventory at 18 months

Target C (N = 7)	Onset		T	Coda		T
p	*lapin* 'rabbit' /lapɛ̃/ [apa]	*parrain* 'godfather' /paʁɛ̃/ [apa]	6	*hippopotame* 'hippopotamus' /ipopotam/ [ɔpta], [taptap]	*requin* 'shark' /ʁəkɛ̃/ [apka]	
b	*ballon* 'big ball' /balɔ̃/ [babo]	*hibou* 'owl' /ibu/ [bobo]	3			
t	*bateau* 'boat' /bato/ [ato]	*partout* /paʁtu/ 'everywhere' [otu]	10	*dauphin* 'dolphin' /dofɛ̃/ [atla]		
d	*dodo* 'sleep (BT)' /dodo/ [dodo]	*dans l'eau* 'in the water' /dɑ̃lo/ [dɑ̃lo]	3			
k	*coucou* 'peek-a-boo' /kuku/ [kuku]	*crapeau* 'toad' /kʁapo/ [ako]	12			
g	*escargot* 'snail' /ɛskaʁgo/ [kago]					
f	*dauphin* 'dolphin' /dofɛ̃/ [afa]	*(l')éléphant* /(l)elefɑ̃/ [afo]	5	*une fleur* 'a flower' /ynflør/ [af]		
s [ç]	*cerceau* 'hoop' /sɛʁso/ [aço]	*pinson* 'chaffinch' /pɛ̃sɔ/ [aço]	5	*poisson* 'fish' /pwasɔ̃/ [açto]		
ʃ	*(le) chat* 'cat' /ləʃa/ [aʃa]					
z	*lézard* 'lizard' /lezaʁ/ [aza]	*crapaud* 'frog' /kʁapo/ [zoʒo] (i)				
z [ʑ]	*musique* 'music' /myzik/ [aʑi]	*nuage* 'cloud' /nɥaʒ/ [aʑa] (i)	3			
m	*animaux* 'animals' /animo/ [emo]	*la main* 'hand' /lamɛ/ [ama, lama]				
n	*baleine* 'whale' /balɛn/ [anɛ]	*sardine* 'sardine' /saʁdin/ [ani]	4			
l	*le lion* 'lion' /ləljɔ̃/ [əlu]	*la main* 'hand' /lamɛ/ [lama]	4	*crapaud* 'frog' /kʁapo/ [zoʒo] (i)		
χ	*les flaques* 'puddles' /leflak/ [aχa]	*micro* 'microphone' /mikʁo/ [aχo]	3	*arbre* 'tree' /aʁbʁ/ [abəχ]	*les cloches* 'the bells' /leklɔʃ/ [aχlo]	3
j	*(il/elle) est là* '(s/he)'s there' /ela/ [eja]	*la lune* 'the moon' /lalyn/ [jadu]	3			

Table 5.23 Béryl's <aCV> template, with and without metathesis

<aCV> *with metathesis*		*Other <aCV> variants*	
crapeau 'toad' /kʁapo/	[ako]	*dauphin* 'dolphin' /dofɛ̃/	[afa]
les flaques 'puddles' /leflak/	[axa, aχa]	*la pieuvre* 'octopus' /lapjoevʁ/	[apø]
les cloches 'the bells' /leklɔʃ/	[aχlo]	*la tête* 'head' /latɛt/	[atɛ]
nuage 'cloud' /nɥaʒ/	[aça]	*marteau* 'hammer' /maʁto/	[ato]
parrain 'godfather' /paʁɛ̃/	[apa]	*micro* 'microphone' /mikʁo/	[aχo]
requin 'shark' /ʁəkɛ̃/	[apka]	*nénuphar* 'water lily' /nenyfaʁ/	[afa]
sardine 'sardine' /saʁdin/	[ani]	*perroquet* 'parrot' /pɛʁokɛ/	[ake]

VCV words have a variety of onset vowels, none of them high. The <aCV> variants include a good deal of metathesis, in which the word-initial consonant is produced medially. In fact, only six of Béryl's 39 <aCVC₀> variants are vowel-initial in the target form and might thus be considered selected, if changes to the vowel quality are overlooked (e.g., *agneaux* 'lambs' [alo], *étoile* 'star' [ata], *hibou* [ibu, abu], and also *arbre* /aʁbʁ/ [abəχ], the only form with coda—with epenthetic schwa to facilitate production of the tri-consonantal cluster). Table 5.23 presents some of the adapted variants, divided into those that involve metathesis, all of which are shown, and some that maintain the target word sequence. (All but two of the VCV targets of variants that show metathesis have [a] in at least one target syllable; the exceptions are *les cloches* and *requin*.)

Although it may be debatable whether the forms with a preceding article—*les flaques, les cloches, le parrain*—truly involve metathesis, other forms cannot be analysed in any other way (*crapeau, nuage, sardine*). This is an exceptional demonstration of the force of a templatic pattern: By fitting words into a pre-existing template Béryl is able to take on the challenge of producing a large number of complex words and also to explore ways of dealing with particular difficulties, such as the frequent consonant-plus-liquid clusters, for which she deploys a number of different phonetic expressions.

5.1.5 Italian: Anna, Nicola

In Chapter 4 we considered data from seven children who were part of a study with recordings only at 15 and 21 months. In order to gain more information about possible template use in Italian we now turn to data from two other children, collected in the same area of northern Italy, around Parma. Eleven children were followed monthly with home recordings from age 10 to 14 months (Majorano & D'Odorico, 2011; thereafter the families came to the lab for 30-minute recordings every other month, from 16–24 months. Keren-Portnoy, Majorano, and Vihman

(2009) reported on the word forms of four of these children, the two most advanced and the two who developed the most slowly. We draw here on Anna, the most rapidly developing child, and Nicola, one of the slower ones. Note, however, that only a single variant of each word target is available for either of these children.

The phoneme inventory of Italian, with its 23 consonants and seven vowels, is not much smaller than that of English (Zanobini, Viterbori, & Saraceno, 2012). The vowels divide symmetrically into front and back high, high-mid and low-mid, and a central low vowel. The consonants include voiced and voiceless stops and affricates /p b t d k g ts dz tʃ dʒ/ and fricatives /f v s z ʃ/, three nasals /m n ɲ/, the liquids /l ʎ r/ and the glides /w j/. In addition, as mentioned in Chapter 4, there are medial geminates but otherwise few codas (either medially or word-finally). Most importantly, the distribution by length in syllables of early-learned words is radically different from that of the other languages we have considered, as monosyllables are rare and disyllables less common than trisyllabic words (Monaghan, Arciuli, & Seva, 2016). Stress placement is variable but falls almost exclusively on the first syllable in disyllables (99%) and on the second syllable in 81% of trisyllabic words (Monaghan et al., 2016).

Anna. Anna produced 27 words in a 20-minute session at 20 months; in the previous recorded session, at 18 months, she produced only 11. As shown in Table 5.24, at 20 months Anna had an unusually large number of consonants that match the target in two or more words, including a full set of voiced and voiceless stops, two nasals (including occurrence as coda in medial clusters) and [l].

Although the extent of Anna's word production is not remarkable for her age, her consonant inventory demonstrates considerably phonetic ability. Her word forms are correspondingly less restricted in terms of consonant variegation than we have seen in other children: She is the only child included in this analysis with consonant change in over half of her word forms—at 85%; this is in accord with the high use of variegation in the seven Italian 21-month-old children whose data we reported in Chapter 4. Three prosodic structures account for more than one form each. First, consonant harmony affects five words, or 19%; all of these show labial harmony (Table 5.25; *vespa* can be considered selected, since Anna is not yet producing /v/). This is a templatic structure.

The two remaining structures both involve consonant variegation; ten of the 21 words target trisyllabic or even longer words. One of two structures, (CV)CVlV, accounts for 30% of the word forms produced and is clearly templatic. This structure reflects Anna's particular preference for producing /l/ as well as her readiness to retain, plan, and produce extra-long words. Like Laurent, Anna disproportionately selects target words with /l/; in addition, she adapts long-word targets either by truncating them or by harmonizing the second-syllable onset consonant to the geminate [l] of the final syllable (Table 5.26). Note that in one case Anna retains the gemination but transposes it to a different word position as well as to a different segment (*piccolo* 'little' /'pik:olo/ [pilil:o]).

Table 5.24 Anna's consonant use at 20 months. Stress is word-initial unless otherwise indicated

Target C (N = 9)	Onset		T	Coda	T
p	*capello* 'hair' /ka'pel:o/ [pɛl:o]	*coperta* 'blanket' /ko'perta/ [pɛt:a]	7		
b	*baffi* 'moustache' /baf:i/ [bap:i]	*bimba* 'child, f.' /bimba/ [bimba]	3		
t	*coperta* 'blanket' /ko'perta/ [pɛt:a]	*seduta* 'is sitting' /se'duta/ [duta]	5		
d	*coda* 'tail' /koda/ [koda]	*dritte* 'straight' /drit:e/ [dit:e]	5		
k	*cadi* 'you fall down' /kadi/ [kadi]	*cane* 'dog' /kane/ [kane]	8		
g	*gallo* 'rooster' /gal:o/ [gal:o]	*grande* 'big' /grande/ [gande]			
dʒ	*giallo* 'yellow' /dʒal:o/ [dʒal:o]				
s	*sedia* 'chair' /sɛdja/ [sea]				
m	*maiale* 'pig' /ma'jale/ [male]	*metto* 'I put' /met:o/ [met:o]	7	*bimba* 'child, f.' /bimba/ [bimba]	
n	*cane* 'dog' /kane/ [kane]	*altri* 'others' /altri/ [nati]	3	*grande* 'big' /grande/ [gande]	
l	*animali* 'animals' /ani'mali/ [mali]	*giallo* 'yellow' /dʒal:o/ [dʒal:o]	8		
r	*ancora* 'again' /aŋ'kora/ [kora]				

Table 5.25 Anna's use of labial harmony

Selected target word	Child form	Adapted target word	Child form
baffi 'moustache' /baf:i/	[bap:i]	*dorme* 'is sleeping' /dorme/	[bom:e]
bimba 'child (f.)' /bimba/	[bimba]	*scarpe* 'shoe' /skarpe/	[pap:e]
vespa 'wasp; Vespa' /vɛspa/	[bep:a]		

Table 5.26 Anna's <(CV)CVlV> template

Selected		Adapted: truncation		Adapted: harmonize to [l]	
bambola 'doll' /'bambola/	[bambala]	*animali* 'animals' /ani'mali/	[mali]	*cavallo* 'horse' /ka'val:o/	[kalol:o]
gallo 'rooster' /gal:o/	[gal:o]	*cappello* 'hat' /ka'p:ɛl:o/	[pɛl:o]	*piccolo* 'little' /'pik:olo/	[pilil:o]
giallo 'yellow' /dʒal:o/	[dʒal:o]	*maiale* 'pig' /ma'jale/	[male]		

Table 5.27 Nicola's consonant use at 24 months

Target C (N = 8)	Onset		T	Coda	T
p	*apri* 'open!' /apri/ [**api**]	*vespa* 'wasp/Vespa' /vɛspa/ [**pɛpːa**]	6		
b	*basta* 'stop' /basta/ [**batːa**]	*buona* /buɔna/ 'good' [**bona**]	3		
t	*trattore* 'track' /traˈtːore/ [**tore**]	*coltello* 'knife' /kolˈtɛlːo/ [**tɛlːo**]	7		
d	*prendi* 'take!' /prɛndi/ [**pɛdi**]	*cadi* 'you fall down' /kadi/ [**adi**]	4		
k	*caffè* 'coffee' /kaˈfɛ/ [**kaˈpɛ**]	*zucchero* 'sugar' /ˈtsukːero/ [**ukːo**]	3		
m	*animali* 'animals' /aniˈmali/ [**mali**]				
n	*carne* 'meat' /karne/ [**ane**]	*pane* 'bread' /pane/ [**ane**]	7		
l	*palla* 'ball' /palːa/ [**alːa**]	*piselli* 'peas' /piˈzɛlːi/ [**ɛlːi**]	6		
r	*cadere* 'to fall down' /kaˈdere/ [**are**]	*trattore* 'track' /traˈtːore/ [**tore**]			

The last structure, disyllabic CVCV (plus a single trisyllabic form without /l/ in the target, *macchina* 'car' [makːaja]), includes 13 words (48%); although four words are adapted by truncation, the structure is essentially adult-like, though not always fully realized. Thus Anna, with her advanced mastery of consonants, is making a start on the Italian challenge of longer word production, with the support of templatic adaptation. (By age 2 years, 27 of Anna's 34 words are trisyllabic or longer and harmony no longer plays a role: Keren-Portnoy et al., 2009.)

Nicola. A relatively large number of Nicola's consonants match the target (Table 5.27), but many occur in very few forms.

Nicola's consonant use is restricted by his tendency to omit pretonic syllables and the onset consonant of initial stressed syllables—a pattern we saw in other Italian children in Chapter 4. Aside from a single monosyllable, *ciao* 'hello', he produces only two prosodic structures, VCV and CVCV. The VCV structure includes only one selected word, *apri* 'open' /apri/ [api]; the remainder are either truncated (e.g., *cadere* 'to fall down' /kaˈdere/ [ere], *cavallo* 'horse' /kaˈvalːo/ [alːo], *forchetta* 'fork' /forˈketːa/ [ɛtːa]) or lack the target onset consonant (*baffi* 'moustache' /bafːi/ [apːi], *chiudo* closed' /kjudo/ [udo], *forno* 'oven' /forno/ [onːo]). One form shows metathesis: *pianta* 'plant' /pianta/ [apːa]. There is no evident pattern to account for onset omission in some words as compared with variegation in others: See, for example, *carne* 'meat' [ane] vs. *cane* 'dog' [kane].

5.1.6 Welsh: Fflur, Gwyn

We will consider possible templatic patterns in the 25wp of two of the Welsh children whose data we included in Chapter 4, Fflur and Gwyn, who produced the most words in the session of interest. We begin with a brief phonetic description of Welsh as spoken in Gwynedd, the area of North Wales where these data were collected.[9]

The consonant inventory includes both voiceless (aspirated) and voiced (lenis) stops, /p t k b d g/; the affricates /tʃ dʒ/ occur in limited positions, due to palatalization of /t d/ before /i/, and in English loanwords. Voiceless fricatives include /f θ s ʃ χ/ and the (highly frequent) lateral /ɬ/ as well as /h/ in initial and medial positions; voiced fricatives include only /v/ and /ð/. Nasals also occur both voiced and voiceless (/m m̥ n n̥ ŋ ŋ̥/, although the voiceless nasals do not occur in words used in isolation but only under certain morphosyntactic conditions (Hannahs, 2013); the details need not concern us here. Similarly, the liquids /l/ and /r/ occur both voiced and voiceless, with /r̥/ occurring under the same conditions as the voiceless nasals. The voiceless lateral fricative, on the other hand, is common in all word positions and is not restricted to particular morphosyntactic contexts. The glides /j/ and /w/ are also subject to devoicing.

The vowels include two long and short front-unrounded and back-rounded pairs /iː ɪ eː ɛ uː ʊ oː ɔ/, the high central-unrounded pair /ɨː ɨ/, the low central pair /a aː/, and an unpaired schwa (Hannahs, 2013). The length contrast occurs only in monosyllables. In addition, there are 13 diphthongs, with the three high vowels serving as second element.

An important phonological property of Welsh is the nature of its accent. Although it is generally held to have penultimate stress, or (for our purposes) initial stress on the disyllabic words that make up much of the children's early lexicon, the manifestation of stress in the case of voiceless stops and also /m ŋ s ɬ/ (Hannahs, 2013) is often a short vowel in the first syllable, a lengthened medial consonant and a vowel subject to final-syllable lengthening (see Vihman et al., 2006, for illustration and analysis).

Fflur. Fflur was 17 months old at her 25wp. She produced 36 words in this session, with 44 variants. Her somewhat unusual consonant inventory is shown in Table 5.28.

Fflur's consonant use is noteworthy in three respects. First, her consonants match the target in two different words surprisingly rarely, given the relatively large inventory of consonants in the input language: There are three each at onset and coda, all coronals at onset (/t, d, n/), both velar /k/ (for /g/, which is often devoiced in target word finals) and /x/ at coda, plus /n/. In general, Fflur's consonants are more likely to match the onset to the second than the first syllable of target words (cf. *banana* [nɑmːa], with metathesis of the first two consonants of the target; *bwni* [hʊni]; *fan'cw* [kʰux]; *moron* [ʔɒwɑn], with gliding of the medial /r/; *mwnci* [gʌgːɪ], with voicing of the medial stop and regressive harmony; *syrthio*

---

[9] I thank Rhonwen Lewis, who went over this section and provided help with the phonetic transcription of the adult target forms as well as with references on Welsh phonetics and phonology.

Table 5.28 Fflur's consonant use at 17 months

Target C (N = 7)	Onset		T	Coda		T
b	*pêl* 'ball' /peːl/ [bɛn]					
t	*eto* 'again' /ɛtɔ/ [tʰɒ]	*nos da* 'good night' /nɔsta/ [tθɑː]	3			
[ts]	*tri* 'three' /tri/ [tsʷiː]					
d	*do* 'yes, I did' /dɔ/ [dɔ]	*drwg* 'bad' /drug/ [dakˣ]	4	*diod* 'drink' /diɔd/ [ʔɒd, dad]		
k	*fancw* 'over there' /vaŋku/ [kʰux]	*dwr* 'water' /dʊr/ [kʰux]	3	*ffork* 'fork' /fɔrk/ [gaʊk]	*drwg* 'empty' /drʊg/ [optionally drʊk] [gʊk]	
g	*gwag* 'empty' /gwɑg/ [ŋgak]	*crocodeil* 'crocodile' /krɔkɔdeɪl/ [gogːogːʊan]	8	*beic* 'bike' /beɪk/ [gɛg]		
[ð]	*blodyn* 'flower' /blɔdin/ [gɔðan]					
[v]	*moron* 'carrot' /mɔrɔn/ [ʔɒvɛn]			*pws* 'puss' /pʊs/ [ʔʊːv]		
s	*syrthio* 'fall' /sərθjɔ/ [ʔʌsːɑ]			*pws* 'puss' /pʊs/ [ʔɑʌːs]		
χ [x]	*Po* (name) /poː/ [xɔ]	*mam* 'mum' /mam/ [xɑːm]		*boch* 'cheek' /bɔχ/ [ʔɒx]	*sos goch* 'red sauce' /sɔsgɔχ/ [ɔʔɔx]	
h	*hwnna* 'here' /hʊna/ [hɛnɛ]	*Po* (name) /poː/ [hɔɑː]	3			
m	*mam* 'mum' /mam/ [mɑm]	*banana* 'banana' /baˈnana/ [nam:ɑ]	4	*mam* 'mum' /mam/ [mɑm]		
n	*na* 'no' /nɑ/ [nɑ]	*bwni* 'bunny' /bʊni/ [hʊni]	6	*moron* 'carrot' /mɔrɔn/ [ʔɒwɑn]	*rhein* 'those' /rɛɪn/ [mɛn]	
[w]	*afal* 'apple' /aval/ [ʌwo]	*moron* 'carrot' /mɔrɔn/ [ʔɒwɑn]				

[ʔʌsːɑ], in which the /s/ moves to medial position by metathesis). It is plausible that Fflur's attention to the second consonant (in all but *syrthio*) relates to the *greater length of this consonant under Welsh accent* (see Vihman & Majorano, 2017). In fact, the onset consonant seems to suffer from a kind of perceptual or attentional neglect, with Fflur's monosyllables as well as disyllables often having glottal stop at onset, as discussed in Chapter 4; this is reminiscent of the effect of phonological geminates in Estonian, Finnish, and Italian.

The second point of difference from other children's inventories is the relatively high number of coda consonants (8 types altogether, compared to 14 at onset), although here again the consonants produced are only occasionally those required by the target. We will see how these unusual aspects of Fflur's production are reflected in her use of prosodic structures.

Finally, Fflur shows a bias toward 'back' sounds: Fourteen variants have velar onsets, 12 velar codas (vs. 10 coronal onsets, 8 coronal codas, 4 labial onsets, 2 labial codas). In addition, the back-rising diphthong [ɑʊ] occurs in variants of five words (*aw, ffork, llaw, moron, puss*), whereas front-rising diphthongs occur in variants of only two (*moron, syrthio*). This back bias is particularly notable in that it is rare; a preference for front-rising diphthongs is in evidence in several children (e.g., Alice and Maarja) and many more children show a preference for labials (like Jude) or coronals (like Maarja) than for velars (but see Menn, 1971 and Stoel-Gammon & Cooper, 1984, for two additional examples of children with a strong velar bias; Vihman & Hochberg, 1986, discuss the still unexplained affinity for coda production in children with a velar bias). The fact that Welsh includes /χ/ as a commonly occurring phoneme—e.g., in the high-incidence *diolch* 'thank you'— may be a factor in Fflur's velar and coda preference. (Berman, 1977, comments that when it is frequent, as in Hebrew, toddlers more readily produce /x/ than other fricatives.)

Fflur produces more one- than two-syllable variants and reaches 20% or more for both CVV_0 and harmony in CVC monosyllables. The open monosyllables are selected, except for two disyllabic targets reduced to their final syllables (*fan'cw* [klʊ], *fanna* [ɳa], both glossed as 'over there'). Two of these monosyllables have the diphthong /aʊ/, the rest are CV. In contrast, the harmony monosyllables are primarily adapted (Table 5.29).

In addition, Fflur has nine CVC variants without harmony—all but three of them with glottal stop or [h] at onset. The GLOTTALVC pattern occurs in six variants (13%), then, all but one adapted; similarly, two variants are selected for $VCVC_0$ and seven more are adapted to it by 'demoting' the onset consonant to a

Table 5.29 Fflur's monosyllabic harmony template

Selected target word	Child form	Adapted target word	Child form
diod 'drink'	dad	*beic* 'bike'	gɛg
gwag 'empty'	ŋgak	*drwg* 'bad'	gʊk, kʊx
mam 'mom'	mam	*dwr* 'water'	kʰʊx
		fan'cw 'over there'	kʰux
		ffork 'fork'	gaʊk
		rhein 'those'	mɛn
		styc 'stuck'	ʔm̩kɔkx

Table 5.30 Fflur's demoted onset (GLOTTALVCVC$_0$) template

Selected target word	Child form	Adapted target word	Child form
A. Monosyllables			
aw 'ow'	ʔax, ʔaʊːtθ	boch 'cheek'	ʔɒx
		diod 'drink'	ʔɒd
		gwallt 'hair'	ʔax
		pêl 'ball'	ʔɛn (cf. also (bɛn])
		pws 'pussy'	ʔɒθ, ʔɑʌːs
B. Disyllables			
afal	ʌwo	bwni 'bunny'	ʔɛɲːɛ, hʊni
eto 'again'	ʔəθax	fyna 'that place'	ʔɛnːæː, ʔəmːɑ
		hwnna 'this'	henɛ, ʔəɲa, ʔɔnːɑ
		moron 'carrot'	ʔɒwɑn, həwɛn
		Po (Teletubby)	hɔɑː
		sos goch 'red sauce'	ɔʔɔx
		syrthio 'fall'	ʔʌsːɑ

glottal. The combined total of 15 demoted onset structures, or 31%, makes this Fflur's most active template (Table 5.30).

Lastly, Fflur has five disyllabic variants with supraglottal word-initial consonants (some with coda) and full or partial harmony across the word; four of these are adapted (*banana, bwni, mwnci, crocodeil*). With 11% use disyllabic harmony may also be considered templatic for this child, although it is not a strong pattern.

Gwyn. Gwyn reached the 25wp at just under 15 months. He produces 42 words in the session, five of them onomatopoeia with stable adult targets, and 53 variants. His consonant inventory is diverse, with seven consonants ([b, d, k, g, m, n, l]) matching the target at onset and three of these ([d, k, n]) in coda as well (Table 5.31). Gwyn also produces several [Cl] clusters at syllable onset (matching the targets /bl kl gl/ in *blodau* 'flowers', *cloc* 'clock', *glaw* 'rain'). Gwyn's articulatory mastery of liquids extends to one successful production of the trilled /r/ in *dai, tri* 'two, three'. (He produces another variant of *tri* with the affricate [dʒ].)

Although Gwyn ventures to attempt sounds that he cannot yet successfully produce as matches to target (see, for example, his one long-word variant, [dixkildadə] for *Dipsy-La-La*, a combination of two Teletubby names that are typically named in that sequence), most of his variants match or are close to their target forms, unlike Jude, for example, who reached the same lexical level at about the same age. Gwyn shows considerable variability for some forms, however, such as the difficult word *diolch* 'thank you': /dijɔlχ/ [djaʊx], but also [djaʊ, ʔaʊx, tʃaʊx] and even [drjaʊf].

Gwyn produces a range of different prosodic structures to criterion. CVV accounts for 27% of his variants, adapted mainly by omission of a coda, often

Table 5.31 Gwyn's consonant use at 17 months

Target C (N = 7)	Onset		T	Coda		T
p				hyp 'hup' /hɪp/ [ʔʌp]	Smot (name) /smot/ [map]	
b	babi 'baby' /babi/ [bab:i]	blodau 'flowers' /blɔdaɨ/ [blab:la:]	8	plop /plɔp/ [blab]		
d	cadw 'fall' /kadʊ/ [bʰad:ʊ]	dau 'two' /daɨ/ [daɪ]	11	bwyd 'food' /bʊɨd/ [bʷʊid]	taid /taɪd/ 'grandfather' [daɪd]	3
dʒ	tri 'three' /tri/ [dʒi:]	mwnci 'monkey' /mʊŋkɪ/ [mʊʔdʒi]				
k	cloc 'clock' /klɔk/ [klɒk]	mwnci 'monkey' /mʊŋkɪ/ [mʊk:i]	4	cloc 'clock' /klɔk/ [klɒk]	cwaccwac/ quack-quack /kwakwak/ [gʊag:ak]	3
g	Bwgan 'ghost' /bʊgan/ [m̩bʊʔgan]	glaw 'rain' /glau/ [glaʊ]	5			
f				giraffe [djɪaf]		
χ [x]				diolch 'thank you' /dijɔlχ/ [djaʊx]		
h	eh-oh 'uh-oh' /ʔʌʔəʊ/ [ʔah:aʊ]					
m	mam 'mom' /mam/ [mam:]	mwy 'more' /mʊɨ/ [mʊi]	6	mam 'mom' /mam/ [mam:]	Bwgan 'spook' /bʊgan/ [həgam]	3
n	nain 'grandmother' /nain/ [naɪ:n]	Noa (name) /nɔa/ [nɔa]		nain 'grandmother' /nain/ [naɪ:n]	sbinc-sbanc 'toad' /spɪnkspank/ [bɪʔdan]	
ŋ				mwnci 'monkey' /mʊŋkɪ/ [mʊŋki]		
l	lawr 'down' /laʊr/ [laʊ]	Lucy [lʊi]	11	Dipsy-La-La [dixkildadə]		
r	dau, tri 'two, three' /daɨtrɪ/ [daɪ.də:dri]					
j	eliffant 'elephant' /ɛlɪfant/ [ʔeɪjʌ]	giraffe [dija, djɪaf]				

alongside variants occurring with coda (see *diolch*, above); one word, *Lucy*, the name of the Welsh speaker who recorded his sessions, is reduced to [lʊi]. Both front- and back-rising diphthongs occur.

Gwyn also produces many CVC variants (19%), seven of them with harmony and all but one selected (the exception is the pet's name *Smot* [mɑp]). However, he also produces 13% of his variants with disyllabic harmony, most of them again selected: The exceptions are *blodau* 'flowers' [blɑb:lɑ:, blɑlɑ] and *mwnci* [gʊg:i], both of which also occur in variants lacking harmony ([abʊla] and [mʊŋki, mʊʔdʒi, mʊk:i], resp.). Thus words with harmony attract Gwyn's attention and he sometimes extends the pattern to other words, but this seems not to be an active template for this chid

Finally, Gwyn produces disyllabic non-harmonic forms, with or without a coda, and also a few VCV forms; none of these reach 20% and none provide convincing evidence of adaptation to any one template, pattern, or schema. Rather, they exhibit Gwyn's willingness to try out different forms, producing [m̩bʊʔgɑn, həgɑm] for *Bwgan* 'ghost, spook', for example. Thus Gwyn provides another example of a child who requires little support from templates at this point in his development.

5.2 Overview: Consonantal resources, variegation, and template use

In Chapter 4 we compared both the first words (and their targets) and the later prosodic structures most used by several children learning each of six languages. In this chapter we have sought to deepen our understanding of the beginning steps in establishing phonological systematicity by looking more closely at individual children's patterns, focusing again on the effects of the input language as well as on the segmental resources—specifically, the consonant inventory—of each child. We are now in a position to make a quantitative comparison of the children's later consonant and word use in all six languages, and in both American and British English (adding in the findings of Chapter 3). This will provide a basis for asking how the children's phonetic abilities may interact with template use.

Table 5.32 shows the use of consonants at onset and coda for each of the 12 children discussed in this chapter and the six American children considered in Chapter 3. (Note that here we tally matching onsets and codas separately.) It also indicates the extent of use of consonant variegation in monosyllables and disyllables (or longer forms), following the criteria laid out in Chapter 4.

At least two findings emerge from Table 5.32. First, the *group differences* are still in evidence, although less sharply so than in Table 4.17: Neither Finnish child produces many consonantal matches and neither produces variegated forms, for example, while, in contrast, the French and Italian children look similar, with a high number of matches at onset and also variegation in disyllables. The Estonian

Table 5.32 Cross-linguistic overview of consonant matches (in at least two words) at onset and coda in relation to extent of supraglottal consonant variegation. US: American English, UK: British English, Est.: Estonian, Fin.: Finnish, Fr.: French, It.: Italian, We.: Welsh. Prop.: proportion, Var.: Variant, Varieg.: Variegation. Cells indicating figures above the mean are shaded

	Matches		Variegation				
	Onsets	Codas	C1–C2 (mono)	C1–C2 (di)	T varieg.	T vars.	Prop. varieg.
Alice (US)	7	0	2	8	10	39	.26
Deborah (US)	6	0	0	0	0	41	.00
Emily (US)	6	0	0	2	2	43	.05
Molly (US)	8	2	6	7	13	47	.28
Sean (US)	6	2	13	4	17	45	.38
Timmy (US)	5	0	0	2	2	43	.05
Jude (UK)	8	0	1	3	4	50	.08
Jack (UK)	3	2	15	10	25	70	.36
Maarja (Est.)	5	2	4	12	16	34	.47
Kaia (Est.)	7	1	6	10	16	53	.30
Eelis (Fin.)	5	0	0	0	0	37	.00
Eliisa (Fin.)	6	0	0	0	0	35	.00
Laurent (Fr.)	8	0	1	13	14	46	.30
Béryl (Fr.)	7	0	0	9	9	79	.11
Anna (It.)	9	0	0	22	22	27	.81
Nicola (It.)	8	0	0	9	9	32	.28
Fflur (We.)	3	3	4	5	8	47	.19
Gwyn (We.)	7	3	3	12	15	53	.28
mean	6	1	3	7	10	44	.23

children show strong consonant production and variegation, in both monosyllables and disyllables. The two Welsh children both show strong coda production.

Interestingly, there is a correlation of .46 between consonant matches to target and proportion of variants with variegation. This means that, as we might expect, variegation depends to some extent on the child's phonetic skills, although some instances derive from exploratory segmental use, as we saw with Jude, for example. Additionally, variegation may also be facilitated by use of a melodic template, as in the case of both Laurent and Anna.

Variegation is found in 23% of the variants of these 18 children (see also Table 4.16, which showed a mean of 26%, based on data from 39 children, including 14 from the present sample). This level of variegation is far lower than the 37% of *targets* with variegation reported even for first-words (Table 4.4), known to be pre-selected for their simple forms. (Recall that at the 25wp the mean variegation in targets was 54% [Table 4.16].) This is again evidence of a connection between difficulty in producing consonant variegation and children's dependence on templates: Much of the difficulty of word production in this period is not about segmental mastery per se but about *planning* and *articulating whole word forms*; this also speaks to the challenge of *retaining whole-word forms in memory*.

The next question is the extent and nature of template use that we could identify by examining individual children's output, across different languages, late in the single-word period. A summary of our findings as to active template use (based on the discussion in Chapter 3 for the American children and this chapter for the other language groups) is given in Table 5.33 and elaborated briefly below (shown as prosodic structure shapes only, to allow tabular presentation). Note that some children were found to be using a template only to a

Table 5.33 Cross-linguistic template use. T: Template, Prop.: Proportion, Var.: Variant, Lg.: Language; CH-mono, CH-di: mono- and disyllabic consonant harmony; RED.: reduplication; Eng.: English. The children are ordered within each structure from most to least proportionate use

Monosyllables				Disyllables			
T struc.	Child name	Prop. of vars.	Lg. group	T struc.	Child name	Prop. vars.	Lg. group
CVV_0	Timmy	.40	US Eng.	CH-di	Jude	.38	UK Eng.
					Eliisa	.37	Finnish
					Timmy	.28	US Eng.
					Deborah	.22	US Eng.
					Maarja	.21	Estonian
					Anna	.19	Italian
					Fflur	.11	Welsh
CVV	Eelis	.32	Finnish	CH-di.,	Kaia	.28	Estonian
	Gwyn	.27	Welsh	RED.	Laurent	.28	French
	Jack	.18	UK Eng.		Béryl	.17	French
	Eliisa	.14	Finnish		Jack	.14	UK Eng.
CH-mono	Fflur	.21	Welsh	VCV	Nicola	.63	Italian
	Maarja	.15	Estonian		Béryl	.63	French
					Eelis	.38	Finnish
					Eliisa	.23	Finnish
CVC	Molly	.36	US Eng.	RED.	Eliisa	.20	Finnish
	Sean	.36	US Eng.				
				C_1VC_2V	Laurent	.47	French
					Anna	.30	Italian
					Molly	.26	US Eng.
Combined mono- and disyllabic pattern							
CVV/CVC/CVVCV	Alice				.69		US English
$VC(VC_0)$	Fflur				.31		Welsh
$(CV)CVV_0N$	Jack				.23		UK English

limited extent (although always in at least 10% of variants), most likely because the pattern was either on the wane or newly emergent. Also, three children had templates that were best understood as combining one- and two-syllable structures; these are listed separately.

Disyllabic consonant harmony is the most used pattern, as could be expected, as it is the child phonological process most discussed in the literature; although not universal, it is clearly very widespread. At least one child in each language group makes some use of it, with or without also using reduplication; one Welsh and one Estonian child make some use of the monosyllabic equivalent. The less commonly reported VCV pattern is used by four children learning three languages, Finnish, French, and Italian, while reduplication, often discussed in the literature on English phonological development, is an active templatic pattern on its own for one Finnish child only.

Given the evidence of a relatively low mean incidence of variegation, we can readily understand the role of consonant harmony and VCV, which address that challenge. The reason why VCV is found in languages like Finnish and Italian, with their medial geminates, has been discussed elsewhere (Vihman & Velleman, 2000; Savinainen-Makkonen, 2000b; Vihman & Majorano, 2017). Vihman and Croft (2007) also discuss the use of VCV in French, with its phrase- (and word-) final accent (see also Wauquier & Yamaguchi, 2013, and for Hebrew, with its dominant iambic pattern, Keren-Portnoy & Segal, 2016; see also Segal, Keren-Portnoy, & Vihman, under review). In the case of each of these structures a longer segment later in the word—whether medial consonant or final vowel—appears to deflect child attention from the word-initial consonant.

Finally, three children each show either some kind of melodic template involving the sequencing of consonants in the word or patterns that combine mono- and disyllabic outputs. As discussed above, both Laurent and Anna have templatic patterns specified for the lateral [l]; with the additional challenge of producing words of more than two syllables, Anna uses harmony as well, repeating the lateral in the next-to-last syllable. Molly, on the other hand, produces words with final consonants with the support of two templates, CVC and C_1VC_2V.

Alice uses her palatal pattern somewhat differently in monosyllables and disyllables, but a similar articulatory gesture seems to underlie both (see Vihman, Velleman, & McCune, 1994; a similar palatal pattern was in evidence in Maarja's earlier word production, affecting both word lengths: Vihman & Vihman, 2011). Fflur imposes a 'demote onset' pattern on both one- and two-syllable words and Jack uses a nasal coda for both word lengths as well. (Noël, one of the French children included in Chapter 4 but not discussed here, made similarly templatic use of nasal codas in both monosyllabic and disyllabic words: See Vihman, 2014, ch. 10 and Table A3.12.)

In all of these cases there is ample evidence from instances of adaptation that in constructing an output plan the child is drawing on an internal model as well as on the target form. The existence of a pre-established plan or favoured set of motoric routines may be assumed to be an important factor underlying the more rapid growth in expressive vocabulary typically seen toward the middle or end of the second year.

5.3 Discussion

5.3.1 Targets and first words

The information regarding the children's first words and their targets in each of the languages under discussion (Chapters 3 and 4) allowed us to gain some purchase on cross-linguistic differences while at the same time revealing how similar the early words are. The basis for that cross-linguistic similarity is important. It can be ascribed to at least two factors: (i) severe constraints on word production in the earliest period, when articulatory routines are few and relatively unpractised; (ii) limitations on phonological memory.

Early articulatory insufficiency has been much discussed (e.g., McAllister Byun, Inkelas, & Rose, 2016) and thus needs no further comment. However, the memory factor has had less attention. Keren-Portnoy et al. (2010) demonstrated that length of experience with consistent and stable use of one or more consonants in the prelinguistic period is significantly correlated with a child's ability to repeat nonwords at age 26 months. However, *familiar words* were more successfully repeated than nonwords, even when the known words included consonants with which the child had less experience: *The familiarity of the whole-word pattern trumped the familiarity of the individual sounds.*

The lesson for us here is that in the period before developing even a small set of often-used word forms a child will find it particularly difficult to retain adult words; the forms that are first attempted, produced, and recognized tend to be those with relatively simple adult target forms—forms that may be expected to have a counterpart, or something close to it, in the child's existing vocal repertoire. This allows the child to take in these forms in the first place and to retain them (in a way that allows subsequent voluntary access) by mapping them onto an internal representation of their own vocal patterns; this, by hypothesis, is how phonological memory is established.

5.3.2 Prosodic structures and templates

We have laid out replicable methods for undertaking a template analysis. The prosodic structure analyses of Chapters 3 and 4 provide a rough cut, sketching out the types of patterning used in each language group and sometimes identifying templatic behaviour (e.g., the use of VCV in Finnish and Italian). The more detailed analyses provided in Chapter 3 as well as here provide strong grounds for arguing, in line with several of the studies reviewed in Chapter 2, that templates play an important if relatively short-lived role in phonological development, particularly in the single-word period.

As discussed in Chapter 3, word forms produced at the end of the single word period show remarkable progress in relation to the children's very first words. Now the child is no longer restricted to producing only what is already in repertoire but can extend familiar patterns to unknown word forms, sometimes 'collecting' similar target words to attempt (selection), sometimes attempting less congenial words, assimilating them to existing schemas through adaptation. As we have seen, however, children differ in the extent to which they avail themselves of this possibility and they do so at different points in their lexical development, some of them having apparently outgrown the need for such a facilitative process by the time they reach the lexical level we have focused on here. In Chapter 6 we consider longitudinal accounts of children learning two additional languages and discuss issues of timing, function, and possible ways of quantifying differences in template use.

The lesson for theories of phonological development is unavoidable, however: Children do form their own preferred output patterns, with strong individual differences within language groups despite ambient language channelling into favoured rhythmic or prosodic patterns. Not all children use templates, but many, perhaps most do, to some extent; these individual pathways must be encompassed in any theoretical account.

6

Issues around child templates

Timing, fading, quantification, and function

6.1 The timing of template emergence and use

As illustrated in the preceding chapters, prosodic structures provide a frame-work for identifying a child's preferred motor plans and also for noting, in comparison with other children in the same group, what the child is *not* attempting to produce. Templates constitute a more elaborated step in the process of learning word forms. We saw in Chapters 3–5 that not all children make use of templates, at least not in any readily recognizable way, although in each of the language groups that we have considered data from at least one or two children can be drawn on to specify templates that shape the child's words beyond the more generic statement of prosodic structure. Thus template use is not 'universal', but it is not restricted to particular languages either, any more than it is limited to a single point in a child's development. We have also seen that it is a concomitant of children's relatively limited inventory of sounds or familiar production routines in comparison with the range of adult word structures and it is, accordingly, a prominent feature of early lexical and phonological development.

Two key questions that arise in connection with the use of phonological templates in development are (i) the timing of their emergence and (ii) the process by which they fade and are replaced by more adult-like forms that show systematic segmental substitutions and contrast (Macken, 1979). In addition, the question of function remains: What role do templates play in development? Can they be considered facilitative of lexical advance? Or do they sometimes hamper such advance? And is the relative advantage or disadvantage of template use perhaps related to the question of timing in relation to a child's level of word use? Before addressing these questions we must consider the issue of quantifi-cation: How can children best be compared, given the extent of individual differences in the age and lexical level at which templates may be found? This chapter will address each of these topics, although data from many more children learning a much wider range of languages would be needed to arrive at definitive conclusions.

Phonological Templates in Development. First edition. Marilyn May Vihman.
© Marilyn May Vihman 2019. First published 2019 by Oxford University Press.

6.2 Differences in timing: Longitudinal analyses

It would be useful for many purposes, applied or clinical as well as theoretical, to know just when templates of any kind may be expected to emerge in a given child's lexical and phonological development. There is no reason to expect a change at a set chronological age, given the wide range of individual variation in age at first word use as well as in rate of lexical advance. Yet even in relation to a child's level of productive word use, which provides a better basis for comparison, it is difficult, perhaps impossible, to arrive at any reliable answer to the question of timing in template emergence.

Diary studies sometimes show template use at a very early point in development (i.e., within the period of the first 50 words: see Menn, 1971; Vihman & Vihman, 2011; Sowers-Wills, 2017). On the other hand, Waterson (1971) discusses her son P's 'little word groups' or 'schemas' only from the point where he had about 155 words in his expressive vocabulary ('about 104 monosyllables, forty-eight disyllables and three or so trisyllables ... The child was already using three–four word sentences': Waterson, 1971/2013, p. 145); this suggests that notable patterns were not observed earlier. Similarly, as we discuss below, Priestly (1977) observed his son Christopher's first uses of a striking idiosyncratic pattern only at a point when he was producing about 100 disyllabic forms. And the bilingual diary studies of both Leopold (1939) and Deuchar and Quay (2000) provide evidence of template use only beyond the point of production of the first 100 words, whereas three other bilingual children, Kaia, Maarja, and Raivo, had readily identifiable templates well before reaching that level (Vihman, 2016).

In observational studies based on regular recordings carried out as part of planned research projects total vocabulary size can only be estimated, based on words identified in the session, as in the studies we have drawn on here, or on the Communicative Developmental Inventory (CDI), in wide use over the past 25 years (cf., e.g., Arriaga, Fenson, Cronan & Pethick, 1998), based on parental observation. Vihman and Miller (1988, p. 156) found that, on average across the 10 children recorded weekly in their study, the cumulative word lists reported by the mothers in the diary logs they were asked to keep (before the CDI was available) tended to include, at any given point, at least twice as many words as could be identified in transcripts of the half-hour recording session. Thus the '4-word point' (4wp) corresponds to 8–9 words in parental report, while the 25wp corresponds to a vocabulary of 50 words or more. As discussed and illustrated in Chapters 3–5, the 25wp can be used as a basis for evaluating a child's template use, as the number of child word forms may then ensure sufficient lexical material for drawing conclusions about patterning, whereas the 4wp is generally found to involve relatively accurate renditions of the adult word forms attempted, typically with little or no strong evidence of patterning (see Menn & Vihman, 2011).

However, even observational data—whether recorded weekly, biweekly, or monthly—differ in this regard: Vihman and Velleman (1989) find evidence of template use in their recordings of the American English learner, Molly, already from age 1;1.15, when she produced only 13 words in the session; the pattern was more firmly established a month later, when the child produced 19 words—at which point the child's mother herself noticed a change:

> She reported that *button, balloon, banana,* and *bunny,* each of which had had its own unique phonetic shape previously, were now all produced as [bʌnːə] or [banːə] – a regression [in accuracy] reflecting the force of Molly's new output pattern.
>
> (Vihman & Velleman, 1989, p. 244)

Similarly, Macken (1979) describes the first signs of whole-word (later termed templatic) patterning in her weekly recordings of the Mexican-American child Si from 1;8, when the child had produced only about 12 words altogether (p. 138). On the other hand, in a close investigation of seven months of word production in three children exposed to British English, beginning with the 25wp, Szreder-Ptasinska (2012) finds evidence of template emergence and later fading in just one of them (Alison, discussed below). Finally, Renner (2017) specifically looked at the relation between vocabulary size (based on the Swedish CDI) and template use (based on half-hour recordings) in 12 Swedish children aged 18 months. She found evidence of template use in the three children who had over 100 but fewer than 300 words but not in the one child with a larger reported vocabulary; for the children with fewer words it was difficult to draw any clear conclusions from the data available.

Not many longitudinal accounts of phonological development provide enough data to evaluate the progress of the child from the earliest word production, before any templatic pattern is observed; only studies of that kind make it possible to judge the timing of the first templates. In an effort to observe both the emergence and the fading of templatic patterning we consider here longitudinal data from studies of three children acquiring Arabic and two acquiring Brazilian Portuguese, before going on to studies of two more children acquiring British English.

6.2.1 Lebanese Arabic: Martin, Lina, Rama

Khattab and Al-Tamimi (2013) trace the first few months of word production for three children recorded monthly from age 9 months to 3 years in Greater Beirut, Lebanon; the data they report cover the period from the 4wp to the 25wp. It is important to note that Lebanese society is generally multilingual, with either English or French, or both, being used in many homes, particularly among the more educated families. Table 6.1 gives the children's names and ages at the start of the

Table 6.1 Lebanese Arabic (Khattab & Al-Tamimi, 2013). Children are ordered by age at start of study

Child name	Age at start of study	Word types produced, including imitations (N sessions)	Proportion of tokens in each language		
			Arabic	French	English
Martin	1;3	11–46 (7)	.77	.13	.06
Lina	1;4	7–64 (8)	.48	.28	.21
Rama	1;6	5–35 (5)	.60	.10	.30

study, along with the total word types produced over the several sessions included in the analysis and the proportion of word tokens in each of the three languages.

The shapes of target words differed by language, as one might expect, with disyllables predominating in Arabic and French but monosyllables in English. Syllable shapes differed as well: Both one- and two-syllable words most often featured geminates in Arabic (CVC:, CVC:V). Khattab and Al-Tamimi find that the proportion of disyllabic *targets* with medial geminates drops quite sharply (from about 26% to 12%) over the period between the two word points, while at the same time the realization of *child words* with geminates increases (from 54% to 65%). The authors comment that:

> What [the children] seem to take some time to acquire is phonological length, and their patterns of acquisition seem to involve experimenting with adding phonetic length to all elements of the target syllable structures rather than just to the phonologically long ones.   (p. 389)

Khattab and Al-Tamimi report that both initial and medial consonants may be geminated in child words and both the initial and the final vowel may be lengthened; this variability also extends to the shape of the word as a whole (e.g., /baːba/ 'daddy' [baːbaː], [babːah], [baːbːaħ], [bːaːbam]), with coda glottals or pharyngeals often being added to open disyllabic target forms. The combination of a large consonant inventory, a structural bias in the adult language toward full CVCV(C) word shapes, and contrastive vowel and consonant length occurring in all possible positions appears to lead to a rather different type of word shape than we have seen in child production in Finnish, for example, in which VCCV was a commonly preferred shape, but not CVCCV (which was common in Italian, however). In tracing, session-by-session, the shapes of target words and of the children's own word forms Khattab and Al-Tamimi provide a clear profile of template use in Lebanese Arabic.

Martin. Martin's most commonly used word shape, CVC:V(C), is in evidence from the 4wp, at 1;3: 79% of his word tokens take that form and also show consonant harmony (Table 6.2). Word-initial consonants are more likely to be

Table 6.2 Selected and adapted word forms: Martin, 4wp (adapted from Khattab & Al-Tamimi, 2013, Table 14.5, p. 391). Consonant doubling is used to represent geminates; % figures are out of all tokens. (Fr. French target word)

1;3: 11 types, 75 tokens					
Main pattern: CVC:V(C) 79%					
Select 32%			**Adapt 47%**		
Target	**Child form**	**Gloss**	**Target**	**Child form**	**Gloss**
nanna	nǽnnǽˑh	food	baːba	bæˑb̥b̥æː	daddy
baʔʔa	ʔǽʔʔəːm	peek-a-boo	teːta	tɪˑttæˑh	grandma
ʔoʔʔo	mʔæʔʔəm	night-night	habbuːba	β̥ʊbbæh	Habbouba
			tɾɛ̃	tɪttaːh	train (Fr.)

reduced than medial consonants; the expression of length is variable across tokens of the same word. This child makes use of more Arabic than French or English and produces primarily disyllables.

In the next two sessions, at 1;5 and 1;6, Martin's output scarcely changes in terms of word types, and he also continues to make use of the template identified at the 4wp (48% of all tokens at 1;5, 63% at 1;6), although he now also uses other patterns as well, including disyllables with long vowels and monosyllables. Consonant harmony no longer affects all disyllables. At 1;7–1;8 the number of different word types produced per session increases somewhat but the main pattern remains the same, accounting for 58% of all tokens. The sessions include a great deal of imitation, generally in the preferred pattern and with adaptation as necessary to fit that pattern (e.g., /fuːfuː/ (nickname) [β̥ʊββ̥uːh], /maɾtin/ (proper name) [tˈæˑtˈɐh]).

In the last two sessions, at 1;9 and 1;10, the number of words produced increases to 29 and then to 46 word types; the diversity of consonant types increases as well. The template continues to be used, mainly in words adapted to fit the pattern; consonant harmony affects some but not all of those words. Interestingly, adaptation continues to contribute heavily to the template, which by the last session again accounts for over 70% of Martin's word tokens (see Table 6.3); other word shapes, such as monosyllables, are largely target-like.

Lina. Lina, who reached the 4wp at 1;4, experienced the most parental input speech in English and French alongside Arabic; accordingly, she produces less than half of her word tokens in Arabic across the eight sessions analysed. Lina's early word shapes (first three sessions) are similar to those of the other children, however, with both French and English words showing assimilation to the predominant CVC:V(C) pattern: e.g., French *oui oui* /wiwi/ [ʔɪwwih]; English *thank you* /θaŋk ju/ [ʔʰæ̈ttʊ]); this likely reflects the input, as French as produced by Lebanese Arabic speakers also tends to show medial consonant lengthening (Khattab & Al-Tamimi, 2013). Lina also produces monosyllables and disyllables

Table 6.3 Selected and adapted word forms: Martin, Session 8 (adapted from Khattab & Al-Tamimi, 2013, Table 14.5, p. 393). Consonant doubling is used to represent geminates; % figures are out of all tokens. (im. imitated; Fr. French target word)

1;10: 46 types, 140 tokens					
Main pattern: CVC:V(C) 71%					
Select 28%			**Adapt 43%**		
Target	**Child form**	**Gloss**	**Target**	**Child form**	**Gloss**
bʊbbo	bəbbuːh	baby	ħakiːm	pʰḭˑˈppʰi̅ˑĩ̂m	doctor
ʕammo	ɲæːnnm̃ɣ̃ʔ	uncle (im.)	balõ	bβ̞ᵂɐˑbbᵂə̃ɑ̃ː	ball (Fr.)
buwwa	gʊwwaːʊ	water (im.)	mɪfteːħ	tᵂəttʰæːtˤ	key
jalla	hæˑllaˑɛ̂x	come on (im.)	ħaliːb	mḛppʰḭːpʔ	milk (im.)
laʔʔa	lð̥ɑˑʔʔaːh	no	mabadde	cɐd̥d̥ɪh	I don't want to

with medial singletons; in accordance with the salience of the medial geminates in disyllables, Lina's medial consonants are the most varied, while word-initially she produces primarily glottals. Although monosyllables are used in increasing numbers in the next two sessions, the adapted words largely fall into the typically Arabic disyllabic pattern with medial geminates (Table 6.4).

Lina's use of the disyllabic template continues to increase in her last two sessions, reaching a peak of 79% at 1;9 and accounting for 57% of her word tokens in the final session, at 1;10, when she makes a lexical leap and produces 41 spontaneous word types. The template is again expressed primarily in adaptations—at this point, mostly Arabic words (Table 6.5), and this is the only pattern to which words are adapted.

Rama. Rama began word use somewhat later than the other two children; she had made heavy of uninterpretable jargon in the early recorded sessions. The considerable vocal practice that Rama experienced over those months may account for her relatively advanced consonant inventory—including fricatives

Table 6.4 Selected and adapted word forms: Lina, Sessions 4–5 (adapted from Khattab & Al-Tamimi, 2013, Table 14.7, p. 400). Consonant doubling is used to represent geminates; % figures are out of all tokens. (im. imitated; Fr. French target word)

1;6–1;7: 25 types, 59 tokens					
Pattern 1: CVC:V(C) 34					
Select 5%			**Adapt 29%**		
Target	**Child form**	**Gloss**	**Target**	**Child form**	**Gloss**
lallo	ʔĩlæˑlləˑh	nickname	ʔɛ̃#dø̃ː	ʕæˑttːø̃ĩ̃	one, two (Fr.)
			ʔaʕt̚ˤi	ʔæʰˑttˢiː	give him (im.)
			tneːn	ʔɪnnɛˑn	two (im.)
			ʃokola	koˡllɐ̞ᵝʕ̞	chocolate (Fr.)

Table 6.5 Selected and adapted word forms: Lina, Session 10 (adapted from Khattab & Al-Tamimi, 2013, Table 14.7, p. 402). Consonant doubling is used to represent geminates; % figures are out of all tokens

1;10: 64 types, 206 tokens					
Main pattern: CVC:V(C) 57%					
Select 12%			**Adapt 45%**		
Target	**Child form**	**Gloss**	**Target**	**Child form**	**Gloss**
tappø	tʰæ·pp̃vʉːʰ	shoes	lɪˤbe	hḛbbɛ̥ːh	doll
waʔʔaʕ	wˈæʔʔæˤ	he dropped	hajdi	ħaːddɛ·h	this
ʔoʔʔo	ʔo̥ʔʔəɪ	oh-oh	dawa	d·ʁ·ɵ̃ʋæh	medicine
			bɾaːvo	b̃wævvɵːh	bravo

and laterals—when recognizable words finally appeared. Although Rama produces many monosyllables (46% of all tokens) in her first two sessions of identifiable word use, likely reflecting the larger proportion of English in her input, the disyllabic geminate pattern is also in evidence, accounting for 40% of tokens. At 1;7 and 1;8 Rama's most used pattern is monosyllable with coda, generally a glide or fricative. The disyllabic pattern accounts for 48% of her tokens but only 28% of her word types, including adaptations such as [tˈatˈa̱h] for /teːta/ 'grandma' and [hæɪddæ·ʰ] for /haj#dah/ 'this (is) nice'.

In the final session monosyllables are the most frequent, accounting for 40% of Rama's word tokens, with disyllables with medial singletons accounting for a further 29%. Most of the words produced are accurate, within the bounds of the child's segmental inventory; there are few adaptations—but those that do occur involve, again, the disyllabic/long medial consonant template (20% of all tokens: Table 6.6).

A single phonological word shape dominates production in the early months of word use of all three children whose data Khattab and Al-Tamimi analysed. Although we noted individual differences in the timing of the 'discovery' and extent of use of this general template, it was the single most used pattern overall

Table 6.6 Selected and adapted word forms: Rama, Session 5 (adapted from Khattab & Al-Tamimi, 2013, Table 14.6, p. 397). Consonant doubling is used to represent geminates; % figures are out of all tokens. im. = imitated

1;8: 35 types, 86 tokens					
Pattern 3: CVC:V(C) 20%					
Select 12%			**Adapt 45%**		
Target	**Child form**	**Gloss**	**Target**	**Child form**	**Gloss**
baddo	bɛddo	he wants	tiktak	tiːttih	sweet
ʒiddo	ʒɪddo̥	grandpa	hajj	ʔəhhaiːh	this
(ʔi)dˤaww	ʔiddaʊh	light (im.)	baħħ	bæħhaʊ	all gone

and it was the only one to attract considerable adaptation, with the children assimilating numerous non-matching word forms to this particular shape. Such an overwhelming influence of a single pattern has not been evident in the other languages we have considered, although CVC is highly characteristic of English (see Vihman, 2014, ch. 8: CVC is often identified as typical of English word use in bilinguals with English as one of their languages).

As far as timing is concerned, only Martin already showed heavy use of the template from the 4wp on. Lina showed some effect of the salience of medial geminates in her production of a greater diversity of consonants in word-medial as compared with initial position (recall Béryl, Chapter 5, and also the heavy use of VCCV in Italian); her use of the disyllabic geminate template fluctuates but emerges strongly as she reaches the 25wp. Rama, finally, never shows a strong preference for the pattern and generally manages to advance phonologically without making much use of a template. We see no evidence of *idiosyncratic* template use in any of these children, however, as Martin and Lina both appear to be strongly channelled into use of CVCCVC by the structure of the adult language.

6.2.2 Brazilian Portuguese: Lucas, Paolo

Oliveira-Guimarães (2013) describes a full year of word production for two children recorded (along with two others) as they acquired Brazilian Portuguese in Belo Horizonte, Minas Gerais, Brazil (Table 6.7; see Oliveira-Guimarães, 2008). The children were recorded monthly from the time when their mothers reported an expressive vocabulary of 20 to 25 words; however, neither child was producing identifiable word combinations when first seen. For one of the children, Paolo, this study began toward the end of the single-word period, the end-point of most of the studies described here so far.

Lucas. Table 6.8 presents Lucas' first recorded words, most of them good matches to their targets. They include three word shapes: reduplicated CVCV, monosyllabic C_0VC and, in the one word *Gisele*, a combination of the two, with a coda on the second syllable, C_1VC_1VC. (Word-final off-glides [j] and [w] derive

Table 6.7 Brazilian Portuguese (Oliveira-Guimarães, 2013). Children are ordered by age at start of study. Range of types and tokens are given for the monthly recording sessions over a full year

Child name	Age at start of study	Range of word types produced	Range of word tokens produced
Lucas	1;9.21	8–119	15–153
Paolo	1;11.13	20–229	88–243

Table 6.8 First word forms: Lucas (adapted from Oliveira-Guimarães, 2013, Table 10.3, p. 296). Word counts include both spontaneous and imitated uses

1;9.21: 8 types, 15 tokens			
Target word	**Gloss**	**Adult form**	**Child form**
Cacá	(name)	kaˈka	taˈta
esse	this	ˈes	ˈeʃ
Gisele	(name)	ʒɪˈzɛlɪ	ziˈziʃ
mamãe	mother	mãˈmãj	ũˈmãj, mãˈmãj
nã não	no	nãˈnãw	nãˈnãw
oi	hi	ˈoj	ˈoj
papai	father	paˈpaj	paˈpaj
Zizi	(name)	ziˈzi	ʒiˈʒi

from the adult model and are part of the vocalic nucleus.) The sibilant coda of the child's form for *esse* is target-based, whereas [ziˈziʃ] for *Gisele* can be considered an adaptation, reflecting the child's early affinity for coda production. The sibilant coda itself reflects harmony with the target sibilants, one palatal, one alveolar; Lucas varies between these in his production of coda sibilants throughout the year (Oliveira-Guimarães, 2013, p. 298), despite the fact that only alveolar sibilants occur word-finally in adult forms in this dialect.

Starting in the next session Lucas adapts words to a reduplicated template, a pattern also reported for other children acquiring Brazilian Portuguese (Baia, 2013), including Paolo, as well as for children acquiring European Portuguese (Correia, 2009; Freitas, 1997): *Gabriel* /gabɾiˈɛw/ [beˈbe], *Pedro* /ˈpedɾu/ [duˈdu]. In Session 3 such adapted forms occur more frequently (e.g., *Fernanda* /fehˈnãda/ [veˈve]; *Izabel* /izaˈbɛw/ [pɛˈpɛ]); an appendix to the chapter lists five selected and eight adapted words showing the reduplication template in this session, which amounts to use in over a third of the 35 words produced spontaneously.

Lucas' production of word tokens with a coda shows a steady increase, rising slowly from 13% in Session 1 to 23% and 28% in Sessions 4 and 5, and then to 45%, a level that is minimally maintained thereafter, with a high point of 64% (overall mean, 35.5%). Oliveira-Guimarães notes that Lucas' coda sibilants occur in words with target sibilants or affricates (cf. *bruxa* 'witch' /ˈbɾuʃa/ [ˈbuʃ], *pode* 'is able, can' /ˈpɔdʒɪ/ [ˈpɔʒ]). Although the child form lacks the open final syllable of the adult form, the sibilant itself is target-based.

However, Lucas also unexpectedly produces a coda nasal in many of his words: Brazilian Portuguese admits of no such coda. A more target-like coda [w] is seen in the first session, in *nã não*; the nasal coda occurs for the first time in Session 4: *tira* 'take it' [ˈtʃiɾa], produced as [ˈdiw, ˈdim]. This corresponds to the point at which coda production overall shows a sharp increase and marks the emergence of 'a genuine template' (Oliveira-Guimarães, 2013, p. 297), which now occurs in parallel with the earlier overuse of the reduplication pattern.

By plotting the extent of use of the off-glide and the nasal coda over the 12 sessions Oliveira-Guimarães shows that the child's innovative use of coda [m] first rises in frequency, with some fluctuation, from Sessions 4 to 8, then declines sharply while overall coda use continues to rise to about 70% of all words; by the final session, off-glides account for just under 60% of all closed-syllable word forms, complementing the use of coda sibilants.

How can the non-target-like coda [m] in the child forms be accounted for? Oliveira-Guimarães provides an analysis of the target word shapes that Lucas produces with coda [m]. In Sessions 2 to 4, as with the sibilant codas, any kind of nasalization in the target word attracts coda [m] production. Overall, the strongest attractor is word-final [ʊ] (e.g., *sapo* 'toad' /ˈsapʊ/ [ʃãm], [saw]). As [ʊ] marks masculine gender in Portuguese, nouns of this form are extremely common. In addition, as Oliveira-Guimarães notes, words with difficult medial segments, such as liquids (e.g., *tira* 'take it' /ˈtʃiɾə/ [ˈdiw, ˈdim]) or clusters (*tigre* 'tiger' /ˈtʃigɾɪ/ [tʃiw]) also attract child use of the off-glide or [m] as coda.

Paolo. In the first recording session Paolo produced more words than expected based on his mother's report and also proved to be both more vocal and more rapidly developing than Lucas. In his first two sessions his words primarily take the form of open monosyllables and reduplicated open disyllables. Only the disyllables include adaptations in both sessions: 54% of all tokens in Session 1, 29% in Session 2 (examples of reduplication from the two sessions are given in Table 6.9). Paolo's word forms tend to be selected, not adapted, and the strongest evidence of template use in his recordings comes from the first two sessions.

Note that Paolo, like Lucas, treats disyllabic words as iambic, regardless of the target stress pattern (Table 6.10). This is a long-standing puzzle in Portuguese linguistics, given that adult words typically have penultimate stress (Santos, 2007; Correia, 2009; Baia & Correia, 2010; Baia & Santos, 2011a, 2011b), leading one to expect child disyllables to be trochaic. Table 6.10 summarizes the stress patterns that Oliveira-Guimarães reports for target words and child forms for both of the children in their early sessions. Here we see that in these sessions the disyllabic

Table 6.9 Early word forms: Paolo (adapted from Oliveira-Guimarães, 2013, Table 10.9, p. 303)

Paolo, 1;11 and 2;0							
Selected				Adapted			
Target word	Gloss	Adult form	Child form	Target word	Gloss	Adult form	Child form
vovó	grandmother	vɔˈvɔ	vɔˈvɔ	Letícia	(name)	leˈtʃisɪa	taˈta
papai	father	paˈpaj	paˈpaj	Luciana	(name)	lusiˈãna	ʔuˈʔu
mamãe	mother	maˈmãj	mãˈmãj	tartaruga	turtle	tartaˈɾʊɡa	taˈta
vovô	grandfather	voˈvo	voˈvo	Roseli	(name)	hozeˈli	ʔiˈʔi

Table 6.10 Word length and stress (in tokens; adapted from Tables 10.8 and 10.10 in Oliveira-Guimarães, 2013, pp. 303f.). The total number of tokens does not match Table 6.8 because each child also produced a few longer forms. The peak of iambic word-form production is marked in **bold face** for each child

	Lucas (first 3 sessions)		*Paolo* (first session)	
	Adult form (total: 72)	Child form (total: 83)	Adult form (total: 64)	Child form (total: 86)
Monosyllables	18 (25%)	45 (37%)	7 (11%)	20 (23%)
Iambic	30 (42%)	42 (**51%**)	27 (42%)	42 (**49%**)
Trochaic	24 (33%)	4 (5%)	30 (47%)	24 (28%)

adult target forms are relatively evenly balanced between the two accentual patterns, whereas both boys' disyllabic word forms are predominantly iambic. Tables 6.8 and 6.9 give reason to suppose that it may be the high frequency of a small number of critical words that are iambic (those for the key family members, *mother, father, grandmother/father*, as well as *no-no*, for example) that leads to the children's overuse of iambic forms.

Paolo also heavily favours labial production in his first two sessions. In 38% of his word forms (Session 1) and then in as much as 64% (Session 2), all of the consonants are labials; the preference is then gradually reversed, as reduplication and harmony loosen their hold on his production and difficult segments (alveo-palatal fricatives and velars) are targeted but replaced by alveolar stops (e.g., *girafa* /ʒiˈrafa/ [diˈafa], *aqui* /aˈki/ [aˈti]).

Session 3 marks a transition between template use and more segmentally oriented production. Only 29% of the child's forms show either harmony or reduplication; in the following session even fewer words are adapted to those forms, and those that do occur may be 'entrenched' forms that arose earlier, possibly with mediation from adult use of the child forms. Oliveira-Guimarães provides as an example the proper name *Roseli* [ʔiˈʔi] (2;2.20). The child also sometimes has recourse to reduplication when he attempts challenging word combinations in later sessions (e.g, *comeu bolo* 'eat cake' /kumewbolu/ [memewˈbolu] (2;5.20; see Lleó, 1990; Vihman, 1996, ch. 9; Vihman & Vihman, 2011; Szreder-Ptasinska, 2012, sec. 3.2.4, and Vihman, Keren-Portnoy, Whitaker, Bidgood, & McGillion, 2013, for similar examples of consonant harmony in child attempts at longer word and phrase targets).

After the first five sessions words are rarely restricted to a single place of articulation. Instead of applying templatic patterns to whole words Paolo now began to make segmentally-specific phonological substitutions, as Oliveira-Guimarães illustrates with the word *tartaruga* /tahtaˈruga/, which the child produced in almost every session. He begins with [taˈta] (Sessions 1–4), lengthens the form in the variants [tataˈluga, tatauˈtugu, tataˈu] (Session 5), and finally abandons the shorter forms entirely in Session 7, by which point he has actually become capable of saying the whole sequence, *tartaruga nada na água* /tahtaɾuganadanagwa/ 'turtle swims in the water' [tata'uganadana'agwa].[1]

The chapter concludes with a discussion of the status of the word as a unit in child and adult phonology. Oliveira-Guimarães' comments on variability, which affected whole-word forms for Lucas but segmental units for Paolo, are relevant here. Lucas showed relatively stable word forms over the entire period of the study, although he often displayed variants expressing the ongoing competition between two structures, CV[m] and CV[w]. Paolo, on the other hand, made a transition to segmentally oriented phonology early on, with whole-word templates no longer constraining his word forms. Nevertheless, the lexical representation as a whole continued to play a phonological role, as difficulty with certain target sounds, such as /s/ or /dʒ/, were dealt with in different ways in different lexical structures. Oliveira-Guimarães concludes that 'a phonological model is needed which recognizes segments as functional units for both adults and children but that allows for the word in lexical representation as well' (2013, pp. 312f.). This echoes the view that Ferguson and Farwell expressed in 1975.

In relation to our question about the longitudinal profile of template use, the data from two children acquiring Brazilian Portuguese show the individual differences in timing that we saw in earlier chapters. From the first recording session, at somewhat different lexical points, both children showed the reduplication that appears to be characteristic of the language, along with a bias toward iambic stress patterning in disyllables. However, whereas one child quickly outgrew the use of templates, maintaining only a few vestigial forms, the other child went on to develop his own idiosyncratic approach to word-form learning, creating one- or two-syllable words with an off-glide or nasal coda for targets consisting mainly of CV-syllables (e.g., *(a) peteca* '(a/the) shuttlecock': 2;2.26 [abe'bem], 2;4.26 [ɛ'tɛʊ]).

6.3 Templates in development: Where do they go?

Longitudinal studies that follow through to well beyond the end of the single-word period and thus could provide further insight into the final step in the U-shaped progression are rare. That final step is the fading out of template use and its replacement by more accurate word forms, with any remaining errors involving systematic segmental substitutions or cluster reduction, for example. Oliveira-Guimarães gives us an idea of this in her description of Paolo's progress. Similarly, Macken (1979) tracked one Mexican-American child's advances in Spanish until the templatic patterns had faded and the child's phonology seemed to be more segmentally-based; Vihman and Vihman (2011) followed one Estonian-English learning child through roughly the same progression, which unfolded mainly within the period of production of her first 100 words.

---

[1] The gloss 'sleeps (in the water)' was a slip in Oliveira-Guimarães (2013).

Szreder-Ptasinska (2012) analysed the word forms produced by three children learning British English over a period of seven months, beginning at about the 25wp. One of these was Jude, discussed here in Chapters 4 and 5. A second child, Rebecca, proved by far the most accurate of the three throughout the period of the study. This child mainly selected words to say that fell within her phonetic repertoire, with minor departures that capitalized on her skill with alveopalatal fricative production, especially in codas; little adaptation and little evidence of template use were seen. The third child, Alison, showed the full profile of template emergence, use and fading away within the period covered by the study.

6.3.1 Emergence and fading of templates: Alison

Szreder-Ptasinska finds that Alison made only small advances in her consonant use over the course of the study. In her first recorded session, at 1;3.21, when she produced 12 words spontaneously (17 variants), she used four consonants accurately (labial and coronal stops, transcribed as voiced, and nasals), all in onset position. Table 6.11, which shows seven months of Alison's consonant use, makes it clear that these consonants are consistently produced as matches to target over the entire period. In coda position only [p] is produced as a match in more than a single word in more than one session (*pop* [pɛp̚], *stop* [æpɸ] at 1;4.24; *help* [hɛɫpʰ], *step* [dʒɛːpʰ] at 1;9.5); the fricatives [ç] and velar or uvular [x, χ] each occur as codas in two or more words in two of the last three sessions, although the corresponding target consonants are inconsistent (and none are matches, by definition, as these fricatives are not part of the adult repertoire).

In the first recorded session harmony forms account for 41% of Alison's variants but only two could be called adapted; no other patterning is in evidence. At 1;4.24, Alison's 25wp (31 words produced spontaneously) and the session with which Szreder-Ptasinska's study begins, the child heavily restricts her target forms, selecting many open monosyllables (20% of her 50 variants) and words with labial harmony (*pop* [pɛp̚], *bubbles* [bʊboʊ]: 14%). She also produces many forms with glottal stop as coda (7 out of 24 monosyllables); unusually, she extends this motoric routine to the first syllable of disyllables, in words with or without harmony (Table 6.12: We label 'selected' words with a medial coda in the target, a common way to produce final stops in Yorkshire). Alison's most used structures in this session are CVC, with or without harmony and with or without glottal stop as coda (26%), and disyllabic harmony, with or without coda in the first syllable (36%). Disregarding word length, harmony accounts for 46% of her variants, while variants with a medial glottal stop or [h] account for 28%. There are 21 variants altogether, of either length, with a glottal coda in the first syllable (42%).

In the following session, at 1;5.23, Alison produced medial glottal codas in only two words, *Pirate Pete* [pɛʔpæʔ] (the only trisyllabic target attempted so far) and *quack-quack* [qɒʔgəʔ], in both of which the coda is motivated by a medial target

Table 6.11 Alison's consonant inventory: Matches at onset and coda. **Bold face** indicates 25wp session. Counts indicate spontaneous words attempted (targets), word forms fitting distinct prosodic structures (variants) and consonants matching the target in *at least two word types in either onset or coda* (not one of each)

Session	1	2	3	4	5	6	7
	1;3.21	**1;4.24**	1;5.23	1;7.0	1;7.24	1;9.5	1;10.7
N spontaneous targets	12	**31**	34	47	27	61	71
N variants	17	**50**	40	119	46	94	85
Total matches	4	**7**	4	7	6	9	7
onset							
p		x		x	x		x
b	x	x	x	x	x	x	x
d	x	x	x	x	x	x	x
h						x	
dʒ				x	x	x	x
h						x	
m	x	x	x	x	x	x	x
n	x	x	x	x	x	x	x
j		x					x
w				x			
coda							
p		x				x	
f						x	

Table 6.12 Alison's use of glottal codas in disyllables at the 25wp: CVʔ/ʰCVC

Selected target word	Child form	Adapted target word	Child form
Consonant harmony			
milk please (i)	mɛʰmuː	*baby (i)*	bɛʰʔbʊː
nightnight	nɪʰʔnaʰː	*ball*	bəʊʔwəʰ
quack quack	dæʔdɛk̚, gæʔgaʊ̯	*bye bye (i)*	baʔbʊ
thank you	daʔdɔʰ	*choo choo*	dʒɪʰʔdʒəʊɸ (i)
yes please (i)	mɛʔmə	*more please*	mɛʰmɔː
		mummy	mɛʔmaʰ
		nana	nəʔnaʰ
		shoes	deɪʔdu
No harmony			
help please	wəʔpʰjəʊ	*boot (i)*	βuʔhʌ
		hija	aɪːʔjɛʰ

6.3 TEMPLATES IN DEVELOPMENT: WHERE DO THEY GO? 177

coda. There is no monosyllabic harmony, but harmony in disyllables accounts for
23% of the variants. In this session Alison's five CVC word forms all have glottal
stop codas (for target obstruent codas). Two additional forms—*bow* [bɒːʔːə] and
box [bʌʔʊ̈h]—have unmotivated medial glottal stop (and an unmotivated additional syllable). No other patterns are in evidence.

At 1;7 Alison produced 108 words in the session, including 61 imitations (119
variants). This is the first session in which Alison attempts words of more than two
syllables. She truncates some long words (*banana* [nːɛnaːː], *computer* [bʊibɜː],
dinosaur [gɑːgaʔ], *museum* [mːumɪː], *teddy bear* [bəbɛː]), but matches the target
syllable count in 12 trisyllabic forms. Harmony continues to play a role in disyllables
(21%) and provides support for production of seven of the 12 trisyllabic forms
(Table 6.13), for a total of 27% harmony forms. A newly productive pattern in this
session is ʔVCV (22%). Almost half of the targets are vowel- or /h/-initial (and so
'selected'); most of the adapted forms have word-initial fricatives—mainly sibilants,
which Alison had not previously attempted—or liquids (e.g., see the no-harmony
variants in Table 6.13, where the highly inaccurate consonant production appears to
reflect a trade-off with word length). Thus *glottal substitution for difficult onsets*
accounts for this pattern; it cannot be considered a whole-word template.

Glottal codas continue to be prominent in this session, with 10 monosyllabic
C₀Vʔ variants, all with target obstruent codas. The earlier glottal-coda disyllabic
template is also in evidence (Table 6.14); words with medial coda, regardless of
harmony or onset consonant, account for 15% of the variants (20% if intervocalic
glottal stop variants are included).

At 1;7.24 Alison was still relying on harmony but no longer produced many
medial glottal codas. At 1;9.5 she produced 41 distinct two-word combinations; by
1;10.7 many combinations were three words long. The templates appear to have
served to support Alison's attempts at challenging segments and sequences; she
may have held back from combining words until she had sufficient mastery of
word-final consonants, within-unit variegation, and perhaps above all greater ease
in mapping heard forms to production patterns—i.e., sufficiently well-trained
phonological memory capacity.

Table 6.13 Alison's first trisyllabic word forms

Consonant harmony		No harmony	
building blocks	bəʊbəbaː	ABC	ʔeibʊɣːɪʰ
choo choo train	dʊdɜdʒɜː	butterfly	ʔɛ hɛwʊː
computer (i)	bʊbubɜ	dinosaur	ʔaːʊɣɒh (i)
cup of tea	gʊgːɔːgɔː	orange juice	ʔɒjɒ.ah
Emily	ʔɛmɛmeh	raa-raa-raa	ʔaʊɣɑːwa̰h
gentleman	dʲɜdɜːdɜː		
paddling pool	pʊpʊpɔː		

Table 6.14 Alison's use of medial glottals in disyllables at 1;7

Medial coda [h]		Medial coda [ʔ]	
bottom	bːəhpə	blanket	baʔbaː
coffee	jəʰ gɒː	mixer	mɪʔ mːiː
help please	ʔəhwɪː	more please	mːːəʔmaː
leopard	ʔɛ̞hpɛ	naughty	nːɜʔneə
office	ʔʌhʔɒː	pictures	m̩bɪːʔːmɜː
party	bahbaː	quack quack	gɒʔ gːaːː
tea pot	bəhpaː	tweet tweet	tɬɪʔdʒiː
		yes please	mɪʔmɪ̃ːːç
Intervocalic [ʔ]		Medial non-glottal coda	
biscuit	biʔiː	lifting	lʊɸdɪː
sausage	ʔɒ ʔəː	scoop	dɪbpʰʊ̞
shoes	ʔiːːʒɵ (i)	shopping	ʔaɸbaː
stuck	gʊːʔə̞		
sugar	ʔa ʔɔ̞ː		
uh-oh	ʔʌːʔɒː		

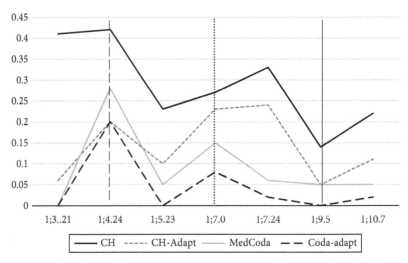

Figure 6.1 Alison's template use over time: Proportion of harmony (CH) and medial glottal coda and of adaptation to these templates. The vertical lines mark the session with the first (i) spontaneous use of 25 words or more (*dashed*), (ii) trisyllabic words (*dotted*), and (iii) productive word combination (*solid*).

Figure 6.1 shows the longitudinal trend in Alison's use of and adaptation to each of her templates (based on proportion of total variants in the session: See Table 6.15). Template use shows two rises and falls over the period of the study, as Alison produces more or less challenging targets and longer strings. For her

Table 6.15 Emergence and fading of Alison's templates. 25wp is in **bold face.** Vars: variants, Prop.: proportion out of all variants in session

	T vars	CH	Prop.	Adapt to CH	Prop.	Medial glottal coda	Prop.	Adapt to med. coda	Prop.
1;3..21	17	7	0.41	1	0.06	0	0.00	0	0.00
1;4.24	**50**	**21**	**0.42**	**10**	**0.20**	**14**	**0.28**	**10**	**0.20**
1;5.23	40	9	0.23	4	0.10	2	0.05	0	0.00
1;7.0	119	32	0.27	27	0.23	18	0.15	9	0.08
1;7.24	51	17	0.33	12	0.24	3	0.06	1	0.02
1;9.5	92	13	0.14	5	0.05	5	0.05	4	0.00
1;10.7	85	18	0.22	9	0.11	5	0.05	2	0.02

strongest template, consonant harmony, we can see that in the first session analysed, at 1;3.21, most words with harmony were selected, whereas at 1;4.24 half were adapted. In the case of the glottal-coda template, on the other hand, we see emergence with adaptation in the same session, with a new increase at 1;7, when long words began to be produced. (See the similar relationship between Maarja's use of consonant harmony and her attempts at long word production in Vihman & Vihman, 2011). As the child's vocal skills improve, there is less adaptation, although the well-practised patterns continue to provide a basis for production well into the period of early syntax (and harmony shows a small rise again as word combination becomes more active and longer strings are produced).

6.3.2 Emergence and fading of templates: Christopher

In the longitudinal studies discussed so far we have seen that an initial templatic pattern may be adapted and changed over time and new patterns may arise over the same period. Priestly's diary account of his son's development over four months of template use provides the most detailed data set available for observing the process of emergence and subsequent fading of a well-specified template as it unfolds week by week. The template takes the 'bisyllabic experimental form' (BEF), CVjVC (e.g., from Week 3 of Priestly's data collection, *blanket* [bajak], *dragon* [dajan], *medicine* and *music* [mɛjas]). (A few 'monosyllabic experimental forms' [MEF] were also recorded, from Week 7 on, but this competing template, CV·C [where the raised dot indicates increased vowel length], is used for only six words.)

Appendix IIa provides Priestly's (1977) list of 70 words adapted to fit the template, reorganized to reflect the chronological order that Priestly describes;[2]

[2] Florence Oxley deserves special thanks for creating this list, as part of her work for the MA in Phonological Development at the University of York in 2014.

this reveals the pathway the child followed as he assimilated more and more words to his template over a period of several weeks and gradually, in parallel (from the second month of template use), corrected the forms, producing the 'ordinary replacement forms' (ORF) that Priestly also lists. The target words are primarily CVCVC disyllables, with clusters occurring in any one or more of the three consonantal slots (cf. *Christmas:* CCVCCVC, *muskox:* CVCCVCC, *present:* CCVCVCC). Some disyllabic words that lack a word-final consonant are also produced according to the template (e.g., *farmer* /fɑmə/ [fajam]), perhaps due to the 'template force', the implicit pressure of a strong inner model that, for a period of time, dominates the child's production.

To gain insight from this rarely exhaustive longitudinal analysis we can look more closely at Christopher's progress over his 13 weeks of template use. Priestly does not mention the child's 'ordinary' monosyllabic word forms, which may be assumed to have been roughly as numerous as his multisyllabic word production (based on our profile of British English in Chapter 4: About half of the children's words were monosyllables).[3] Accordingly, Christopher's template appears to have come into effect when the child had an expressive vocabulary of some 200–300 words.

Priestly provides a list of the initial 68 'bisyllabic ordinary forms', or words that the child was producing more or less accurately in Week 4 of his observation and registering of the child's use of templates, when Christopher was 1;10. This list includes 17 words that already fit the template in their ordinary adult form ('selected' forms, to set beside the 'adapted' forms that are the focus of Priestly's account). These words have a medial yod in the target as pronounced in Southern British English (e.g., *lion, deer, whale*). Some of the 'adapted' forms (e.g., *carrot* [kajat]) also fit the pattern in the expected child rendition, given the regular process of liquid gliding; those forms are not then template-based, strictly speaking. However, child forms that can be 'explained away' (i.e., accounted for without invoking templatic patterning) are exceptional here, as Priestly points out.

The majority of Christopher's BEF words—the 'idiosyncratic strategy' that Priestly so insightfully identified—fit the notion of a child phonological template as we conceive of it here, as an extension of an existing motor plan that has developed through accurate production of a small number of words. This second step, from selecting to adapting, opens the way for the child to attempt challenging forms that he may now be able to express in a recognizable way, albeit at the cost of temporarily setting aside any chance of achieving accurate production in favour of maximizing numbers of output forms. In other words, a strongly experienced production pattern has become available that permits the child to bypass less well-

---

[3] See also Smith (1973), who provides an appendix listing all of the words he recorded for his son Amahl, also learning British English, over a two-year period. 'Stage I', recorded at age 2;2, included 126 monosyllables out of a total vocabulary of 255 (p. 43). Similarly, Alison, in the study reported above, produces an average of 46% monosyllabic variants over the seven months.

practised elements or sequences presented by the target words. Considerable creativity may enter into the rearrangement of articulatory gestures or segments that results in the child's output form; Priestly's discussion focuses on analysis of those child adjustments.

The final step in the evolution and decline of template use involves replacement of the experimental forms by regular ('ordinary') child forms that match the target in most ways, but with segmental substitution or cluster reduction as needed.[4] In Christopher's case this was first observed already in Week 4, when *sucker*, noted in Week 3 as [fajak], is replaced by [fʌkə], and in Week 5, when *banana*, produced as [bajan] in accord with the template in Weeks 3, 4, and 6, is produced as [bánan]. Appendix IIb presents the data week by week, so that we can see the variation in the child's production over time (following the first mention variants are in italics, to distinguish *'old'* vs. 'new' forms).

Appendix IIb makes it easy to see inter-lexical effects, such as the use of [kajal] for both *candle* and *carol* and [majas] for both *medicine* and *music* in Week 3, [kajat] for *carrot, cupboard* and *covered* and [fajan] for both *flannel* and *fountain* in Week 5. In Week 6 the difficult form *chocolate* (/ˈtʃɒklət/)—noted as [kajak] in Weeks 3, 6, and 9, as [kɔjak] in Week 7—is produced as the ORF [kákat]: Although this form is not a close match to the target, it reflects regular phonological processes, harmonizing the initial affricate to the coda of the first syllable in the adult form and simplifying the medial cluster. (Vowel harmony is only apparent, as Priestly normalizes 'what was assumed to be free variation between [a] and [ə]' [1977, p. 218].) Note that here, as in many instances, the 'replacement form' coexists with an experimental form, which reappears two weeks later. Similarly, *monster* is produced in Week 5 as [mɛjan] but in Week 6 as both [majɒs] and the ORF [mostə], while *porridge* is recorded as both [pajɒs] and the ORF [pɒrɪs] as late as Week 12. That is, the template is in competition with the child's emergent ability to produce closer approximations of the targets.

This is the story that unfolds as we examine Priestly's data with the benefit of the chronological organization. A few more ORFs occur in Weeks 7 to 9; the remaining words achieve a roughly adult-like form only in the last four weeks of data collection. The actual week in which the replacement is noted is of no particular significance as the child's spontaneous word uses fluctuate, presumably depending on occasions for use, form-priming within the discourse from his own as well as others' uses, and so on. Priestly made a point of eliciting as many forms as possible in Week 12, to complete his record. What is clear is that the process of replacement of templatic forms by regular forms extends over a good two months, with competing forms commonly coexisting with the templatic forms.

---

[4] Priestly provides ordinary replacement forms (ORF) just once each, in the week when they are first noted; stress is marked on these forms but not on the experimental forms, where neither syllable was clearly stressed: Priestly, 1977/2013, p. 218. See also Vihman, DePaolis, & Davis, 1998, on child production of English stress and its effect on adult perception.

6.4 Quantifying template use

We have observed that, in each of the language groups we have considered, at least two of the children whose early word-form data are available for analysis provide evidence of template use. In addition, Baia and Correia (2010) report template use in European Portuguese; Macken (1978, 1979) provides template descriptions for two children learning Mexican Spanish in California; Kehoe (2015) provides evidence of such use in children learning German, European Spanish, or both; Vihman and Croft (2007) provide evidence of template use in a child learning German (based on Elsen, 1991, 1996) and one learning Hindi and English (based on Bhaya Nair, 1991); and Szreder (2013) describes template use in a child acquiring Polish. Templatic tonal patterns have been identified in Cantonese-English and Mandarin-English bilingual children (Mok & Lee, 2018 and Choo, Vihman, & Keren-Portnoy, 2019, resp.). Thus out of the relatively small sample of languages for which such an analysis has been undertaken, all include one or more children who exhibit identifiable templatic behaviour as part of their early lexical and phonological learning. Other studies report template use in Hebrew (Keren-Portnoy & Segal, 2016), Norwegian (Garmann, Kristoffersen, & Simonsen, 2017), and Swedish (Renner, 2017). Current work in progress is addressing template use in children acquiring Farsi, Pashto, and Urdu.

Nevertheless, as we have seen, not all children provide evidence of such use. Furthermore, in studies of children with phonological difficulties or delay, templates have sometimes been found to be part of the problem: A child can become 'stuck' in a pattern that makes further advance more difficult (Velleman, 1994; Velleman & Vihman, 2002; Vihman et al., 2013; see also Velleman, 2016). Taken together, then, the fact that some children show little or no reliance on templates while others seem to develop too much of a dependence on them suggests that it would be helpful to have a way to objectively compare template use in children learning the same language. This would not only help us to arrive at a better understanding of the possible developmental function of templates but could also lead to a useful diagnostic tool for clinical work. In this section we will look at a study of expressive late talkers that proposes a way to quantify template use, the essential basis for making such a comparison; that study also provides insight into the relationship of template use to other phonetic and phonological advances that might serve as predictors of later linguistic ability.

Note that the studies we have described here have already broadly attempted quantification in some sense, although the unit used for calculating use has varied. Khattab and Al-Tamimi (2013), for example, provided percentage use of templates over all *child word tokens*; Kehoe (2015), following Ingram (2002), Keren-Portnoy, Majorano, and Vihman (2009), and Majorano and D'Odorico (2011), calculated the percentage use of templatic forms over *word types* included in the analysis, with analysis restricted to one child variant per word (see also Szreder-

Ptasinska, 2012). Our own approach here, as well as in Vihman (2016), has been to consider the proportion of *word variants* affected by template use—a measure that is neither purely lexical or phonological (since variants of the same word may fall into different prosodic categories) nor entirely phonetic (since the number of uses of a form or set of forms that fall into a single prosodic category is disregarded). By including all distinct prosodic variants for each word type rather than picking one representative variant this approach aims to gain as much insight as possible into the resources available to the child and also to reveal any emergent sense of a phonological system that the child may seem to have, based on his or her perception or experience of lexical similarities (that is, based on emergent *lexical engagement*, in Leach and Samuel's terms).

All of these measures have in common the application to the data of an analysis based on the proportion of child forms conforming to a particular pattern. Whether types, tokens, or variants provide the most reliable basis for comparison across children in different studies or languages is an empirical question that has yet to be directly addressed (e.g., by a study that undertakes and compares more than one approach). Note that whichever measure is chosen, for between-child comparison it is best applied to lexically defined milestones, in longitudinal observational studies, or to size of cumulative lexicon, in diary studies, given the wide range of individual variability in the timing and relative rate of word learning.

6.4.1 Expressive late talker study: Developing a score for template use

Vihman et al. (2013) developed a template score that takes into account not only the numbers of word types or variants that fit a given pattern but also the relationship of those child word forms to their adult target forms. The study was designed to investigate the possible role of template formation and use in the linguistic development of late talkers whose comprehension skills are within the norm. Vihman et al. (2013) analysed template use and a number of other lexical and phonological measures based on transcription of recordings obtained in a naturalistic setting for 21 potential late talkers acquiring British English.

An initial visit was made to families who expressed an interest in participating and whose child, at age two or over, was producing fewer than 50 words and few if any word combinations, based on the Oxford CDI (Hamilton, Plunkett, & Schafer, 2000). This was followed by repeated phone contact until the child was reported to be producing some 50 words. Half-hour home recordings then continued to be made until the child produced at least 25 different words spontaneously in a single session (25wp). This session constituted Time 1; the study recorded the children again about 14 months later (Time 2) in order to compare phonological and lexical development at the end of the single-word period with linguistic advance over a comparable period for all of the children. The study also included a control group of 11 typically developing children (TDs) recorded as part of an earlier study (Keren-Portnoy, Vihman, DePaolis, Whitaker, & Williams, 2010; Jude, whose data were presented in Chapters 4–5, was the youngest of these). The children's ages at Time 1 ranged from 15 to 36 months.

All of the children were tested on the Reynell Developmental Language Scales III (Edwards et al., 1997) at age 2;6 in order to formally identify the late talkers. Ten of the 21 children followed as potential late talkers (LTs) fell within the age-norm for expressive language when tested on the Reynell-III; these 10 children were retained in the study as 'transitional LTs' (TLTs), or 'late bloomers' (Mirak & Rescorla 1998; Jack, whose 25wp phonology is described in Chapter 5, was one of these). The remaining 11 children constituted the LT group. In the final sample the age ranges of the three groups at the 25wp were largely distinct (see Table 6.16). No TDs overlap in age with any LTs at the 25wp, although the TLTs overlap with some members of both of those groups. Thus the division into groups based on performance on the Reynell-III was strongly correlated with age at the 25wp.

Notice that the TLT and LT groups, whose expressive scores are at least four months behind the norms for their age but whose comprehension skills are age-appropriate, tend to produce more word combinations in the 25wp session than do the TDs, although all of the children can be characterized as being within the single-word period. On the other hand, whereas number of *word types* establishes the timing of the session to be analysed and is thus comparable across the groups (TD: 36, TLT 40, LT 39), mean (T)LT *word-token* production is lower than that of the TDs.

In addition to the defining lexical measure, *age at 25wp*, the Time 1 analyses in Vihman et al. (2013) include the count of word tokens ('*volubility*': See Table 6.16) and two measures of phonetic advance (*size of consonant inventory*—based on a random selection of 25 of the word types used spontaneously by each child, to equalize sample size) and extent of *consonant variegation*, adapted from Stoel-Gammon's (1989) Mean Babbling Level analysis, which distinguishes vocalizations with (1) no true consonant, (2) no more than one true consonant type, and (3) more than one true consonant type. The measure was applied to all word tokens produced in the session and constituted an average based on mean level per word. In addition, two measures of phonological advance were included: (1) *Percent Consonants Correct* (PCC: Shriberg, Austin, Lewis, McSweeny, & Wilson, 1997) and (2) the *Pscore*, devised to measure template use. This is a novel approach to assessing phonological advance, closely related to the methods presented here in Chapters 3–5. It goes beyond those methods, however, in providing a specific score for each session analysed, which can then be used for comparative purposes. Accordingly, in what follows we draw extensively on Vihman et al. (2013) to define and illustrate this measure.

Table 6.16 Late talker study: Age range and numbers of word tokens and word combinations in 25wp session. (Adapted from Vihman et al., 2013.) TD: 'typically developing', TLT: 'transitional late talker', LT: 'late talker'

Group: N	TD: 11	TLT: 10	LT: 11
N male	6	6	8
Mean age (range) in mos. (Time 1)	21.08 (15–26)	26.8 (25–28)	31.65 (27–36)
Mean word types	36	40	39
Mean word tokens	123.34	117.73	118
Mean word combinations	1.1	2.6	2.8
Age range/Reynell expressive	3;0.11–3;1.18	2;5.28–2;6.21	2;5.8–2;11.13
Reynell receptive score	3;00–5;5	2;5–3;1	2;3–2;11
Reynell expressive score	2;9–3;11	2;2–2;9	1;9–2;4

The Pscore is arrived at as follows:

We first established the main *generic* prosodic structures used, based on number and order of C[onsonant] and V[owel] slots (CV, CVC, CVCV ...). To these we added patterns *specified* by particular manner of consonant (e.g., CVC with fricative or nasal specified for the coda slot) or particular vowel or diphthong or consonantal sequence. Table [6.17] shows the patterns included, ordered by total uses in our sample, and the scores that we assigned them. We categorized all of the words analyzed for each child in terms of (1) overall prosodic structure and (2) whether or not they could be considered 'accurate', within the child's production limits.   (Vihman et al., 2013, pp. 54f.)

The goal ... is to define idiosyncratic pattern use ... on a gradient scale, with words adapted to 'specified' patterns providing the strongest indicators of such use, whereas words based only on a generic pattern and closely adhering to the adult target form (selected) provide little such evidence. Accordingly, Pscore points were assigned as follows: 1 point to 'selected' words that fit generic patterns (e.g., *no* [nəʊ]); 2 points to 'selected' words that fit *specified* patterns, including ... consonant harmony, as seen in *bubbles* [Table 6.17]; 2 points to word forms *adapted* to fit a generic category (e.g., *boat* [bəʊ:], produced by a child who sometimes produces codas); 3 points to words *adapted* to fit a *specified* category (e.g., [Lewis'] *Harvey* ...). To arrive at a single score for each child we average the child's individual word scores, yielding *mean score per word*. The Pscore assigns more points to forms that are (a) more constrained and (b) less accurate and is thus not only a measure of pattern formation, generalization or systematization, but also an error score, potentially indicating the extent to which a child's output is guided by individual limitations.

(Vihman et al., 2013, p. 55)

To repeat, the Pscore expresses the number of *points per word* given for each child, where child word variants that are *selected* for the pattern are given a lower score than variants that are *adapted*. Also, prosodic categories *specified for particular*

Table 6.17 Phonological template patterns and scoring (adapted from Vihman et al., 2013), ordered by extent of use (2nd column) for the 32 children in the study. The examples given for each pattern derive from the child who made the most use of it. The counts are based on the procedures described in this book.[1] **Bold face** marks the late talkers whom we profile below. RED: reduplication, Mono: monosyllable, Disyl.: disyllable, Fric: fricative

Word shape	Uses	Child	Group	Select: gloss	Select: form	Select score	Adapt: gloss	Adapt: form	Adapt score
CVV	250	Colin	TLT	no	nəʊ	1	boat	bəʊ:	2
C1VC1V	**169**	**Lewis**	**LT**	**bubbles**	**bʌbɔ:**	**2**	**Harvey**	**bæbi:**	**3**
C1VC2	161	Jennifer	TD	pink	pɪkʰ	1			
CV	114	Jude	TD	sky	kʰa	1	flower	la	2
CH-disyl.	81	Ian	TD	monkey	maŋgi	1			
CVFRIC	73	Elise	LT	eyes	aɪs	2	bike	baɪs	3
VCV	64	Julie	TLT	(there) we go	iːgəʊ	1	jigsaw	iʃɔ:	2
CVCVC	53	Ian	TD	break it	baɪkɪt	1			
CVVHIGH	**41**	**Jeremy**	**LT**	**go**	**gɔu:**	**2**	**two**	**tau:**	**3**
CVNASAL	38	Jane	TLT	green	giːn	2	camera	kʰæm	3
CVGLIDEV	28	Jack	TLT			2	straw-berries	dauːwi	3
RED	**22**	**Liam**	**LT**	**nana**	**nɑːna**	**2**	**spot**	**babɑ:**	**3**
CV?	18	Carl	TLT	foot	ɛfʰʌʔ	1	Thomas	ətɑʔ	2
CH-mono.	18	Clarissa	TLT	cake	gekʰ	2	dog	gaɡkʰ	3
C1VC1VC	15	Dean	TLT	saucers	tʌtaːs	2	carrots	kækɫaːs	3
CVCVFRIC	13	Elise	TD			2	rabbit (i)	haʔpiːs:	3
VGLIDEV	12	Tony	LT	away	aweɪ	2	flowers	aːwe	3
C	7	Andy	TD	sh	s:	1	moo	m::	2
CVi	7	Tomos	TD	bye	baːɪ	1	plane	peɪ	2
CVCi	4	Sylvia	TD	potty	poti	2	beer	biːdi	3
CVCVi	4	Owen	TD	marmite	mə'maɪ	2	Harri	fɪə'waɪ	3
CVFRICV	3	Andy	TD	what's that	wʌsɛʔ	2	tortoise	daza	3

Note: [1] Note that this analysis differs from that of the 2013 paper, in which only one token (or variant) was included per type.

sound classes or segments (such as CVFRIC or CVlV) are awarded more points than *generic* prosodic categories, to reflect the assumption that the more segmentally constrained templates express a more active or more deeply entrenched pattern or motoric routine than do generic patterns such as CVC or VCV. Aside from Vihman et al. (2013), such distinctions have so far been included as part of a quantitative measure, to our knowledge, only in Szreder-Ptasinska's (2012) thesis and in Garmann et al. (2017).

At Time 2, finally, the transcriptions of the home recordings were used to assess *phonological accuracy* (PCC), *morphology* (based on provision of morphemes in obligatory contexts: Brown, 1973), *lexicon* (indexed by diversity of verb types and function words) and *syntax* (mean length of utterance, or MLU: Brown, 1973, and Index of Productive Syntax: Scarborough, 1990).

The mean Pscores are, for TDs 1.69, for TLTs, 1.68, and for LTs, 1.87.[5] To give a better idea of the calibration, Jude scored 1.56 (in the lower third), Jack, 1.9 (in the top third). Overall, about half of the LTs had high template use while the others did not. To illustrate the method used to arrive at Pscores we draw on three of the LTs who had particularly strong templatic patterns, Lewis (Pscore 2.53), Liam (2.11), and Jeremy (1.96) (see also Vihman, DePaolis, & Keren-Portnoy, 2009, where templates are described for two more LTs, Elise [2.05] and Tony [1.69]). We will also consider the consonant inventories of each of these children in relation to their relative reliance on templates.

Lewis. Lewis was 30 months old at the 25wp; he produced 29 words spontaneously in the session, including onomatopoeia with stable adult models. The child had a tightly constrained set of word-production patterns, almost all of them disyllabic; this alone sets his data apart in an English context. His consonant inventory was limited to onset position and included just four consonants used in more than one word each (Table 6.18).

Table 6.18 Lewis' consonant inventory at 30 months. Consonants in **bold face** are those used as matches to target in at least two words. Adapted words are also in **bold face**

Target C (N = 4)	Onset		T
b	*baby* [bibiː]	*football* [bʊbɔː]	7
d	***panda*** [dɔdʌʰ]	*daddy* [dadiːʰ]	7
tʃ	*train/choo-choo* [tʃː]		
h	*in there* [hiː[j]uᵂ]		
m	*grandma/ granddad* [mʊma]	*man* [məma]	5
n	***Spencer*** [nanaː]	*nee-nor* (fire-engine sound) [niːnɔː]	
w	***Sarah*** [wɜːwə]	***brother*** [bəwɔː]	
ɹ	***zebra*** [əɹəɹɜː]		

Table 6.19 Scoring for Lewis (including scored structures only). Numbers in *italics* indicate the total score for each column; shaded rows indicate the score to be used for each structure

	CVV	VCV	RED	C_1VC_1V	CVGLIDEV	T		Pscore
	4	*5*	*7*	*14*	*6*	*36*		
N select	3	0	1	7	1	12		
N adapt	1	5	6	7	5	24		
T/select	6	0	2	14	2	24		
T/adapt	3	10	18	21	15	67	91	2.53
select	2	1	2	2	2			
adapt	3	2	3	3	3			

   Lewis produced a total of 36 variants, in five prosodic structures that account for over 10% of the variants each: Reduplication (19%, e.g., *baby, football, Spencer*), consonant harmony (39%, e.g., *bubbles* [bʌbɑ:], *daddy, Sarah*), CVGLIDEV (17%, e.g., *brother*), CVV (11%, restricted to onomatopoeia, such as *baa* [bæ:::]), and VCV (14%, e.g., a variant for *grandma/granddad* [æmɒ:]).
   Table 6.19 provides the score sheet used to arrive at the Pscore for this child; a similar one is presented for each of these children. The bottom two rows (grey shaded) give the score for each structure, adding one point for 'adapt'; the more fully specified structures (reduplication, harmony, glide, and also CVV, which specifies a diphthong or long vowel) receive an additional point each. The top row gives the total number of variants in each structure, totalling the number selected and adapted, so that the total at the far right counts all the variants identified in the session. The next two rows (select, adapt) give the number of selected and adapted variants in each structure; the next two rows (T/select and T/adapt) give the score for these, multiplying number adapted, for example, by the adapt score for that structure (e.g., 5 reduplicated variants adapted to express non-reduplicated targets, multiplied by 3, gives a score of 15 for Lewis' adapted reduplications, like *football* and *Spencer*). The top-row column headed T totals all the cells to the left of that column; the single score in the next column totals the select and adapt scores overall, while the Pscore is arrived at by dividing that overall total by the total number of variants included in the analysis. (The format can easily be created on an excel sheet that also computes the Pscore.)
   Liam. Liam was 36 months old at the 25wp. Like Lewis, his phonological patterns are highly constrained, although he shows more phonetic diversity. Although Liam uses no voiceless onsets, he does have words with more than one consonant type (variegated forms, such as *tortoise* [dɛdas]) and in addition to

Table 6.20 Liam's consonant inventory at 36 months. Consonants in **bold face** are those used as matches to target in at least two words. Adapted words are also in **bold face**

Target C (N = 6)	Onset		T	Coda		T
b	*baby* [baba:]	*please mummy* [bɪmʊmɪ:]	8			
d	*cheeky* [dadɪ]	*tortoise* [dɛdas]	10			
g	*go* [gəɒ:]					
ʔ	*uh-oh* [ʊʔʊ]					
s				*leaf* [θɛs]	*yes* [jɛs]	3
v	***Ross*** [**vɒv**]			***Ross*** [**vɒv**]		
m	*mama* [mama]	*me* [mɪ]	5	*mum* [mʊm]		
n	*nana* [nɑ:na]	*no* [nəʊ]				
l	*laalaa* [lɒ:la]					
j	*cat* (meow?) [jɒ:]	*yes* [jɛs]	3			

stops, nasals, glottals, and glides he produces fricatives, mainly in coda position. Altogether, Liam makes use of six consonants in at least two words or word positions (Table 6.20).

Table 6.21 shows the structures and tallies used to arrive at Liam's Pscore. Notice that the structures Liam uses are different from those of Lewis; only the relevant structures are shown. Liam's structures are: CV (22%, e.g., *me*), CVV (25%, e.g., *no*), CVFRIC (8%, e.g., *yes*), reduplication (25%, e.g., *mama*), and harmony (19%, e.g., *cheeky*). Few of Liam's words are clearly adapted; examples are mainly found among his reduplicated words, such as *biscuit* [bɪbɪ] or *spot* [babɑ:].

Table 6.21 Scoring for Liam (including scored structures only).). Numbers in *italics* indicate the total score for each column; shaded rows indicate the score to be used for each structure

	CV	CVV	CVFRIC	RED	$C_1VC_1V_0$	T		Pscore
	8	*9*	*3*	*9*	*7*	*36*		
select	5	9	3	5	2	24		
adapt	3	0	0	4	5	12		
T/select	5	18	6	10	4	43		
T/adapt	6	0	0	12	15	33	76	2.11
select	1	2	2	2	2			
adapt	2	3	3	3	3			

The two boys have about the same numbers of variants and structures, but Lewis has far more adapted variants. Lewis' higher Pscore expresses his considerably more constrained production patterns.

Jeremy. Jeremy reached the 25wp at 28 months, when he produced 47 words within the session. His consonant inventory is shown in Table 6.22. This child has more phonetic resources than Lewis or Liam. His stable consonant count is higher and he produces several word-final consonant matches. However, unlike Liam, he lacks fricatives almost entirely, producing mainly sonorant codas.

Table 6.23 provides Jeremy's score sheet. Like Lewis and Liam, Jeremy too has five structures, but he also has half again as many variants as the other two boys. Like Liam, Jeremy has a higher count of selected than of adapted variants, but he also produces proportionately more adapted forms than Liam does. Only one of the structures Jeremy uses is generic, the default CV (16%, e.g., *bear*; note that all of the variants in this structure have lengthened vowels; variants with diphthongs are numerous enough to form a separate prosodic structure), CVV$_{HIGH}$ (25%, e.g., *knife*), CVNASAL (16%, e.g., *coin*), harmony (20%, e.g., *window* [aninəu]), and CVGLIDEV (10%, e.g., *wheel* [wi:[j]əʊ]).

Table 6.22 Jeremy's consonant inventory at 28 months. Consonants in **bold face** are those used in at least two words as matches. Adapted words are also in **bold face**

Target C (N = 8)	Onset		T	Coda		T
p	*pepper*[m̩pep pəu:]					
b	*byebye* [bæbaɪ:]	*bear* [bɛ::]	7			
t	*two* [tu:]	*toottoot* [tu:tu:]	4			
d	*stairs* (im.) [dɛ::]	*sink* [dɪn]	4			
k	*car key* [kʰa:kʰiæʔ]			*drink* [aʊlədənk]		
g	*go* [gəɒ:]	*coin* [əugɔɪ::n]	9			
ʔ	*uh-oh* [ɒʔəu]					
χ	*cheese* [χʰi::]					
h	*hand* [hænʔ]	*house* [haʊ]	4			
m	*moon* [mu:]	*mummy* [əma:mi]		**ball** [bɛ:m]		
n	*knife* [ʰnəɪ]	*nose* [nɲɛ:u]	6	*all gone* (im.) [əʔgɒn:]	*hand* [hænʔ]	7
l	*chair* [lɛ:]]			*wheel* [wiɫ]		
j	*yeah* [jeʰ]					
w	*wheel* [wiɫ]					

Table 6.23 Scoring for Jeremy (including scored structures only). Numbers in *italics* indicate the total score for each column; shaded rows indicate the score to be used for each structure

	CV	CVHIGHV	CVN	C₁VC₁V	CVGLIDEV			Pscore
	15	*13*	*8*	*10*	*5*	*51*		
select	14	9	7	5	3	38		
adapt	1	4	1	5	2	13		
T/select	14	18	14	10	6	62		
T/adapt	2	12	3	15	6	38	100	1.96
select	1	2	2	2	2			
adapt	2	3	3	3	3			

6.4.2 Overall results and discussion

Statistical tests showed no significant differences between groups at Times 1 or 2 on any measure other than age at 25wp, the basis for the grouping in the first place. This is an important finding, in that most LT studies have conducted age-based comparisons of TDs and LTs (Paul & Jennings, 1992; Mirak & Rescorla, 1998; Carson, Klee, Carson & Hime, 2003), with the result that LTs are predictably found to be less voluble, less lexically advanced, and less phonetically skilled or phonologically advanced than their faster-developing peers at the same age. Here the comparison was developmentally based instead and was thus able to reveal that the LTs (all of whom have typical comprehension skills in this sample) are not qualitatively different from the TDs at either time point when lexical levels are equated: A delayed start means delays at later developmental points as well, but there was no evidence of slower progress *between* the two points for the TLTs or LTs in comparison with the TDs. Instead, some of the typically developing children made relatively slow progress over the intervening year and some of the late talkers progressed fast enough to no longer count as 'late'.

The samples included in this study were too small to provide definitive results as regards the key question of interest—the possible relation of templates at Time 1 to linguistic advance at Time 2; it must be considered exploratory. Nevertheless, it has its interest as a first attempt to relate template use to broader aspects of development. The primary hypothesis that the study was designed to test was the paradoxical idea that although template use necessarily implies inaccurate production (as seen in an inverse correlation of −0.39 for overall Pscore with PCC), template use—seen as a sign of systematicity, as part of the pattern of non-linear advance also typically seen in overregularization in morphology, for example— might actually prove to be a *positive* indicator for a child's later development. The idea was based on evidence from earlier studies that typically developing children rely on templates as a temporary measure when their interest in communication and their growing understanding of the value of speech production fuels an ambition to attempt more challenging words than their articulatory and mnemonic resources are successfully able to cope with; Alison, described above, has provided an excellent example of this. The extension of a familiar motoric routine to assimilate more difficult words can be seen as a bold move that can serve the child well in the short term (Szreder-Ptasinska, 2012; Vihman, 2016). In the event, however, the study demonstrated the contrary, perhaps unsurprising result: The strongest predictors of good advances between the two sampling points were a large consonant inventory and high variegation, and to a lesser extent accurate matches, or high PCC, at Time 1. Template use played only a minor role and a negative one.

Two sets of statistically significant correlations were found. The first picked out, as most strongly related to Time 2 measures, (i) late achievement of 25wp, (ii) small consonant inventory, and (iii) low variegation at Time 1, along with both (iv) high volubility and (v) low accuracy—but not template use. The Time 2 measures most strongly associated with these were low accuracy (PCC) and also, to some extent, poor morphology and lexico-syntactic scores. This significant correlation of different measures taken 14 months apart points up the importance of strong phonetic and phonological foundations in the single-word period for making solid advances later in morphology and lexico-syntactic knowledge as well as in phonology. As Vihman et al. conclude, 'phonetic and phonological advance are inextricably bound up with word learning, and word learning is likely a critical foundation for advances in grammar' (2013, p. 65).

A secondary set of correlations picked out the template measure, Pscore, along with low accuracy and to a lesser extent volubility but no other Time 1 measure, and found them to be most strongly related to low morphology scores at Time 2. In other words, far from marking potential for advance, heavy reliance on template use among the 32 children was most predictive of difficulty with morphology a year later (although this effect was less strongly reflected in the data than the basic finding of the relationship of phonetic factors to later grammatical advance). This puts the emphasis on template use as a response to output constraints rather than as a sign of systematicity. Vihman et al. explain the finding as indicating that 'dependence on templates, or holistic matches to target, may sometimes be a useful "holding strategy" while in other instances proving a negative indicator' (2013, p. 65). It is perhaps worth noting that a t-test for the difference between TD and LT Pscores approached significance (p=.09, two-tailed):

> An extended period of holistic phonology could be paralleled by an extended period of holistic (i.e., not yet truly productive) morphology (Vihman, 1982). Note that successful acquisition of morphology requires, for some functional

morphemes, prior analysis of words into stem and affix. Thus the Pscore appears to offer a usable predictor of later outcomes for morphology, although this is not what we had anticipated.   (Vihman, 2013, p. 66)

Reflecting on the failure of high template use to serve, as expected, as a positive indicator for advance in the LTs, Vihman et al. ruefully conclude that:

> our attempt to meaningfully capture and compare pattern or template use at a single developmental point was likely misconceived: Previous studies suggest that such use may fluctuate over time and, most importantly, that the timing of its emergence and period of sway differs by child.   (Vihman, 2013, p. 66)

6.5 Function of child templates

The function of templates in early phonological development is difficult to establish. Different children face different problems or challenges; the value of templates is thus unlikely to be the same for different children or to play a role in lexical development at the same point. We have seen that, in the case of late talkers, strong use of templates may be primarily a response to articulatory or phonetic limitations. Szreder-Ptasinska (2012) also found evidence that level of articulatory control was a factor in template use and suggested further that selection and adaptation might play different roles in lexical development. Selection is widely reported (Stoel-Gammon, 2011) and is seen in most children; the essence of templatic behaviour is the process of adaptation, or assimilation of challenging forms to an existing child pattern. In Szreder-Ptasinska's study it was only adaptation, not selection, that was both (i) preceded and followed by increased variability in production and (ii) positively related to lexical growth. Furthermore, selection provided an 'entry point', but the key factor affecting the emergence of templates was the size of a child's consonant inventory, with a small inventory resulting in the strongest reliance on templates (2012, p. 202).

We have viewed children's phonological templates as involving either (i) the extension of a *motoric routine* to assimilate less familiar patterns in input speech or (ii) *(secondary) distributional learning*, based on a small but growing sample of articulatorily familiar vocal shapes (as proposed in Vihman, 2014, ch. 2). Under either interpretation the primary function is *representation (memory)*, which is basic to lexical learning. The template makes it possible to bring an unknown pattern—of greater complexity than the child's existing repertoire—within the compass of her articulatory and planning mechanisms. At the level of intention, the function may be seen as *social*: Being able to produce, however approximately, a wide range of adult target forms makes it possible for the child to participate in verbal exchanges with others. Increasing the diversity of the verbal units she can contribute to these exchanges will be satisfying on many levels, not only that of successful communication (see Locke, 1993).

Why should templates appear to be, on the whole, a positive indicator of potential for lexical advance in typically developing children while at the same time, on the evidence from the late talker study reviewed above, also sometimes signalling potential delay? The link with the child's underlying phonetic competence may be the most important clue: For a child who has good phonetic skills from early on but who makes (implicit) use of template formation to leap forward lexically (see, for example, Si in Macken, 1979, or the several longitudinal studies provided here), the template serves as a shortcut to lexical production while at the same time expanding the ability to reliably internalize or represent at least some aspects of unfamiliar adult word forms, providing additional experience with aspects of those forms at a motoric and proprioceptive level. This experience can prepare and facilitate the later step of progressing to a more advanced, more segmentally accurate level of word production, as we see in the diary records of Christopher (Priestly, 1977) and Maarja (Vihman & Vihman, 2011), and the observational studies of Si (Macken, 1979) and Jude and Alison (Szreder-Ptasinska, 2012), among others.

In contrast, Jeremy, Lewis, or Liam still had, at about age three, limited phonetic skills while nevertheless having an interest in language and communication considerably more sophisticated than that of a one-year-old. For a child like that, extended reliance on a relatively constraining template risks becoming a trap (Velleman & Vihman, 2002). Here the template may serve as an easy way around production problems at the expense of phonetic advance and hence also of advances in other areas of language development.

Templates reflect a child's sensitivity to structures that are within his compass and they can effectively limit demands on his inadequate phonetic resources. But how might template use advance *phonological learning*—given that templates necessarily correspond to inaccurate production of word forms? We hypothesize that in providing at least some proprioceptive experience with challenging words template-based production must acquaint the child with a range of unfamiliar phonological possibilities. Although the child is not producing the words in their adult language form, in assimilating them to his own representational patterns he may be presumed to be gaining experience with their articulatory make-up. Priestly's detailed account of Christopher's parallel production of 'experimental' and 'ordinary' forms helps us to see how this can happen.

In exemplar terms, we conceptualize perception of both others' speech and one's own vocal output as resulting in representational clusters or clouds of heard forms. Such clouds necessarily include multiple tokens varying along a great many different parameters, mainly perhaps as regards phonetic aspects of segmental realization. Taking into account the drop in child word-form variability sometimes observed in conjunction with template formation (Vihman & Velleman, 1989; Szreder-Ptasinska, 2012), we can assume that exemplars based on the child's own preferred output pattern will cluster relatively tightly for a given word type; knowledge of these forms will include links to the proprioceptive aspects of the motoric routine as well as its auditory effect (see the discussion of variability in Sosa & Stoel-Gammon, 2006). At the same time, a separate but related exemplar cloud represents the adult target form as the child has retained it. As a record of the child's 'intake' rather than of the actual adult input speech forms, the exemplars constituting the child's representations of adult forms may be conceived of as being more or less precise, with gaps for poorly recorded aspects, such as unstressed syllables or the consonant not produced in a target consonant cluster (for an early expression of such a view, see Ingram, 1974b; for experimental evidence, see Vihman, Nakai, DePaolis, & Hallé, 2004; Renner, 2017). Furthermore, exemplars are thought to change continuously with time and additional exposure to the input (Vihman, DePaolis, & Keren-Portnoy, 2014; Vihman, 2017).

The suggestion that phonological memory is an important factor linking template use to lexical advance is based on evidence that the ability to represent and recall unfamiliar sound sequences or word forms is closely related to vocal practice and phonological experience (see Beckman & Edwards, 2000a; Edwards, Beckman, & Munson, 2004; Beckman, Munson, & Edwards, 2007; Munson, Edwards, & Beckman, 2012, in addition to Jones, Macken, & Nicolls, 2004 and Keren-Portnoy et al., 2010). We can conceive of the effect of verbal practice on improvements in memory for word forms, or phonological memory, as due to an increase in robust, neurophysiologically grounded knowledge of forms (segments, syllables, whole-word shapes), which permits on-line mapping of heard forms to existing representational patterns or exemplar clouds and, in the case of child output-based exemplars, to the articulatory subroutines that underpin them.

As the child's consonant inventory grows with increasing production experience, exemplars of adult forms will gain in representational precision; on the evidence, template formation typically supports that link, meaning that word production, even if inaccurate, involves a linking of adult forms with multimodally represented child forms. Whether or not this then leads to advances in accuracy will depend on child sensitivity to the differences between the exemplar clusters based on adults' as compared with his own production. This is an individual matter; we are far from understanding the mechanism of a shift from (i) primary reliance, for production, on internal representations (which we suppose to underlie long-lasting template use) to (ii) reliance on external input; the shift is undoubtedly gradual and most likely intermittent, as we see from the Priestly account (see also the discussion in Menn, Schmidt, & Nicholas, 2013). Further research involving dense recordings of production accompanied by experimental techniques such as eye-tracking or Event-Related Potentials, which require no overt behavioural response or voluntary cooperation on the child's part, are needed to shed light on this question (see, for example, Renner's [2017] small-scale eye-tracking demonstration of the effect of children's phonological patterns on their attention to adult models); computational modelling could also elucidate the processes involved as the initial template-based network is replaced by one that is more segmentally-based.

7

Relation of child to adult
templates, I

Parallels in core grammar

At the outset of this investigation we posed the question of the relation of child phonological templates to templates as understood in current linguistic theory. The question arises for several reasons, or rather perhaps for a single reason that can be posed from different perspectives. First, we have illustrated, in children learning one or more of eight languages, the prevalence of overused prosodic structures and, in many cases, more fully specified templates at a particular point in lexical development. This constitutes evidence enough to establish the phenomenon of templates as a factor in child language development—which naturally leads one to wonder whether the templates identified in adult languages are in any useful sense comparable.

Second, the function of child templates remains open to debate. Certainly their use reflects in part the evident articulatory or, more precisely, neurophysiological limitations of one- to two-year-olds, as emphasized by McAllister Byun and Tessier (2016), for example. We argue that memory for language, which itself increases in scope and fidelity as experience and thus familiarity with word-form representation and use increases, is an equally important basis for the use of constrained, pre-established patterns for word production. Critically, we argue that not only maturation but also experience in articulating speech or speech-like forms advances a child's ability to remember words (DePaolis, Keren-Portnoy, & Vihman, 2016). But how might the role of templatic constraints in early lexical development relate to the uses of templates in adult language?

Some researchers favour the idea of 'continuity', such that whatever elements obtain in the adult linguistic system must be present already in the child (e.g., Prince & Smolensky, 2004 [1993]). In contrast, we consider it unproblematic to posit discontinuity in aspects of lexical and phonological development; indeed it is a central tenet of Dynamic Systems Theory (Thelen & Smith, 1994) that both continuity and discontinuity are to be expected and are consistently found in multiple aspects of development, given sufficiently fine-grained analysis. In any case comparing child phonological templates with templates posited for adult language from the point of view of somewhat differing theoretical frameworks can provide insight into the range of possible templatic functions.

Phonological Templates in Development. First edition. Marilyn May Vihman.
© Marilyn May Vihman 2019. First published 2019 by Oxford University Press.

Finally, given that the term 'template' is used in both adult and child language research, we need to consider the definitions and illustrations of the construct as it is applied in studies of adult languages to determine whether or not the phenomenon can be thought of as meaning essentially the same thing in both domains. If it can be understood in that way, then we might be justified in tracing the commonality between adult and child templates to deeper roots in human cognitive function.

We begin our overview of proposals for a role for templates in adult core grammar with McCarthy's work on Semitic structure in the early 1980s, which laid the foundation for theorizing around prosodic shapes as a formal constraint on structure. In what follows in this chapter we will consider a range of proposals as to the role of templates in adult language, including their occurrence at the interface of phonology and morphology, variable shape templates, and an experimental approach to templatic patterning.

7.1 Prosodic Morphology

Based on his analyses of Arabic, a Semitic language radically different in morphological structure from that of most other well-studied languages, McCarthy (1979, 1981, 1982) extended ideas developed within the framework of autosegmental (Goldsmith, 1976) and prosodic phonology (Selkirk, 1980) to a theory of non-concatenative morphology. In a succinct early statement of the approach McCarthy (1982) characterizes the construct of a 'prosodic template' as follows:

> The central notion is that information about the canonical pattern of segments in a form is represented on a different tier from information about the kinds of segments occurring in a form. The canonical pattern tier is called the prosodic template... (pp. 191f.)

The canonical patterns of morphemes 'can be stipulated independently of morpheme identity' (p. 192). This far-reaching innovation is the likely basis for the use of the terms 'canonical pattern' and 'template' in studies of phonological development (Menn, 1983; Macken, 1992, 1995).

McCarthy and Prince (1986, 1990, and elsewhere) offer a strong theoretical defence of Prosodic Morphology; their contribution to Goldsmith's *Handbook of Phonological Theory* (1995) provides an accessible account of the approach as it had evolved to that point. The theory is rooted in three basic claims:

(1) *Prosodic Morphology Hypothesis*: A prosodic template consists of a fixed or invariant shape specified only in terms of the 'authentic units of prosody' (McCarthy and Prince, 1995, p. 318)—namely, the units of the prosodic hierarchy (mora, syllable, foot, prosodic word). No mention of particular segments may be included, nor can a shape such as VCV be specified, as this does not constitute a 'prosodically definable unit' (p. 319).

(2) *Template satisfaction condition*: Templatic constraints are to be met obligatorily, as determined by 'the principles of prosody, both universal and
language-specific' (p. 318).

(3) *Prosodic circumscription*: A domain of application for 'morphological
operations' may be identified ('circumscribed') on the basis of either
prosodic or morphological criteria (root, stem, base, affix).

Prosodic Morphology plays a role in adult grammar primarily in the case of
reduplication and root-and-pattern morphology (non-concatenative grammar),
such as is found mainly in Semitic languages; truncation is an additional domain
in which the prosodic constraints may apply (Mester, 1990). In all of these cases,
according to the theory, a *fixed 'canonical' or 'templatic' shape*—expressed in
terms of the *prosodic units of the hierarchy*, as defined within the language in
question—applies to a *full or partial copy of the base* (whether in the form of an
affix or an integrated output derived from root or base and pattern), which
supplies the *segmental melody* of the output form.

7.1.1 Arabic plural formation: The operation of a prosodic template

McCarthy and Prince (1990) describe the principles of Prosodic Morphology in
relation to the highly complex Arabic 'broken plural'. Their analysis involves
imposition of 'a fixed light-heavy syllable sequence (an iambic foot) on the
singular noun base' (1995, p. 319). A key point is that the plural cannot be said
to consist of a morpheme with a specifiable segmental identity of its own; instead,
it is the combination of the (segmentally specified) base and (fixed-shape) template (together with a vocalic melody associated with the inflection) that produces
the required output form; furthermore, it is not the whole singular form to which
the template applies but a prosodically defined portion of it (that is, the portion
selected by 'prosodic circumscription').

  Table 7.1 (based on McCarthy & Prince, 1990, 1995) illustrates all of the Arabic
nominal classes for which the plural solely, or primarily, takes the form of the
iambic template VCVV. The left-most column provides a class number, for convenience of reference, along with the skeletal or prosodic representation of the
singular form (with -*at* added for feminine gender). Both the *circumscribed portion
of the base* to which the template applies and its *templatic replacement in the plural*
are indicated in **bold face**. (There are a number of exceptions and distinct patterns,
but the forms given here represent by far the most common type.) Following the
principles of prosodic phonology and morphology, the onset consonant, which is
obligatory in Arabic, is irrelevant to the prosodic unit that defines the pattern: It is a
'prosodically null position' (McCarthy & Prince, 1990, p. 245). The plural forms

Table 7.1 Arabic productive plural and diminutive inflection (from McCarthy & Prince, 1986 and 1995). **Bold face** as in the original. (v here = vowel)

	Singular	*Plural*	*Gloss*
I. CvCC	ħukm	/ħakaam/	judgement
II. CvCvC	ʕinab	/ʕanaab/	grape
III. CvvCvC+ at	ʔaanis+at	ʔawaanis	cheerful
	faakih+at	fawaakih	fruit
IV. CvvCv(v)C	jaamuus	jawaamiis	buffalo
V. CvCvvC + at	ħaluub+at	ħalaaʔib	milch camel
	jaziir+at	jazaaʔir	island
	kariim+at	karaaʔim	noble
	sahaab+at	sahaaʔib	cloud
VI. CvCCv(v)C	jundub	janaadib	locust
	sulṭaan	salaaṭiin	sultan

I and II, bracketed by diagonals, mark abstract representations to which stem-initial metathesis applies to arrive at the actual surface form, which is [ʔaCC...]: [ʔaħkaam] 'judgements', [ʔaʕnaab] 'grapes'. Thus the table provides the idealized structural pattern for each plural form, not the actual forms that surface in speech.

McCarthy and Prince (1990) point out a number of ways in which the forms of the plural depend on the prosodic structure of the singular. In Classes I and II, in which the singular forms are bimoraic (CVC[C] or CVCV[C]: 'internal' codas are moraic but word-final codas are considered to be extra-metrical in Arabic prosody and are thus excluded from the mora count), the plural is disyllabic; where the singular is longer, as in the remaining classes, the plural is trisyllabic. Also, wherever the singular has a long vowel, the form is broken up by introduction of the glide /w/ in the plural, as in Classes III and IV, or /ʔ/, as in Class V (/w/ is 'realized as ʔ under certain phonological conditions': 1990, p. 218).

McCarthy and Prince (1990) propose a prosodic template to account for the regularities that they identify in the way the plural relates to the singular; this template is in effect the *skeletal base of the noun plural*, with the consonantal melody of the stem filling in the C slots and the vocalic melody of the plural filling in the V slots. By the 'Template satisfaction condition', whatever patterning the template specifies must apply obligatorily wherever conditions allow; no optional elements can be included in the template. Accordingly, they propose that the iambic-foot template applies *only to the first two moras of the stem* (the portion identified in bold face for each item on Table 7.1; recall that the onset consonant is disregarded for the purpose of defining the prosodic template), allowing for more idiosyncratic aspects of the derivation to be accounted for in other ways. Later argumentation, based in part on the stress system, justifies the claim that *the first two moras constitute the minimal word in Arabic*, demonstrating that an 'authentic prosodic unit', defined in ways specific to the grammar of this language, motivates the circumscription of a portion of the base.

An example or two will suffice to illustrate the steps in the analysis. The usual plural vowel melody is /a – i/. The template is imposed on the first two moras of the singular base—for example, the first two moras of *jundub* 'locust', namely, *[j]un-*; applying the template to just this portion of the base form and allowing /a/, the first vowel of the plural melody, to spread over the outcome of that operation, we arrive at (iambic) *janaa-*, to which the remainder of the form is then added, with the second part of the plural melody /i/ replacing the second-syllable /u/ of the base: *janaadib*; we can derive *salaaṭiin* from *sultaan* in just the same way, *[s]ul- > salaa- > salaaṭiin*, with spreading of the plural /i/ to the long vowel of the remaining syllable of the base.

Understanding the complex details of Semitic grammar—which differ from one Semitic language to another, but which generally retain non-concatenative structure—is not essential for our purposes, although it is worth noting that McCarthy and Prince's proposal has received validation from both psycholinguistic experiment (Boudelaa & Marslen-Wilson, 2004) and computational modelling of learnability (Dawdy-Hesterberg & Pierrehumbert, 2014). (For current debate and experimental evidence as to the nature of representations in Semitic languages more generally, see, for example, Frost, Forster, & Deutsch, 1997; Shimron, 2003; Ussishkin, 2005; Berent, Vaknin, & Marcus, 2007; Deutsch & Meir, 2011; Schluter, 2013; Ussishkin, Dawson, Wedel, & Schluter, 2015.) To anyone unfamiliar with Arabic the pattern may seem obscure and riddled with complications, but it has strong resonance for a second language learner, suggesting that the rhythmic alternation of short/long syllables and consistent vocalic melody can readily be felt.

From the research on templates in adult languages the field of phonological development has gained a formal theoretical basis for dealing with the typically non-concatenative ('whole-word') nature of early child phonological representations. Thus Wauquier (2014) comments that 'theoretical tools proposed within autosegmental theory (particularly through the analysis of Semitic languages) can shed light on acquisition data and formalize the strategies employed by children in the setting up [of] their phonological representations' (p. 220). For example, since harmony, the single most common phonological process or prosodic constraint affecting early child words, is most efficiently described by reference to a separate consonantal tier, phonological development has been well served by the model of autosegmental representation (Menn, 1978). Similarly, the idea of base melody segments mapping onto a fixed output shape to account for grammatical alternations (as in Arabic) inspired Fikkert's (1994) analysis of children's acquisition of Dutch stress.

Thus the existence of a theoretical model that recognizes the phenomenon of an obligatory prosodic output shape in adult language has provided an important impetus to further research on child phonological templates, or fixed prosodic patterns whose segmental identity changes from word to word. Furthermore, the distinction between the constructs of *'mapping templates'* and *'prosodic delimiters'*, or templates that, in a more passive way, define the prosodic shape of a base form (see examples from Cupeño and Hausa, below) corresponds to the parallel (but functionally very different) distinction between child 'adaptation' and 'selection' of adult word targets. (We will note, both in this chapter and the next, several instances in which the distinction between 'selecting' and 'adapting' clarifies the application of templates described for adult languages.) On the other hand, the child data described here in Chapters 3–6 fail to meet the critical requirement of Prosodic Morphology that only the 'authentic units of prosody' may play a role in templates. We return to this issue in the final section of this chapter.

7.2 Typological approach to templatic description

One place to look for answers to the question of the relationship of child to adult templates is the recent effort of Good (2011, 2016) to develop a typology to unite templates posited in the very different domains of morphophonology, morphosyntax, and syntax. As one might expect, Good defines the construct 'template' as broadly as possible, initially characterizing it as 'a fixed linear structure, whether in terms of the arrangement of its subconstituents or its overall length' (2016, p. 1). More precisely, Good offers the rather surprising definition of a template as 'an analytical device used to characterize the linear realization of a linguistic constituent whose linear stipulations are unexpected from the point of view of a given linguist's approach to linguistic analysis' (p. 7); to this he adds that 'the characterization of a given pattern as templatic is the product of a particular linguistic analysis' (p. 9). These characterizations are intentionally broad (and theoretically neutral), to leave open the possibility of identifying as many different types of templates as possible, with the stated goal of creating a suitably flexible but well-defined typology. The limitation to what is 'unexpected from the point of view of a given linguist's approach' is intended to help distinguish templates from constructions more generally.

The most striking morphophonological template that Good describes (based on Hyman, 2010) is drawn from the Northwest Bantu language, Tiene. In this case, quite exceptionally in general and also in Bantu languages specifically, a moraic length restriction of the kind predicted by prosodic theory is supplemented by a restriction on *segmental order*, which frequently results in metathesis of the consonants of root and affix; this is a process seldom observed in adult grammar. These patterns are complex; they illustrate perhaps the most extreme way in which a templatic stipulation can interact with the segmentalism of a base form. However, we must note that the pattern is primarily historical; it is not analysable synchronically as shown here.

Table 7.2 Causative verb forms in Tiene (adapted from Good, 2016, supplemented with information from Hyman, 2010). The synchronic situation can be analysed in different ways, e.g. Vs for I. and II. versus infixal sV for III, IV (Larry M. Hyman, p.c.)

Stem & gloss	Stem + Causative & gloss	Effect of affix	Derived stem
I. monosyllabic V-stem			
-lɛ 'eat'	-lées-ɛ 'feed'	CV+V**s**	CVV**s**
II. Stem ends in coronal (alveolar or palatal)			
-bany-a 'be judged'	-baas-a 'cause to be judged'	CV~~C~~+V**s**	CVV**s**
-mat-a 'go away'	-maas-a 'cause to go away'	CV~~C~~+V**s**	CVV**s**
-pal-a 'arrive'	-paas-a 'cause to arrive'	CV~~C~~+V**s**	CVV**s**
-piin-a 'be black'	-piis-ɛ 'blacken'	CV~~VC~~+V**s**	CVV**s**
III. Stem ends in non-coronal (non-nasal)			
-lab-a 'walk'	-lasab-a 'cause to walk'	CVC+V**s**	CV**s**VC
-lók-a 'vomit'	-lósɛk-ɛ 'cause to vomit'	CVC+V**s**	CV**s**VC
IV. Stem ends in non-coronal nasal			
-suɔm-ɔ 'borrow'	-sɔsɔb-ɔ 'lend'	CV~~V~~C_2+V**s**	CV**s**V$C_{2\text{-}denasalized}$
-yóm-a 'become dry'	-yóseb-ɛ 'make dry'	CVC_2+V**s**	CV**s**V$C_{2\text{-}denasalized}$

Note: X indicates deletion of stem segment under affixation; C indicates consonant affected by metathesis under affixation. Vowel changes in suffix are due to a form of harmony with stem; stem-final vowels are disregarded in the Effect of affix and Derived stem columns. **Bold face** marks the affixal segments per se in the derived stem.

Tables 7.2–7.4 illustrate the intriguingly complex phonological effects of the templatic restrictions. (In Hyman, 2010, two additional verbal derivational affixes are shown to behave in the same way.) To clarify the complex processes involved, we have added to the tables that Good provides a third column that spells out the effect of combining stem and affix and a fourth column that shows the template-conforming shape of the derived stem, with bold face for the affixal elements still evident in that stem. (Note that in the first column, for all but the monosyllabic V-stem forms, Good parses off the final vowel of the verbal stem as it is usually given; the second column gives the stem with the affix attached.) Following Hyman (2010), the affixes are treated here as having the shape -VC. We discuss the relevant templatic constraints below.[1]

---

[1] Based on a review of the phonological acquisition literature, Hyman (2010) came to the dispiriting conclusion that 'data from child language phonology also seems to be of little help in understanding Tiene' (p. 165). However, his source was Macken's (1992) strong claim that 'in melody templates [in acquisition], coronals are sequenced to the right of non-coronals' (p. 264), which is actually based on data from no more than three or four children. In the table of documented melodic patterns provided in Vihman (2014), Table 10.2, pp. 300f., data from several children appear to support Macken's claim but data from others go against it. Even now, 25 years later, it remains premature to state 'universals' of child melodic templates, which occur in only a small minority of the still limited number of cases of template use that have been described.

Table 7.3 Applicative verb forms in Tiene (adapted from Good, 2016, supplemented with information from Hyman, 2010)

Stem & gloss	Stem + Applicative & gloss	Effect of affix	Derived stem
I. monosyllabic V-stem			
-tá 'throw, strike'	-téel-ɛ 'throw to/for'	CV+Vl	CVVl
-síɛ 'whittle'	- síil-ɛ 'whittle for'	CV$\bar{\text{V}}$+Vl	CVVl
II. Stem ends in coronal			
-bót-a 'give birth'	-bóot-ɛ 'give birth for'	CVC$_2$+Vł	CVVC$_2$
-kas-a 'fight for'	-kaas-a 'fight on behalf of'	CVC$_2$+Vł	CVVC$_2$
-sɔ́n-a 'write'	-sɔ́on-ɔ 'write for'	CVC$_2$+Vł	CVVC$_2$
-kony-a- 'nibble'	-koony-ɛ 'nibble for'	CVC$_2$+Vł	CVVC$_2$
-yal-a 'spread'	-yaal-a 'spread for'	CVC$_2$+Vł	CVVC$_2$
III. Stem ends in non-coronal (non-nasal)			
-yɔb-ɔ 'bathe'	-yɔlɔb-a 'bathe for'	CVC$_2$+Vl	CVlVC$_2$
-yók-a 'hear'	-yólek-ɛ 'listen for'	CVC$_2$+Vl	CVlVC$_2$
IV. Stem ends in non-coronal nasal			
-dum-a 'run fast'	-dunem-ɛ 'run fast for'	CVC$_2$+Vl$_{\text{nasalized}}$	CVnVC$_2$
-lɔŋ-a 'load'	-lɔnɔŋ-ɔ 'load for'	CVC$_2$+Vl$_{\text{nasalized}}$	CVnVC$_2$
-súom-a 'buy'	-sónem-ɛ 'buy for'	CV$\bar{\text{V}}$C$_2$+Vl$_{\text{nasalized}}$	CVnVC$_2$

Note: Ӿ indicates deletion of stem segment under affixation; *C* indicates consonant affected by metathesis under affixation. Vowel changes in suffix are due to a form of harmony with stem; stem-final vowels are disregarded in the Effect of affix and Derived stem columns. **Bold face** marks the affixal segments per se in the derived stem.

Good (2016) describes the Tiene patterns as '"slotting" morphological material into the verb stem wherever strict phonotactic constraints allow' (p. 155). Following Hyman (2010), he lists four such constraints (p. 157, italics added here):

  (i) A derived verb stem [i.e., the stem in the 2nd column, without the final vowel] is *bimoraic* (i.e., consisting of either one long vowel or two short vowels)

  (ii) C_2 *must be coronal* in a -C$_1$VC$_2$VC$_3$V- structure

  (iii) C_3 *must be non-coronal* in a -C$_1$VC$_2$VC$_3$V- structure

  (iv) C_2 *and* C_3 *must show nasal harmony* in a -C$_1$VC$_2$VC$_3$V- structure

Good treats these constraints as reflecting the action of two distinct templates, one regulating permitted length, the other segmental sequencing. The length constraint (i) stipulates a maximum of two morae in a derived stem. Accordingly, wherever a two-vowel stem (i.e., for the stems included in Tables 7.2–7.4, -*faas*- 'drive through', -*kaa*- 'fasten', -*piin*- 'be black', -*síe*- 'whittle', -*suɔm*- 'borrow', -*súom*- 'buy', and *yaat*- 'split') is combined with any of these -VC- affixes, a vowel is omitted in the derived stem.

The constraints on segmental ordering (ii–iv) lead to more complex changes under affixation. If the affix itself is (strong) coronal /s/, it replaces a coronal stem

Table 7.4 Stative verb forms in Tiene (adapted from Good, 2016, supplemented with information from Hyman, 2010)

Stem & gloss	Stem + Stative & gloss	Effect of affix	Derived stem
I. monosyllabic V-stem			
-kaa 'fasten'	-kaal-a 'be fastened'	CVV̶+Vl	CVV**l**
II. Stem ends in coronal			
-ból-a 'break'	-bólεk-ε 'be broken'	CVC$_2$+V**k**	CVC$_2$V**k**
-faas-a 'drive through'	-fasak-a 'be driven through'	CVV̶C$_2$+V**k**	CVC$_2$V**k**
-yaat-a- 'split'	-yatak-a- 'be split'	CVV̶C$_2$+V**k**	CVC$_2$V**k**
-vwuny-a 'mix'	-vwunyeŋ-ε 'be mixed'	CVC$_2$+V**k**$_{nasalized}$	CVC$_2$V**ŋ**
-sɔ́n-ɔ 'write'	-sɔ́n-ɔŋ-ɔ 'be written'	CVC$_2$+V**k**$_{nasalized}$	CVC$_2$V**ŋ**
III. Stem ends in non-coronal (non-nasal)			
-kab-a 'divide'	-kalab-a 'be divided'	CVC$_2$+V**l**	CV**l**VC$_2$
-nyak-a 'tear'	-nyalak-a 'be torn'	CVC$_2$+V**l**	CV**l**VC$_2$
IV. Stem ends in non-coronal nasal			
-kam-a 'twist'	-kanam-a 'be turned over' (with semantic shift)	CVC$_2$+V**l**$_{nasalized}$	CV**n**VC$_2$

Note: X̶ indicates deletion of stem segment under affixation; *C* indicates consonant affected by metathesis under affixation. Vowel changes in suffix are due to a form of harmony with stem; stem-final vowels are disregarded in the Effect of affix and Derived stem columns. **Bold face** marks the affixal segments per se in the derived stem.

C$_2$ (see Table 7.2, II), but if it is (weak) coronal /l/, it is the stem C that is retained and the affixal /l/ that is deleted (7.3, II). In both cases incorporation of the affix to create the derived stem effectively extends the stem by one vowel (-mat- + -Vs- > -maas- 'go away'; -bót- + -Vl- > -bóot- 'give birth'). In other words, the difference in the effect of the segmental constraints in the case of Causative /s/ vs. Applicative /l/ can be taken to reflect the relative strength of the two consonants involved; the resulting applicative forms have come to be distinctive by virtue of the long vowel of their derived stem rather than by the /l/ of the affix, which appears in only a subset of the actual derived stems. Finally, if the stem ends in a non-coronal, combination with a coronal affix results in metathesis (Table 7.2 and 7.3, III), as stipulated by constraint (iii).

To conform with constraint (iv), stems with nasals denasalize if the affixal consonant is oral (and has no corresponding nasal in the language, as is the case with /s/: see Table 7.2, IV), while non-nasal affixal /l/ is replaced by /n/ when combined with a nasal stem (Table 7.3, IV).

The Stative is particularly complex, due to apparent suppletion: After either a CV(V) stem or a non-coronal stem (whether oral or nasal), the affixal allomorph is /l/ (Table 7.4, I, III, IV), resulting in a derived stem indistinguishable from the Applicative. However, after a coronal stem the Stative is -(V)k-, so that no metathesis is needed to conform with the constraints. Like /l/, affixal /k/ is replaced by the corresponding nasal (/ŋ/) after stem nasal (Table 7.4, *-vwuny-a* > *-vwunyeŋ-* 'mix'; *-són-ɔ* > *-són-ɔŋ-* 'write'). Note, however, that the velar nasal occurs only rarely in Tiene, according to Hyman (2010). In the forms with the affixal allomorph /k/ there is no homophony with the Applicative.

For adult language morphology, the extent of templatic activity here seems highly unusual. Both metathesis and consonant harmony are seen only rarely in morphological descriptions of adult languages (although metatheses do occur in the Arabic plural, for example, as noted above); in general, changes to non-contiguous segmental sequencing are unusual. Yet of the effects we are likely to encounter in core adult grammar, these are perhaps the most reminiscent of child phonological templates.

7.3 Templates at the interface of phonology and morphology

Inkelas (2014) is specifically concerned with the 'interplay of morphology and phonology'; accordingly, her definition of template disregards the morphosyntactic or syntactic constructions that Good includes in his typology: 'Prosodic templates are morphological constructions . . . which directly constrain the phonological shape of the derived stem' (p. 84). From her thoroughgoing review of morphophonological templates of three broadly different types we consider here only those that affect the 'core grammar', leaving discussion and illustration of what we term 'marginal phenomena' (basically, lexical patterns, as observed in colloquial shortenings, slang, hypocoristics, and echo-words) for Chapter 8.

Inkelas (2014, pp. 88f.) begins by illustrating what she calls '*isolated templaticity*', or templates that are restricted to a single construction within a language. The English comparative and superlative affixes *-er* and *-est* provide excellent examples. These affixes attach only to a monosyllabic base (*calm-er, dens-er, weird-er*), or a disyllabic base whose second syllable is either a syllabic sonorant consonant (*subtl-er*) or /i/ (*crazi-er*). (McCarthy & Prince, 1990, claim that the affixes attach only to minimal feet [p. 236].) Inkelas reports that, exceptionally, adjectives in *-y* may take the inflectional suffixes regardless of length; she gives *slippery* and *shadowy* as examples. However, on closer examination, an additional requirement is that the first syllable of the base be stressed.[2] Table 7.5 illustrates the various patterns that are allowed, disallowed, or uncertain (showing only the comparative suffix, as the superlative is governed by the same constraints). Derived stems seem to resist the inflectional affixes (see Table 7.4C, although not 7.4B).[3]

---

[2] Adjectives derived with the prefix *un-* constitute exceptions to this rule: cf. *un-'happi-er, un-'lucki-est*, etc. This is a 'bracketing paradox' (Fabb, 1988), as the morphological derivation—first *happi-er*, then *un-happier*—is at odds with the meaning, which is not 'not happier' but 'more unhappy'.

[3] The table incorporates most of Inkelas' examples, supplemented with a number of our own; the (un)acceptability judgements are informally based on a small survey of friends and family members, all native speakers of American English.

Table 7.5 English comparative (and superlative): Bases allowing inflectional suffix. Forms of doubtful acceptability are marked with '?', unacceptable forms with *. Derived stems are *italicized*

A. Monosyllable (σ)
calm-er, dens-er, fin-er, near-er, new-er, poor-er, short-er, strange-(e)r, tall-er, weird-er
B. Disyllable, second syllable in -/i/ (σ + Ci): Stress on 1st syllable
crazi-er, fanci-er, pretti-er, silli-er, *live-li-er, murk-i-er, seem-li-er*
C. Disyllable, second syllable a sonorant consonant (σ + C$_{SON}$): Stress on 1st syllable
-/ən/, -/ərn/ common-er, stubborn-er, sudden-er ?human-er, ?sodden-er *?hid-den-er, ?lead-en-er, ?silk-en-er*
-/əl/ ample-(e)r, ?fickle-(e)r, gentle-(e)r, humble-(e)r, little-(e)r, noble-(e)r, simple-(e)r, subtle-(e)r **cheer-ful-er, *use-ful-er*
-/ər/ ? tender-er - *but* ?bitter -er, ?dour-er, ?sour-er, *eager-er, *somber-er

D. Disyllable, second syllable neither a sonorant nor /i/ (σσ)	
Stress on 1st syllable	*Stress not on 1st syllable*
curious-er, stupid-er, shallow-er ?furious-er, ?vacant-er, **fool-ish-er, *gorgeous-er*	*devout-er, *divin-er, *ideal-er *august-er, ?intens-er, ?obtus-er (McCarthy & Prince, 1990)

E. Tri- or quadrisyllable ending in /i/ (σσ + Ci)	
Stress on 1st syllable	*Stress not on 1st syllable*
finicki-er, ricketi-er *shadow-i-er, slip-peri-er* ?uppeti-er, *?colick-i-er,* *?neighbour-li-er, ?velvet-i-er*	*persnicketi-er

F. Longer words not ending in -y (σσσ+)	
Stress on 1st syllable	*Stress not on 1st syllable*
*beautiful-er, *ramshackle-r, *affabl-er **out-going-er*	*adorable-er, *gigantic-er, *gregarious-er, *horrendous-er, *important-er, *intelligent-er, *outrageous-er, *preliminari-er, *stupendous-er **creat-ive-er, *supplet-ive-er* **extra-ordinari-er,* **hallucinat-ori-er,* **success-ful-er*

G. Participles	
Present	*Past*
**alarm-ing-er, *revolting-er*	**pollut-ed-er, *confus-ed-er*

The 'grey area' where what is acceptable varies by individual speaker includes items in Table 7.5C through E:

- Disyllabic bases in /əl/ elicit some disagreement: Some speakers reduce such a base to a monosyllable (*subtle* /sʌtəl/: *subtler* /sʌt-lər/), others produce a disyllabic base /sʌtəl-ər/ and reject the monosyllabic-base variants;
- (American English) bases ending in unstressed /ər/ are problematic, perhaps because of the resultant sequence of two *r*-codas in unstressed syllables (monosyllables in /-r/ are not excluded: compare *nearer, poorer* with ?*bitterer*, ?*sourer* /sawərər/, ?*dourer* /dawərər/); this is similar to the avoidance of suffix -*ing* for the denominal verb *lighten-ing*, with its unstressed homophonic final syllable (whereas *cling-ing* is not a problem) or the unacceptability of adverbial -*ly* for *friendly* (cf. Bybee, 2001, p. 128).
- Disyllabic bases with a second syllable that is neither /i/ nor a sonorant generally do not accept the suffixes, although not only *stupid-er* but also *furious-er* seem acceptable—the latter likely due to the enculturation of Lewis Carroll's jocular innovation, 'curiouser and curiouser'.
- Trisyllabic bases in /i/ are variably acceptable (and only when initial-syllable-stressed); derived forms do not seem to eschew the suffixes in this case.

Where the inflected form is not acceptable, speakers have to resort to the periphrastic construction with *more* or *most*. Here, then, the template merely delimits the base to which the affixes can apply. Although one can express the possibilities at least partially in terms of the units of the prosodic hierarchy, the combination of constraints is idiosyncratic and a certain amount of segmental specification must be included.

A second often-discussed example is the Cupeño habilitative (McCarthy & Prince, 1990, pp. 234f., 241f.; Inkelas, 2014, pp. 89f.). In this case the derived or output form as a whole is specified by the template: The habilitative, when formed on a consonant-final stem, must be *trisyllabic, with antepenultimate stress*; the stress of the stem, which can fall on any syllable, is maintained, however, and syllables are added as necessary (through vowel reduplication and glottal stop epenthesis) to satisfy the template. If the stem is trisyllabic and has first-syllable stress, it does not change (Table 7.6.C).

Here, as Inkelas notes, the templatic constraint cannot be expressed in terms of any of the 'authentic' prosodic units (foot, syllable, mora). On the other hand, the distinction between 'selection' (in the case of forms that already have antepenultimate stress, as in C) and 'adaptation' (where additional syllables are needed to fill out the template, as in A and B) applies quite naturally. Analogously to the application of these terms to child template-based forms in relation to their adult models, 'selected' means that the circumscribed portion of the stem fits the output template as is, while 'adapted' forms require some addition to that circumscribed portion.

Verb + Noun compounds in Hausa are similarly reminiscent of selection and adaptation in child templates (Table 7.7). The template constrains the deverbal

Table 7.6 Cupeño habilitative formation (adapted from Inkelas, 2014; original source, McCarthy, 2000)

	gloss	*stem*	*habilitative*
A.	be angry	čáŋnəw	čáŋnəʔəw
	joke	čəkúkʷilʸ	čəkúkʷiʔilʸ
B.	husk	čál	čáʔaʔal
	hiccup	həlʸə́p	həlʸə́ʔəʔəp
C.	sing enemy songs	pínəʔwəx	pínəʔwəx
	fall	xáləyəw	xáləyəw

Table 7.7 Hausa verb + noun compounds (adapted from Inkelas, 2014; original source, Newman, 2000). Changed vowels or tones are in bold face

/tʃí + fàːráː/ → [tʃìː-fàːrá]	'eat-locust' (bird name)
/bí + bángòː/ → [bìː-bángò]	'follow-wall' (leakage from roof along wall; wall ivy)
/gàː + rúwàː/ → [gàː-rúwá]	'here-is-water' (selling water in Jerry cans)

noun that results from combining a monosyllabic verb with a disyllabic noun: The verb must be bimoraic (long vowel), with low tone, and the final vowel of the noun must be short. Where these conditions are met by the verb and noun that enter into the combination, no change occurs; where that is not the case, vowels are shortened or lengthened and the tone replaced as necessary.

Inkelas (2014) comments that 'every output meets the same phonological description, regardless of whether or not an alternation has taken place to achieve it. What is constant is the shape, not the process' (p. 93). This contrasts with compounding as a general rule in Hausa, where no such constraints apply. The comment applies equally well to the Cupeño templatic constraint (Table 7.6), where we see that some forms undergo no change at all and are thus not formally marked for the habilitative.

In her next section Inkelas describes 'systematic stem templaticity' (pp. 94ff.), with illustration from the Tiene case discussed above and also a complex template in Yowlumne, which also affects several different constructions. In Yowlumne, both roots and some affixes are associated with templates, expressed as a prosodic pattern, σ_μ, $\sigma_{\mu\mu}$, $\sigma_\mu\sigma_{\mu\mu}$ (or CVC, CVVC, or CVCVVC). Where the affix requires a template different from that of the root, the form changes to fit that requirement. Here the template is defined in recognized prosodic terms and imposes no segmental constraints.

The last set of templates Inkelas discusses as such involve 'pervasive templaticity', or multiple effects on unrelated constructions in the language. In each case, one from Lardil, the other Japanese, content words are required to have a minimal length of two morae, whether monomorphemic or not in the case of Lardil, but only when composing a derived form in Japanese. A striking illustration of the latter is the case of CV number roots (see Itô, 1990). For simple counting, the numbers take forms like *ni* 'two', *shi* 'four', *go* 'five', *ku* 'nine', but when combined into a sequence, as in reciting a telephone number, the vowels are lengthened in accordance with the templatic constraint.

7.3.1 Prosodic constraints and morphological alternation in Estonian

The adult-language templates discernible in core grammar tend to have rhythmic effects, requiring a set length in syllables, in most cases, and often specifying the distribution of stress patterns or segmental length across a derived word. The phonology of Estonian is centred on quantitative contrasts in units of different sizes—vowels, consonants, syllables, and even whole inflectional paradigms. Templates as such have not so far been proposed to account for the inflectional alternations found in Estonian (although Pöchträger, 2006, 2010, proposes a Government Phonology approach to the Estonian quantitative distinctions, which are treated as reflecting a 'total amount of room', analogous to the templates of Semitic languages); however, the rhythmic characteristics of both the phonology itself and the basic nominal and verbal inflectional paradigms seem sufficiently suggestive to be worth considering as we pursue our search for parallels in adult language for the kinds of templatic patterns that underlie children's earliest systems of lexical and phonological representation.

Note first that content words are minimally bimoraic in Estonian. In addition, monosyllabic content words are necessarily 'overlong' ('third degree of length', or Q3 [Lehiste, 1960], indicated by a grave accent before the relevant form, to indicate that lengthening affects the entire syllabic rime [Viks, 1992]). Monosyllables can take the shape CVV (`*maa* 'earth, ground, country'), CVCC (`*toll* 'customs', `*tulp* 'tulip', `*tekk* 'blanket') or $CVVCC_0$ (`*tool* 'chair', `*täis* 'full', `*kuusk* 'spruce tree').[4] CVC is not permissible: Word-final consonants do not contribute to prosodic weight in Estonian (Prince, 1980), although C_1 of a word-medial cluster, whether geminate or not, does add a mora to the preceding syllable.[5]

---

[4] Estonian orthography, which is largely transparent, is used here, with the addition of the grave accent to mark Q3. The vowel *ä* is low front /æ/, *õ* is mid-back unrounded /ɤ/. Palatalization is not marked but is irrelevant to this discussion.

[5] Inflected monosyllables are also necessarily Q3: cf. `*maa-l* 'in the country' (`*maa* + adessive -*l*); `*suu-s* 'in the mouth' (`*suu* + inessive -*s*), `*vii-s* 'took away' (`*vii*- 'take away', + -*s* 'past'). In contrast, in accordance with the principles of Prosodic Morphology, unstressed monosyllabic function words that cliticize to a content word are exempt from the minimal word constraint: Compare, for example, `*maa* with (unstressed) pronominal *ma* 'I' (short for the full pronoun, *mina*), necessarily followed by the inflected verb form: e.g., *ma 'tulen* 'I'm coming, I'll come' (whereas *mina* can occur on its own, but adds a nuance of emphasis when used in full before a verb form).

The Estonian quantitative system has long been of interest to phonologists, since a three-way contrast in both vowel and consonant length is cross-linguistically rare and a challenge to the binarity assumptions underlying many theoretical approaches. Both vowels and consonants contrast three degrees of length in the (generally word-initial) stressed syllable: cf., for /o/, Q1 *koli* 'trash', Q2 *kooli* 'school, gen. sg.', Q3 `*kooli* 'school, prt. sg.'; for /l/, Q1 *koli* 'trash', Q2 *kolli* 'ghost, gen. sg.', Q3 `*kolli* 'ghost, prt. sg.' (Ehala, 2003). However, analysts generally agree that although length contrasts can be demonstrated for virtually all segments, it is the syllable, not the individual segment, that varies between long and overlong (E. Vihman, 1974). The syllabic nature of the long : overlong contrast is particularly clear phonetically in the case of words whose stressed syllable has a complex nucleus, including either a diphthong or an internal consonantal coda, or both: In these cases the difference in the measurable length of a Q2 vs. Q3 syllable is spread across the entire nucleus, so that no one segment can be fairly characterized as 'long' or 'short' (Tauli, 1968; Lehiste, 1970; Eek & Meister, 2003, 2004). The long : overlong contrast often occurs, with contrasting grammatical meanings, within the same paradigm (e.g., Q2 *koo.li* 'school, gen.sg.', Q3 `*koo.li* 'school, prt./illat. sg.' or Q2 *lil.le* 'flower, gen. sg.', Q3 `*lil.le* 'flower, prt. sg.'). Prince (1980) uses the Estonian quantity system to demonstrate the value of metrical theory; he analyses Q3 syllables as constituting a prosodic foot, which successfully accounts for several of their unique properties.

Lippus, Asu, Teras, and Tuisk (2013) carried out a thorough review of the phonetic factors underlying the Estonian quantitative contrasts in spontaneous recorded speech. They confirmed earlier suggestions from various phoneticians, generally based on read speech (cf. Lehiste, 1960; Eek & Meister, 1997; Krull, 1997), that quantity contrasts are effectively carried not by the first (stressed) syllable alone but by the *disyllabic foot as a whole*: Unstressed (generally non-initial) syllables, which cannot show quantity contrast on their own, vary in duration in such a way as to partially balance first syllables of differing lengths, achieving something like isochrony over the disyllable (cf. also Eek & Meister, 1997; Lehiste, 2003). In particular, the length ratio between first and second syllable plays an important role in the perception of Q2 vs. Q3, whose stressed syllables are less clearly distinct in purely durational terms than are Q1 vs. Q2. The Q2 : Q3 difference in the relative location of the shift from rising to falling pitch—'early' in the stressed syllable for Q3 but not for Q2—plays a role in the perception of the contrast as well. Note that the *absolute durational distance* of this pitch change from syllable onset (between 60 and 90ms) is much the same in words of all three quantities

A system of quantitative alternations also pervades Estonian inflection (Blevins, 2006, 2007, 2008), as suggested by the examples given above of Q2 and Q3 occurring within the same nominal paradigm. Although by no means all nouns, verbs, or adjectives show these alternations, many paradigms include both 'strong' and 'weak' forms, which may be based on duration alone (generally Q2 vs. Q3) or

Table 7.8 Alternation of weak and strong forms in Estonian nominal paradigms. Nom 'nominative', Gen 'genitive', Prt 'partitive', Iness 'inessive', Adess 'adessive', Com 'comitative'. Estonian forms are given orthographically. Recall that Estonian lacks a voicing contrast. Word-initially, where no differences in quantity are possible, only the voiceless-stop symbols are used; elsewhere the symbols for voiced obstruents are used for (lenis) stops occurring in Q1 syllables (*tigu* 'snail'), while single voiceless (tense) stops are written for Q2 syllables, double voiceless (long and tense) stops for Q3 syllables. The final obstruent of *rand* falls outside of the syllable nucleus and is lenis / *rant*/. *rant*/; it contrasts in this position with possible tense stops, written with the voiceless symbol (e.g., *part* 'duck' / *part*:/)

Case	A Quant. alternation: Vowel 'school'	B Quant. alternation: Consonant (i) 'rooster'	C Quant. alternation: Consonant (ii) 'acid'	D Qual. alternation: Consonant change (i) 'snail'[1]	E Qual. alternation: Consonant change (ii) 'cane'	E Qual. alternation: Cluster change (iii) 'shore'	G No alternation 'fish'
Nom	'kool	'kukk	hape	tigu	'kepp	'rand	kala
Gen	kooli	kuke	'happe	'teo	kepi	ranna	kala
Prt	'kooli	'kukke	hapet	tigu	'keppi	'randa	kala
Iness	koolis	kukes	'happes	'teos	kepis	rannas	kalas
Adess	koolil	kukel	'happel	'teol	kepil	rannal	kalal
Comit	kooliga	kukega	'happega	'teoga	kepiga	rannaga	kalaga

Note:

[1] Note that although *'teo* 'snail, gen. sg.' is a weak form, in the sense that it lacks the medial consonant of the strong nominative *tigu*, as a monosyllable it necessarily takes the form of a Q3 accented foot, as do the 'semantic' cases that it implies (*'teos*, *'teol*, *'teoga*, etc.). Blevins (2007) comments that 'Estonian often continues to treat Q3 syllables as the disyllables from which they are historically derived' (p. 251)—recalling Prince's (1980) analysis of Q3 syllables as prosodic feet.

on qualitative 'consonant gradation', with a consonant in the strong form being modified or omitted in the weak form. Table 7.8 illustrates the alternations between weak and strong forms as carried by quantitative differences in vowels (A) or consonants (B, C), or by qualitative changes to a medial consonant or cluster (D, E, F); forms declined as in (G), which completes the declension class with vowel-final partitive singular ('first declension', in Blevins' analysis), have no stem alternation. (For the sake of exemplary exposition only three of the 11 'semantic' cases are shown here, with the singular form of each noun; all of these cases are formed regularly by affixation to the genitive singular stem.)

A key point, as Blevins argues, is that neither strong nor weak forms are associated with any one case or grammatical meaning (contrast the paradigms of *kukk* 'rooster' and *hape* 'acid' in Table 7.8); instead, the alternations are properties of the paradigms as a whole. In fact, in Blevins' (2008) analysis, words with a strong nominative and a weak genitive case form ('weakening' inflections) all fall into his first declension, while words like *hape*, with the no longer productive 'strengthening' pattern, fall into the only other declension class that features gradation (disregarding recent loanwords).[6]

Similarly, Blevins (2007) shows for the verb system that one conjugational class includes all of the 'weakening' verbs, with a strong infinitive, for example (`õppi-da* 'to learn'), alternating with a weak set of present tense forms (*õpi-n* 'I'm learning', *õpi-d* 'you're learning', etc.), while another class includes all of the 'strengthening' verbs, which alternate in the complementary way (*hüpa-ta* 'to jump'; `hüppa-n* 'I'm jumping', `hüppa-d* 'you're jumping', etc.). (In Blevins' analysis a third regular conjugation includes only invariant verb stems, while a certain number of verbs showing diverse irregularities fit into none of the regular classes.) Here again, 'it is the distribution of strong and weak stems that is contrastive...The patterns that determine the three prosodic classes are all morphological, in the sense that they are neither lexically idiosyncratic nor phonologically conditioned' (Blevins, 2007, p. 254).

The alternation between strong and weak forms is thus basic to the Estonian grammatical system. Although it does not affect all inflected words, it does mark the single largest declensional class (Granlund et al., 2019) and is a characteristic feature of the core vocabulary. One could argue that the alternation itself is in some sense templatic, although no such construct follows from the theoretical account as it stands. That is, for the many content words marked by quantitative or qualitative gradation, morphological meanings are signalled by *whole-word patterns that abstract away from the segmental sequences involved, are rooted in the metrical foot and involve alternation between forms well characterized as 'weak'*

---

[6] For other ways of describing the classes see, for example, Kaalep (2012); using Kaalep's system as a basis for investigating children's acquisition of nouns in Estonian, Granlund et al. (2019) provide some figures for the distributional frequency of nouns among the different declensional classes.

and 'strong'. As with the quite different Arabic templatic system, the rhythmic character of these alternations facilitates acquisition for second-language learners. Also, the large number of old loanwords (such as `*kool* 'school': cf. German *Schule*, Old High German *skuola*; `*rand* 'shore': cf. German *Strand*) that have long since been fully assimilated into the alternating inflectional patterns may well reflect a now untraceable period of morphological productivity for these patterns.

More broadly, it is striking that the theoretical advances for which the complexities of Estonian phonology (Prince, 1980) and morphology (Blevins, 2006) have been used as proving grounds both involve moving away from 'bottom-up' (phonetic, segmental) or maximally analytic (structuralist, morpheme-stem-based) approaches toward a word level of analysis that affords a more holistic perspective on the patterning involved.

7.4 Reduplication in core grammar

Singh (2005) defines reduplication as 'a morphological process that allows speakers to form new words from old words by adjoining the latter in their entirety (complete reduplication) or some recognizable and definable part of the old words to themselves (partial reduplication)' (p. 263). Partial reduplication in particular provides parallels with child prosodic templates because the 'recognizable and definable part of the old word[s]' is 'phonologically characterizable' (Inkelas, 2014, p. 114). Partial reduplication involves a formal element that is something more than an individual segment or pair of segments but something less than a full morphological constituent, such as a root, stem, or word. The interest for our purposes, then, is in comparing these subparts to the kind of phonological patterns we observe in infants. We will again restrict our discussion to grammatically relevant uses of reduplication, reserving discussion of purely lexical uses for Chapter 8.

Inkelas' (2014) account makes clear the relevance of partial reduplication for our comparison with child templates: This process 'does not in general seem to duplicate an existing phonological constituent (e.g. syllable) of the base. Rather, partial reduplicants tend to have *their own invariant overall shape, to which copied base segments are compelled to conform*' (2014, p. 117, our italics). Inkelas' example, from the Oceanic language Mokilese, involves the expression of progressive aspect through *prefixation of a bimoraic syllable* (where codas are included in the mora count): See Table 7.9.

The fixed constraint on the shape of the reduplicant necessarily involves adaptation of the phonological sequence of the base, in which 'either less or more than the prosodic constituent [may be copied] . . . , as long as the segments that are copied can be reconfigured to form the desired shape' (Inkelas, 2014, p. 117). The reduplicant respects neither the syllabic division of the base (*pɔd* from *pɔ.dok*, *and* from *an.dip*) nor segmental length (*dii* from *di.ar*, *urr* from *u.ruur*).

Table 7.9 Partial reduplication in Mokilese (adapted from Inkelas, 2014, pp. 117f.; the data are originally from Harrison, 1973, 1976)

Base	Reduplicated form	Gloss: V / V-ing
pɔdok	pɔd-pɔdok	'plant'
kasɔ	kas-kasɔ	'throw'
nikid	nik-nikid	'save'
soorɔk	soo-soorɔk	'tear'
diar	dii-diar	'find'
wia	wii-wia	'do'
andip	and-andip	'spit'
uruur	urr-uruur	'laugh'
alu	all-alu	'walk'

The one thing that all of the variant shapes of the Mokilese reduplicant-copy have in common is that they add to the base form a single bimoraic syllable, whether in the shape CVC, CVV or VC.C.[7]

A characteristic of partial reduplicants familiar from phonological development is their tendency to reduce consonant clusters to simple onsets and omit codas entirely. Within Base-Reduplicant Correspondence Theory (McCarthy & Prince, 1995) this is treated as 'The Emergence of the Unmarked', or TETU. As Inkelas remarks, however, there is reason to think that a historical process of erosion of what was once full reduplication can account for such phonological reductions. Furthermore, from the point of view of communicative expression, loss of contrast in a reduplicant affix is unlikely to affect comprehension, given the continued presence of the reduplicated base; the gradual erosion of the form involved is thus a plausible consequence of conversational speech processes (see Bybee, 2006).

7.5 Variable shape templates

Scheer (2016) provides an overview of the uses of templatic solutions in linguistic analyses of morphology from the perspective of Government or CV-Phonology, including templatic analyses that go well beyond those we have noted so far. Scheer (2003) broadly characterizes a template as assigning 'a fixed amount of consonantal or vocalic volume to a given morphological and/or semantic category' (p. 97); Scheer (2016) specifies further that 'templates are...about the management of syntagmatic space: quantity distinctions count (long vs. short

---

[7] Inkelas' discussion of Mokilese reduplication, drawing on McCarthy & Prince (1996), notes that the vowel-initial verb forms take a VC.C prefix, which, when added to the base forms, spreads over two syllables (an.dan.dip).

vowels, two vs. three consonants etc.), while quality distinctions are irrelevant (a vs. i, t vs. m etc.)' (p. 91). He comments that Prosodic Morphology has proven useful ('has been successful') in the three domains of reduplication, minimal word constraints, and language games, but he resists the idea of universal prosodic constituents, noting that:

> templatic activity does not appear to be predictable across languages: it is a parametric possibility that languages may or may not make use of. Even though it is a typical feature of Semitic, it is not true that all Semitic languages are clearly templatic. Nor is it true that only Semitic languages are templatic. There are no other typological features either that have been found to systematically cluster with templaticity ... [Furthermore] the size restrictions imposed on strings are variable within and across languages, and do not appear to correlate with any other property, or to be predictable. Semitic templates accommodate three, four or more consonantal slots, minimal word constraints may impose one or two syllables (moras), what is called Variable Shape Templates ... may impose two, three, four or more moras. These templatic requirements may define a minimal, a maximal or an exact size.   (p. 92)

Whereas languages with non-concatenative morphology, including most although not all Semitic languages, have what Scheer identifies as 'Fixed Shape Templates (FST)', other languages may instead show 'Variable Shape Templates (VST)', in which morpheme size is restricted but the shape is not fixed in terms of a specific vowel or consonant count. FST involve constraints on lexical morphemes, such as the verbal roots of Arabic and also the reduplicative shapes discussed above. In contrast, VST can be invoked to deal with templatic restrictions that affect output strings, including affixes as well as roots or stems.

Scheer classifies the Tiene constraint identified by Hyman (2010) as a VST, in that it is not the root that is constrained but the particular combination of root and derivational affix. In a parallel case from Ibibio (Niger-Congo; based on Akinlabi & Urua, 2002), a suffix of the shape -CV (with vowel harmony) combines only with bimoraic roots (including codas in the moraic count). Whereas Akinlabi and Urua treat the phenomenon in Prosodic Morphology terms, as involving a fixed template requirement that the output shape be a heavy-light trochaic foot, Scheer characterizes both the Tiene and the Ibibio templates as affecting only the root, although triggered by the specific (invariable) suffix. (The Estonian paradigmatic alternations described above might also fit Scheer's conception of a VST.)

A number of non-Semitic languages—including other members of the Afro-Asiatic family, such as Egyptian (Benjaballah & Reintges, 2009) and some Berber languages (Lahrouchi, 2003; Bendjaballah & Haiden, 2013)—have been analysed as showing grammatical templates. For example, Benjaballah and Reintges (2009) trace reduplicative constructions from Ancient Egyptian to Coptic, using both phonological and syntactic analysis. Carvalho (2003, 2006) focuses on metaphony in the Portuguese verb, identifying a single template and three vocalic

Table 7.10 Variable shape template (Czech): Root and iterative verb stem. Long vowels are written here with VV, to bring out the patterning; Scheer gives the Czech spelling, with an acute accent

Root	Infinitival stem	Gloss	Iterative form	Gloss	Changes effected
			Selected		
haaj-	haaj-i-t	defend	haaj-e-t	defend repeatedly	none
hlaas-	hlaas-i-t	announce	ohlaaš-e-t	announce repeatedly	none
maav-	maav-nou-t	wave	maav-a-t	wave repeatedly	none
chyt-	chyt-i-t	grasp	-chyc-ova-t	grasp repeatedly	none
hust-	hust-i-t	thicken	-hušt-ova-t	thicken repeatedly	none
tlac-	tlac-i-t	push	tlac-ova-t	push repeatedly	none
			Adapted		
sad-	sad-i-t	plant	saaz-e-t	plant repeatedly	stem V lengthened
skoč-	skoč-i-t	jump	skaak-a-t	jump repeatedly	stem V lengthened
ciit-	ciit-i-t	feel	cit'-ova-t	feel repeatedly	stem V shortened
chvaal-	chvaal-i-t	praise	chval-ova-t	praise repeatedly	stem V shortened

melodies, which he contrasts with the Semitic system: Portuguese morphology is catenative, or based on segmental sequencing, and the template is 'both semantically "poor" and morphologically widespread' (2003, p. 13)—or, in Inkelas' terms, 'pervasive'. Other studies have analysed Germanic languages along similar lines (e.g., Ségéral & Scheer, 1998; Bendjaballah & Haiden, 2003; Caratini, 2009).

Scheer's central interest is in what he sees as the templatic nature of some Indo-European languages, such as Czech (see Scheer, 2003, 2004), which are not traditionally treated as having whole-word shape constraints. As an example he describes the derivation of Czech iterative verb stems from non-iteratives, which involves combining root + thematic vowel + infinitive suffix –t (Table 7.10; Scheer, 2003, mentions several other morphological categories that exemplify the same or a similar templatic constraint). Note that Scheer's account of a Czech template that requires 'an exact amount of vocalic volume' (2016, p. 93) as a key to vowel length alternations treats consonants as non-moraic.

The templatic constraint requires that the output form that results from the combination of all three elements consist of exactly three moras. For verbs with a long-vowel root and a single-vowel thematic connector (-e- or -a-; the connector varies by conjugation) or a short-vowel root and the bimoraic thematic connector -ova-, the three-mora requirement is satisfied and no change is observed in the iterative ('selected' forms, Table 7.7). Where the thematic connector is bimoraic (-*ou*- or -*ova*-) and the root vowel is long, the vowel is shortened to meet the three-mora-length constraint on the iterative derived stem; where the root has a short vowel and the thematic element has only one mora, the root is lengthened ('adapted' forms, Table 7.7).

In each case the root alone changes to meet the demands of the templatic restriction—but the template affects only derived forms, not suffixes themselves or lexical items per se. The affix triggers (but does not itself undergo changes to conform to) the template. An important final point is that although only derived forms exhibit such templatic patterning, the forms in question are no longer productive (and in some cases the derived form has shifted in meaning until it can no longer be considered an iterative counterpart to the plain stem: Scheer, 2004, lists nine such pairs). Although these forms, like those of Tiene, are superficially part of 'core grammar', then, both of these phenomena have lost active grammatical function and should perhaps be considered lexical at this point.

The distinction Scheer (2016) draws between fixed and variable templates indicates a limitation of the Prosodic Morphology approach, as

> VST cannot be characterized in terms of an invariable – and hence storable –
> sequence of Cs and Vs. Rather, the exponence of VST is a constraint that imposes
> a certain weight to a morpho-syntactically defined portion of the string. That is,
> the exponence involves computation, rather than a lexical object.   (p. 96)

For Scheer, this raises the question of the function of the template, which cannot serve—as it does in Arabic, for example—to mark 'the morphological and semantic identity of the object at hand' (p. 96). However, given that, as noted above, the Czech iterative derivational forms are identifiable mainly on historical grounds, with layers of change in form and meaning obscuring the patterns that may once have played a productive grammatical role, it is hard to see how 'computation' could be involved—and the question of (synchronic) function seems moot.

7.6 Output templates in innovative word formation

Using experimental methods to provoke innovative word formation, Pierrehumbert and Nair (1995) provide an important additional perspective on output templates. Their study cannot well be considered to reflect either 'core grammar' or 'language at play', inasmuch as it is a word game designed, following Treiman (1983), to shed light on syllable structure; no meanings attach to the novel forms elicited as part of the game. Strictly speaking, then, the template cannot readily be ascribed to either grammar or lexicon, but the study does provide an insight into adult word learning.

Pierrehumbert and Nair report a meticulously controlled set of experiments in which monolingual English-speaking participants were asked, in response to a series of auditorily presented English words, to provide novel spoken output forms including a specific infix, either VC (/-əl-, -ək-, -ət-/, intended to test effects on clusters) or /-ɹ-/. Participants were first trained to criterion on adding the experimental infix to monosyllabic words (e.g., *boy* + /-əl/ > /bəlɔj/) and then tested on words like *stub, tub, stubby, tubby*, for word-onset /(s)t/, or *brook, rung, brooklyn, rookie*, for /(b)ɹ/. This deliberately provided participants with 'quandaries' as to the required output form (e.g., *stub* + /-əl/ > /səltʌb/? /stəlʌb/?; *brook* + /-ət/ > /bətɹʊk/? /bɹətʊk/?).

The results of the first two experiments revealed a strong preference for inserting the infix after a word-initial consonant, regardless of the length or stress pattern of the input form (while splitting C + liquid but not /sC/ clusters, for reasons that need not concern us here). However, the third experiment included vowel-initial words, which are less common in English; here stress was found to play a role, with participants placing the *-r*-infix before either the first- or the second-syllable vowel, but with a tendency to modify the stressed rather than the unstressed syllable. Interestingly, the treatment of *consonant-initial words* differed in this experiment from the previous one, due to an apparent *carry-over effect from the vowel-initial words:* Here, consonants were more likely to be inserted before a stressed second syllable (e.g., *bikini* /bəkɹini/ rather than /bɹəkini/—but only *after* some vowel-initial words had been so produced in response to earlier test items.

The study is clearly relevant for our understanding of adult templates, although our issue is distinct from that of the authors, who are concerned with resolving the debate between alternative theories of internal syllable structure (hierarchical onset-rhyme vs. the 'flatter' prosodic analysis into syllables and moras). The key finding, for our purposes, is that 'subjects did not acquire a rule for manipulating the input, but rather a target format or template for the result' (p. 105). The authors comment that 'these templates were extremely detailed, reflecting only the most conservative generalizations of the model forms. That is, *the target templates encode everything that is true of examples already encountered*' (p. 105; italics added). This presumed 'over-specificity' (monosyllabicity, for example) meant that when longer words with distinct stress patterns were presented, participants had to make a choice as to which aspect of the template to model in their response. Critically, as indicated above, the priming effect on consonant-initial words of the prior processing of vowel-initial words meant that participants' on-line experience could alter their interpretation of the output template: 'The output template for the experiment is not necessarily frozen at the end of the training phase, but may also be affected by outputs produced during the test phase' (p. 108). This suggests that, as Thelen and Smith would also argue, *even adult representations are dynamic and subject to change with experience.*

Furthermore, the 'over-specificity' of the output format meant that, to accommodate longer outputs, some aspects of the templatic constraints had to be violated. As Pierrehumbert and Nair point out, the idea of constraint violation is now embraced by mainstream phonological theory. However, the constraints that they propose to account for their results are

> both stochastic and formative-specific, since the new infixes in the experiments have the phonological status of new formatives. Optimality Theory... provides no support for such constraints. Constraints are claimed to be universal... and non-stochastic... Furthermore, Optimality Theory draws a strong distinction between the grammar and the lexicon, with constraints residing in the grammar and not in the lexicon...   (p. 110)

Pierrehumbert and Nair approvingly mention Declarative Phonology (see now Coleman, Bethin, & John, 1998) as an approach that makes no such strong distinction and conclude that their results support the view that 'constraints and lexical items should be represented in the same way' (p. 110).

7.7 Adult and child templates, I

We have been describing templates in accordance with uses of the term in the literature on adult grammar. We now consider again in what sense these adult patterns may be taken to resemble child phonological templates. We have cited a number of definitions of templates that have been used in relation to adult grammar. In one of the earliest statements, McCarthy (1982) referred to the 'canonical patterns of morphemes' (p. 192); McCarthy and Prince (1995) referred with greater theoretical specificity to 'a fixed or invariant shape' consisting only of the 'authentic units of prosody' (p. 318). Good (2016) spoke broadly of 'a fixed linear structure' (p. 1) and 'the linear realization of a linguistic constituent...' (p. 7). Inkelas (2014) provided a more tightly defined characterization: 'Prosodic templates are morphological constructions... which directly constrain the phonological shape of the derived stem' (p. 84). All of these definitions bring out the syntagmatic nature of templates, although some have seen them as mainly phonological, others as mainly morphological, and yet others as specifically marking the phonology–morphology interface.

The templates we have used to illustrate these views also differ in their essentials. Some play an active role in grammatical processing while others reflect historical processes and are scarcely identifiable in synchronic alternations. Most specify the permitted length of either root or derived stem, in terms of moras or syllables; sometimes the position of stress or a particular tone pattern is also part of the specification (English comparative/superlative, Cupeño, Hausa). In only one case—that of certain verbal morphemes in Tiene—did the template also include segmental specification. Finally, in several cases the input to a particular morphological output already met the requirements of the template, so that no change was required between stem and output; we termed such instances 'selection', in contrast with the majority of cases, in which change to the base in the sequencing of segments, tones or syllables was needed to satisfy the templatic constraint ('adaptation').

Good (2016) comments, in relation to the discussion of child templates in Vihman and Croft (2007), that he would term these 'morphophonological' rather than phonological, 'since the relevant constraints apply at the level of the word, rather than a purely phonological unit' (p. 8). However, it is questionable to ascribe 'morpho[phono]logy' to child forms that as yet provide no evidence of analysis of words into smaller meaning-bearing units (or morphemes) or of integration into larger systems (such as paradigms), based on form–meaning relations. In fact, little morphological knowledge can typically be demonstrated in the period in which developmental templates are most often observed; instead, children sometimes treat (adult) morphological variation as phonological at this point (Peters & Menn, 1993; Vihman, 1996, p. 225). In other words, morphology has no status in the relevant developmental period, which often precedes any sign of its productive use. Thus in this period the word is the primary domain of infant production and thus of word-form retention or representation and access; early child phonology indeed operates at the level of the word.

A key point here is that adult grammars generally have little reason to create novel lexical forms; what is active in adult grammar is the use of productive processes to build larger meaningful constructions, particularly when the range of options is large enough to preclude the lexical option of listing. According to McCarthy & Prince (1995), templates involve a 'prosodic reparsing of a copy of the base' (p. 247). But how often do adults need to copy the base or map one form onto another, outside of an experimental study? The majority of examples in the literature involve reduplication, truncation, or non-concatenative morphology used to express particular grammatical meanings. In contrast, child templates may map input—or the child's intake of the input—to any of their output representations. Each word form must be learned; use of a template to supply one part of a novel form can lessen the burden on memory. Furthermore, in the period before morphological analysis begins to play a role the word is a basic or primitive unit for the child, an unanalysed whole (see Vihman, 2017).

The treatment of phonological templates in the adult-language literature is, as Good notes, generally posited in terms of universals: 'Available phonological templates are either drawn from a universal inventory ... or are highly constrained by universal phonological principles' (2016, p. 17). A central point of Prosodic Morphology is the limitation of prosodic constituents to minimum and maximum lengths as defined in terms of the putatively universal units of the prosodic hierarchy: mora, syllable, foot, and prosodic word; these units are claimed to provide a necessary and sufficient (universal) set for expressing the nature of prosodic constraints on morphology. These claims have provided a strong impetus for research in the field, an influence in some ways analogous to the effect of Chomsky's more radical claims, in 1965, as to the nature of language acquisition, which effectively launched the field of language acquisition.

However, typologists have criticized the 'universal principles' embedded in such widely used theoretical constructs as the prosodic hierarchy on the grounds that these principles are based on limited evidence, typically restricted to a relatively small sample of well-studied languages (Evans & Levinson, 2009; Schiering, Bickel, & Hildebrandt, 2010; see also Nichols, 2007). Furthermore, Inkelas (2014) notes at several points in her discussion of templates in adult grammar that the formal limitation of the descriptive language to a closed inventory of universal constituents does not do justice to the full range of phenomena actually observed in the world's languages. It does not appear to be the case, based on the available empirical evidence, that the 'authentic units' prescribed by the prosodic hierarchy can successfully account for any and all of the patterns that might be viewed as 'templatic'.

Similarly, attempts to trace stages of emergent knowledge in phonological development based on the prosodic hierarchy (e.g., Fikkert, 1994; Demuth, 1996) have not, on the whole, been convincing: The empirical data have not generally supported the assumption of either (i) a universal order of emergence of prosodic units or (ii) the existence of a fixed set of such units. Other factors— including ambient language effects, often seen as reducing to frequency effects— have been found to be equally or more important in shaping the course of development (see Kehoe & Stoel-Gammon, 1997, 2001; Demuth & Johnson, 2003; Taelman, 2004; Demuth, Culbertson, & Alter, 2006; Fikkert & Levelt, 2008). And as our surveys in Chapters 3–6 suggest, the patterning of templatic constraints arrived at by individual children, within and across languages, also offers little support to the notion of a closed universal inventory of possible constituents or word shapes. More specifically, a VCV pattern is clearly demon-strable in children learning a number of languages in which the onset consonant is less perceptually salient due to iambic patterning, as in French or Hebrew (Keren-Portnoy & Segal, 2016), or to medial geminate consonants, as in Finnish, Italian, or Hindi (Vihman & Croft, 2007); in Welsh, consonant lengthening under accent has the same effect (see Chapter 5). This casts doubt on the strong claims of Prosodic Morphology. In short, in neither adults nor children has a fixed set of constituents been found to express the full range of possibilities for linear com-bination that may be specified by templatic constraints.

Based on the evidence marshalled here, a key characteristic of child templates is that they are schematic patterns encompassing a whole functional unit—a whole word or remembered phrase, not individual segments or contiguous segmental sequences; their relation to the adult target forms from which they derive is holistic in the sense that some aspects of the adult word are represented, but not necessarily all aspects and not necessarily in the linear sequence found in the adult target form. The child data that provide the most convincing evidence of child systematization and organization involve both (pre-)selection of targets that constitute a good match to a child's existing production routines and adaptation of adult forms to fit the child's preferred patterns. Furthermore, we saw that in the most striking cases of template use segmental specification goes beyond global prosodic structure, establishing fixed consonantal (or, more rarely, vocalic) melodies. Our data set makes it clear that this characterization is valid not for one but for many children, learning a variety of languages and applying a small range of different prosodic structures.

We have observed no limitation of developmental templates to the 'authentic units of prosody'. It is surely possible to pick out instances in which these particular prosodic units play a role in the organization of phonological patterns for one child or another. However, our goal has been to identify, in a data-first or 'bottom-up' way, any kind of systematicity that the children may be inducing from the input and from their own output forms, without invoking prior (innate) access to specifically linguistic principles. That endeavour requires exhaustive analyses of each child's production at set points in time. The result here has been the heterogeneous collection of templatic patterns summarized in Table 5.33, some applying to monosyllables, others to disyllables, and yet others specifying segmentally constrained words of either word length.

To arrive at a deeper understanding of the function of templates in adults and children, however, we should expand our coverage to include 'language at play'. Purely lexical templatic patterns are often involved in hypocoristics and other colloquial, innovative uses, such as everyday slang; the patterning also extends to 'echo reduplication'. Here, as we shall see, the templatic constraints appear to signal the special character of a minor area of the lexicon and of derivational grammar.

8

Relation of child to adult templates, II
Language at play

Templates have been identified in lexical as well as in core grammatical domains. The lexical uses may be considered 'marginal', belonging to special registers or speech styles rather than to the linguistic resources (basic inflection, part-of-speech markers and so on) deployed in virtually every verbal interaction; the term 'extra-grammatical' is sometimes used for these phenomena (Doleschal & Thornton, 2000; Mattiello, 2013). However, the domains of lexical clipping, hypocoristic formation, and rhyming compounds, or echo-pairs, all allow scope for the creation of innovative lexical forms as they are deployed in informal situations, in communication with friends and family—that is, in insider or in-group talk.

Usage in these domains is also necessarily constrained by the phonology of the language; where innovative forms are involved, this creates a 'workspace' (or a 'field of play') for the speaker not entirely unlike that of the child and similarly subject to templatic constraints on whole-word forms. As Ronneberger-Sibold (1996) put it in her account of 'preferred shapes in German and French', encompassing clippings or shortenings and also acronyms pronounced as words (e.g., French *HLM* /aʃɛlɛm/, for *Habitation à Loyer Modéré* or 'rent-controlled housing'), these forms afford the speaker

> the rare opportunity to create new words unhampered by the constraints of the normal word-formation rules. The (almost) unique condition which these new words must fulfil is to be a practical tool for frequent use, i.e., they have to satisfy only the language users' needs for shortness, for ease of pronunciation and perception, and for distinctiveness. (p. 263)

This is the area that we consider here, under the rubric 'language at play', in the expectation that novel forms may reveal underlying synchronic patterns that will lend themselves to a more robust comparison with child phonological innovation than is possible with the often unproductive templates identified in core grammar. In fact, phenomena that fall under this general topic—including hypocoristics (e.g., Mester, 1991, on Japanese; Yip, 1992, on Chinese; Plénat, 1984, 1994 and Scullen, 1997, on French; Scheer, 2003, on Czech; studies of Australian English use this term for the category of short colloquial forms as a whole: see Simpson, 2006; Kidd, Kemp, & Quinn, 2011), language games and secret languages (e.g., Plénat, 1991,

Phonological Templates in Development. First edition. Marilyn May Vihman.
© Marilyn May Vihman 2019. First published 2019 by Oxford University Press.

1995), and echo words (e.g., Morin, 1972; Southern, 2005; Sóskuthy, 2012; see also the review in Inkelas, 2014)—have long been of interest to phonologists. Indeed McCarthy and Prince (1990) draw on several of these phenomena to illustrate and justify the principles of Prosodic Morphology. The three phenomena that we discuss at some length below are all based on spoken language. However, we will also briefly discuss an Australian English clipping construction (Spradling, 2016) that appears to have begun as a way of accommodating the character limits imposed by tweets and text messages; it is in current use in speech as well.

We start from the assumption that new word creation may reveal something more about the nature of template use in adults than we were able to discern in reviewing the core-grammar literature, given 'the rare opportunity' identified by Ronneberger-Sibold. In fact, other characteristics of such novel word formation that this investigator mentions also evoke the situation of the word-learning child. Ronneberger-Sibold points out that 'shortenings' normally arise in small groups of speakers defined by their common background and interests, where both high frequency of use and 'the desire of the members of the group to demonstrate that they are insiders' (1996, p. 268) are the key factors favouring novel formations. The requirement to maintain lexical contrast in order to ensure effective communication is typically minimal in these cases, given a common frame of reference among interlocutors. Maintenance of contrast is of especially little importance in the case of echo-pairs, given that the base form is present alongside the rhyme (cf. Southern, 2005: 'A crucial factor ... is the transparency of the echo-replacement and the continuing comprehensibility and availability to speakers of the original, undeformed base word', p. 15). Accordingly, phonological factors should be primary—just as they are with children in the early word-learning period, when in most cases family members or other 'insiders' likely to be attempting to converse with them can readily discern a child's intended meaning. Based on all this, novel lexical formations—often expressive of humour, irony, or other affective attitudes, many of them 'slang' terms—provide an ideal locus for making a comparison between adult language forms and child template use.

In this chapter we focus on a few cases of such inventive, colloquial, or slang usage, picking up on parallels with child templates that go somewhat beyond what we saw in Chapter 7. Our data are drawn primarily from the three languages with which the author has the greatest familiarity, English, Estonian, and French. For Estonian and French we provide as data a subset of colloquial forms with a long history but also a strong contemporary presence. In French, forms demonstrating these patterns have been documented for nearly 200 years; the earliest forms originated as student slang (though many of these are now archaic or simply old-fashioned sounding). The Estonian forms, which first attracted linguistic attention only in the 1990s, appear to be experiencing a current vogue, but some clearly date from early in the last century at the latest. For English we report on rhyming compounds, which have a recorded history of over 700 years; these forms remain highly popular in contemporary speech and fiction writing.

8.1 Clippings with suffixation: French short forms

Clipping and hypocoristic formation are closely related; the processes, at least in the languages under study here, are similar. However, personal names (particularly 'pet names' or diminutives) are far more readily deduced from context and may accordingly show more extreme adaptations than is practical for words used in more strictly referential contexts. Lists of the wide range of French hypocoristics reveal this quite clearly (e.g., Plénat, 1984, 1994; Scullen, 1997). We will first discuss the set of forms that account for the largest proportion of shortenings in French and will then consider more briefly the much-studied hypocoristics or pet-name formations.

The prosodic structure of French has been the subject of a good deal of controversy and theoretical debate, in relation to both adult and child phonology. A key issue in contemporary accounts is the question of whether French can properly be considered either an 'iambic' or a 'trochaic' language, or neither (Andreassen & Eychenne, 2013; Wauquier & Yamaguchi, 2013). Additionally, the minimal prosodic word has been defined in different ways; the questions of whether or not French is quantity-sensitive (in other words, whether or not the coda counts as a mora, meaning that syllables may have either one mora or two) and whether or not onset vowels may be extra-metrical (Plénat, 1994) have all been discussed and differently decided in different studies, sometimes by the same researcher at different times. On the other hand, accounts formulated within the theoretical framework of Natural Morphology disregard these issues, although their concerns are much the same (e.g., Ronneberg-Sibold, 1996, wants to determine, through comparison of French and German 'shortenings', whether 'language users have anything like "the phonetically ideal new root"' [p. 263]). As we will see, the forms in -o make up a large subset of French clippings or short forms and have been characterized with some success under the principles of Prosodic Morphology.[1]

---

[1] A far more limited but intriguing current French template takes the shape $rV_1\{CV_1\}_2$ (where the C may be a cluster). Plénat and Roche (2003) list eight such forms (in **bold face** below), commenting that 'some trisyllabic patterns can be found in French . . . , all colloquial or slang formations' (p. 2); at least two more are documented. A possible model is *rococo*, which appears to have shifted from its conventional reference to eighteenth-century architecture to the colloquial sense of 'old-fashioned, excessively ornamented'. **Raplapla(t)** 'tired' may derive from *(être) à plat* 'to be wiped out, bushed' (lit. 'flat'); *rototo* 'burp' (especially in reference to babies) is presumably based on *rot* 'a burp', which motivates the initial syllable, and **roudoudou** 'toffee; sweetie' has a plausible origin in *doux* 'sweet'; all of these would then be derived by adaptation of an existing lexical unit to the templatic pattern. However, the remaining forms—*radadas* 'sexual activity', *ragnagna* 'menstrual period', *rififi* 'trouble', *riquiqui* 'skimpy', *roploplo* 'breasts', *ronfionfion* 'blunt instrument'—defy easy ascription to any base word. (I am indebted to Olivier Bonami for drawing my attention to these forms.)

8.1.1 Templates in -o

French colloquial forms ending in -o, created by truncation from longer words with a medial -o, already began to attract academic interest 100 years ago (cf. Kjellman, 1920; Heinemann, 1953). According to French lexicography (see the website of the Centre National de Ressources Textuelles et Lexicales [CNRTL]: http://www.cnrtl.fr/, and also Antoine, 2000), many such forms were current already in the nineteenth century (e.g., kilo[gramme] [1835], [jardin] zoo [logique] 'zoo' [1847]; aristo[crate] [1849], photo[graphe] 'photographer' [1864], mélo[drame] 'melodrama' [1872]; philo[sophie] 'philosophy' [1880], métro[politain] 'subway, underground rail' [1891], porno[graphique] 'pornographic' [1893], restau[rant] 'restaurant' [1899]). Truncation or shortening has long been common in everyday usage in French: For example, ciné is attested in print for cinéma (itself a shortening of the full form, cinématographie) from 1905. But many short forms—like petit-déj[euner] 'breakfast', d'ac[cord] 'okay, agreed', sympa[thique] 'nice, agreeable', etc.—are only shortenings (Scullen, 1997, provides a 'representative sample' of nearly 300; Antoine, 2000, lists 911 truncated forms).

Weeda (1992, cited in Scullen, 1997) noted that forms ending in -o are the single most common French option for truncation, and also that the -o need not be an addition to a base form, as implied by the term 'suffix', but may instead derive from the base itself, as in the forms cited above (e.g., collabo < collabo[rateur] 'collaborator'); this would fit with the shortening pattern more generally. In other cases the -o suffix may replace an existing suffix (gaucho < gauch[-iste] +o 'leftist') or may simply be added to what is left after truncation, adapting the form to prosodic constraints on the output rather than either prosodic or morphological conditions on the longer base form (e.g., clando < cland[estin] +o 'secret, clandestine').

Both Weeda and Scullen define the -o in these forms as a suffix, due to the fact that many forms go beyond mere truncation, replacing other suffixes, occasionally augmenting rather than shortening, and so on. Weeda proposed the term 'brico-lant' for forms that are truncated and end in -o but undergo no 'suffixation', like kilo[gramme]; Ronneberger-Sibold (1996) further distinguishes the suffixed forms that follow regular distributional criteria, like gaucho, from 'pseudo-suffixed' forms that show various irregularities. Kilani-Schoch and Dressler (1993 [K-S&D]) provide extensive analysis of the forms that involve the addition of -o, arguing that the two types of o-forms are inherently different (the 'bricolants' being constrained purely phonologically, the derivation of the suffixed o-forms reflecting phonological, morphological, and lexical considerations) and should not be treated as aspects of a single phenomenon, despite the fact that native speakers do not distinguish between them. Here we will persist in using the terminology adopted in relation to child forms, dividing the -o forms into 'selected' (those with o in the base form) and 'adapted' (those lacking o in the base: See Appendices IIa and IIb, resp.²). For our purposes, the two types share the critical property of conforming to a single template.

It is important to note that many of the short forms in -*o* are marked 'colloquial' or 'slang' in on-line dictionaries; the informal usage—often with an added affective or pragmatically nuanced connotation, whether humorous, ironic, or, perhaps most typically, pejorative—is a critical part of their meaning. To illustrate this, note the following forms, all of which differ from their bases only by the change in final vowel from /i/ to /o/ (or truncation of /i/ and suffixation of /o/)³:

avaro 'hitch, personal setback' < *avarie* 'accident, loss' (1874)

garno 'furnished flat, cheap hotel room (used by prostitutes)' < garni 'furnished' (1867)

ramollo 'senile (or senile person); flabby, limp' < *ramolli* 'softened' (1923) (with a 'quite strong pejorative nuance', due to ending in -*o*: Antoine, 2000)

Most of these forms involve not only a move into colloquial register but also a shift to a purely metaphorical, largely negative connotation.

Many of the short forms show some degree of semantic shift away from the meaning of the base; this does not always involve a pejorative sense: The slang term *dispo* (< *disponible*), for example, is restricted to an immediate practical and personal meaning, 'available [to meet with you]', whereas the base form *disponible* has the broader sense not only of 'available' but also 'ready to listen, open-minded' and even (in relation to property) 'unappropriated'. Similarly, *raido* is used with the meaning 'tough, difficult (to do)', whereas the base form *raide* means 'stiff' and also 'steep (slope)'. (See Fradin & Kerleroux, 2009, for the proposal that, in general, derivation involves the singling out of just one sense from polysemic base lexemes.) However, the literal or referential meaning of the forms need not be different from that of their base; the suffixed form often seems to be used primarily to index the informal, colloquial or slang register that the speaker is affecting.⁴

Of the 318 forms for which dates are mentioned in our sources (64% of the total), about a third (99: 20% of all the *o*-forms listed in the appendices; 31% of the forms with dates) were recorded in dictionaries between the early 1800s and 1919, over a period of over 100 years. On the other hand, the same number (99) were first recorded in 1968 or later (i.e., 50 years ago, all but one—*Sarko* < *Sarkozy*,

---

² Note that the 340 *o*-forms provided by Antoine (2000) make up 68% of our total of almost 500 such forms. They include 87% of our 'selected' forms but only 50% of our adapted forms. This may reflect an increase in innovative *o*-forms over the last 20 years.

³ As in the Appendices, we provide year of earliest mention here, when available.

⁴ Kidd et al. (2011) come to much the same conclusion regarding the widespread use in Australian English (AusE.) of short forms, mainly in -*ie* or -*o*: 'Australian hypocoristics [i.e., short forms] do not alter the meaning of the base form ... Instead, as an informal register, their use has pragmatic effect ... [serving to] promote social cohesion between speakers' (p. 367). For experimental demonstration of this effect, see Kidd, Kemp, Kashima, & Quinn (2016).

Table 8.1 Short forms in -o: Length in syllables based on output form

	CV	CVCV	CVCVCV	CVCVCVCV	Total
select	9	181	58	7	255 (.51)
adapt	0	130	104	10	244 (.49)
	9 (.02)	311 (.62)	162 (.32)	17 (.03)	499

French president from 2007–12—recorded within the 30-year period prior to the publication of our three main sources (Kilani-Schoch & Dressler, 1993; Scullen, 1997; Antoine, 2000). Thus at some point in the mid-century, presumably based on an accumulation of *o*-forms in current use, the template increased in its power to attract novel forms, and these continue to be added (e.g., *déco/reco* < *déconnecté/ reconnecté* 'connected/disconnected [from the internet]'; *texto* 'text message').[5]

The pattern is a productive source of derived formations, marked for their stylistic value and the associated 'attitude', which may be characterized as one of light irony or pejorative implication (*accro* 'addict' < *accroché* 'attached', *mégalo* < *mégalomane* 'megalomaniac'). A semantically and pragmatically unrelated use of the form is to shorten the names of professions (which are often quite lengthy: *cardio* < *cardiologist* 'cardiologist', *ostéo* < *osthéopathe* 'osteopath', *stomato* < *stomatologue* 'dentist', and, with adaptation, *mécano* < *mécanicien* 'mechanic'). Several forms show not truncation but augmentation by addition of the suffix to a shorter form (e.g., *frèro* 'little brother' < *frère* 'brother'; *classico* < *classique* 'classic'; *duro* < *dur* 'difficult'; *raido* 'tough, hard to do' < *raide* 'stiff'), demonstrating that *pragmatic nuance* is sometimes the primary factor leading to 'short-form' use.

The 499 forms that we have identified, based on the literature (especially Kilani-Schoch & Dressler, 1993, and Scullen, 1997), web chats, dictionaries (primarily Antoine, 2000), on-line sources (such as the CNRTL), and personal experience, divide quite evenly into those that can and those that cannot be fully accounted for by shortening alone (51% selected, 49% adapted: see Apps. IIIa, IIIb; recall that 'selected' here refers to forms in which no new material is added to the base).

Table 8.1 shows the distribution by length in syllables (indicated by CV, CVCV, etc.) of the output forms listed in Appendix III(a, b). As with the child forms, we disregard the distinction between C and CC; in fact, there are some medial three-consonant clusters (*folklo* < *folklorique* 'eccentric, offbeat, weird', *monstrico* 'little monster' < *monstre* 'monster'). There are no word-final consonants as the forms end in -*o* by definition (although variants of several of them are sometimes written

---

[5] As evidence of the current productivity of these forms note this remark, made by a 16-year-old boy: *Celle là, il faut qu'elle arrête de mytho.* 'She's just got to stop lying.'—in which, remarkably, the short form *mytho* < *mythomane* 'fantasist, liar' is used as a verb with neither derivation nor inflection to accommodate French grammar. The same uninflected form appears after the hashtag in a subway poster advertising mobile-phone banking, #*zéro mytho*, presumably meaning 'no lies' or 'we can be trusted'. (I thank Olivier Bonami for both of these examples.)

with final -*s*; it is unclear just how often that /s/ is actually pronounced). Note also that while the vast majority of forms are derived from their bases through truncation of material that *follows* the segmental sequence preserved in the short form, a few are derived through apheresis, or truncation of material that *precedes* the sequence preserved in the short form (e.g., *bleau* < *Fontaine]bleau*; *fiot* /fjo/ < *ra]fiot* 'boat', *pédo* < *tor]pédo* 'torpedo'). All of these cases are 'selected' words, in which the apheresis appears to have resulted from opportunistic use of the syllable in /o/ from the source word to create a short form that satisfies the template. (In Appendix IIIa the truncated material is marked off with a square bracket; because the adapted forms often have a more complex relationship with the base, as we discuss and illustrate below, the truncated portion is not marked in Appendix IIIb.)

As can be seen in Table 8.1, more than half of the short forms are disyllabic (62%). Similarly, of the 99 forms that can be traced back over 100 years (i.e., prior to 1919: 42 selected, 57 adapted), 66% are disyllabic. For the sample as a whole, 58% of the disyllabic forms are selected, as against 36% of the trisyllabic forms; the corresponding proportions for the earliest recorded short forms are 52% selected disyllables vs. only 17% selected trisyllables. Disyllabic short forms have more often been selected, then, with simple truncation sufficient to yield a form fitting the template, but the selection for truncation of longer bases with a medial -*o*- has considerably increased over the past century.

More information about the history of these forms would be helpful, but we can see that speakers have long created trisyllabic short forms where they readily suggest themselves and perhaps also where a disyllabic form might be less immediately intelligible (*démago* < *démagogue* 'demagogue', *intello* < *intellectuel* 'intellectual'—in lieu of **démo, *into*); disyllabic and trisyllabic variants do sometimes co-occur (*familo/familisto* < *familistère* 'group housing', *moblo/mobilo* < *mobilisation* 'mobilization', *ordo/ordino* < *ordinateur* 'computer'). Note that the bases for selected forms are, on average, one syllable longer than the bases for adapted forms (3.87 vs. 2.73). This reflects the fact that while the selected forms are for the most part genuine shortenings or truncations, the adapted forms include both truncation and a variety of additions, as we discuss below (thus bases may be mono- or disyllabic). This is one of the points that Kilani-Schoch and Dressler bring out to distinguish the two types. We argue, however, that both types are channelled, or filtered (whether by selection or adaptation), to fit the same output template.

8.1.2 Analysis of adapted forms in -o

The identifying feature of the forms of interest is their common ending in -*o*; in addition, most of them involve truncation of a longer base. As discussed above, for the *selected* short forms no suffix need be invoked, strictly speaking, as the related base form already includes an *o* and that is the point at which the latter part of the word is normally cut off, *regardless of syllable structure or morphological constituency*: see, for example, *désinto < désintoxication*, cut off between nucleus and coda of the third syllable.

Adapted short forms involve not only shortening but also the addition of the suffix *-o*, if not further changes to the truncated form itself (e.g., *apéro < apér[itif]* 'a drink before a meal'; *congélo < congél[ateur]* 'freezer'). The further changes include reduplication, syncope, and, in several cases, the addition of a consonant or cluster not warranted by the base form itself.[6] We list here all of the formal changes that we are aware of; they affect 103 word forms altogether (42% of the adapted sample, 21% of the full collection). Recall that the final *-s* included in the spelling of some o-forms may or may not be pronounced.

(1) Reduplication (N=10)
   bobo < bourgeois-bohème 'a bourgeois trying to pass as a bohemian'
   coco < communiste 'communist'. Also used for *commandant* 'commander',
      cocaïne 'cocaine', *[oeuf à la] coque* 'soft-boiled egg'. (These are listed and
      counted separately.)
   gogo 'credulous person, sucker' *< gober* 'to trick' (this is a rare case of
      part-of-speech change in *o*-form derivation). Also used for *gozier* 'throat'.
   jojo < joli(e) 'pretty'
   lolo < lorette 'beautiful woman, courtesan (slang)'
   zozo 'simpleton, clown, weirdo' *< Joseph* /ʒoˈzɛf/; documented, 1894
   (Cf. also baby talk terms not included in the sample: *bobo* 'a small hurt'
      [used in print, 1869; the source word is not obvious]; *dodo < do[rmir]*
      'to sleep'; *lolo < l'eau* /lo/ 'water' [also used for *lait* /le/ 'milk']; *nounou <*
      nourrice 'nurse'; *popot < pot* /po/ 'potty'; *toto < auto* /oto/ 'car'; *zozio*
      /zozjo/ *< les oiseaux* /[lezwa]zo/ 'birds'; *zozo < les oreilles* /[le]zo[rej]/
      'ears'.)

(2) Syncope and other form-medial omissions (N = 9, if the forms in fn. 6 are
   included here)
   biclo < bicyclette 'bicycle' /bi.[si.]kl[ɛt]/ + /o/
   civlo < civil 'civic' /si.v[i]l/ + /o/
   moblo < (garde) mobile 'militia' /mɔ.b[i]l/ + /o/
   moblo < mobilisation 'mobilization' /mɔ.b[i.]l[i.za.sjɔ̃]/ + /o/
   réglo 'straight, law-abiding' *< régulier* 'regular': /re.g[u.]l[je]/ + /o/

(3) Augmentation with -o (N=30)

In words like *franco* and *tardo*, the consonant preceding the suffix is silent in the likely base form. Its use in the short form may have been suggested by other forms

---

[6] At least four forms have /o/ somewhere in the source word but are considered adapted here because truncation + /o/ affords a more straightforward analysis: *cello < cell[uloid]*; *dico < dic[tionnaire]* 'dictionary', *exhibo < exhib[itionniste]* 'exhibitionist, flasher'; *réviso < révis[ionniste]* 'revisionist'.

of the word, as indicated for *tardo*; alternatively, the consonant might simply be due to historicizing orthography, as is more plausible for *blanco, franco*. Several such cases can also be found in the next subsection. (For evidence of the relative psycholinguistic effects of morphological vs. orthographic relatedness in French, see Pacton et al., 2018.) Note also that at least two of these short forms are most naturally derived from the feminine form of the adjective (*follo, froido*), although derivations based on the masculine form are the general rule (CNRTL).

> *blanco* < *blanc* 'white' /blɑ̃/ + /ko/?
>
> *bobino* < *bobine* 'watch (slang)'
>
> *calmos* < *calme* 'calm'
>
> *cantalo(s)* < *cantal* 'a type of cheese'
>
> *chemino(t)* < *chemin (de fer)* 'railroad worker'
>
> *chéro(t)* < *cher* 'expensive'
>
> *chicos* < *chic* 'elegant'
>
> *classicos* < *classique* 'classic'
>
> *coolos* < *cool* 'calm' (English loan)
>
> *débilos* < *débile* 'idiot, idiotic'
>
> *dingo* < *dingue* 'crazy'
>
> *duro* < *dur* 'hard'
>
> *follo* < *folle* 'crazy, f.'
>
> *franco* /fʁɑ̃ko/ < *franchement* 'frankly' /fʁɑ̃[ʃmɑ̃]/ + /ko/; cf. *franc* + V-onset word, which creates a liaison in /k/: e.g., *si vous voulez mon franc avis* /fʁɑ̃kavi/ 'if you want my honest opinion...' (the CNRTL suggests that the form is influenced by the Italian loanword, *franco* 'free of charge')
>
> *frèro* 'little brother' < *frère* 'brother'
>
> *froido* < *froide* 'cold, f.' /fʁwad/
>
> *légitimo* < *légitime* 'legitimate'
>
> *mésigo, tésigo* <*mézigue, tézigue* /mezig/, /tezig/ 'I, you (sg., informal)'. The base forms are documented in a slang dictionary of 1827 and have identifiable origins dating back to the sixteenth century (see *mézigue*, http://www.cnrtl.fr)
>
> *mollo* 'softly, gently' < *molle* 'soft, lacking energy'
>
> *muflo* < *mufle* 'boor, lout'
>
> *musico(s)* 'musician' < *musique* 'music'
>
> *nisco* < German *nix* (K-S&D) or *nichts* 'nothing'
>
> *raido* 'difficult to do' < *raide* 'stiff'
>
> *ringardos* < *ringard* 'tacky, out of fashion'
>
> *serbo* < *Serbe* 'Serbian'
>
> *tardo* < *tard* 'late (adv.)' /taʁ/; cf. *tarder* /taʁde/ 'to be late', *tardif*/-ve 'late (adj., m/f.)'
>
> *texto* < *text* 'text message'
>
> *tracos* < *trac* 'stage fright'
>
> *turco* < *turc* 'Turk'

(4) Addition of a consonant before *-o*, creating a $-CC_0V$ suffix (N = 58)

This is the largest category; several distinct suffixes occur. However, the forms in /Co/ cannot be accounted for in any unified way. In some cases, as indicated above, the consonantal onset to the suffix appears to have been suggested by other forms of the word (cf. *clodo, hosto, médico*). But many others—especially those making use of /l/—remain a puzzle.

Several forms take the suffix *-go*, some with locational or directional meaning. In addition, there are proper names of places or identities (nationalities, origins) in /(i)ko/ or /(i)go/.

/(i)ko/, /(i)go/
icigo < ici 'here' /isi/ + /go/ (with augmentation)
labago < là-bas 'over there' /laba/ + /go/ (with augmentation)
lago < là 'there' /la/ + /go/ (with augmentation)

Espago, Espingo < Espagne 'Spain' /ɛspa[ɲ]/ + /go/, /ɛsp[aɲ]/ + /ɛ̃go/
Versigo > Versailles /vɛʀs[aj]/ +/igo/

alsaco < Alsace, alsacien 'Alsace, Alsatian' /alza[s]/, /alza[sjɛ̃]/ + /ko/
arbicot < arabe 'Arab' /aʀ[a]b/ + /iko/ (with syncope and also augmentation)
belgico < belge 'Belgian' /bɛlʒ/ + /iko/ (with augmentation); cf. *(la) Belgique* 'Belgium'
corsico < corse 'Corsican' /kɔʀs/ + /iko/ (with augmentation)
italgo < Italie, italien 'Italian' /ital[i]/, /ital[jɛ̃]/ + /go/ (from 1901)
parigo < parisien 'Parisian' /paʀi[zjɛ̃]/ + /go/
prusco < prussien 'Prussian' /pʀys[jɛ̃]/ + /ko/
romanigo < romanichel 'gypsy' /ʀomani[ʃɛl]/ + /go/
rusco < russe 'Russian' /ʀys/ + /ko/ (with augmentation)

The remaining forms, which are more diverse in function, also reflect a mix of truncation and augmentation along with the suffixation of -o.

/ʒo/
l'airjo 'unsettled, undecided' < *en l'air* 'in the air', fig. /[ɑ̃]lɛʀ/ + /ʒo/
arjo < en arrière 'behind' (in time or place) /[ɔ̃n]aʀ[jɛʀ]/+ /ʒo/
dargeot, derjo < derrière 'bum, butt' /dɛʀ[jɛʀ]/+ /ʒo/
derjo < derrière 'behind' /dɛʀ[jɛʀ]/+ /ʒo/
verjo < verni 'varnished' /vɛʀ[ni]/+ /ʒo/

/(s)to, do/
clodo < clochard 'tramp' /klo[ʃaʀd]/; cf. *clocharde* 'bum, f.', *clochardiser* 'to live like a tramp'
coinsto < coin 'corner': /kwɛ̃/ + /sto/
crado < crasseux 'filthy' /kʀa[sø]/ + /do/
cuisto < cuisinier 'cook' /kwiz[inje]/ + /to/
curetot < curé 'priest' /kyʀ[e]/+ /to/
gauldo < Gauloise 'cigarette brand' /gol[waz]/ + /do/
frometot < fromage 'cheese' /fʀɔm[aʒ]/ + /to/

hosto < hôpital 'hospital' (/s/ based on historical root *hos-*, as in *hospice?*)

obligado > obligatoirement 'obligatorily' /ɔbliga[twarmɛ̃]/ (influenced by Spanish, with the support of the template?)

pristo < prisonnier 'prisoner' /priz[onje]/ + /to/

proto < proviseur 'lycée director' /pʀo[vizør]/ + /to/

/(i)ko/, /go/

These suffixes—together with those referring to places and identities—account for 30 of the 58 adapted forms with added consonant. There is orthographic <*c*> or <*g*> (but phonological /s/ or /ʒ/) in several of these forms, with /(i)ko/ or /(i)go/, resp., in the corresponding suffixes; this suggests likely influence of spelling on the short form—although the phonological context is also relevant, dictating voiceless stop after voiceless consonant (as in *censco*, *pensco*), voiced stop after vowel or sonorant (*auxigot*, *mendigo*). Uncertainty as to choice of suffix results in the co-existence of alternates such as *pharmaco/go*, *rhumaco/go*, *robico/go*, where *pharmaco*, at least, could be expected to prevail, in accord with the ending -*cien* in the base.

auxigot < auxiliaire 'prisoner-aide, trusty' /ɔksi[ljɛʀ]/ + /go/

censco < censeur 'censor' /sɑ̃s[œʀ]/ + /ko/

chirurgo < chirurgien 'surgeon' /ʃiryr[ʒjɛ̃]/ + /go/

frigo < Frigidaire 'refrigerator' (brand name) /fʀi[ʒidɛʀ]/ + /go/

fromego < fromage 'cheese' /fʀɔm[aʒ]/ + /go/

médico < médecin 'doctor' /mɛd[sɛ̃]/ + /iko/ (cf. *médical* 'medical', *médicament* 'medicine')

mendigot < mendiant 'tramp' /mɛd[jɛ̃]/ + /igo/

méningo 'person suffering from meningitis' < *méningite* 'meningitis' /menɛ̃[ʒit]/ + /go/

milico < milicien 'national guard' /mili[sjɛ̃]/ + /ko/

monstrico < monstre 'monster' /mɔ̃stʀ/ + /iko/ (with augmentation)

pensco < pensionnaire 'boarder, lodger' /pɑ̃s[jɔnɛʀ]/ + /ko/

pharmaco, pharmago < pharmacien 'pharmacist' /farma[sjɛ̃]/ + /ko/ or /go/

rhumago < rhumatisme 'rhumatism' /ʀyma[tism]/ + /go/

robico, robigo < robinet 'faucet' /ʀɔbi[nɛ]/ + /ko/ or /go/

saligot < salaud 'swine' (as metaphorically applied to people) /sal[o]/ + /go/

sergo < sergent 'sargeant' /sɛʀ[ʒɑ̃]/ + /go/

/l/

Alforlo < Maison(s)-Alfort /alfɔʀ/ + /lo/

amerlo < américain 'American' /amɛʀ[ikɛ̃]/ + /lo/

artiflo < artilleur 'artillery man' /aʀti[jœʀ[/ + /flo/

dirlo 'director (of a school or hotel)' < *directeur* 'director' /diʀ[ɛktœʀ]/ + /lo/

fromlo < fromage 'cheese' (see also *fromego*, above)

gourdiflo < gourde 'idiot' /guʀd/ + /iflo/

invalo < *invitation* 'invitation' /ɛ̃v[it]a/ + /lo/
mercelo < *mercier* 'haberdasher' /mɛʀs[je]/ + /lo/
travelo < *travestie* 'transvestite' /tʀavɛ[sti]/ + /lo/
virolo < *virage* 'bend in the road' /viʀ[aʒ]/ + /o/ + /lo/
/j/
coffiot < *coffre-fort* /kɔf[ʀfɔʀ]/ + /jo/
hiviot < *hiver* 'winter' /iv[ɛʀ]/ + /jo/

Scullen (1997) undertakes a thoroughgoing analysis of a sample of about 1000 French words in a range of non-standard categories: short forms in -*o* alongside other abbreviations, acronyms, compounds, hypocoristics, reduplications, echo words, and language games. Her goal is to explore the fit of the French data with the principles of Prosodic Morphology. She finds that a number of adjustments are needed, including application of the principle of the 'loose minimal word' that Itô and Mester (1992) invoke to account for certain phenomena in Japanese.

Briefly, Scullen extends the possible word types by allowing (i) the iambic foot (the minimal word in French, based on Scullen's evidence and arguments) to be supplemented by (ii) a 'loose' iambic foot (an iambic foot followed by an unfooted syllable) and (iii) 'compound words' made up of two feet ('maximum binary' foot structure). With these additions, Scullen finds that the morphologically innovative words in her sample largely conform to the principles. More specifically, 97% of the short forms in her large sample and 100% of the reduplicated forms (p. 95) conform to the requirement that the output constitute 'a well-formed Prosodic Word of restricted length' (pp. 71f.)—i.e., one of the three word types mentioned above, never exceeding two iambic feet.

Scullen emphasizes the point made earlier, that the systematicity of these short forms cannot be found in the input or in its mapping to the output, neither of which follows any clear principles. Instead, it is only the output form whose patterning systematically adheres to the formal requirements: maximally one or two iambic feet, where the second syllable of either foot may be 'heavy' (closed with a coda consonant), but a word can include no more than two feet or four moras.

All of the derivation types in -*o* included in our sample are shown in Table 8.2, along with the prosodic analysis of foot types, following Scullen. The types that conform to Scullen's constraints, including the prosodic length limit, are in **bold face**.

It is clear from Table 8.2 that the vast majority of forms in our sample (97%) conform to the principles Scullen has set out, based on previous work in Prosodic Morphology but with adjustments for the specific characteristics of the French data. In fact, 84% fit either an iambic foot (LL or 'light-light': CoVCoV) or an iambic foot with one unfooted syllable ([H]L, [LL]L); only 3% fall into the last single-foot option, [LH]L, while 10% are best analysed as made up of two feet. Just 2% of the total sample—9 selected monomoraic CV forms (like *pro* < *professionel*

Table 8.2 Prosodic analysis of forms in -o

Prosodic structure	Select			Adapt			Total	prop.
	Example	N	prop.	Example	N	prop.		
L	pro	9	0.05		0	n/a	9	0.02
[LL]	**mytho**	138	0.55	sado	801	0.33	219	0.44
[H]L	**perso**	41	0.16	bolcho	49	0.20	90	0.18
[LL]L	**collabo**	40	0.15	socialo	71	0.29	111	0.22
[LH]L	**aristo**	6	0.02	anarcho	11	0.05	17	0.03
[H][LL]	**magneto**	13	0.05	aspiro	21	0.09	35	0.06
[LL][LL]	**endocrino**	4	0.02	capitalo	8	0.03	12	0.02
[LL][H]L	intradermo	1	0.00	familisto	1	0.00	2	0.00
[H][H]L	opthalmo	1	0.00	Alforlo	1	0.00	2	0.00
[H][LL]L	porte-hélico	1	0.00	accélero	1	0.00	2	0.00
[LL][H][LL]	sténodactylo	1	0.00		0	n/a	1	0.00
		255			244		499	

'professional') and a handful of over-long forms—fail to conform to any of the expected shapes. Thus it is safe to say that the principles of Prosodic Morphology, under a loose interpretation, characterize the data very well.

Scullen draws some additional conclusions about her data set as a whole, based on the prosodic analysis. First, she notes that several forms show variability, with different outcomes of truncation, although there is far less variation in the subset of words derived with -o. What is more striking and more critical for interpreting the derivation process, however, is the impossibility of predicting from a standard or base form just what the short form will be; Japanese also has clippings not predictable from the shape of the input form. Scullen argues that this is evidence that the clippings in both languages are lexical, not morphological; this is why she proposes that the template be viewed as serving as a (lexical) 'filter' rather than a (morphological) mapping target.

The short forms could equally well be interpreted in terms of Bybee's (2001) 'product-oriented schema', which 'generalizes over forms of a specific category, but does not specify how to derive that category from some other', in contrast to a 'source-oriented schema', which 'act[s] on a specific input to change it in well-defined ways into an output of a certain form' (p. 126; see also Kidd et al., 2011, who illustrate how Bybee's lexical network model of morphology could accommodate the analysis of short forms in Australian English). As Bybee points out, templatic schemas are generally 'product-oriented' and thus allow for speaker creativity in deriving the output form from any particular input.

Turning to our primary concern with possible parallels with template use in children at the early stages of phonological development, the emphasis on the output shape corresponds well to the child data that we have described. There too the mapping is not always reliable (although it is sometimes possible to predict how a child will say a new word: See Menn, Schmidt, & Nicholas, 2013). That is, a child's application of a template tends not to be entirely systematic, even at a single point in time; in many cases the mapping varies from one production to another (see Chapter 6 and Appendix IIb for examples from Priestly, 1977). Generally speaking, then, child template use reflects a process similar to what we see here in the French short forms in -*o*. There is an 'input' (for the French adult, this is the base; for the child it is the adult target word) and an output. The output form is more constrained than the base, with *prosodic aspects typically fixed* (length in syllables or in feet and moras, with some optionality). *Segmental aspects may also be specified*, such as the final *o* or the more extended suffix in the case of French adapted forms. In the case of the children, a medial or final consonant may be specified, as well as a discontinuous melody—that is, a consonantal or vocalic sequence. This is reminiscent of Semitic root-and-pattern templatic morphology but has no analogy in (adult) French short forms.

The functions of adult and child templates are clearly different: The child is primarily concerned with producing adult-like forms, with accuracy less critical than a drive, in the period of most intense template use, to increase lexical diversity in the face of limited phonological resources. The template provides support not only for production per se but also for the registering and retention of new representations and for access to these representations in the moment of use.

As mentioned above, Ronneberger-Sibold (1996) sees the adult language user as having three 'needs' in creating abbreviated forms, 'shortness,…ease of pronunciation and perception, and…distinctiveness' (p. 263). Adherence to the prosodic patterning of the ambient language or broadly 'universal' pattern-ing can be taken to satisfy the need for 'ease…'; this is nicely captured by the notion of the 'prosodic minimal word' and the principles of Prosodic Morphology. Adults have an additional interest in marking their speech as belonging to the informal register by using 'breezy' word forms that are typically quicker to say than the full forms; the truncation process in itself lends an ironically dismissive or humorous twist by dropping some of the expected segmental material.

8.1.3 Hypocoristics

Hypocoristics, also known as pet names or nicknames, are common cross-linguistically and are often arrived at by truncation, although suffixing (and thus lengthening) with a diminutive marker is common as well (e.g., French *Paula* > *Paulette*; in Bulgarian, *Mahaela* > *Mihaelka, Radostina* > *Radostinka* for females,

Momchil > Momchicho, Bogdan > Bogdancho for males[7]). In French they are highly varied in pattern, with multiple alternative forms of the same name, although any one individual is likely to be known by only one or two of them. It was possible to find one or more variant short forms for 156 different French first names by drawing again on the existing literature, the internet and personal experience (see Appendix IV). Scullen (1997) lists a 'representative sample' of 191 'reduplicated hypocoristics', including forms that are only partially reduplicated— i.e., with vowel or consonant harmony or reduplication of the onset syllable—as well as fully reduplicated forms, with or without a final consonant. Our sample overlaps somewhat with her fully and partially reduplicated forms; the combined list would reach well over 300 forms. This indicates how extensive the list must be, although many of the variants provided in earlier studies are rare or non-existent in contemporary usage. Variants for a single name can range as high as 16 or more (e.g., for *Dominique*) and reflect at least a dozen different phonological patterns; for the 156 names we count 276 short forms (treating all variants of each base name separately). Beyond the patterns we note below our sample also includes 16 hypocoristics created by addition of the suffix *-ou*, with or without truncation or reduplication of some part of the base (e.g., *Alain > Alinou, Béatrice > Batou, Brigitte > Brijou, Bijou* ['jewel'], *Didier > Didou, Anne > Nanou*), or both (*Edouard > Doudou, Isabelle > Zazou* [both with apheresis as well]).

Table 8.3 categorizes the variants included in our sample in terms of prosodic units (left-most column), template shape (i.e., output shape, using the terminology of phonological development where relevant: e.g., consonant harmony, reduplication) and type frequency within the sample, followed by examples; for the full list, see Appendix IV. Several examples are given for the more frequently used patterns, to illustrate the variability in the relationship between short form and base. For example, the closed monosyllable *Tophe* derives from the final syllable of its base form, *Christophe, Gus* from the middle syllable of *Augustin* and *Chris* from the onset syllable of *Christelle*. Both *Guitte* and *Mèche* draw on non-adjacent segments to create the monosyllabic hypocoristic. We discuss in more detail below the most heavily used category, fully reduplicated disyllables.

As is evident from Table 8.3, the basic [LL] iambic foot structure characterizes by far the most hypocoristics (70%); fully or partially reduplicated forms account for 47% of the variants overall. Beyond that, with the sole exception of the three open monosyllabic forms, all the structures in our sample fit Scullen's proposed prosodic word analysis. The fully reduplicated disyllables are the single most common category, accounting for over a third of the names in our sample. These forms vary considerably in the ways in which they relate to their bases; as with the short forms in *-o*, there is no way to predict which types of hypocoristic will be used for a given base name.

---

[7] I thank Kremena Koleva for supplying these examples.

Table 8.3 French hypocoristics: Analysis into prosodic words and template type

	Template	N	prop.	Name	Short form
[L]	Open monosyllable	3	.01	*Dominique*	Do
[H]	Closed monosyllable	15	.07	*Augustin* *Christelle* *Christophe* *Marguerite* *Michelle*	Gus Chris Tophe Guitte Mèche
	Closed monosyllable, consonant harmony	3	.01	*Benoit* *Eveline,* *Jaqueline*	Bèbe /bɛb/ Nine /nin/
[LL]	Reduplicated disyllable	77	.34	*Brigitte* *Carole*	Bibi, Bribri Coco
	Consonant harmony	18	.08	*Fabrice* *Marie-Emilie*	Babi Mami
	Vowel harmony	14	.06	*Bénédicte* *Geneviève*	Béné Givi, Geuneu
	No harmony	50	.22	*Alfred* *Elisabeth*	Frédo Lisa
[LH]	Closed disyllable	15	.07	*Alphonsine* *Jacqueline*	Phonsine Kiline
[HH]	Closed 1st and 2nd syllables	2	.01	*Ernestine*	Nestine
[LH]	Partial reduplication	31	.14	*Alfred Marc*	Féfed Mamarc
	Total	228			

Table 8.4 shows the relationships of short form to base in the 77 phonological variants of fully reduplicated hypocoristics: They are instructively similar to the mappings from target to child template in our cross-linguistic data, as we discuss below. Note that, in the case of final syllable reduplication, word-final consonants are deleted wherever they occur (e.g., *Odile* /didi/, *Paulette* /popo/). Cluster reduction and denasalization occur variably as options in the reduplicated short-form names and may be seen in only one of the two syllables of the short form; we combine for the count any variants of a name that fit within the same category in Table 8.4, like the three forms of *Claude*.

(A) The *monosyllabic* first names are unproblematic: The reduplicated short form may or may not include an initial cluster but omits the coda and reduplicates the CC_0V sequence.

(B) Perhaps surprisingly, given French final-vowel lengthening under accent, names in the largest category (13 fully reduplicated disyllables) retain and repeat the *first syllable*, omitting whatever follows (i.e., one or more syllables: cf. *Frédéric*).

(C) Another 14 forms retain a *later syllable*, final in disyllabic names, either second or third in trisyllabic names (cf. *Dominique, Augustin*).

Table 8.4 Reduplicated hypocoristic variants: Relationships to the base name form[1] (Number: percentage of all fully reduplicated forms)

Relationship to base form	Base name form	Variants	Base name form	Variants
A. Truncate monosyllabic base (3: 4%)	Claire /klɛr/	/keke/	Pierre /pjɛr/	/pjepje/, /pepe/
	Claude /klod/	/kloklo/, /kloko/, /koko/		
B. Retain 1st syllable (33: 43%)	Brigitte /brizit/	/bribri/, /bibi/	Lilliane /liljan/	/lili/
	Chantal /ʃãtal/	/ʃaʃa/	Paulette /polɛt/	/popo/
	Fréderic /fredərik/	/frefe/	Sophie	/soso/
C. Truncate first syllable(s) (14: 18%)	André /ãdre/	/dede/	Eveline /ɛvlin/	/vivi/
	Augustin /ogystɛ̃/	/tɛ̃tɛ̃/	François /frãswa/	/swaswa/, /sasa/
	Dominique /dominik/	/mimi/	Romuald /romɥald/	/mymy/
D. Truncate, metathesize (27 [including D$_1$ and D$_2$]: 35%)	Anne /an/, Christianne /kristjan/	/nana/	Lucienne /lüsiɛn/	/nene/
	Carole /karɔl/	/koko/	Madeleine /madlɛn/	/nana/
	Hughes /üg/, Hughette /ügɛt/	/gygy/	Thérèse /terɛz/	/zeze/
D$_1$. *Select* to CiCi (10: 13% of total in D)	Angeline /ãʒlin/	/ʒiʒi/	Jaqueline /ʒaklin/	/kiki/
	Béatrice /beatris/	/bibi/	Marie /mari/	/mimi/
	Bénédicte /benedikt/	/bibi/	Rachide /raʃid/	/riri/
	Catherine /katrin/	/titi/	Valérie /valri/	/lili/
	Félix /feliks/	/fifi/	Yves /iv/	/vivi/
D$_2$. *Adapt* to CiCi (3: 4% of total in D)	Daniel /danjɛl/	/nini/	Pierre /pjɛr/	/pipi/
	Geneviève /ʒønvjɛv/	/ʒiʒi/		

Note:
[1] Note that some vowel changes reflect French phonological alternation between mid-vowels in open vs. closed syllables (e.g., *Carole* /karɔl/ > *Coco* /koko/, *Pierre* /pjɛr/ > *Pépé* /pepe/).

(D) This category of forms, which shows only a *holistic* relation to the base, is the second most common of the reduplicated name variants (35%): These names show a kind of reorganization of the base-form segmental sequence that is rare in adult word derivation.[8] The names are derived in various ways, but most include only segments found in the base form, combined and repeated; the output syllable itself does not occur as such in any of the base forms. Two are based on monosyllabic VC names (*Anne, Hughes*); *Christianne* and *Huguette* may be influenced by the existence of the forms /nana/ and /gygy/ for *Anne* and *Hughes*, respectively. Other names in this category must be analysed as showing metathesis after truncation (*Lucienne* > -*enne* > *néné*, *Thérèse* > -*èse* > *zézé*) or more radical recombination (*Eveline* > /veve/, *Madeleine* > /nana/, reminiscent of the child form [nana] < *Annalena*, reported in Elsen, 1996; see also Vihman & Croft, 2007).

(D_1, D_2) These subcategories of D, accounting for about half the forms, include names that fit the more fully specified template CiCi. D_1 lists the selected forms, with base names that include both the consonant and an accented rhyme in /i/; these conform to the general description of D. D_2 lists three adapted forms in which the base provides only the consonant of the output, not the vowel, so that these forms go beyond the 'recombination' seen in the remaining 24 forms.

Finally, we can consider the 31 partially reduplicated forms, all of which take the form CVCVC. The reduplicated syllable may draw on the final syllable of the base (*Adolphe* > *Dodolphe*, *Marcel* > *Cécel*), or on the sole syllable of a monosyllabic name (*Paul* > *Popol*); the coda is always omitted in the reduplicant. The consonant of the reduplicant is sometimes taken from a non-final syllable (*Dominique* > *Mimique*). In most cases the vowel of the final syllable is mapped to the output; of the five words that stand as exceptions to this pattern, four have /a/ as the vowel of the reduplicant, retained from the pre-final syllable (*Bernadette* > *Nanette*, *Isabelle* > *Babelle*); all of them have the melody /a...e/, suggesting another possible templatic influence on hypocoristics.

As mentioned above, Scullen (1997) focuses on prosodic analysis of the various word types she covers in her thesis; this is also the focus of most of the work on French hypocoristics as well as on clipped forms (e.g., Plénat, 1994). However, the nature of the segmental derivation of short form from base is also of interest. Specifically, the way these pet names are derived is more similar to the child adaptations of adult word forms than any other derivation we have so far encountered—variously providing examples of harmony, or partial reduplication, reduplication, metathesis, holistic adaptation based on non-contiguous segments and mapping to a fixed template based on only a minimal 'hook' in the base form.

The similarity of these hypocoristics to child forms may not be accidental: This is one area where child forms may influence adult language, as children struggle to

---

[8] Note that some of the baby-talk reduplications mentioned above, under Template in -*o*, are similarly formed (e.g., *zozo* < *les oreilles*).

produce their own or their siblings' names; their efforts often appeal to adults in the family and may thus take root.[9] By extension, the reduplicated baby-talk forms mentioned earlier (*dodo, jojo*) could have formed in the same way. Although it is unlikely that all of these forms derive from specific children's mispronunciations of the target name, the patterning may have had its source in individual instances of this kind, with subsequent generalization to other names.

We should also note the presence of a relatively high proportion of short forms in -*o* among the hypocoristics. Where these form part of the base (as in *Carole* [koko], *Théophile* [toto]), the /o/ could be expected—although the part of the base name to be retained in the short form may well be influenced by the presence in that part of a favoured segment (e.g., the three monosyllabic CV hypocoristics in our base, specifically, those fitting the prosodically ill-formed monomoraic word shape, all take the form Co [*Do, Flo, Jo*]; 18 of the 77 fully reduplicated variants are of the form CoCo [23%]). More interestingly, 17 (34%) of the no-harmony disyllables end in -*o*; half of these lack an /o/ in the base form; instead, the -*o* is suffixed, with either truncation (*Frédo,* for both *Alfred* and *Fréderic, Madeau* < *Madeleine*) or augmentation (*Jacquot, Jeannot, Marco, Paulo, Pierrot*) to the stem. These are precisely the patterns found in adapted short forms in -*o* in the lexicon examined above. (For comparison, disregarding the CiCi forms in the subcategories of D, only two forms in /i/ lack a model in the base: *Danielle > Dani* and *Éléonore > Eli*; no other vowels participate in this type of derivation.)

8.2 Clippings with suffixation: Estonian short forms and hypocoristics

The Estonian short forms to be presented here are similar to the French forms in -*o* not only phonologically, as clippings or shortened forms of base words, but also pragmatically, in their general domain of use as colloquial terms mostly shared among members of the same social subgroup. These forms have been the focus of fewer prior investigations than the French forms; the material available is thus necessarily more limited. Perhaps not coincidentally but as a reflection of a shift in theoretical interest to the whole-word or syntagmatic level of structure, the existing literature on Estonian slang forms dates from the 1990s, when analogous French studies became more common as well. Our sample was initially based on informal observation, followed by research in two on-line dictionaries with search engines and a small informal survey (Vihman & Vihman, 2017); this was then supplemented by forms reported by Loog (1991), Tender (1994, 1996), Hennoste (2000), Hussar and Faster (2015), Kasik (2015), and Pari (2016).

---

[9] I thank Virve-Anneli Vihman for proposing this interpretation.

To briefly illustrate the pattern to be described, consider the following forms: *õps* /ˋ ʊps/ < *õpetaja* /ˋʊpɛtaja/ 'teacher', *õlts* /ˋʊlts/ < *õlu* 'beer', *vants* /ˋvants/ < *vanaisa* 'grandfather'. Altogether we have identified 118 such short forms, of which 93 (79%) are adapted (Appendix V). In the Appendix we also include 43 hypocoristics, mostly from Hussar and Faster (2015); all of these are adapted to fit the template. As the hypocoristics are formed in the same way as the other short forms, we include the two sets here in a single analysis.

It is possible to distinguish Estonian short forms derived from the native vocabulary, like *jamps* < *jama* 'nonsense', from those based on recent loanwords, like *burks* < Eng. *burger*. However, many commonly used words are very old borrowings (e.g., *pliks* < *plika* 'girl', long since adapted from Swedish *flicka*), and some more recent loanwords have likely been part of the language for at least a century (e.g., *kemps* < *kemmergu* 'toilet', *vets* < *veetsee* (WC) 'toilet'; *kops* < *kopikas*, Russian *kopek* + diminutive marker *-kas*). Accordingly, we will not attempt to draw a line between native and loanword sources; their phonological treatment is indistinguishable.

The template can be formally characterized as follows. The output conforms to the minimal Estonian prosodic word, requiring at least two moras (see Chapter 7). The form consists of a single heavy (bimoraic) foot, or [H]. The syllabic nucleus cannot be adequately specified in moras alone, however, as it may include a short vowel or diphthong but only rarely a long vowel; furthermore, the rhyme must include an obstruent followed by *-s*:

$$C_0V_1(V_2)(C_{[son]})C_{[obs]}s$$

As a general rule, the base selected or circumscribed for template formation consists of the segmental material *up to and including the stressed syllable*, whether that syllable is initial or not (Vihman & Vihman, 2017), with the addition of a homorganic stop if the consonant is a sonorant (see the short forms provided here so far); /k/ is inserted if the stressed syllable is vowel-final (*tšauks* 'bye' < Italian *ciao* 'hello, bye' [Loog, 1991]; *tiuks* < *Tiiu*). However, the vast majority of the short forms we have identified and all of the hypocoristics are monosyllabic, regardless of the length of the source form. This follows from the Estonian accentual system, in which stress generally falls on the first syllable (as noted in Chapter 4).

A small number of recent loanwords—*antibiots* < *antibiˈootikum* 'antibiotic'; *narkots* < *narˈkootikum* 'drugs'; *lokats* < *loˈkaator* '(radio-, ultrasound-) locator'— are disyllabic, with the characteristic stop + *s* marking the end of the short form (cf. also *daˋvaiks* < Russian *daˈvai* 'sure, let's do it!'). Similarly, native words derived with at least one common suffix, the feminine-noun-formative *-anna*, are exceptional in attracting non-initial stress (cf. *ˈlaulja: laulˈjanna* 'singer, m.: singer, f.'; *ˈsober: sõbˈranna* 'friend: girlfriend'); this allows *sõˈbrants* 'girlfriend' to be derived from *sõbranna*, creating a form distinct from *sõps*, from *sõber* 'friend'. However, there is little consistency in the treatment of non-initial-stressed loanwords, as the unstressed initial syllable is just as often circumscribed to create the required monosyllabic short form: cf. *dots* < *do'sent* 'docent', *karts* < *garde'roob* 'cloakroom' (cf. French *garderobe*), *kilts* < *kilo'meeter* 'kilometer', *liks* < *li'köör* 'liqueur', *mops* < *mo'biil* 'mobile phone').

The following restrictions or characteristics of the short forms and their derivation apply to all the forms we are aware of:

1. *Vocalic nucleus*
   a. Long vowels are generally shortened (e.g., *nöps* < *nööp* 'button'; *ramps* < *raamatukogu* 'library'; *Pets* < *Peeter*, *Tints* < *Tiina*; cf. also the disyllabic short-form borrowings mentioned above).[10]
   b. Diphthongs are retained as such (*tõuks* 'scooter' < *tõukeratas* 'scooter', *Toits* < *Toivo*).[11] This difference in the way long vowels and diphthongs are treated sets the template apart from the general vocabulary, where (i) long vowels occur without restriction before multi-consonant codas in monosyllables (cf. *juust* 'cheese', *keerd* 'spiral, coil', *paavst* 'pope') and (ii) long and complex vocalic nuclei generally pattern in the same way (see Chapter 7 [7.3.1]).

2. *Coda*
   a. Long (or tense) and short (or lax) consonants are neutralized in forming a cluster with suffixal /s/ (*jops* < *jope* 'jacket'; *kõps* < *krõbe* 'crisp, potato chip'; *Mats* < *Madis*; *kots* < *kodu* 'home').
   b. Where the circumscribed portion of the base ends in a sonorant (nasal or liquid), a homorganic stop is epenthesized before /s/ (*jamps* < *jama* 'nonsense'; *Lõunts* < *Lõunakeskus* 'Southern Mall'; *dolts* < *dollar*; *Kalts* < *Kalle*). However, /r/ is treated variably: It may be preserved, with the addition of /t/ (*eurts* < *euro*, *Sirts* < *Siret*), or /t/ may replace the /r/ (*näts* < *närimiskum* 'chewing gum'). Similarly, stop plus /r/ clusters mostly retain the /r/ (*porks* < *porgand* 'carrot'; *burks* < *burger*; *Arts* < *Arda*, *Kerts* < *Kertu*, but see *Ats* < *Artur*, *Maks* < *Markus*—perhaps influenced by the German name *Max*).
   c. It is unclear whether the stem-final consonant should be identified as 'stop' or 'obstruent'. Estonian has only three native-language fricatives, /v/, /s/, and /h/, and no affricates. A base in /-s/ gives C_0Vs-s; we list three such short forms (*küss* < *küsimus* 'question', *muss* < *musi* 'kiss', and *muss*

---

[10] Among the rare exceptions are two outdated forms, *kraap(jalg)* 'scrape(leg)' < *kraap-i-ma* 'to scrape' and *kaaps* 'bowler hat' < *kaabu*. These look like short forms in -Cs, but neither is in active use. The only current short-form exception to vowel-shortening is *kleeps* < *kleebispilt* 'sticker'.

[11] One apparent exception is *sonks* < *soeng* 'hair-do'. We have not so far identified other instances of a short form nucleus derived from a sequence in which V_2 is a mid-vowel, a more recent type of diphthong in Estonian (Asu, Lippus, Pajusalu, & Teras, 2016). It is thus impossible to judge whether this instance of reduction to a monophthong is general or not.

< *muusika* 'music'), but the formation cannot be distinguished from a competing short-form or template, CVCC (cf. *kunn < kuningas* 'king'; *Tõnn < Tõnis, Mell < Meelis*, and others).

d. Neither /vs/ nor /hs/ are permissible clusters. The only examples of bases ending in /v/ are hypocoristics (*Raits < Raivo, Toits < Toivo*); these suggest that /v/ is replaced by /t/ to provide a stem-final consonant compatible with the suffixal /s/. Where the first consonant of the base is /h/ it is similarly replaced by /t/ (e.g., *käts < kähmlus* 'scuffle') or omitted (*tots < tohter* 'doctor'). A single hypocoristic with intervocalic /h/ unpredictably gives /ks/ (*Riks < Riho*—but note that the source-name may derive from *Richard*, itself sometimes shortened to *Riki* or *Riks*).

Table 8.5 provides one example of template formation from each of the phonologically distinct stem-types; Appendix V provides the full list and some additional comments. Syncope may be resorted to when the base does not lend itself to the usual derivational mechanism: In words derived with the suffix *-kas* (e.g., *telekas* 'television') the second consonant is included in the short form, with loss of the second vowel (*telks*). As *-kas* is often used as a diminutive suffix, the hypocoristics include many forms with this suffix; the suffixal /k/ is included in the shorter form in every case (cf. *Toiks < Toivokas, Velks < Velvokas*).

The template for deriving short forms can readily be conceptualized, as Scullen (1997) proposes for French, as a filter on outputs. Unlike French short forms in *-o*, however, the relation of output to base is largely predictable, as described above, so that the short form can equally well be considered to involve a mapping of base to template. The short forms are also more restricted in shape than the French forms. In both cases the words conform to the prosodic minimality requirements of the language but, as noted, the Estonian forms largely constitute a single bimoraic foot. The /s/ that marks all of the forms is arguably suffixal in spite of the fact that, like French /o/, it cannot be said to add any identifiable grammatical or semantic meaning to the forms so derived.

It is important to note that whereas French short forms typically need bear no additional morphological marking, the Estonian forms are inflected as required by the structure of the case system, through the addition of a vowel to the stem ending in *–s*. The vowel used is most often the default /i/ deployed in recent loans (cf. *läheme rampsi* /ˈrampsi/ 'let's go to the library [illat. sg.]'; *õpsid* 'teachers [nom. pl.]'). However, some older forms use /u/ (cf. *vetsu, kempsu*, both meaning 'to the toilet [illat. sg.]'). At least one form is recorded with either vowel (*jätsi/u* 'jazz, prt. sg.' < *džäss*).[12]

The Estonian short forms, like the French, can be assumed to have a lengthy history; some are known to have been in active use for at least 80–90 years. Some

---

[12] Recall that only four unstressed vowels occur in Estonian in the native lexicon, /i, e, a, u/; neither /a/ nor /e/ are currently productive stem-vowel options, although both occur commonly in existing stems.

Table 8.5 Estonian short forms. **Bold face** marks the portion of the base retained in the short form. The left-most column shows the base-final consonant, cluster, or nucleus to which the suffix attaches. Stress is on the first syllable unless otherwise indicated. Q3 is marked on the short forms, as in Ch. 7

Base-final C	Base form	Gloss	Short form
A. Monomoraic base rime			
/p/	**krõb**e /krʊpe/	crisp, potato chip	krõps /ˈkrʊps/
/t/	**nat**uke /natːukːe/	a little bit	nats /ˈnats/
/k/	**mög**in /mʊkin/	goo, gunk	möks /ˈmöks/
/m/	**limon**aad /limonaːt/	lemonade (prt. sg.)	limps(i) /ˈlimps(i)/
/n/	**kin**o /kino/	cinema (illat. sg.)	kints /ˈkints(i)/
/ŋ/	**soeng** /soɛŋk/	hair-do	sonks /ˈsɔŋks/
/l/	**õl**u /ʊlu/	beer	õlts /ˈʊlts/
/r/	**näri**miskumm /næːrimiskumː/	chewing gum	näts /ˈnæts/
B. Bimoraic base rime			
VC	**kok**teil /kokteil/	cocktail	koks /ˈkoks/
	kopikas /kopːikas/	< Russian *kopek* (small unit of money)	kops /ˈkops/
	hammustama /hamː ustama/	to bite	amps /ˈamps/
	konspekt /konspekt/	lecture notes, conspectus	konts /ˈkonts/
	pingpong /piŋpɔŋ/	pingpong	pinks /ˈpiŋks/
	dollar /tolːar/	dollar	dolts /ˈtolts/
	burger /purker/	burger	purks /ˈpurks/
V:	**jää**tis /jæːtːis/	icecream	jäts /ˈjæts/
	Jaapanlane /jaːpːanlane/	Japanese	japs /ˈjaps/
	nark:ootik:um /narˈkːoːtːikːum	drugs	narkots /narˈkots/
V₁V₂	**säut**suma /sæutsuma/	to tweet	säuts /ˈsæuts/
	euro /euro/	euro	eurts /ˈeurts/
C. Hypocoristics			
/p/	**Krib**u (cat's name)		Krips
/p:/	**Tep**po (surname)		Teps
/t/	**And**reus, **Andr**es, **Andr**us		Ants
/t:/	**Get**ter, **Ket**li		Gets, Kets
/k/	**Ang**ela		Anks
/k:/	**Mark**us		Maks
/v/	**Toi**vo		Toits
/h/	**Ri**ho		Riks
/m/	**Rom**et (surname)		Romps

/n/	**Indr**ek		Ints
/ŋ/	**Ingr**id		Inks
/l/	**Kall**e		Kalts
/lv/	**Velv**o		Velts
/r/	**Sir**et		Sirts
/rt/	**Ard**a		Arts
/rt:/	**Artur, Kert**u		Ats, Kerts
/rk/	**Pirg**it		Pirks
/rm/	**Tarm**o		Tarms, Tarmps, Tarts
/V/	**Tiiu**		Tiuks
long vowel	**Eer**o		Erts
	Peeter		Pets
diphthong	**Toiv**o		Toits

forms have essentially faded from use, as their meanings are no longer relevant (cf. *vamps* < *vammus* 'doublet; vest', for example). At the same time, new forms continue to be created (cf. *kints* < *kino* 'film', *säuts* 'tweet' < *säutsuma* 'to tweet'), which testifies to the ongoing productivity of the template. Little information is available to indicate when the forms may have first begun to constitute a unique colloquial or slang form of lexical expression, however. A point of interest is that many of the semantic areas covered are similar in Estonian and French. For example, both show the unusual formation of short, parallel slang expressions derived from the first and second singular pronouns (see Appendices IIIb and V; the Estonian forms—e.g., *mints* 'me, mine', as in *läheme mintsi* 'let's go to my place'—are current, however, whereas Scullen's French examples (*mésigo, tésigo*) come from Heinemann, 1953; neither Antoine, 2000, nor the CNRTL includes them).

As noted above, most of the Estonian short forms are not only truncated from longer forms but adapted as well; there are far fewer forms here that resemble Weeda's 'bricolants', the selected o-forms in French. Nevertheless, word forms of this shape are well supported in the lexicon, as the output shape is of very high frequency and in fact the short forms closely resemble a commonly occurring and highly diverse set of onomatopoeia. To gain an idea of the frequency of occurrence of monosyllables that might have served as phonological models for the observed productive uses of the template we conducted a search of two Estonian on-line dictionaries with search engines, *Eesti õigekeelsussõnaraamat ÕS 2013* ('Estonian Dictionary of Correct Usage')[13] and *Eesti keele seletav sõnaraamat* ('Estonian language explanatory dictionary'),[14] using the possible output

---

[13] http://www.eki.ee/   [14] http://www.eki.ee/dict/ekss/

Table 8.6 Frequency of occurrence of monosyllables whose rime consists of a V (x axis) and CC_0 (y axis) + s. Shading = none found. Overall total, 351

Monosyllables only

	ps	ts	ks	mps	nts	nks	lps	lts	lks	rps	rts	rks
ü	4	16	3	1							1	
ö	2	2	2		1			1			3	
ä	3	10	11	1	4						6	1
õ	4	3	13	3	3			1			1	
o	19	7	13	3	3	11	1		3		5	
i	13	15	16	3	3				3	1	12	
e	4	3	7					2			3	
u	7	10	20	1	5		1		1		7	
a	13	8	10		8		1	3			6	
T	69	74	95	12	27	11	3	7	7	1	44	1

form-endings <-V +C(C)s> as exhaustively as possible. This meant entering the nine vowels that may occur in the stressed syllable (*i, e, ä, ü, ö, õ, u, o, a*) plus each of the stops (*p, t, k*) and the clusters sonorant + stop, followed by *s*. (The phonetic transparency of Estonian orthography makes such a search possible.)

Table 8.6 shows the outcome, omitting compound words already represented as monosyllabic stems, abbreviations, dialect forms, variants of the same form with the same meaning, and function words ending in *-ks* (which marks both the nominal translative case and the verbal conditional mood), such as *miks* 'why (i.e., for what)?', *kelleks* 'for whom?'. As shown in the table, a total of 351 monosyllabic words in -VC(C)s were found in this way; this is a conservative estimate, as the dictionaries stop at 100 examples of any given search term, which was exceeded by the available forms in several cases (very large numbers being accounted for by compounds and in some cases multisyllabic word forms).

There are also about 60 disyllables ending in the four vowels permitted in non-initial (unstressed) position (*i, e, u, a* + stop + s), but these are heavily dominated by the unproductive derivational suffixes *-its* and *-ats* (with meanings like 'tool for doing X'). Since all but a very few of the templatic forms of interest here are monosyllables, the disyllabic frequencies do not seem relevant and were not tallied.

The number of onomatopoeic forms that take the shape of the target output—like *kõmps* 'clomp', *lõmps* 'bite, mouthful', *plumps* 'sound of oar hitting water, cork hitting ceiling', etc.—is remarkable. On a conservative count (disregarding the distinction between adverbial or interjectional and nominal use), 39% of the forms in VCs and 35% of the forms in sonorant+Cs are onomatopoeic, with definitions in *EKSS* such as 'gives the sound/impression of…'; many of these words mean things like 'a blow', 'a slap', or 'a sudden sound', etc. These forms are often used singly or in combination to convey the sound of walking through mud or slush, for example; they also provide BT forms for the sounds animals make, such as *prääks-prääks* 'quack-quack' and *piuks* 'peep'. Note that, in contrast to the short-form template, there is no stricture against long vowels in these forms.

These commonly used descriptive forms are likely to have contributed to the pattern becoming a productive marker of slang forms that are not only short but often also expressive of affection (like the hypocoristics); similarly, the short forms, like many of the onomatopoeia, may give a sense of suddenness, briskness, or snappiness. However, some of the older forms have a negative connotation (cf. *mats* 'country bumpkin', from the hypocoristic *Mats < Madis* (cf. Eng. *hillbilly*), *saks < sakslane* 'German', meaning 'someone who acts like a lord' (cf. Eng. *hoity-toity*) or *frits < Fritz*, meaning 'German soldier' (cf. 1940s US Eng. *Jap* 'Japanese enemy').

A few uncommon uses can be noted as well.

(1) A bilingual Estonian-English-speaking 9-year-old who uses English with her mother derived *momps* from English *mom*. Another bilingual child used *comps* (/komps/) < Eng. *computer* (cf. Est. *arvuti*). There may be other instances: English is currently a natural place from which to source slang terms in Estonian, as knowledge of English, supported by the media, begins early and is widespread. In fact, we include in our list some words derived from English bases, like *gramps*, reported by university students who took our survey. (Both *pops* and *gramps* are used in English as well, although not *momps*.) Also from the survey, note *tänks* (from *tänan* 'thank you': *tänts* would be expected; the form is surely a nod to English *thanks*), with its joking echoic reply, *palks* /ˈpalⁱks/ < *palun* 'please', i.e., 'you're welcome' (again, *palts* would be expected by the regular mapping).

(2) An interesting loan-translation from Russian that exploits the common currency of the template is *läks*, literally 'went'; this is used in primary school games in counting out: *üks, kaks, kolm, läks*, 'one, two, three, go' (the first person plural imperative form *lähme* 'let's go!', could be used but would lack the rhythmic match to the numbers), and it also occurs on its own to mean 'ready, let's go'. The Russian *poshli* 'went', also used colloquially to mean 'we're ready, let's go, let's get going', is the presumed meaning-related model for this usage.

(3) There are a very few instances in which, as in the more numerous French cases of augmentation, the 'short form' is longer than its base. To *davaiks* 'let's do it' < Russian *davai* 'come on; let's'!' and *tšauks* 'hello, bye' < Italian *ciao*, mentioned earlier, we can add *heiks* or *heips* 'hey, hello' < Finnish *hei* 'hey'. In these cases the addition of the suffix itself provides the pragmatic 'meaning' of the derivation: The international flavour lent to the expressions by the borrowed base forms, along with the added 'short-form' suffix, no doubt supports the value of such terms as social identity markers for contemporary young people (see the related phenomena in Australian English, described below).

(4) The term for the hazing of university freshman (known as *rebased* 'foxes') is *reps-imine*—i.e., literally 'fox-ing'. The denominal base *reps-* clearly derives regularly from *rebane* 'fox', but we are unaware of any mention of the form *reps* on its own.

Both Kidd et al. (2011) and Spradling (2016) have analysed the parallel phenomenon of short-form constructions in current use in Australian English; -*s* is the
only consonantal suffix reported by either of them. Kidd et al. elicited a variety of
'hypocoristics' (using the term more broadly than elsewhere to refer to 'short
forms', in accordance with the Australian English literature) from 115 Australians
divided into three age groups, young (17–39), middle-aged (40–59), and old
(60–84); the forms in -*s*, which were among the least common of several subtypes,
were largely cited only by the two younger groups. The main examples were
maybe > *maybs*, *mobile phone* > *mobs*, *people* > *peeps*, *whatever* > *whatevs*,
definitely > *defs*, and *probably* > *probs*. Note that, as in Estonian, these words
are truncated after the consonant that follows the stressed syllable (and note the
similarity of, for example, *whatevs* to *sōbrants*, both of them rare disyllabic
instances derived from base words with second-syllable stress; some of Spradling's
examples, below, fit here as well).[15]

Drawing on tweets and texts as well as spoken language, Spradling (2016)
focuses on forms like *totes atrosh* < *totally atrocious*; her examples include *adorbs*
< *adorable*; *arbz* < *arbitrary*; *awfs* > *awful*; *deplorbz* < *deplorable*; *Deuts* < *Deuter-
onomy*; *grodes* < *grody*; *hopes* < *hopeful*; *inevs* < *inevitable*; *verbates* < *verbatim*;
wellbz < *wellbeing*).[16] Spradling reports that 'totesers' ('totes users') 'are generally in
their teens and twenties, and use totes in speech and electronic communication for
stylistic reasons, such as signaling group affiliation' (p. 275); in a footnote she adds
that 'the construction may also have been popularized by character limits imposed
on electronic communication' (i.e., tweets or text messages). The phenomenon is
thus in some ways both formally and functionally similar to the Estonian short
forms in -*s*.

The Estonian short forms and related hypocoristics have a long history in the
adult language and have come to play a particularly lively part in today's world. To
return to our theme, they provide yet another example of adult word formation
based on a set template grounded in the phonological and prosodic constraints of
the language but with its own distinctive 'filter' or 'mapping rules'. The function of
such a template can be debated, but the principles invoked by researchers dealing
with French apply here as well. Some forms are genuinely shorter and so perhaps
easier to say and remember (e.g., *Vaps*, *kemps*); some are used colloquially in an
affective or pejorative sense (*jamps*, *mats*, *saks*), and some combine shortening
with function as an identity marker (*kaups*, *ramps*). Newer coinages especially seem

---

[15] Following Weeda (1992), Simpson (2006) interprets Australian English 'hypocoristics' as phonological templates mapping words of variable length to either one- or two-syllable forms; the latter most
commonly involve forms ending in /i/ or /o/. This has the advantage (which applies equally well to both
the French and the Estonian short forms) of accommodating simple shortening (our 'selection') as
readily as shortening with suffixation (our 'adaptation').

[16] Most of the forms with a final sibilant appear to be adapted. Exceptions include *bluebz* <
blueberries and *ginorms* < *ginormous*.

to be used in the latter function, like the Australian *totes* construction, setting adolescent or young adult users apart from the larger society (e.g., *õps, kints, davaiks* or *sünks* 'cool' < *sünge* 'dark, grim'); this corresponds to Ronneberger-Sibold's third proposed function, distinctiveness.

The Estonian forms, unlike the French hypocoristics, for example, cannot plausibly be related to early child forms in any concrete way as they constitute unlikely phonological simplifications, with their heavy coda clusters. The parallel is rather in the use of a highly familiar prosodic shape, and with segmental stipulation as well, as a basis for novel word formation: Although the function of the word forms thus arrived at is different, the process is reminiscent of children's reliance on familiar prosodic shapes, sometimes further elaborated into fixed, segmentally specified templates, to support and facilitate the word-learning process.

8.3 Rhyming compounds

Linguists have collected 'echo words' in English for nearly 200 years. A notable early example is Wheatley's 1866 dictionary—but Wheatley himself cites an earlier collection (Booth, 1835), which includes 112 forms. However, the most complete annotated collection available is no doubt Thun (1963), which includes nearly 2000 such forms. Of these, 675 are distinct 'rhyming compounds', in which only the word-initial consonants differ across the paired words (*bigwig*); other compounds involve vowel change or 'ablaut' in the stressed syllable (*shilly-shally*) and a third type shows full reduplication (*goody-goody*). Various terms are used for these forms, including the broader 'reduplicated words' (Wheatley) or 'reduplicatives' (Thun) and 'echo-pairs' (Sóskuthy, 2012) or 'echo words'. Here we will use 'rhyming compounds' to refer to any lexical unit made up of two word-like forms that differ only or mainly in the onset consonant of the two forms (Word1 and Word2). In some cases the 'compound' will be a conventional unit, a word made up of two real words (*nitwit, stalk-talk*) or a conventionalized phrase marked by rhyme (*fair share, true blue*), in others a nonsense form or a word and its nonsense 'echo'.

For rhyming compounds, as Thun points out, the question of the 'motivation' of the compound arises, especially where two real words in current use are concerned: How can one distinguish compounds that just happen to combine words that rhyme, like *cookbook* (see the parallel forms, *baby book, handbook, notebook*, etc.), from compounds that have likely been combined or retained as lexical items at least in part due to the rhyming effect? For example, *redhead* has no parallel in other hair-colour compounds, which are expressed instead in other ways (*blonde, brunette*); it seems likely that the rhyme is one reason why the term *redhead* persists in the lexicon. Hladký (1998) lists the properties that guided his exhaustive compilation of compounds found in previous studies. For the rhyming compounds Hladký proposes as 'central' (and therefore to be included in his list)[17] (i) exocentric compounds like **redhead**, (ii) compounds involving a semantic shift in (at least) one element (**toy boy**) or (iii) a transferred or metaphorical meaning (**brain drain**), (iv) compounds that are grammatically irregular (**fly-by**, **no-go**), (iv) compounds with full rhymes (**dream team**) but not those with partial rhyme (**peelie-wallie**, **whipper-snapper**), and (v) compounds with regular syllabic patterning (**jeepers-creepers**, but not *chock-a-block*).

Rhyming compounds are the most common type of reduplication in English (Hladký, 1998). We generally follow the guidance of Thun and Hladký as regards the definition of rhyming compounds for the most problematic category, combinations of two words in current use ('real words'). We exclude compounds in which the rhyme appears to be essentially irrelevant to the composition of the word. That is, when the form seems likely the most logical expression for a given meaning (cf. *backpack*, say—although the rhyme may have contributed to the choice of this compound over a possible alternative, **backbag*), we exclude it, whereas we retain combinations apparently in use because of the effect of the rhyme, along with the connotation of the two elements combined (e.g., *double trouble*). However, we have disregarded the strict interpretation of 'rhyme' in Hladký's last two principles; we note irregularities in syllable count in Appendix VI. We include set phrases (*real deal*) as well as what are generally written as and felt to be compounds, but exclude conjoined phrases (*huff and puff, fair and square, by hook or by crook*), although some of these might be considered single lexical items as well. We also exclude proper names (*Andy-Pandy*), onomatopoeia (*boohoo, bow-wow, teehee, yoo-hoo*), and forms that occur only in nursery rhymes (*Humpty-Dumpty*).

Some examples cited by Wheatley that are still in common use can serve to illustrate further what is meant by the term rhyming compound: *hanky-panky* (cited from 1864, where the meaning is given as 'mystery'), *higgledy-piggeldy* (with the current meaning), *hoity-toity* ('flighty, giddy, thoughtless'; contrast the contemporary meaning of 'haughty or snobbish'), and *hocus-pocus* ('a cheat, hoax'). The meanings have clearly drifted in 150 years, but the format remains productive: cf. *bleedie-peedies* (G. Swift, 1983, *Waterland*, p. 301); *hippy-dippy* (*New Yorker*, 8/18/17); *snuggle-buggle* (R. Ford, 1986, *The Sportswriter*, p. 108); cf. also *Trump-slump*, a reference to a fall in the numbers of tourists visiting the United States, attributed by some to President Trump's unpopularity internationally (*Forbes*, 8/7/2017).

A collection of 211 words that are in use today, primarily in American and British English, will serve here as the basis for analysis; these words are listed in Appendix VI. In order to maximize the database of word types to be used for

---

[17] The examples in bold face are Hladký's; the others derive from the present compilation.

testing identifiable phonological tendencies we include all of the 32 rhyming compounds Hladký (1998) lists as being among the 69 most frequent reduplicatives; we also include several compounds listed only in Mattiello (2013). A few words are evident borrowings (*charivari, hoi poloi, kowtow*), whose currency in English likely owes something to their rhyming form—as suggested by the deformation of *hara-kiri* to create the more satisfyingly rhyming compound *harikari*. (Wheatley defines *mumbo-jumbo* as 'an African bugbear' and *powwow* as 'name given to the feasts, dances, etc., of the red men; preliminary war expeditions, and adopted into political talk to signify an uproarious meeting for a political purpose' [citing *Bartlett's Dictionary of Americanisms*], but these terms have taken on broader reference now and are not categorized as loanwords here.) Other expressions are more recent coinages, like *chick flick* or *flower power*. Of 192 distinct rhyming compounds in Wheatley's collection of over 600 partially reduplicated expressions (including the complementary set of alliterative or ablaut compounds as well as some one-off mentions from dictionaries and a number of separately listed variants of forms with essentially the same meaning), 43 (22%) also appear in this twenty-first century collection.[18] Alternatively, out of the present collection of rhyming compounds 20% were in use already in Wheatley's day. In short, there has been considerable lexical turnover in the 150 years since Wheatley published his list, yet many forms remain in use, and the productivity of the forms also remains high.

It was noted in each of the earlier studies that forms with /h/ as Word1 onset consonant are particularly common. Wheatley claims that nearly half of all the compounds he has identified take this form; of his rhyming compounds, by our count, 72 (37.5%) are *h*-initial. The comparable figure for Thun is 216 (32%); no other single consonant accounts for the Word1 onset in even as many as 70 (10%) of the compounds Thun lists.

What is not mentioned in these earlier studies, however, is the even more strikingly disproportionate occurrence of rhyming compounds whose second element begins with a labial. In Wheatley's collection we count 100 rhyming compounds (52%) with labials as Word2 onset. (For Thun's larger collection we have not made the count; Thun provides his own count of Word1 but not Word2 onsets.[19]) From Table 8.7 we see that in the present collection the proportion of Word2 labial onsets is also high, at 44%; for comparison, in the English CELEX corpus roughly 29% of all types begin with a labial (/p, b, f, v, m, w/).[20] Word1

---

[18] Hladký (1998) counts 305 rhyming words in Wheatley; we have excluded specifically Scottish or other dialect variants, forms that Wheatley could not confidently trace to a source, and other entries that seemed questionable for one reason or another.

[19] Thun does mention the frequent occurrence of /w/ and sometimes /m/ as Word2 onsets, but only for cases with Word1 stop onset (40% of these have /w/ or /m/ as Word2 onset); he does not specify Word2 onset for the remaining Word1 onset consonants nor generalize to the occurrence of labials overall.

[20] We thank Márton Sóskuthy for checking this.

Table 8.7 Phonological shape of rhyming compounds in English

Word1 onset	Word2 onset labial	Word2 onset not labial	Total	
V	8	7	15	
h	21	24	45	21%
C	63	88	151	
total	92	119	211	
	44%	56%		

Table 8.8 Lexical status of compound types. Prop: proportion

Compound type	Word2 onset labial	prop.	Word2 onset not labial	prop.	Total	prop.
Real word	23	.33	46	.67	69	*.33*
Nonsense word	33	.46	39	.53	73	.35
Word + rhyme	23	.53	18	.46	54	.34
Rhyme + word	6		7			
Shortened words[1]	4		3		7	*.03*
Loanword	3		6		9	.07
	92	.44	119	.56	211	

[1] E.g., *sci fi, Tex Mex, lit crit.*

onsets in /h/ make up 21% of the total, a smaller proportion as compared with either Wheatley or Thun.

Table 8.8 breaks down the rhyming compounds by lexical status. The compilation as a whole divides fairly equally into three word types: (i) real-word and (ii) nonsense-word compounds and (iii) 'word and rhyme' (in either order). The third type consists of cases where only one element (in **bold face**) is a currently identifiable word (e.g., *easy-peasy*), while the other element is either a nonsense rhyme or a real word that, although recognizable, has little to do with the meaning of the whole, its presence in the compound or phrase being largely due to its formal or phonological contribution (e.g., **eager** *beaver,* **phony***-baloney,* **good-***should* or the several compounds whose second element is a first name evidently chosen primarily for the rhyme, such as **silly** *billy,* **plain** *jane,* **even** *stephen*). These forms are more likely than not to have Word2 labial onset (53%), with nonsense words being the next most affected by the pattern (46%). Complementarily, compounds and phrases made up entirely of real words (*blame game, deadhead*) are the least affected at 33%, or just over the level expected, given the figure of 29% labial-onset words in CELEX.

The word + rhyme/rhyme + word compounds can be considered 'adapted', in contrast to the real-word rhyming compounds, which may have been 'selected' for (or retained in use due to) their existing rhyme (which is semantically as well as phonologically motivated). The nonsense words do not fit into this distinction, as they cannot really be considered compounds at all. These nonsense forms might nevertheless have supported an unconscious bias toward rhyming compounds with Word2 labial onset, as suggested by the fact that they have by far the longest history. Of the 43 compounds that occur in both Wheatley and the current collection, 35 (81%) are nonsense words that admit of no further analysis (and all 43 incorporate at least one nonsense word); alternatively, half of our nonsense words (35 out of 73) had already appeared in Wheatley, as compared with 20% of our collection as a whole (43/211). Furthermore, the disproportionate representation of labials as Word2 onsets is highest in these long-established nonsense-word compounds (79% of the nonsense compounds with Word2 labial onset are also found in Wheatley, as compared with 44% of those with non-labial onsets to Word2).[21]

Benczes (2012) notes the relatively restricted set of semantic domains to which 'nonsensical rhyming compounds' refer and provides an account of the most common of these. She finds that the prevailing category involves the meanings of disorder and confusion, which are expressed by rhyming compounds in other European languages as well. The high proportion of nonsense compounds beginning with /h/ appear to go back to the very earliest forms (e.g., *hiddy-giddy, hodge-podge, hurly-burly*—each of which originally included at least one meaningful element), from which a productive schema may have been extracted, with more flexible segmentalism in later forms (Benczes, 2012, p. 311). The schema, which can be expressed formulaically as $W_h[rime]W_2[rime]$ (in which W = Word-onset), would then have also given rise—by virtue of its meaningful relation to the recitation of magic spells and also 'nursery words', with their preference for reduplication—to related schemas or templates that no longer specify initial /h/ but take the more general form $W_1[rime]W_2[rime]$. The prominence of Word2 labial-onset compounds in these forms might simply have originated then in an incidental bias in the early Word1 h-onset forms.

A recent web-based corpus analysis of echo-pairs in Hungarian, based on tokens, not types, reveals a far more striking Word2 labial-onset effect than we see in any English collection (Sóskuthy, 2012: cf. *cica-mica* 'cat, diminutive', *csiga-biga* 'snail, diminutive', *Ancsi-Pancsi* 'Anna'). Because a corpus based on informal text samples seemed likely to constitute the most fruitful source, given the 'playful

---

[21] We have excluded hypocoristics from our sample; they occur only rarely as rhyming compounds. However, it is worth mentioning that all those that we are aware of—Mattiello lists four, to which we can add, from personal experience: *Linda Pinda, Ellie Belly, Sleepy Beepy* (addressed to a baby), and *Hungry Bungry* (to a cat)—have Word2 labial onsets. Cf. also *Silly Milly*, used dismissively by Virginia Woolf's father Leslie Stephen to refer to his Quaker activist and theologian sister, Caroline Emilia Stephen (Lyndall Gordon, 2017, *Outsiders*, pp. 237f.).

and intimate contexts' most conducive to use of the template (p. 118), Sóskuthy drew on the Hungarian Webcorpus for his search. (Although the corpus is available only in orthographic, not phonetic form, the search is feasible because Hungarian, like Estonian, has a relatively transparent spelling-to-sound relationship.) The search specified 'all strings consisting of two identical parts where only the initial onsets differ' (p. 118) and included the same sets of compound types as we set out in Table 8.8 (except for 'shortened words').

Within Sóskuthy's 'reduplicated word' category, which combines our 'word +rhyme' and 'rhyme+word' categories, fully 98% of the tokens found in the corpus search had labial onsets to the second element (for types the figure is 87.4% 'word-and-rhyme' [Sóskuthy, p.c.]); /b, p, m/ account for close to 91%, with minor contributions from /f, v/, the only other Hungarian labials. Sóskuthy points out that 'reduplicated words' are the only rhyming compounds to exhibit a typical morphological process, in which one element reduplicates the other and adapts it to fit a template. In the case of real-word compounds, as discussed above, the rhyming effect may be secondary to straightforward semantic considerations, whereas for the iconic compounds that Sóskuthy identifies (roughly corresponding to our 'nonsense compounds', although we have excluded onomatopoeia from the English list), some degree of sound symbolism may affect the formation. Thus Sóskuthy finds it unsurprising that the Word2 labial-onset bias should be most strongly represented in these reduplicated-word types, as it is in our database as well.

Like Benczes, Sóskuthy appeals to Bybee's (2001) 'product-oriented schema' to account for the data. An advantage of this approach is that the phonological generalizations embodied in the schema—in this case, 'altered repetition of the same phonological sequence, labial-initial second component' (Sóskuthy, 2012, p. 132), among other things, along with the associated semantic connotations (diminutive, hypocoristic, playful)—are not categorical; other novel formations may embody one or another of this cluster of schema-like characteristics. This provides a theoretical parallel for the evidence we find of both *h*-initial and Word2 labial-onset tendencies in the English rhyming compounds, based on analysis of a much smaller database (of types, not tokens) than Sóskuthy's. (The fact that Sóskuthy finds a higher proportion of Word2 labial onsets in a count of tokens than of types suggests, again, that the echo-pairs that include the labials are somehow the most appealing or the most accessible to language users.)

One category of rhyming compounds that we have not included in our database is the enduringly productive Yiddish-influenced *shm*-compounds expressing, in English, a dismissive attitude toward the base word, as in *love-shmove*—or *crisis-shmisis* (the first reported use in English, based on the Oxford English Dictionary: Nevins & Vaux, 2003). In a scholarly treatise, drawing on multiple languages and considerable historical documentation, Southern (2005) traces these echo-pairs, twins or doublets back to a double origin in Germanic, the basic source language for Yiddish, and East Slavic, which was in turn influenced by Turkic.

The interplay between the Yiddish ... stand-alone configurational matrices and Turkic-derived East Slavic *m*-initial echo twins ... result[ed] in the new Eastern Yiddish ... echo-pair structures in *shm*- ... The highest-frequency Eastern Yiddish pairs' baseword onsets seem to be phonologically distributed in roughly similar proportions (and with similar onset-type preferences, favoring labials and labial clusters) to those displayed by comparable data in Yiddish-influenced English.   (p. 21)

These playful connotations ..., disparaging for single words ... and ironically mocking ... for echo-twins ... then passed wholesale into U.S. English and other Englishes adoptively as intentionally ephemeral echo-pairs, with growing productivity, particularly in ludic/comedic register U.S. English.   (p. 22)

Southern provides the following account of the spread of *m*-initial echo-words from Turkic to Slavic:

East Slavic expressive-based echo-doublets in *m*- ... show the unmistakable and deep-seated effects of contact-induced linguistic influence from Turkic ... Turkic *m*- echo-pairs seem to have originated as Turkic-internal morphological structures ... Twin formulas [i.e., rhyming compounds] are ... attested in a range of differently structured languages emanating out from the Turkic contact area. Their obligatorily affective component everywhere – paralleled by other distinctly Slavic-based morphological and phonological expressives ... – points to likely morphological or morphosyntactic borrowing ... Abundant evidence from coterminous Iranian and South Asian languages in particular shows that this 'X and/or whatever' rhymed reduplication pattern was an areal feature of expressive morphology, with systematic pairing rules involving (1) a labial-initial second element and (2) a dismissive-similarity semantic component.   (p. 26)

Southern identifies the ultimate likely origins of the echo-phrase in two Turkish *m*-initial particles, one expressing negation, the other interrogative meaning, both posited for the earliest period of Turkic (Common Turkic). Strikingly, the Turkic native lexicon lacks word-initial /m/ and is structurally agglutinative, with suffixing only. Thus two elements of the echo-construction, attested as early as the eleventh century (Middle Turkic), are atypical for these languages: word-initial /m/ (seen only in the second element of the phrase) and any kind of onset-consonant mutation or prefixing. This means that the English *shm*-pairs, with a clear source in Yiddish, can be traced back to an expressive construction likely to have originated in a language in which the echo-phrase was a grammatical anomaly; Southern quotes Jakobson and Waugh (1979, p. 206) to the effect that 'grammatically "counter-normative" features are fertile ground for the proliferation of expressive or affectively charged phenomena' (p. 59). (Recall again Ronneberger-Sibold's third criterion of 'distinctiveness'.)

Returning to Hungarian, we can see where the near-absolute occurrence of a Word2 labial-onset bias in the reduplicated-word constructions may have gotten its start, as Hungarian linguistic history is deeply bound up with that of Turkish, over centuries of partially bilingual speech communities. None of this answers the question as to why we find the bias in native English reduplicative compounds: English is by no means culturally or geographically close to any of the areas over which the echo-phrases spread. Thus the puzzle of the origins of the bias remains.

To take up again our broader theme of adult–child parallels in template formation, the shapes of these words cannot be specified in terms of segmental sequence alone, as Thun also notes in his chapter devoted to the 'form and formation' of reduplicative compounds, nor is the metrical or prosodic structure sufficient. As with any reduplication, the shapes of both base and output must be specified at some level; this is one way in which the compound formations resemble child phonological templates, paralleling their whole-word relationship to a target form. In addition, in English as in Hungarian, Word2 labial-onset compounds are particularly favoured in those cases in which one of the words is included on largely phonological grounds, for the rhyme it provides to the first element.

The relatively higher representation of the Word2 labial-onset and *h*-initial compounds among the older English forms means that both of these segmentally stipulated elements must have been losing ground, at least proportionately, ever since such data was first collected, as the rhyming principle comes to be used more generally to support novel combinations of real words; this is precisely the period over which the Yiddish-derived *shm*-compounds began to gain in productivity in American English. The parallel timing of the diminishing influence of the labial onset schema in English and the emergence of the popular Yiddish-English compound type thus precludes any plausible cause-and-effect relationship between the two. Instead, we can speculate that the formation of rhyming compounds has been templatic in English for centuries. The earliest known instances are *h*-initial; subsequently the compounds may have come to be formed preferentially with second elements beginning with a labial for reasons that remain obscure. These were tendencies, not categorical constraints, but they have left a sufficient trace in current usage to suggest a strong and long-lasting phonological bias in an important subtype of lexical innovation.

8.4 Adult and child templates, II

In this chapter we have considered adult constructions that allow for more leeway or more radical departures from typical morphological relations than are seen in the core grammar. We found good reason to accept Ronneberger-Sibold's proposals as to the goals of shortenings, namely, the creation of lexical forms that are 'short', 'easy', and 'distinctive'. The English rhyming compounds differ from the French and Estonian templates in that they are not literally 'short forms', but their rhyming pattern renders them not only distinctive but also 'easy'—as suggested by psycholinguistic studies showing that repeated rimes (but not repeated onsets) facilitate access to word forms, specifically in cases where the primes match the prosodic structure of the intended forms (Wheeldon, 2003; see also Rapp & Samuel, 2002). This would mean that Word1 will naturally prime Word2 in a rhyming compound.

The creativity allowed for in these constructions is especially apparent in the case of the French and Estonian short forms and hypocoristics. Examples of recent coinages would be French *texto* '(phone) text, SMS'; Estonian *säuts* 'tweet' (now used for social messaging as well as birdsong), *mops* 'mobile phone'; cf. also AusE. *mobs*—but note also the rare, possibly one-off rhyming compounds *bleedie-peedies, roola-boola, gloomy-doomy, good-should, hully-gully, numbly-crumbly, snuggle-buggle, stalk-talk* and *tinkle-chink*, all found in novels written within the last 40 years.[22] In these cases, as we have seen, the grammar of the language in question retains its full sway as regards prosodic constraints on outputs, yet the users depart from existing forms in sometimes unpredictable ways in forming the novel expressions: They may disregard principles of syllabification or prosodification as they circumscribe bits of the existing, conventional lexical forms or proper names to squeeze or stretch them into a template bearing its own affective or social connotations. The domain of 'language at play' seems particularly conducive to such innovation.

To what extent does such adult word formation present a parallel with the template uses observed in development? The similarities are both superficial and more deeply rooted.

(i) The existence of a *well-practised pattern* is critical for the child, whose templatic elaboration always draws on highly familiar output shapes or motoric routines. Similarly, in the case of not only the short forms but also the forms that enter into novel rhyming compounds (whether real words or nonsense forms), a *well-stocked bank of familiar word shapes* lies behind the innovative forms, which fit within the bounds of the usual constraints on words in the language. This is the essence of the idea of selection co-occurring with adaptation. That is, like child templates, adult templates *both select familiar patterns and adapt forms to fit into them*, thus extending usage potential to unlimited numbers of words.

(ii) The *prosodic structure* of the templatic pattern is critical: A template is always a holistic pattern, typically specified in terms of number of syllables (as in the case of the largely monosyllabic Estonian short forms) or metrical feet (a better framework for describing the more variable French short forms in -*o*); the English

---

[22] Several derive from Richard Ford's 1986 *The Sportswriter*, which also includes uses of the more conventional *humdrum, higgledy-piggledy, hurdy-gurdy, phony-baloney*, and *razzle-dazzle* as well as one instance of the Yiddish-based compound type, *Vicky-Schmicky*.

rhyming compounds are also very largely made up of monosyllabic or trochaic disyllabic bases, resulting in output forms that repeat those high-frequency shapes.

(iii) *Segmental specification* goes beyond what formal prosodic accounts allow for. Such specification is not seen in every child phonological template, but it occurs commonly enough, based on the rather restricted child data available so far, to warrant inclusion in our understanding of what such a template may consist of. The segmental elements in the Estonian and French short forms are a crucial part of their identity. They do not call child templates to mind in any specific detail, although both specified final vowels (like French -o) and codas (like Estonian -Cs) do occur. The English Word2 labial onset bias, similarly, calls to mind children's use of a fixed onset to the second syllable (e.g., [l] in the case of both Laurent and Anna, Chapter 5).

(iv) Note that no child templates have been observed in which the fixed element is the *word-initial consonant* (see the table of template melodies, Vihman, 2014, pp. 300f.). The only adult templatic pattern with a fixed onset consonant that we have encountered so far is the Word1 *h-* seen in English rhyming compounds. The rarity of Word1-onset specification may not be coincidental: Insofar as templates are aids to memory, the initial consonant must be the element least in need of pre-specification. (See the literature on lexical access errors: The first consonant is the most likely to be remembered, especially in the case of adults [Aitchison, 1972; Aitchison & Straf, 1981; Fay & Cutler, 1977; Vihman, 1981; see also Jaeger, 2005].)

(v) *The kinds of adaptations observed differ from one case to another.* Both the French and the Estonian short forms generally restrict themselves to truncation before suffixation, although additional processes (augmentation, syncope) are seen occasionally. The French hypocoristics, which depend on reduplication rather than fixed segmental specification, are far freer in their modulations of the original name, making use, as child templates often do, of metathesis and other holistic adaptations of the segmental material in the base to form the reduplicated pet name (see also Mattiello, 2013, on hypocoristics in English).

This rather free use of segmental material can be ascribed to the uniquely defining context of use for such forms, where the principles of lexical contrast and avoidance of ambiguity have the lowest priority. A parallel can again be cited with child template use, in which the risk of being misunderstood is a minor concern at best: Much of children's early word use is more in the nature of 'joining the conversational game' than of communicating information of any kind, and the typically routine contexts of use with familiar interlocutors make clarity or contrast low priorities for the child.

The rhyming compounds are less obviously related to our argument. The *prosodic shape is restricted*: The combination into a single lexical unit of two forms that differ only by onset consonant characterizes most of the items in our database; almost all the forms derive from one- or two-syllable bases. We made much of the *segmental specifications* that can be seen in a large subset of the rhyming compounds: the high incidence of forms with Word1 *h*-onset—currently affecting about one-fifth of the forms—presumably harks back to the Middle English origins of these forms, centuries ago. More strikingly, the occurrence of a labial as Word2 onset affects almost half the forms overall and over half of the partly-nonsense compounds. Although the origins of the pattern are unknown, at some point an unconscious bias must have developed, such that the addition of a labial-initial word form to complete a rhyming compound led to an intuitively satisfying shape, a kind of aesthetic attractor.[23]

The relationship to child templates can then be stated in global terms: The continuing popularity of these semi-nonsensical English compounds, regularly used in everyday discourse and in contemporary novels, can be understood in terms of the distinctiveness and aesthetic appeal of the rhythmic play involved; the implicit relationship to nursery rhymes and the associated intimate and affectively marked context may play a role as well, as Benczes (2012) has argued. Child templates reflect sensitivity to an emergent pattern in their own word use, a familiar sensorimotor routine that can assimilate words of less familiar shapes, supporting both articulatory and memory processes. The templates that we have discussed in this chapter offer a deeply-rooted adult parallel with the creative adaptations of the child, providing snappy, hyper-familiar forms that evoke membership in an inner circle, as in French and Estonian (or Australian English), or evoking the nursery-like rhythms of a rhyming compound. All of these innovative means of word formation, whether by adult or child, are deeply rooted in the sensitivity to formal patterning of the human mind.

---

[23] The same principle likely applies to the formation of lexical clusters bearing the same phonestheme, such as English verbs ending in -*le* (e.g., *crumple, tipple, topple, babble, bumble, cobble, dabble, dribble, fumble, quibble, scribble, prattle, whittle, dawdle, doodle, fiddle, muddle, toddle, waddle, wheedle, trickle, bungle, giggle, haggle, scuffle, waffle, jostle, tussle, drizzle, fizzle, mizzle*—all with the connotation of doing something unseriously, or in an inexpert or incomplete way (over 100 such verbs are readily arrived at). (Thanks to Virve-Anneli and Raivo Vihman for initiating this compilation; see also the Appendix to Benczes, 2019, where the 66 words ending in -*le* account for about one-third of the multisyllabic, non-compound words of 'imitative origin' culled from the OED.)

9

Conclusion

In the first chapter we laid out two basic questions about phonological patterns or templates. The first related to the balance to be observed between the different factors that can be taken to shape these patterns in development (Vihman, 2015): biological or neurophysiological constraints, differing ambient language structures, and individual child differences. The second referred to the relationship of child to adult patterns and the possible implications of this relationship for adult phonology or morphology. Over the course of the book we have addressed these questions in various ways. We demonstrated the effect of common maturational constraints on babble and first words in all of the language groups whose data we analysed (Chapters 3 and 4), while at the same time considering ambient language effects, providing summary typologies in the form of an overview of prosodic structure use in Chapter 4 and of cross-linguistic template use in Chapters 5 and 6. In the concluding section of Chapter 6 we considered the function of templates in phonological development, while in Chapters 7 and 8 we reported templatic phenomena in adult grammars and colloquial usage. Here, we begin our concluding discussion by recapitulating in brief the overall developmental story presented in this book, reviewing three 'moments' or phases that can be distinguished in the course of early phonological and lexical advances.

9.1 Three moments in early phonological and lexical development

In the first 'moment' (briefly described in Chapter 1 and further illustrated and discussed in Chapters 3 and 4), infants who have been producing speech-like vocalizations for some months respond to familiar situations associated with one or more easily produced word forms by producing one of those words in the relevant routine context. Such word use, which typically results in a form similar enough to its adult model to be readily identified by anyone who knows the child, is likely to motivate a social response (Goldstein & Schwade, 2008; Laing & Bergelson, 2017). That response can serve in turn to model the adult form, creating a productive cycle of use and perceptual experience of the form (see Pearson's [2007] 'input-proficiency-use' model of bilingual children's experience).

Phonological Templates in Development. First edition. Marilyn May Vihman.
© Marilyn May Vihman 2019. First published 2019 by Oxford University Press.

Thus 'item learning', one plausible way for a child to be launched into first word use,[1] is highly reminiscent of the process Thelen and Smith see as accounting for walking—a multidimensional behaviour, with 'organic components and the context ... [being] equally causal and privileged' (1994, p. 17). For word learning the 'organic components' are individual advances in articulatory skills and variable retention of input forms, while social responses provide context.

In the second 'moment' (Chapters 3–6), after the accumulation of more varied word knowledge through item learning as well as continued vocal practice, now guided by the increasing numbers of words already attempted (Elbers & Ton, 1985), the child will begin to experience the self-organizing internal process of lexical engagement (Leach & Samuel, 2007). At the same time, improvements in working memory, or representational capacity, mean that the child can now mentally access more than one word at a time (McCune, 1995, 2008). At this point, then, the child can begin to apprehend the similarities between disparate word forms. By hypothesis, this advance underlies the implicit induction of common patterns in the child's own output repertoire or, alternatively, leads to the extension of one or more existing word-production routines to new, somewhat less closely related and more challenging word-form targets. In other words, this provides the basis for template use.

A period of exploration and heightened variability culminates in the first lexical organization or systematicity (Vihman & Velleman, 1989, 2000; Szreder-Ptasinska, 2012): The emergent network of related forms provides an internal model of phonological patterns—that is, an increasingly serviceable phonological memory—onto which novel forms are implicitly mapped. Thus where the child had previously learned individual lexical items, she now begins to 'collect' words of a similar structure (selection) and to categorize as yet untried, more challenging adult models into what gradually becomes a stable, although impermanent, templatic pattern (adaptation) (Vihman & Velleman, 2000; Vihman & Croft, 2007). Once word learning is well enough established to yield lexical engagement,[2] every new word learned enters into and affects the network of previously known words, altering

---

[1] At least one alternative route to first word use can be glimpsed in the case of 'progressive idioms', such as Hildegard Leopold's first word, *pretty* [pɹ̥ə̣ti] (whispered), at 10 months, presumably based on frequently hearing the word directed to herself (Leopold, 1939); regular word use emerged only two months later. Similarly, at 11 months the Estonian-English-learning child Kaia repeatedly whispered her first word, *kiisu/kitty* [kịtʊ] (the adult target cannot be definitively established, as the forms in either language constitute plausible models and in fact both may have contributed to the child's representation), in rapt response to the passage of one of the family's month-old kittens; she produced no other recognizable words for three months. In both cases the child form was well in advance of what might have been expected (and Hildegard's form was later reduced to the more predictable [bidi]); there is no record of a social response in either case. In fact, Vihman (2016, p. 81) interprets Kaia's form as 'a personal marker of attentional focus'—in other words, a form not intentionally directed to others at all.

[2] Word use in the earliest period is notorious for its fragility and transience. Diarists have frequently commented on the mysterious disappearance of words used with some frequency over a period of days or even weeks (see Bloom, 1973, for example). The process of lexical engagement may not yet have become a robust or reliable part of the word learning process in such cases.

neighbourhood densities and creating new associative links in both form and meaning. This implies a dynamic process of adjustment and readjustment that will necessarily slow in the course of development but that continues to operate imperceptibly over the lifespan (Wedel, Jackson, & Kaplan, 2013; Sóskuthy & Hay, 2017).

In the third 'moment'—to which we have given only cursory attention here—the child has made progress in developing her articulatory resources. With the benefit of more robust and more diversified production skills, which contribute to an ever more effective phonological memory, she can begin to map new adult word forms to more closely related output phonological sequences, eventually bypassing any previously established templatic patterns to produce forms that largely respect the segmental sequences of their models (while nevertheless applying regular phonological processes, such as cluster reduction, stopping of fricatives, gliding of liquids, etc., as necessary; Chapter 6 reports some examples of the shift into post-templatic systematicity). This is the period of early word combination and morphological development, when whole-word processes such as consonant harmony, truncation, and metathesis become increasingly rare (Grunwell, 1982; Vihman & Greenlee, 1987, illustrate mixed segment-based and holistic phonological production in ten three-year-olds, including the six children whose data are analysed in Chapter 3).[3]

As mentioned in Chapter 1, our basic conceptualization of the course of early phonological development is similar to that of other child phonologists, but there are differences in emphasis and in our understanding of development per se. We agree with Davis and MacNeilage (1995, 2000; MacNeilage & Davis, 2001), for example, that 'frame and content' or mandibular open-close action is basic to child speech production; it underlies 'canonical babbling' and is followed some months later by first attempts at words. However, we see that children's first identifiable words make use of whatever vocal patterns the child has become familiar with through babbling (Vihman, Macken, Miller, Simmons, & Miller, 1985). We fail to find the orderly pattern of emergence of segmental contrasts that Jakobson (1941/1968) described (see also critiques in Olmsted, 1966; Ferguson & Garnica, 1975; and Kiparsky & Menn, 1977). Instead, we see the first words as deriving from independent episodes of item learning, often with little if any consistency in phonological patterning (Menn & Vihman, 2011). And in the next phase, instead of the gradual releasing of C-V associations that Davis, MacNeilage, and Matyear (2002) anticipated as a natural concomitant of increasing word use, we see

[3] We can cite here a concrete example of systematic phonological substitution, stop for fricative, alongside a whole-word adaptation of a challenging word to an existing pattern, from a study of morphological acquisition in Eegimaa, a Joola language of the Casamance in southern Senegal (Sagna, Brown, Vihman, & Vihman, 2018). In his first recording, at age 2;2, Jandy produced several forms that show stopping of /s/ to [c] or of /v/ to [b] (e.g., [koccon] *kosoŋ* 'pig' [< Fr. *cochon*], [cíndo] *súndo* 'home' and, with the default nominal prefix *e-*, [e-bbu] *e-vvu* 'fly'). However, one 'whole word error' occurs: [kiccit] *bi-sikkit* 'biscuit' (< Fr. *biscuit*, with reinterpretation of the first syllable of the loanword as the prefix *bi*): In the child form, the prefix is omitted and the first two obstruents of the reanalysed root form metathesized, but a medial-position geminate stop is retained.

systematization and a regression in accuracy (see also Macken & Ferguson, 1983; Menn, 1983; Menn, Schmidt, & Nicholas, 2013).

We provided cross-linguistic evidence of (implicit) pre-selection of word forms in the first phase, indicating that the target forms initially attempted by children learning the several languages represented are constrained in similar ways, presumably due to commonality in the underlying neurophysiological basis for vocal practice: Most target words are mono- or disyllabic and include only a single 'true' (supraglottal) consonant type; that consonant is typically a stop or a nasal. These constraints also characterize the first word forms children themselves produce in the languages we have considered. In other words, the first words produced largely reflect 'the dynamics of selection', as MacNeilage anticipated in 1979: 'The child's first words can be seen as . . . a matter of choosing from the babbling repertoire a set of approximations to adult word forms' (p. 30). It is difficult to avoid the conclusion that, cross-linguistically, it is motoric limitations that constrain children as they move into more rapid word learning, while at the same time communicative and cognitive advances affect child understanding of the function of talk in a social context and inform a dawning appreciation of the symbolic value of language (Bates, 1979; Vihman & McCune, 1994). This fuels a strong drive to increase the expressive lexicon.

We argued that the primary function of templates is to bridge the gap between limited articulatory capacity and that growing lexical ambition. Accordingly, we provided data and analysis to demonstrate that in the second phase, as the pace of lexical advances increases, children extend their word production by fitting adult target forms into the motoric routines or prosodic structures with which they have become familiar in the first phase. We focused primarily on this second moment, when we can detect signs of generalization, whether in broad terms, involving preferred prosodic structures, or more specifically, as the child makes an implicit search for opportunities to use the segments or segmental sequences that happen to be accessible to him. Importantly, the resultant regression in accuracy demonstrates the kind of non-linearity that Dynamic Systems Theory posits for development: The first relatively simple words, amenable to production with just the limited resources the child has developed through vocal practice, come to be complemented by child attempts at more challenging, often longer word targets, with little or no change to their existing motor routines. This shift from relatively accurate first words to more radically modified later words has been amply documented, and the developmental profile—the 'U-shaped curve'—has long been familiar from other areas of language development, most notably the acquisition of past tense in English (Cazden, 1968). (Tessier, 2019, has provided a sharply contrasting approach to explaining regression in phonological development, framed in Optimality Theory—although she concedes that templates of the kind reported by Priestly, 1977, cannot readily be explained by her account).

In their A[rticulatory]-map Model (discussed below), McAllister Byun, Inkelas, and Rose (2016) emphasize accuracy as the primary developmental goal. In contrast, we argue that, although accuracy is necessarily the ultimate measure of success in learning to produce words, the child's primary challenge in a period of rapid lexical growth is to gain not only motoric control but also its necessary complement, the ability to retain forms in memory (whether in whole or in part) well enough to access them at will. In dynamic systems terms, both articulatory skill and phonological memory are likely control parameters, gateways for lexical advance and important sources of individual differences (see Aitchison & Chiat, 1981).

Edelman (1992) saw memory as resulting 'from a process of continual recate-gorization. By its nature, memory is procedural and involves continual motor activity and repeated rehearsal in different contexts' (p. 102). As Thelen and Smith (1994) elaborate:

> Each memory is dynamically constructed from many, but not all, of the previously facilitated [neural] connections...Because the perceptual categories are themselves probabilistic and context-bound, so are the memories that are based on these categories themselves fluid and inexact...Because infants' experience acting and thinking in many different contexts...is limited primarily by their motor skills, what infants remember should be tied closely to the perceptual-motor situation in which the associations were established.   (p. 203)

Here the templates, or favoured prosodic structures, appear to serve an important function: One need not remember everything about a word form in order to produce it if one's attention is channelled by a dominant shape or phonological sequence. Having a limited range of output types simplifies access to representations as well as on-line production while at the same time permitting more ambitious word choices. (Furthermore, the child's conversational partners, adults or older siblings, can readily accommodate the child's idiosyncratic ways of saying words if they are also relatively consistent.) This means that, in the second phase described above in particular, the motive to achieve accuracy in production plays a relatively minor role. Instead, lexical diversity is most likely the primary goal for most infants as long as articulatory skills lag behind cognitive and communicative development.

Experience producing words that are similar to if not fully matched to their adult target should support the child in gaining better representational access to the adult form. Phonological memory is critical in this process. Memory for word forms develops through use (Jones, Macken, & Nicolls, 2004; Keren-Portnoy, Vihman, DePaolis, Whitaker, & Williams, 2010; Parra, Hoff, & Core, 2011); production-based implicit memory for a well-practised articulatory routine or prosodic structure supports word-form retention, even if not all elements of the word are retained. Production of a truncated, harmonized, or restructured word form will familiarize the child with the form to some extent despite the failure to match the target; furthermore, even inaccurate production should result in more opportunities to hear others produce the word in conversational exchange.

After a few days, weeks, or months of this kind of experience, the child may make a seemingly sudden leap, abandoning many if not all of her idiosyncratic forms in favour of more adult-like production. This replacement of templates, which occurs in parallel with advances in articulatory skills in the third moment we have described, may give the impression of 'across-the-board' change, especially if, as is generally the case, the density of the recordings is insufficient to allow close tracking of development. ('In order to study transitions as they happen, the time scale of observation must be smaller than the time scale of change': Thelen & Smith, 1994, p. 252; cf. also Lieven & Behrens, 2012 on the effects of sampling density.) The resultant improvement in production is sometimes interpreted as evidence that the child has now gained access to abstract adult phonological structure (e.g., Rose, 2018). However, the kind of close tracking of changes to a child's word forms that a diarist like Priestly provides demonstrates the extent of variability involved, with 'correction' to target-like forms occurring in parallel, over a period of many weeks, with the deployment of new (inaccurate) template-based forms (see Chapter 6).

9.2 System-building: Phonology and the lexicon

The idea of grammar as a network connecting similar elements at all levels—segments, syllables, morphemes, words, and larger units—was lost sight of over the last century, a period dominated by reductionist analyses under the influence of structural and generative linguistics. It was clearly understood by earlier linguists, however, as is evident from this passage, cited by Ackerman and Malouf (2018):

> . . . we have shown that the acquisition and use of language would be impossible if language were represented by a mass of isolated words. Words are connected to each other directly: 1) through association by similarity and 2) through association by contiguity. From these arise nests or systems and series of words. The associations by similarity make possible creativity in language.
>
> (Kruszewski, 1883, pp. 68f., as cited in J. R. Williams, 1993, p. 85)

The view that the parts not only 'construct' the whole but that the system as a whole also has (unpredictable or unanticipated) effects on the parts is critical to current ideas about 'word-based morphology' (see Chapter 1). Furthermore, the reference in the passage quoted to acquisition, or what is now termed 'the learnability problem', points up the relevance of such approaches for our themes here.[4] The emergence and implications of systematicity are critical for understanding early lexical and phonological development—and they arise again and again, as new systems are created in the course of the assimilation or integration of

---

[4] Note, however, that translations differ: In Koerner's 1995 edition of Kruszewski's *Writings in General Linguistics* the word *assimilation* is used in the same passage in lieu of *acquisition* (p. 100).

new bits of knowledge, at new levels of organization (see Karmiloff-Smith's [1992] 're-representation').

We return again to the importance of distinguishing two aspects of word learning. The first is 'lexical configuration', in which a particular form is first registered and appropriately linked with its situational meaning ('item learning')—although both form and meaning may be modulated, in the child's case, by limitations on both articulatory skills and semantic or pragmatic understanding (see the two-step model of word learning, with a focus on reference, in McMurray, Horst, & Samuelson, 2012). After a period of internal consolidation and/or repeated encounters with the word, the newly learned word form begins to be 'lexically engaged', finding a place in the child's larger network of known words. The formation of one or more templates reflects that engagement and interaction among the forms the child has come to know well through repeated hearing and use. This is a highly compelling picture of lexical and phonological development: It enables us to conceptualize how, through word learning and representation, a networked system self-organizes, with similar units linking with (and thus co-activating) one another—monosyllabic words with other monosyllables, stressed syllables with other stressed syllables, onsets with onsets, harmonized whole-word consonantal sequences with other such sequences, and so on.

Because word-learning research along these lines is relatively recent (cf. Gaskell & Dumay, 2003; Leach & Samuel, 2007; Lindsay & Gaskell, 2013; Tamminen & Gaskell, 2013; Brown & Gaskell, 2014) and has not so far included infant studies, we have little information as to the key organizing elements, but we can assume that they are the units familiar from phonological theory (e.g., features, moras, syllables, feet), with the specifics differing by language, depending on typical word length, morphological complexity and so on. One source of data revealing something of the lexical network is the study of malapropisms, or lexical items mis-selected on the basis of similarity in form (e.g., in adults: Fay & Cutler, 1977; Zwicky, 1978–9; Vitevitch, 1997; in children: Aitchison, 1972; Aitchison & Straf, 1981; Vihman, 1981; Jaeger, 2005).

Recent studies using computational modelling represent linguistic knowledge in multiply layered and linked systems or networks. For adults, for example, Shook and Marian (2013) focus on the particular problem posed by bilingual comprehension, modelling the well-established effects of cross-linguistic interaction in lexical processing via a network in which formally similar exemplars cluster together, regardless of their source language. For infants, Mayor and Plunkett (2014) extend McClelland and Elman's (1986) TRACE model to simulate word-form recognition, finding that lexical knowledge strongly constrains perceptual processes. (See also Werker & Curtin, 2005; Curtin, Byers-Heinlein & Werker, 2011.) Considerable further insight into emergent phonological knowledge could be gained from a model of infant advances in speech production that would combine the steps that Leach and Samuel (2007) propose for word-form learning with those envisioned by McMurray et al. (2012) for word use: Although both proposals address the systematization of the lexicon rather than phonological grammar per se, in our understanding advances in phonological knowledge are dependent on that emergent systematization.

The adaptation of words either to generic prosodic structures or to more fully specified templates is good evidence that a child has begun to reach the level of lexical engagement: It is only when words activate one another, or are simultaneously represented, that familiar word forms can begin to influence the shape of newly learned items. Taking a strictly motoric approach—assuming that the child automatically extends a motoric routine to new words—might lead one to argue that such an inference is too strong, but in most of the examples we have identified, especially in the case of the more fully specified templates, the extension of a routine to a new word is not fully 'automatic'; instead, there is adaptation or reorganization, with elements of the target form creatively reallocated to fit the child's preferred pattern (see Priestly's examples, App. II, or [kiccit] < *bisikkit* 'biscuit', in fn. 2, this chapter). This is a strong sign of engagement, categorization, and incipient lexical networking. The gradual self-organization of known words into a phonological network follows from usage-based ideas; evidence of templatic activity in the single-word period gives some insight into the way that grammatical regularities can emerge out of the words the child knows. Note, however, that this account makes no explicit reference to 'the phonological grammar', as invoked in constraint-based and other generative accounts (e.g., Fikkert, 1994; Morrisette, Dinnsen, & Gierut, 2003; Fikkert & Levelt, 2008; McAllister Byun et al., 2016; Tessier, 2019).

9.3 Current models of phonological development

At least two models of infant speech perception and word learning are currently available: Jusczyk's (1992, 1993, 1997) WRAPSA model, touched on in Chapter 1, and Werker and Curtin's (2005) PRIMIR model, updated to include bilingual development in Curtin et al. (2011; Vihman, 2014, ch. 9, provides overviews of both WRAPSA and PRIMIR). Neither of these addresses production, however. On the production side, there has long been a divide, noted earlier, between (i) formal generative models, which generally assume innate foreknowledge of linguistic principles, embedded in the construct of Universal Grammar (e.g., Smith, 1973, 2010; Fikkert, 1994), and (ii) emergentist models, which take a usage-based perspective (for a review of formalist and functionalist theoretical perspectives, see Vihman, 2014, chs. 9 and 10, resp.). Recently this divide has begun to break down, with two current models incorporating aspects of both approaches; interestingly, exemplar ideas are basic to both of them.

As summarized in Chapter 3, Menn and her colleagues' (Menn, Schmidt, & Nicholas, 2009, 2013) 'Linked-Attractor model' finds a role for rules, constraints, and templates, drawing broadly on existing theoretical formulations (including both formalist or generative constraint-based and functionalist connectionist models). The long-term goal of this ambitious model is to combine these approaches into a far more sweeping synthesis that would address aspects of both perception (early category formation as well as later word recognition) and production (prelinguistic vocalizations and word use), and also the interaction or 'mapping' between the two. Notably, although the model remains sketchy so far, it is intended to allow for the (multimodal) dynamics of variation and change that are so fundamental to development.

In a somewhat similar vein, in two recent papers McAllister Byun and her colleagues have sought to integrate emergentist or usage-based and production-based ideas with formalist generative models (McAllister Byun & Tessier, 2016; McAllister Byun et al., 2016). It is worth noting the difference in emphasis between these otherwise compatible approaches. Menn et al. draw on rules and constraints for the contribution these elements of previous theoretical approaches can make to what is essentially a 'whole-word phonology' model expressed in terms of 'attractors'. The conceptualization is strongly rooted in the principles of neural activation; the goal is ultimately to achieve better understanding of how neurolinguistic knowledge actually develops and is represented over the lifespan.

McAllister Byun and her colleagues agree with much of what Menn et al. propose. They emphasize the role of motoric limitations in constraining early production and they also see emergent systematicity as deriving, at least in part, from generalizations over a child's own patterns. Both of their 2016 papers also draw at least in passing on notions of memory and templates, not typically considered in constraint-based models. In contrast with Menn and her colleagues, however, both of the contributions of McAllister Byun and her colleagues insist on the validity and centrality of abstract elements of phonology, or 'the grammar' (see also Rose, 2018); McAllister Byun et al. go further in shaping these ideas into an optimality theoretic account. As this approach differs in many ways from that adopted in this book we provide here a critical summary of both McAllister Byun and Tessier (2016)'s integrative overview of current emergentist and formal-grammar accounts and the formalist proposals of McAllister Byun et al.'s (2016) 'A-map model', comparing the latter approach to ours and to the overarching developmental perspective of Dynamic Systems Theory.

McAllister Byun and Tessier (2016) provide an extensive and sympathetic account of the evidence available in support of the role of production in constructing phonological knowledge. They situate their proposals between the extremes of well-established views within the formal phonology literature—that is, the view that child phonology is simply a variant of adult phonology, with differently ordered rules or constraints (e.g., Smith, 1973; Pater & Barlow, 2003; Dinnsen, 2008), and the view that child patterns reflect mere 'performance' and accordingly need not be given serious consideration in any theoretical model

(Hale & Reiss, 2008). McAllister Byun and Tessier themselves hypothesize that 'children's grammars are constructed under the influence of performance factors' (p. 445). Thus they emphasize the role of 'motor influences', relating to the limitations imposed by immature and/or inexperienced neurophysiological capacities, and the consequent importance of 'each individual speaker's previous history of speech production' (p. 431)—or in other words, practice or 'usage'. (See also Tessier, 2015.)

As part of their dialogue with formalist approaches McAllister Byun and Tessier distinguish between 'restrictions and alternations that are unambiguously classified as phonological in adult grammars' (i.e., morphophonological alternations) and 'systematic sound patterns in child speech that are not modeled by adult speakers' (i.e., the well-established phonological processes that affect late-learned segments and sequences, such as fricative stopping) or, more problematic for phonological theory, patterns that 'lack counterparts in all of phonological typology', such as the most widespread of child patterns, consonant harmony (pp. 432f.). Morphophonological alternations have received very little attention in the developmental literature (and indeed McAllister Byun and Tessier's examples date back 30 or 40 years); they can be expected to emerge considerably later than the period of template use that has been our focus here. In general, these authors argue that 'if we make the assumption that mature and developing phonologies reflect different permutations of the same basic elements, it is difficult to capture the full range of child speech patterns without generating incorrect predictions for the possible range of grammars in adult typology' (p. 433).

After discussing the evidence for a role for production in phonological learning, McAllister Byun and Tessier focus on a defence of the idea of emergent (rather than universal-grammar-based) segments, features and constraints (see also Fikkert & Levelt, 2008). They support the idea of early representations being 'holistic', 'targeting the gestalt of the word rather than sublexical elements' (p. 440), and draw on the work of Munson, Edwards, and Beckman (2012) to show that segmental knowledge grows in relation to (and as a probable concomitant of) vocabulary size, not age.

McAllister Byun and Tessier also cite with approval Metsala and Walley's (1998) 'Lexical Restructuring Hypothesis', which sees emergent segmental representation as a response to the pressure of increasing neighbourhood density. Note, however, that both corpus analyses, such as Ota and Green (2012), and experimental studies of word-form recognition, such as Fernald, Swingley, and Pinto (2001), have provided counterevidence to this hypothesis. In fact, as suggested in Chapter 8, there is little reason to assume that infants at the early stages of word learning experience a need to keep word forms distinct; lexical contrast is of least importance in the context of child discourse, which typically involves highly familiar interlocutors and focuses on the here-and-now. Even at age three, children show a willingness to adjust, without apparent discomfort, to sudden conversational shifts due to mutual misunderstanding (Vihman, 1981).[5] Instead of seeing the emergence of more fully or more accurately specified segmental representations as a response to lexical pressure we may ascribe this developmental shift to lexical growth itself, which provides steadily increasing exposure both to target word forms and to the feedback afforded by repeated deployment of those forms in the child's own production (see Chapter 6).

As one might expect, McAllister Byun et al. (2016) present some of the same ideas as McAllister Byun and Tessier (2016), yet the shape of the argument is quite different, with constraint-based formalism taking centre stage along with a side-lining of the notion of holistic early representations. What unites the two papers is an emphasis on the role of motor factors, or articulatory limitations, in shaping early phonology. What most sharply separates them is McAllister Byun et al.'s goal of accounting for child phonology within the framework of Optimality Theory. This paper focuses on patterns that are specific to children, including phonological templates. The authors' stated goal is to account for such patterns 'without abandoning the assumption that child grammars draw from the broad space of possible adult grammars' (p. 141).

McAllister Byun et al. (2016) start from a very different conceptualization of both adult and child grammar from the one presented here. These researchers see 'child-specific phonological patterns' as a problem for phonological theory, as indicated in their definition of these patterns as 'any systematic patterning of sounds found in the speech of children but not in adult typology' (p. 141). That is, these patterns challenge a theoretical preference for child-to-adult continuity in phonological systems, based on universal constraints. McAllister Byun et al. accept the idea that early child forms may be holistically represented: 'For very young children, exemplar memory may be organized primarily at a coarse-grained (e.g. word) level' (p. 152). Also, these authors argue—similarly to Menn et al. (2013), as they point out—that the child's internal model is based on both their own and others' outputs. And although, like McAllister Byun and Tessier (2016), they see articulatory limitations as the key factor shaping outputs, they also acknowledge a role for memory, noting that 'both adult and child learners acquire new word-meaning mappings more quickly and accurately when they already possess the corresponding articulatory routine in memory' (p. 149).

In the A-map account the child faces two 'grammatical pressures', (i) to match the adult string but also (ii) to do so consistently, with a stable, well-practised motor plan. The competing constraints that they propose to express this tension

---

[5] To illustrate, see this brief conversational exchange (from Vihman, 1981, p. 248): 'One child (N) announces, "We have a palm tree at home".

Other child (A): Does it have fruit on it?

N: No, it has nuts on it.

A: We have a plum tree too.

They then go on to discuss plums.'

derive from the grammatical module: 'PRECISE' requires reduction in variability as the child's motor plans come under more intentional control; this requirement effectively falls into disuse in typical adult production. 'ACCURATE' expresses the requirement to match output to internal episodic traces of the adult form. The key idea is that these constraints, although most active in the early period of lexical and phonological development, persist in adult grammars and may play a role there under special conditions, as in cases of aphasia, for example.

As they develop their formalism McAllister Byun and her colleagues seem to lose track of some of the ideas they have embraced, however. Templates are mentioned, but how such patterns may evolve, affect other targets, and then fade from use receives no attention; similarly, the role of production in memory is plausibly related to Hickok and Poeppel's (2004, 2007) account of a possible neural basis ('a string that undergoes auditory-motor transformation is encoded more specifically and more robustly than a string processed at a purely auditory level in the ventral stream', p. 149), but these ideas are not integrated into the constraint-based account.

The model makes no explicit distinction between different developmental phases, with their differing consequences for the relationship of child and adult forms. McAllister Byun and her colleagues predict, in a concluding section, that the interaction of their constraints should result in low accuracy (of segmental production) early on, along with high variability due to the child's lack of a stable motor plan; this should be followed by low accuracy and low variability (or greater stability), and then 'at least a brief interval of heightened variability' before correct production stabilizes (p. 167). If we take this to refer to phonological development over the entire early period, the predictions do not accord with the existing evidence from multiple studies of children learning a wide range of languages. If they relate, instead, to the second and third phases of word learning outlined above, the fit is better, although the templatic patterning that we have presented cannot easily be interpreted within the A-map framework.

McAllister Byun et al. support their argument for grammatically conditioned effects on production with evidence from a single child acquiring Portuguese. However, the short phrases they provide as examples of the effects of adult grammar (specifically, resyllabification rules) all appear to be 'frozen' or rote-learned expressions rather than child-initiated word combinations. As such, these child productions appear to reflect adult phonological patterning rather than being, as suggested, child applications of positional stopping across word-boundary (p. 161).

Finally, they suggest, rather surprisingly, that 'the relative weighting of PRECISE and ACCURATE within a child's phonology should show relatively stable effects across multiple phonological patterns' (p. 168), implying a categorical division of learning types or strategies between different children. Ferguson and Farwell (1975) also commented on the individual differences in phonological learning that they observed and Macken (1992, 1995) proposed that child learners fall into distinct 'harmony' vs. 'melody' types, based on their template use. Note, however, that although Vihman and Greenlee (1987), whom McAllister Byun et al. cite in this connection, proposed distinguishing child learning styles as 'systematic and stable' vs. 'exploratory and variable', it is now apparent—not least in the light of Dynamic Systems ideas—that such broad characterization glosses over all of the pertinent process needed to inform our understanding of development. It is not clear how seriously McAllister Byun and her colleagues take the idea that weightings are set child-by-child rather than moment-by-moment, or how the dynamics of development could be accommodated in such a model.

9.4 The function of child and adult templates

At the broadest level, child templates serve a *social function*, facilitating entry into verbal exchanges based on the child's emergent capacity to attempt a wider range of challenging adult target forms, however inaccurately. The situational context will often make the child's meaning clear enough to be understood, especially once a template has taken hold and begun to be used consistently for a time. In addition, whether child templates are taken to reflect (secondary) distributional learning, based on a limited sample of familiar vocal shapes, or the more direct extension of a motor routine, assimilating less familiar word forms, the development of such an internal model will serve a *memory function*, supporting retention and phonological representation, however approximate, of increasing numbers of forms.

Additionally, given the social context of development, even inaccurate 'adapted' word forms are likely to motivate adult responses, which should be particularly informative when the child has just produced a form. (Note that contingent responses have long been observed to support word learning: Tomasello & Farrar, 1986; Akhtar, Dunham, & Dunham, 1991; Carpenter, Nagell, & Tomasello, 1998; Rollins, 2003; Masur, Flynn, & Eichorst, 2005; McGillion, Pine, Herbert, & Matthews, 2017b.) Sporadic priming by an immediate model may account for some of the variability reported in the more detailed studies, when template-based and 'ordinary' forms occur in parallel. Thus, we see in Priestly's (1977) data (App. II) that adapted child forms may co-exist for days or weeks with a more advanced, more adult-like form, although in a diary study like Priestly's we lack information as to the discourse context. In general, no close longitudinal tracking has yet been attempted to test the relationship of moment-by-moment variability in production to priming effects from input speech, but it would seem worthwhile to look for such an effect.

Generally speaking, templates appear to facilitate and speed word learning. However, no one has yet addressed the paradox of how templates might support phonological advance, given that they would appear in the nature of things to limit a child's motivation or opportunity to extend their range of experience with production. We can speculate that templates serve word learning by providing both (i) *direct articulatory experience*, in production, with some portion of the required phonetic sequence and (ii) *repeated perceptual experience*, in the course of individual episodes, with both the adult model and the child's own variants. Under an exemplar model this would clearly have the ultimate effect of highlighting the missing elements and consolidating memory of the adult form.

Generative models, with their continuing distinction between competence and performance, look for ways to accommodate child and adult differences within a phonological grammar informed by innately programmed principles or constraints. Here we have taken a different approach, looking above all for insight into the developmental process where child production is concerned and assuming that grammar is not innately inscribed, not categorical and not the same at different points in development. Furthermore, like Thelen and Smith (1994), we find the long-standing division between competence and performance to be counterproductive for research purposes as well as out of step with contemporary psycholinguistic and neurolinguistic understanding of the way that language is learned, processed and produced.

Our foray, in Chapter 8, into productive templatic patterning in adult usage was intended as an exploration of adult–child similarities at a deeper level. We argue that adult creativity in word formation is rooted in the same biological pattern-finding propensities as those that channel early phonological and lexical development.[6] There are several similarities in the phonological processes involved, such as (i) reliance, in both cases, on an existing stock of highly frequent or familiar forms, (ii) implicit imposition of templatic requirements in terms of a limitation on length in syllables or metrical feet, and (iii) possible further specification as to particular onset or coda consonants.

Furthermore, short forms and rhyming compounds, which express a range of affective and pragmatic meanings associated with informal situations and familiar social settings, derive from a playful, innovatory mindset on the part of their users. This supports creativity, giving rise to productive extension of the adult lexicon. There is thus an inherent similarity in the settings, the intimate exchanges of friends and family (or an implicit allusion to such exchanges, in long-established colloquial forms), in which adults feel free to expand the lexical resources of their language and in which children take their first steps in word learning. The specific functions served by those very different activities are not the same, but it is perhaps no coincidence that 'language at play' is basic to both.

---

[6] For a sharply contrasting account of the deep biological origins of adult–child similarities in phonological processing and pattern finding, see Berent (2013).

Children and language groups (Chapter 4)

Sources for the data used in Chapter 4 are given for each group as a whole, except where separate published sources are appropriate for different children. Children are ordered within groups by age at the data point analysed here. Target words include imitations.

UK English (All but Jude: Menn & Vihman, 2011; DePaolis et al., 2016)			
Child name (age)	**Target words**	**Prosodic variants**	
Jude (1;3) Keren-Portnoy et al., 2010	42	50	
Ella (1;4)	34	55	
Rachel (1;5)	61	75	
Lewis (1;6)	31	32	
Patrick (1;6.5)	27	36	
Tobias (1;7)	34	46	
Flora (1;7)	46	50	
Tania (1;7)	37	45	
mean	**39**	**49**	

Estonian Based on diary reports: 30+ target words per child (70th to 100th)			
	Target words (English)	**Prosodic variants (English)**	**Proportion of English variants**
Maarja (1;4–1;5) Vihman, 2016; Vihman & Vihman, 2011	34 (17)	50 (22)	.44
Virve (1;5–1;7) Vihman, 1976; Vihman & Croft, 2007	36	39	0
Raivo (1;6–1;8) Vihman, 1981, 2014, 2016	53 (11)	63 (15)	.24
Kaia (1;7–1;8) Vihman, 2016	57 (20)	59 (20)	20 (.34)
Madli (1;8) Kõrgvee, 2001	44	48	0
mean	**45**	**52**	

Continued

Continued

Finnish			
Child name (age)	**Target words**	**Prosodic variants**	
Sini (1;3) Savinainen-Makkonen, 2001	53	60	
Eliisa (1;3.5) Kunnari, 2000, 2003; Vihman & Velleman, 2000; Vihman & Kunnari, 2006	30	35	
Mira (1;5) Kunnari, 2000, 2003; Vihman & Velleman, 2000	29	32	
Atte (1;8) Kunnari, 2000, 2003; Vihman & Velleman, 2000; Vihman & Kunnari, 2006	26	29	
Eelis (1;10) Kunnari, 2000, 2003; Vihman, 2014	33	37	
mean	**33**	**38**	
French			
Child name (age)	**Target words**	**Prosodic variants**	
Carole (1;2.5) Boysson-Bardies & Vihman, 1991	27	44	
Laurent (1;5.5) Boysson-Bardies & Vihman, 1991; Vihman, 1993	29	46	
Charles (1;6) Boysson-Bardies & Vihman, 1991; Vihman, 1996	27	36	
Noël (1;6) Boysson-Bardies & Vihman, 1991; Vihman, 2014	30	44	
mean	**28**	**43**	
Italian (1;9) Vihman & Majorano, 2017			
Child name	**Target words**	**Prosodic variants**	
A.P.	32	34	
C.L.	47	50	
G.A.	33	33	
G.C.	32	33	

I.S.	46	47	
J.A.	33	36	
L.L.	57	60	
mean	**40**	**42**	

Welsh
Vihman, 2000

Child name (age)	Target words	Prosodic variants	
Elen (1;5)	34	39	
Fflur (1;5)	36	48	
Gwyn (1;5)	42	53	
Carys (1;6)	31	35	
mean	**36**	**44**	

C's adapted productions in chronological order (based on Priestly 1977, Appendix II)

The week numbers indicate when the forms were first observed, starting at child age 1;10.2. Most child words have equal stress on both syllables; otherwise, stress is on the initial syllable (Priestly, 1977/2013, p. 218); it is marked on ORF forms only. BEF: Bisyllabic experimental form, MEF: Monosyllabic experimental form, ORF: Ordinary replacement form. (Stress is marked on the adult form only when it is not on the initial syllable.)

	Lexical item	Target form	Child form	Week	BEF/MEF/ORF
1	banana	bəˈnɒnə	a) bajan b) bánan	3, 4, 6 5	BEF ORF
2	doughnut	downʌt	a) dɛjawt b) dǽnɔt	3, 7 8	BEF ORF
3	chocolate	tʃɒklɪt kajæk	a) kajak b) kɔjak c) kæ·k d) kákat e) kákɪt	3, 6, 9 7 7 6 9	BEF BEF MEF ORF ORF
4	carol	kærəl	a) kajal b) kǽrəl	3 12	BEF ORF
5	candle	kændəl	a) kajal b) kǽndəl	3 12	BEF ORF
6	farmer	fɑmə	a) fajam b) fɑmə	3, 6 6	BEF ORF
7	sucker	sʌkə	a) fajak b) fʌkə c) sʌkə	3, 6 4 12	BEF ORF ORF
8	blanket	blæŋkɪt	a) bajak b) bǽkɪt	3, 6 11	BEF ORF
9	dragon	drægən	a) dajan b) dajak c) dǽgən	3 4 10	BEF BEF ORF
10	medicine	mɛtsən	a) mɛjas b) mɛtsən	3 12	BEF ORF
11	music	mjuwzɪk	a) mɛjas b) mijus c) mýzɪk	3 6 12	BEF BEF ORF

12	records	rɛkɔdz	a) rɛjas	3	BEF
			b) rɛkas	10	ORF
13	peanut	pijnʌt	a) pijat	4, 8	BEF
			b) pijnat	9	ORF
14	(tooth)paste	pɛjst	a) pija	4	BEF
			b) péjs	12	ORF
15	panda	pændə	a) pajan	4	BEF
			b) pǽndə	9	ORF
16	powder	pawdə	a) pajat	4	BEF
			b) páwdə	11	ORF
17	police-car	pə'liskɑ	a) pija	4	BEF
			b) pəlískɑ	13	ORF
18	bison	bajsən	a) bajas	4	BEF
			b) bájsən	12	ORF
19	tiger	tajgə	a) tajak	4	BEF
			b) tajaŋ	4, 6	BEF
			c) kajaŋ	9	BEF
			d) tájgə	10	ORF
20	turkey	təkij	a) tajak	4	BEF
			b) təkij	12	ORF
21	Jesus	dʒijzəs	a) dʒijas	4	BEF
			b) dʒijzəs	13	ORF
22	garage	gærɑʒ	a) gajas	4	BEF
			b) gáras	10	ORF
23	finger	fɪŋgə	a) fijak	4, 7	BEF
			b) fajak	5	BEF
			c) fɪŋgə	10	ORF
24	present	prɛzənt	a) pɛjas	4	BEF
			b) prɛzət	13	ORF
25	Brenda	brɛndə	a) bɛjan	4	BEF
			b) bɛndə	10	ORF
26	Christmas	krɪsməs	a) kijas	4	BEF
			b) kɪsəs	12	ORF
27	spider	spajdə	a) bajat	4	BEF
			b) bájdə	8	ORF
28	streamer	strimə	a) mijat	4	BEF
			b) dijmə	12	ORF
29	whisker	wɪskə	a) wijak	4	BEF
			b) wɪsə	12	ORF
30	whistle	wɪsəl	a) wijas	4	BEF
			b) wijus	6	BEF
			c) wɪsu	12	ORF
31	hanger	hæŋə	a) hajaŋ	4	BEF
			b) hǽŋə	12	ORF

Continued

Continued

	Lexical item	Target form	Child form	Week	BEF/MEF/ORF
32	monster	mɒnstə	a) majɒs b) mɛjan c) majɒs d) mɒstə	4 5 6 6	BEF BEF BEF ORF
33	rabbit	ræbɪt	a) rajat b) rajap c) ræ·p d) ræbɪt	4 5, 7 10, 11 9	BEF BEF MEF ORF
34	rhinoceros	raj'nɒsərəs	a) rajas b) rajɒs c) ràjnɒ́s	4 7 12	BEF BEF ORF
35	elephant	ɛlɪfənt	a) ɛjat b) ɛ·t c) ɛlət	4, 6 10, 12 8	BEF MEF ORF
36	parrot	pærət	a) pajat b) pǽrət	5, 9, 11 13	BEF ORF
37	porridge	pɒrɪdʒ	a) pajas b) pajɒs c) pɒrɪs	5 12 12	BEF BEF ORF
38	Tobin	towbɪn	a) bajam b) bæ·m c) tówbɪn	5, 7 7 12	BEF MEF ORF
39	carrot	kærət	a) kajat b) kæ·t c) kærət	5, 9 12 12	BEF MEF ORF
40	cupboard	kʌbəd	a) kajat b) pʌbəd	5, 9 12	BEF ORF
41	covered (wagon)	kʌvəd	a) kajat b) kʌvəd	5 13	BEF ORF
42	coaster	kowstə	a) kajows b) kówsə	5 8	BEF ORF
43	aerial	ɛrɪjal	a) ɛjal b) ɛrijal	5, 12 13	BEF ORF
44	accident	æksɪdənt	a) ajak b) ǽkas	5 11	BEF ORF
45	Oscar	ɒskə	a) ɔjas b) ɒsə	5 8	BEF ORF
46	berries	bɛrijz	a) bɛjas b) bɛrijs	6 13	BEF ORF
47	fountain	fawntɪn	a) fajan b) fáwtɪn	6 12	BEF ORF
48	flannel	flænəl	a) fajan b) fajal c) fǽnəl	6 6 10	BEF BEF ORF

49	woman	wύmən	a) wajum	6	BEF
			b) wύbən	12	ORF
50	mouth-organ	mawθɔgən	a) majɒŋ	6	BEF
			b) máwtɔgə	8	ORF
51	lizard	lɪzəd	a) zijan	6	BEF
			b) lɪzət	12	ORF
52	emu	ijmjuw	a) ijumum	6	BEF
			b) ijum	6	BEF
			c) ijmju	12	ORF
53	orange	ɒrɪndʒ	a) ajat	6	BEF
			b) ajɒt	7	BEF
			c) ɒrɪn	11	ORF
			d) ɒrɪdz	12	ORF
54	pillow	pɪlow	a) pijal	7	BEF
			b) pijow	8	BEF
			c) pilow	13	ORF
55	basket	bɑskɪt	a) bajak	7	BEF
			b) básak	12	ORF
56	gingerbread-man	dʒɪndʒəbrɛdmæn	a) bijan	7	BEF
			b) dʒɪnəmæn	12	ORF
57	Jennifer	dʒɛnɪfə	a) dʒɛjan	7	BEF
			b) dʒɛnə	12	ORF
58	garbage-bag	gɑbɪdʒbæg	a) bajak	7	BEF
			b) bægɪdʒ	12	ORF
59	seven	sɛvən	a) sɛjan	7	BEF
			b) sɛvən	7	ORF
60	hydrant	hajdrənt	a) hajat	7	BEF
			b) hájdət	12	ORF
61	melon	mɛlən	a) mɛjan	7	BEF
			b) mɛ·n	12	MEF
			c) mɛlən	12	ORF
62	musk-ox	mʌskɒks	a) majɒks	7	BEF
			b) máksɒks	10	ORF
63	runner	rʌnə	a) rajan	7	BEF
			b) ránə	10	ORF
64	squirrel	skwɪrəl	a) gúrjel	10, 13	ORF
			b) gijal	12	BEF
65	tomorrow	təmɒrow	pajɒm	unassigned	BEF
66	soldier	sowldʒə	sɔjat	unassigned	BEF
67	shoulder	ʃowldə	sɔjat	unassigned	BEF
68	headache	hɛdɛjk	hajak	unassigned	BEF
69	minute	mɪnɪt	mijat	unassigned	BEF
70	engine	ɛndʒɪn	ɛjan	unassigned	BEF

Week-by-week listing of C's adapted productions (based on Priestly 1977, Appendix II)

Word forms that occur more than once in the same form in different weeks are in italics after the first mention.

Week	Target word	BEF	MEF	ORF
3				
	banana	bajan		
	blanket	bajak		
	candle	kajal		
	carol	kajal		
	chocolate	kajak		
	doughnut	dɛjawt		
	dragon	dajan		
	farmer	fajam		
	medicine	mɛjas		
	music	mɛjas		
	records	rɛjas		
	sucker	fajak		
4				
	banana	*bajan*		
	bison	bajas		
	Brenda	bɛjan		
	Christmas	kijas		
	dragon	dajak		
	elephant	ɛjat		
	finger	fijak		
	garage	gajas		
	hanger	hajaŋ		

	Jesus	dʒijas		
	monster	majɒs		
	panda	pajan		
	peanut	pijat		
	police-car	pija		
	powder	pajat		
	present	pɛjas		
	rabbit	rajat		
	rhinoceros	rajas		
	spider	bajat		
	streamer	mijat		
	sucker			fʌkə
	tiger	tajak, tajaŋ		
	(tooth)paste	pija		
	turkey	tajak		
	whisker	wijak		
	whistle	wijas		
5				
	accident	ajak		
	aerial	ɛjal		
	banana			bánan
	carrot	kajat		
	coaster	kajows		
	covered (wagon)	kajat		
	cupboard	kajat		
	finger	fajak		
	monster	mɛjan		
	Oscar	ɔjas		
	parrot	pajat		
	porridge	pajas		
	rabbit	rajap		
	Tobin	bajam		
6				
	banana	*bajan*		
	berries	bɛjas		

Continued

Continued

Week	Target word	BEF	MEF	ORF
	blanket	*bajak*		
	chocolate	*kajak*		kákat
	elephant	*ɛjat*		
	emu	ijumum, ijum		
	farmer	*fajam*		fɑmə
	flannel	fajan, fajal		
	fountain	fajan		
	lizard	zijan		
	monster	majɒs		mɒstə
	mouth-organ	majɒŋ		
	music	mijus		
	orange	ajat		
	sucker	*fajak*		
	tiger	*tajaŋ*		
	whistle	wijus		
	woman	wajum		
7				
	basket	bajak		
	chocolate	kɔjak	kæ·k	
	doughnut	*dɛjawt*		
	finger	*fijak*		
	garbage-bag	bajak		
	gingerbread-man	bijan		
	hydrant	hajat		
	Jennifer	dʒɛjan		
	melon	mɛjan		
	musk-ox	majɒks		
	orange	ajɒt		
	pillow	pijal		
	rabbit	*rajap*		
	rhinoceros	rajɒs		
	runner	rajan		
	seven	sɛjan		sɛvən
	Tobin	*bajam*	bæ·m	

8				
	coaster			kówsə
	doughnut			dǽnɔt
	elephant			ɛlət
	mouth-organ			máwtɔgə
	Oscar			ɒsə
	peanut	*pijat*		
	pillow	pijow		
	spider			bájdə
9				
	carrot	*kajat*		
	chocolate	*kajak*		kákɪt
	coaster			kówsə
	cupboard	*kajat*		
	panda			pǽndə
	parrot	*pajat*		
	peanut			pijnat
	rabbit			rǽbɪt
	tiger	kajaŋ		
10				
	Brenda			bɛndə
	dragon			dǽgən
	elephant		ɛ·t	
	finger			fɪŋgə
	flannel			fǽnəl
	garage			gáras
	musk-ox			máksɒks
	rabbit		ræ·p	
	records			rɛjas
	runner			ránə
	squirrel			gúrjel
	tiger			tájgə
11				
	accident			ǽkas

Continued

Continued

Week	Target word	BEF	MEF	ORF
	blanket			bǽkɪt
	orange			ɒrɪn
	parrot	*pajat*		
	powder			páwdə
	rabbit		rǽ·p	
12				
	aerial	*ɛjal*		
	basket			básak
	bison			bájsən
	candle			kǽndəl
	carol			kǽrəl
	carrot		kæ·t	kǽrət
	Christmas			kɪsəs
	cupboard			pʌbəd
	elephant		ɛ·t	
	emu			ijmju
	fountain			fáwtɪn
	garbage-bag			bǽgɪʤ
	gingerbread-man			ʤɪnəmæn
	hanger			hǽŋə
	hydrant			hájdət
	Jennifer			ʤɛnə
	lizard			lɪzət
	medicine			mɛtsən
	melon		mɛ·n	mɛlən
	music			mýzɪk
	orange			ɒrɪdz
	(tooth)paste			péjs
	porridge	*pajɒs*		pɒrɪs
	rhinoceros			ràjnʊ́s
	squirrel	*gijal*		
	streamer			dijmə

	sucker			sʌkə
	Tobin			tówbɪn
	turkey			təkij
	whisker			wɪsə
	whistle			wɪsu
	woman			wʊbən
13				
	aerial			ɛrijal
	berries			bɛrijs
	covered			kʌvəd
	Jesus			ʤijzəs
	parrot			pǽrət
	pillow			pilow
	police-car			pəlíska
	present			prɛzət
	squirrel			*gúrjel*

French truncated forms
in -o (selected)

A single square bracket marks the truncated portion of selected words. Sources are indicated in short forms by (i) *italics*: Scullen (1997); (ii) **bold**: Antoine (2000);[1] in right-most column, (iii) CNRTL (Centre National de Ressources Textuelles et Lexicales: http://www.cnrtl.fr/). Year of earliest documented use is given, where available, in parentheses.

Foot struc.	Selected	Base form	Gloss and comments
HL	**abdo(s)**	abdo[mineau	stomach muscles (1950)
LL	**accro**	accro[ché 'attached'	addicted, hooked (both literal and figurative, 1980)
LL	*ado*	ado[lescent	teenager (1950s in pedagogical circles; more general use from 1970s)
LLL	*aéro*	aéro[gramme	aerogram
LL	**agglo**	agglo[méré	chipboard (1931)
LL	**agro**	agro[nomie	agronomy (to designate National Institute or its students, by 1906; among students, since 1974)
LHL	**allergo**	allergo[logie	allergy specialist (medical jargon, 1976)
HLL	**archéo**	archéo[logie	archaeology (1950s; briefly used to mean superannuated political approach: 1973)
LHL	*aristo*	aristo[crate	aristocrat (1849)
LL	**asso**	asso[ciation	association
HL	*astro*	astro[logie	astrology (1980)
HL	**(moteur) atmo**	atmo[sphérique	non-turbocharged (motor) (1988)
LL	*auto*	(i) auto[mobile]: (ii) auto[matique	(i) car (1897); (ii) automatic (1974)
LL	**auto (d')**	d'auto[rité	immediately, without further ado (1835)
HLL	**balnéo**	balnéo[thérapie	balneotherapy (rare in English)
LL	**baro**	baro[mètre	barometer
LL	**beaujo**	beaujo[lais	wine from Beaujolais region (1956)
LLL	**biblio**	bibilio[graphie	bibliography (1950s)
LLL	**biblio**	biblio[thèque	library (early 20th C)
LL	**bigo**	bigo[phone	telephone (slang; based on a loud musical instrument used in carnivals) (1950)
LHL	**bihebdo**	bihebdo[madaire	biweekly (magazine)
LL	**bio**	bio[graphie	biography (by 1979)
LL	**bio**	bio[logique	biological (1970s)

[1] My thanks to Olivier Bonami for alerting me to the existence of this invaluable source.

L	bleau	Fontaine]bleau	Fontainebleau military academy (apheresis)
LL	**blenno**	blenno[rragie	blennorrhagia, a symptom of gonorrhoea, sometimes used to refer to gonorrhoea (by 1930)
LL	**braco**	braco[nnier	poacher (1925)
LL	**broncho**	broncho[pneumonie	type of pneumonia (by 1930)
LLL	**cabrio**	cabrio[let	convertible (1986)
LLL	**cambrio(t)**	cambrio[leur	burglar (1895)
HLL	**cardio**	cardio[logiste	cardiologist (by 1979)
LL	*catho*	catho[lique	Catholic (by 1924)
LLL	**cellulo**	cellulo[ïd	celluloid (1929)
HL	**chimio**	chimio[thérapie	chemotherapy
LL	**chipo**	chipo[lata	chipolata, a type of sausage; figurative use for penis (1970s)
LL	*choco*	choco[lat	chocolate
LL	**chromo**	chromo-[lithographie	pejor.: 'colour image in poor taste' (1877)
LL	**chrono**	chrono[metre, chrono[métreur	chronometer; time-keeper (by 1900)
HL	**claustro**	claustro[phobe	claustrophobic (1979)
LL	**clito**	clito[ris	clitoris (1941)
L	*co*	co[pie	copy (1980)
LL	**co-pro**	co-pro[duction	co-production
LLL	*collabo*	collabo[rateur	collaborator (1867; pejor. from 1940)
LL	*colo*	colo[nie de vacances	summer camp (1947)
LL	*compo*	compo[sition	composition (no longer in use) (1875)
LL	*conso*	conso[mmation	consummation, drink (1957)
LL	*corio*	Corio[lis	name of a fountain
HL	**corpo**	corpo[ration	corporation (by 1939)
HL	cosmo	cosmo[graphie	cosmography
LL	*croco*	croco[dile	crocodile (leather) (1937)
LL	**cyclo**	cyclo[moteur	type of motorized vehicle (1960s)
LLL	*dactylo*	dactylo[graphe	typist (1923)
LHL	**décalco**	décalco[manie	decal
LL	**déco**	déco[ration	decoration, wallpaper (by 1980)
LL	**déco**	déco[nnecté	disconnected (from internet)
LL	**décro**	décro[che 'disconnect'	kick a drug habit (1983)
LLL	*démago*	démago[gue	demagogue (pejor.) (1972)
LL	**démo**	démo[nstration	demonstration, demo (1981)
LL	déo	déo[dorant	deodorant
LLL	*dermato*	dermato[logiste	dermatologist (1965)
LLL	**désinto**	désinto[xication	rehab (medical slang) (1981)
LLL	*diapo*	diapo[sitif	photographic slide (1971)
HL	**disco**	disco[thèque	disco (1979)
HL	dispo	dispo[nible 'available, open-minded; unoccupied'	at your disposition, available
HL	*docto*	doctor[rat	doctorate
LL	**droico, droit-co**	droit-co[mmun	ordinary (not political) prisoner (1970)
LLL	**dynamo**	dynamo[-électrique	generator (1881)

Continued

Continued

Foot struc.	Selected	Base form	Gloss and comments
LL	**écho**	echo[graphie	ultrasound (1984)
LL	*éco*	éco[nomie, éco[nomique	economics, economy
LLL	éco po	éco[nomie] po [litique	political economy (1950)
LLL	*écolo*	écolo[gique, -[giste	ecological, ecologist (1970)
LLL	*édito*	édito[rial	editorial (1967)
LHL	**électro**	électro[ménager	household appliances (1984)
LL	émos	émotion	
LLLL	*encéphalo*	électro]encéphalo-[gramme	encephalogram
LLLL	endocrino	endocrino[logiste	endocrinologist
HL	**ethno**	ethno[logie	ethnology (by 1979)
HL	*expo*	expo[sition	exposition (1983)
LL	**favo**	favo[ri	favourite (horse racing term) (1966)
HL	**fibro**	fibro[ciment	a building material (1950s)
HL	**filmo**	filmo[graphie	filmography (1981)
L	*fiot*	ra]fiot	boat (apheresis)
LL	**fluo**	fluo[rescent	fluorescent (1979)
HL	*folklo*	folklo[rique	eccentric, offbeat, weird (1962)
LL	*frigo*	frigo[rifié	freezing (outdated) (1919)
HLL	**galvano**	galvano[type	a printing technique (printers' slang) (1864)
HL	**gastro**	gastro-[enterologue, -[enterite	stomach specialist (1977); more current: stomach upset
HL	gastro	gastro[nomie	gastronomy
LL	**gazo**	gazo[gène	gas generator (1942)
LL	*géo*	géo[graphie, -[métrie	geography, geometry (1870s)
LL	**gonio**	gonio[mètre	goniometer (by 1939)
LL	*gono*	gono[rrhée	gonorrhoea
LL	**grapho**	grapho[logie	graphology
LLL	*gynéco*	gynéco[logie, -[logue,	gynaecologist, gynaecology (medical terms) (1967)
LL	**gyro**	gyro[phare	flashing light
HL	*hebdo*	hebdo[madaire	weekly (1954)
HL	**hecto**	hecto[gramme/hecto [litre	hectogram (1877), hectolitre
LLL	**hélico**	hélico[pter	helicopter (1929)
LL	*héro*	héro[ine	heroine (1960)
LLL	**hétéro**	hétéro[sexuel	heterosexual (by 1964)
LL	**homo**	homo[sexuel	homosexual (1973)
LL	**hypo**	hypo[khâgne	preparatory class for advanced studies in arts and literature (1980)
LL	**immo**	immo[bilier	real estate
LL	**impro**	impro[visation	improvisation (1980)
LL	**inco**	inco[rrigible	incorrigible (1921)
LL	**inco**	inco[nnu	unknown (1988)
LL	*info*	infor[mation	information (by 1977)

LL	*ino*	ino[ccupé	lazy inmate (slang)
LLL	**interro**	interro[gation	interrogation (1981)
LLHL	**intradermo**	intradermo-[réaction	skin test (1944)
LL	**intro**	intro[duction	introduction (by 1979)
LL	**kilo**	kilo[gramme	kilogramme (1835)
HL	**klepto**	klepto[mane	kleptomaniac
L	**Kro**	Kro[nenbourg	a type of beer (1979)
LL	**labo**	labo[ratoire	laboratory (by 1939)
LLL	**lacrymo**	lacrymo[gène	tear gas (1975)
LL	limo	limo[nade	lemonade
LL	**lino**	lino[léum, lino[type	linoleum, linotype (1936)
LL	**litho**	litho[graphe	lithograph (1938)
LL	**loco**	loco[motive	locomotive (rail worker slang) (1878)
LL	**logo**	logo[type	logotype (1970)
HL	*Macdo*	McDo[nald	McDonald's (1981)
LL	**macro**	macro[photo-graphie; -instruction	close-up; macro (computing technology: instructions for assembler to generate sequence of further instructions)
HLL	**magneto**	magnéto[phone	tape-recorder (1981)
LL	*majo*	majo[ritaire	majority
LL	**mano**	mano[mètre	manometer (technical slang) (1980)
LL	**mao**	mao[ïste	Maoist (1965)
LL	**maso**	maso[chiste	masochist (pejor.) (1968)
LL	**mayo**	mayo[nnaise	mayonnaise (by 1982)
LLL	*mégalo*	mégalo[mane	megalomaniac (pejor. due to ending in -o: Antoine, 2000) (1949)
LLL	**mélanco**	mélanco[lique	melancholic (1977)
LL	*mélo*	mélo[drame	melodrama (1872)
LL	**mémo**	mémorandum	memorandum (1974)
HLL	**mercuro**	mercuro[chrome	mercurochrome (1958)
LL	**méso**	mésothérapie	a type of plastic surgery (1984)
LLL	*météo*	météo[rologique	meteorological (1917)
LL	*métro*	métro[politain	subway, underground rail (1891)
LL	*micro*	micro[phone; -[ordinateur	microphone; personal computer (1915)
LL	**miso**	miso[gyne	misogynist (1976)
L	*mo*	mo[(g)nière	individual (slang)
LL	**mono**	mono[phonie; mono[ski	monophony, a musical style; monoski (1960)
HLL	*morphino*	morphino[mane	morphine addict
LL	*moto*	moto[cyclette	motor scooter (1898)
LL	*mytho*	mytho[logie	mythology
LL	**mytho**	mytho[mane	fantasist, liar; lie (pejor. nuance due to ending in -o: Antoine, 2000) (1976)
HL	**myxo**	myxo[matose	virus that affects rabbits (breeder term)
LL	**napo**	napo[léon	gold coin (1887); a type of pastry
LL	**natio**	nation[naliste	nationalist
LL	**nécro**	nécro[logique	obituary (1976)
LL	**négo**	négo[ciation	negotiation (1993)
LL	*neuro*	neuro[logie, neuro[logue	neurology, neurologist

Continued

Continued

Foot struc.	Selected	Base form	Gloss and comments
LL	**nitro**	nitro[glycérine	nitroglycerine (technical slang)
LL	**nono**	non-o[ccupé	unoccupied zone (obsolete) (1941)
LL	**nympho**	nympho[mane	nymphomaniac (pejor. nuance underlined by ending in -o: Antoine, 2000) (1981)
HL	**octo**	octo[génaire	eighty-year-old, in their 80s (1975)
HHL	*opthalmo*	opthalmo[logiste	ophthalmologist
HLL	**osthéo**	ostéo[pathe	osteopath
LLLL	**oto-rhino**	oto-rhino [-laryngologiste	oto-rhino-laryngologist (1949)
LL	**pano**	pano[ramique	panoramic (1981)
LLL	*parano*	parano[îde	paranoid (1970)
LL	*patho*	patho[logie	pathology
LL	**patro, patzo, padzo**	patro[nage	youth club (1928, 1926, 1935)
LLL	**pédago**	pédago[gue	pedagogue (pejor. nuance given by ending in -o: Antoine, 2000)
LL	**pédo**	pédo[phile	paedophile; homosexual (1978)
LL	*pédo*	tor]pédo	torpedo (apheresis)
LL	**pensio**	pension[nnaire	boarder, lodger (1927)
HL	*perco*	perco[lateur	percolator (1927)
HL	perfo	perfo[rmance	performance
HL	**perlo(t)**	sem]perlot	tobacco (slang; apheresis) (1925)
HL	**perso**	perso[nnelle, perso[nnellement	personal (1973); personally (1982)
LL	*phallo*	phallo[crate	male chauvinist (1965)
LL	*phéno*	phéno[menal	phenomenal
LL	*philo*	philo[sophie	philosophy (1880)
LL	**phono**	phono[graphe	phonograph (1935)
LL	*photo*	photo[graphe, photo[graphie	photograph, photography, photographer (1864)
LL	**phyto**	phytothérapie	herbal medicine (1991)
HL	*pictho*	pictho[gorne	wine (slang)
LL	**placo**	placo[plâtre	plasterboard (after 1968)
LL	**pneumo**	pneumo[thorax	artificial thorax (a treatment for tuberculosis) (1911?)
LL	**polio**	polio[myélite, polio[myélitique	polio(myelitis) (1965)
HL	*porno*	porno[graphique	pornographic (1893)
HLLL	**porte-hélico**	porte-hélicoptère	helicopter carrier (after 1963)
HLL	**post-synchro**	post-synchronisation	a film-making technique (cinema slang) (1976)
LL	**préo**	préoblitéré	pre-cancelled stamp (collectors' term) (1979)
L	*pro*	pro[fessionel	professional (1912)
LL	**promo**	promo[tion	promotion (advertising term)
LL	**promo**	promo[tion	cohort, class in school (1850)
LL	**prono**	prono[stic	forecast (1980)
LL	**proto**	proto[type	prototype (sports term)(1960)

LL	provo	provo[cateur	provocateur (CNRTL)
LL	**pseudo**	pseudo[nyme	pseudonym (by 1991)
LL	*psycho*	psycho[logie, -[logue	psychology, psychologist (1906)
LL	*radio*	radio[gramme, radio[graphie, etc.	radiogram, radiography, etc. (1907)
LL	**rando**	rando[nnée	ramble, hike (N)
LL	**reco**	reco[nnaissance	reconnaissance
LL	reco	reconnecté	reconnected (to internet)
LL	**repro**	repro[duction, repro[graphie	reproduction, reprography (1974)
HL	*resto*	restau[rant	restaurant (1899)
LL	*rétro*	rétro[grade; retro [spective; rétro [viseur	backwards, retrograde (1974); retrospective (1975); driving mirror (1946)
LLL	**revalo**	revalo[risation	improvement; pay rise (1987)
LL	*rhéto*	rhéto[rique	rhetorical
LL	**rhino**	rhino[céros	rhinoceros (from English?)
LL	**rhino**	rhino[-pharyngite	stuffy nose (1988)
LL	**rhodo**	rhodo[dendron	rhododendron (1983)
LLL	**rhumato**	rhumatologue	rheumatologist
LLLL	**sado-maso**	sado-maso[chiste	sado-masochist (1970)
HL	Sarko	Sarko[zy	French President, 2007–12
HL	*saxo*	saxo[phone	saxophone (early 20th C)
LL	**scato**	scatologique	scatological (1981)
HL	**schizo**	schizo[phrénie, schizo[phrène	schizophrenia, schizophrenic (1960)
LLL	**science éco**	science éco[nomique	economics
HL	**Sciences Po**	sciences po[litiques	political science (1981)
LHL	Sébasto	Sébasto[pol	Sebastopol
LL	**sémio**	sémio[tique, sémio[logie	semiotics
LLL	**séropo**	séropo[sitif	HIV positive (1989)
HL	**sismo**	sismo[graphe	seismograph (1984)
LL	*socio*	socio[logie	sociology (1924)
LL	**sono**	sono[risation	adding soundtrack to a film (1967)
LL	**sopo**	sopo[rifique	soporific
LLL	**spéléo**	spéléo[logue	spelunking (1985)
HLL	**spermato**	spermato[zoïde	sperm (1947)
LLL	**stakhano**	stakhano[viste	workaholic (pejor. due to ending in -o: Antoine, 2000)
LLL	**staphylo**	staphylo[coque	staph infection (1983)
LL	**sténo**	sténo[graphe	typist (1913)
LLHLL	**stenodactylo**	stenodactylo [graphe, -[graphie	shorthand typing, typist (1911)
LLL	**stéréo**	stéréo[phonique	stereo(phonic) (1957)
LL	**stétho**	stéthoscope	stethoscope (1979)
LLL	**stomato**	stomato[logue	stomatologist (1863) CNRTL
HL	**strepto**	strepto[coque, strepto[mycine	streptococcus; streptomycin, an antibiotic used in treating tuberculosis (1954)
LL	**strobo**	strobe[scope	strobe light
LL	**stylo**	stylo[graphe	fountain pen, ballpoint pen; full form is out of use (1912)

Continued

Continued

Foot struc.	Selected	Base form	Gloss and comments
LL	**suppo**	suppo[sitoire	suppository
LL	**synchro**	synchronisé, synchronisation	synchronized, in synch (1974)
HL	**techno**	techno[logie	technology (1985)
LLL	**territo**	(brigade) territo [riale	police force (dated)
LLL	**thalasso**	thalasso[thérapie	seawater cure (1960)
LL	théo	théo[logie	theology
LLL	**thoraco**	thoraco[plastie	thoracoplasty (part of treatment for tuberculosis)
LL	**topo**	topo[graphie	topographical map; by extension, summary, run-down (1855)
HLL	*toxico*	toxico[mane/-manie	drug addict/addiction (1977)
HL	**toxo**	toxo[plasmose	toxoplasmosis, a parasitic infection
LLL	**trachéo**	trachea[tomie	tracheotomy (1978)
HL	**transfo**	transfo[rmateur	transformer (1980)
HL	**trichlo**	trichlo[réthylène	trichloroethylene, a compound used as a solvent but also as an intoxicant (1975)
LL	**trigo**	trigo[nométrie	trigonometry (1889)
HL	**turbo**	turbo-[compresseur	turbocharger (mid-20th C)
LL	*typo*	(le) typo[graphe, (la) typo[logie	typesetter, -setting (1874)
LL	**vapo**	vapo[risateur	vaporizer, spray
LL	**vélo**	vélo[cipède	bicycle (1889)
HL	**vibro**	vibro[masseur	vibrator
LLL	vidéo	vidéo[fréquence	video (1949)
LLL	**volo (à)**	à volo[nté	at will, as much as you like (1930)
LL	**xéno**	xéno[phobe	xenophobe (1986)
LL	**xylo**	xylo[phone	xylophone, woodpile (machine for writing or sewing)
LL	**yougo**	yougo[slave	Yugoslavian (by 1978)
L	*zoo*	(jardin) zoo[logique	zoo (1847)

French truncated forms in -o (adapted)

Sources are indicated in the short forms by (i) *italics*: Scullen (1997); (ii) **bold**: Antoine (2000); (iii) SMALL CAPS: Kilani-Schoch & Dressler (1993) (K-S&D); in right-most column, (iv) CNRTL (Centre National de Ressources Textuelles et Lexicales: http://www.cnrtl.fr/). Year of earliest documented use is given in parentheses, where available. Pejor. = pejorative.

Foot struc.	Adapted	Base form	Gloss and comments
HLLL	ACCÉLÉRO	accélérateur	accelerator (analogical formation: K-S&D)
LHL	ACROSTO	acrostiche	acrostic
LHL	AFFECTO	affectueux/affectif?	affectionate (or emotional?) (K-S&D)
LL	AFRO	(coiffure) africain	afro; African (K-S&D)
HLL	*ALCO(O)LO*	alcoolique	alcoholic (pejor.) (1979)
HHL	*Alforlo*	*Maison-Alfort*	name of a city
HLL	ALSACO	Alsacien	Alsatian (m.) (1927)
LHL	*AMERLO(t)*	américain	American (pejor. in earlier years) (1934)
LHL	*ANARCHO*	anarchiste	anarchist (1889)
LLL	*APÉRO*	apéritif	aperitif (1901)
HLL	ARBICO(T)	Arabe	Arab
HL	*arjo (en)*	en arrière	behind (1934)
HLL	**artiflot**	artilleur (artificier + fiflot 'fantassin': K-S&D)	artillery man (1901) ('fireworks expert + foot soldier')
HLL	ASPIRO	aspirateur	vacuum cleaner
LLL	ATTERRO	atterrissage	landing (analogical formation: K-S&D)
HLL	**AUXIGOT**	auxiliaire	prisoner who serves as cleaner (trusty; 1922); also 'accomplice' (K-S&D)
LLL	*AVARO*	avarie	hitch, personal setback (rare use of f. base: CNRTL) (1874)
LHL	AVERTO	avertissement	warning
LL	**bachot**	baccalauréat (< bachelier)	school-leaving certificate (originally derived from *bachelor*: 1857)
HLL	**barbitos**	barbituriques	barbiturates
HL	*Basto*	la Bastille	the Bastille
HLL	*belgico*	la Belgique	Belgian
LL	BENZO	benzine	benzine
LL	*biclo*	bicyclette	bicycle
LL	*blanco*	blanquiste	political term

Continued

Continued

Foot struc.	Adapted	Base form	Gloss and comments
LL	*blanco*	vin blanc	white (wine) (CNRTL) (1972)
LLL	*bobino*	bobine	watch (slang)
LL	bobo	bourgeois-bohemian	bourgeois trying to pass as a bohemian
HL	**BOLCHO**	bolchévique	Bolshevik (dated) (1947)
HL	BOSCO	bossu	hunchback (19th C dictionaries: CNRTL)
LL	BRANCO	brancardier	stretcher-bearer (dated)
LL	**broco**	broquanteur	dealer in second-hand goods (1936)
LLL	BRUTALO	brutalement	
LLL	CALENDO	calendrier, Calendes	calendar
HL	**CALMO(s)**	calme	calmly, calm down! (1968)
LLL	**CAMARO**	camarade	companion, friend (1845)
LLL	*camembo*	camembert (or brie)	a type of cheese (1939)
LLL	*cantalo(s)*	cantal	cantal (type of cheese)
LLLL	**capitalo**	capitaliste	capitalist (1893)
HLL	CARBURO	carburateur	carburettor (1982) (analogical formation: K-S&D)
LLL	CAVALO	cavalier	horseman, rider; escort
LL	**cello**	celluloïd	celluloid (1981)
HL	CENSCO	censeur	censor
HL	*CERTO*	certificat	certificate (1966) CNRTL
HL	charlot	Charlie Chaplin	
LLL	CHEMINO(T)	chemin (de fer)	railroad worker (1899) CNRTL
LL	*CHÉROT*	cher	expensive
LL	chicos	chic	posh, overly fancy
LHL	chirurgo	chirurgien	surgeon (1974) CNRTL
LLL	CIBOULO	ciboulette?	chives
HL	*CIVLO*	civil	civil
LL	clando	clandestin	clandestine immigrant (1980) CNRTL
LLL	classico(s)	classique	classic
LLL	*clérico*	clérical	clerical
LL	**CLODO(t)**	clochard < clodion (K-S&D, who refer to Heinemann, 1953)	tramp (1926)
LL	**COCO**	cocaïne	cocaine (1912)
LL	**coco**	communiste	communist (1941)
LL	coco	commandant	commander
LL	coco	[oeuf à la] coque	soft-boiled egg
LL	**coffiot**	coffre-fort	safe (N) (1912)
HL	*coinsto*	coin	corner
LLL	commodo	commodier	commode
LLL	**congélo**	congélateur	freezer (1980)
LLL	**CONVALO**	convalescence	convalescence (1928)
LL	COOLOS	cool	cool (slang)
LL	**copo**	copain	pal, buddy
LL	COPO	coopérative	co-op
HLL	CORSICO	la Corse	Corsica

HL	**COSTO**	costume	costume
LL	**CRADO**	crasseux	filthy (applies to people and to behaviour) (1935)
LL	CRÉDO	crédit	credit
HL	CRYPTO	cryptique	cryptic, in cypher (Reverso)
HL	**CUISTO(T)**	cuisinier	cook (1894) (deriving from *cuistancier mlitaire* 'military cook': K-S&D)
HL	CURETOT	curé	priest
HL	CYCLO	cycliste	cyclist
HL	**dargeot, derjo**	derrière	bum, butt (1928)
LLL	débilos	débile	feeble-minded
LL	**délo**	délivrance	prisoner's base (a child's game, 1945)
HL	**DERJO**	derrière	behind (adv.) (1930)
LL	**deusio**	deuxièmement	secondly (1926)
LL	**DICO**	dictionnaire	dictionary (1885)
LL	DINGO[1]	dingue	crazy (1907)
LHL	**DIRECTO(s)**	directement	immediately (1878)
HL	**DIRLO**	directeur/directrice	director (m/f) (especially of hotel or school) (1912)
HLL	**DISCRÈTO(s)**	discrètement	discretely
HL	**DORTO**	dortoir	dormitory (1834)
LL	*duro*	dur	difficult
LLL	**ÉBÉNO**	ébéniste	cabinet-maker (dated) (1889)
LHL	**ÉLECTRO**	électricien	electrician (1960) (analogical formation: K-S&D)
LLLL	ENCÉPHALO	encéphalite	encephalitis, a person suffering from encephalitis
LLL	**enduro**	competition motocycliste d'endurance	endurance race (1970)
LL	**engo**	engagement	kick-off (by 1950)
LLL	engueulo	enguelade	scolding (1966) CNRTL
LLL	ÉPILO	épileptique	epileptic
HLL	*espago, espingo*	espagnol	Spanish (1982)
HLL	*exhibo*	exhibition[nniste	exhibitionist, flasher (1977)
HL	EXO	exercise	exercise (1977) (analogical formation: K-S&D)
LL	**FACHO**	fasciste	fascist (1950s)
LLL, LLHL	*FAMILO, familisto*	familistère	group housing
LL	FOLLO	folle (f.)	crazy, mad
LL	**franco**	franchement	straight away, without hesitation; also (as adj.) loyal (1879)
LL	frèro	petit frère	little brother
LL	*frigo*	Frigidaire	refrigerator (or fridge), from name of early commercial brand Frigidaire (1920s)
LL	FROIDO	froidement	coldly
HL	**FROMLO(t),** *frometot, fromego,* FROMAGO	fromage	cheese (1944)

Continued

Continued

Foot struc.	Adapted	Base form	Gloss and comments
HL	**garno**	garni	furnished flat, cheap hotel room (1867)
LL	*GAUCHO*	gauchiste	leftist (1968)
HL	**gauldo**	Gauloise	type of cigarette (1974)
HL	gerbos	< gerber 'to vomit'	gross, disgusting
LL	**gogo**	gobeur	credulous person, sucker (1834)
LL	gogo	gosier	throat, larynx
HLL	*gourdiflo*	gourde	idiot
LL	*GRAT(T)O(S)*	gratuit, gratuitement	for free (1983), likely influenced by *gratis* (Antoine, 2000)
LL	**hivio**	hiver	winter (dated) (1883)
HL	HOSTO	hôpital	hospital (1919)
HLL	**HYSTÉRO**	hystérique	neurotic (1957)
LLL	*ICIGO*	ici	here (slang)
LLL	*INTELLO*	intellectuel	intellectual (pejor., due to suffix -o: Antoine, 2000) (1977)
LLL	**invalo**	invalide	disabled (1857)
LLL	INVALO	(les) Invalides	the Invalides (CNRTL)
LLL	**invalo**	invitation	invitation
LHL	ITALGO, **ITALO**	italien	Italian (pejor.) (1894)
LL	**jojo**	joli(e)	nice, great (1852) (used only in ironic sense)
LL	**jojo**	Joseph	puritan (pejor.) (1867)
HL	*l'airjo*	en l'air	undecided, lit. 'in the air'
LLL	*LABAGO*	là bas	over there
LL	*lago*	là	there
LLL	*Laribo*	Lariboisière	name of a prison
LLL	**lazaro**	lazaret	military prison (dated) (1886)
LLLL	*légitimo*	légitime	legitimate
LL	*lento*	lentement	slowly
LL	**limo**	limousine	var. of *limou*, under influence of Eng. *limo.* (1985)
LLL	LOCATO	locataire	tenant
LL	lolo	lorette	beautiful woman (slang); street walker (dated)
LL	*LUCO*	(le) luxembourg	Luxembourg gardens (CNRTL)
LL	*LUDO*	ludique	pertaining to play; playful
LLL	*MACHINO*	machiniste	stagehand (1951)
LL	*MACHO*	machiste, machisme	macho, machismo
LLL	*Madago*	Madagascar	Madagascar
LL	*MAGO*	magasin	store (dated)
LL	*malo*	malade (N)	a sick person (1918: K-S&D)
HL	**MARJO, margeot**	marginal	dropout (1988)
HL	MARXO	marxiste	Marxist
LL	*MATOS*	matériel	gear, equipment, hardware (musician and technician slang) (1983)
LLL	*MÉCANO*	mécanicien	mechanic (road and railroad slang) (1907)

LLL	**MÉDICO**	médecin	doctor (dated) (1910) (cf. also *médical* 'medical'; analogical formation: K-S&D)
LLL	MENDIGO	mendiant	tramp (1875)
LLL	MÉNINGO	méningite	person suffering from meningitis (1918) CNRTL
HLL	*mercelot*	mercier	haberdasher
LLL	*mésigo*, MÉZIGO	mézigue	me (slang)
LLL	*métalo*/**métallo**	métallurgiste	metallurgist (1921)
LLL	MILICO	milicien	militia man, national guard
LLLL	MILITARO	militariste	militarist
LLL	*mobilo*	mobilisation	mobilization
HL	*moblo*	garde mobile	militia
HL	*moblo*	mobilisation	mobilization
LL	modo	modérateur	moderator
LL	*MOLLO*	molle(ment)	weakly (Scullen); softly-softly, with caution (1933)
LL	**mono**	moniteur/-trice	monitor, counsellor (camp, sports, technical, m/f) (1981)
LLL	*monstrico*	monstre	monster
LHL	Montparno	Montparnasse	Montparnasse (CNRTL)
HL	MUFLO	mufle	boor, lout
LLL	*MUSICO(s)*	musicien	musician (1919)
HL	NISCO	< German *nix* (K-S&D) or *nichts*	nothing
HLL	NORMALO	Normalien	student at the École Normale Supérieure
HL	**objo**	objecteur de conscience	conscientious objector (1987)
HLLL	**obligado**	obligatoirement	under pressure; influenced by Spanish (1977)
HLL	**ordino**	ordinateur	computer (1984)
HL	**ordo**	ordinateur	computer (1970)
LLL	OUVRIO	ouvrier	worker
LL	**pako**	pakistanais	Pakistani (1989), < pakistoche (1983)
LLLL	*parachuto*	parachutiste	parachutist
LLL	**PARIGOT**	parisien	Parisian (1886)
LLL	*pédero*, pédalo	pédéraste, (dated) pédale	homosexual (1953) CNRTL
LL	**PÉNO**	penalty	sports penalty (by 1939) (cf. also < *pénitence* 'penitence, punishment': K-S&D)
HL	PENSCO	pensionnaire	boarder, lodger (see also *pension* [App. IIa]) (analogical formation: K-S&D)
LLL	**PHARMACO**/-GO	pharmacien	pharmacist (dated) (1859, 1901)
LL	pipo	candidat à l'école polytechnique	unclear deriv.; < polyt? cf. Hippolyte > pipo (1860)
LLL	**POPULO**	populace, populaire	crowd (pejor.) (1867)
HL	**PORTO(s)**	portugais	Portuguese (pejor.) (1975)
LLLL	*possibilo*	possibiliste	political term (1920)
LL	POULO	poulailler	chicken house (dated) (analogical formation: K-S&D)

Continued

Continued

Foot struc.	Adapted	Base form	Gloss and comments
HL	PRISTO	prisonnier	prisoner (mid-20th C: K-S&D)
HL	PROBLO	problème	problem (1966)
LL	**PROJO**	projecteur	spotlight (1955)
LL	**PROLO**	prolétaire	proletarian (pejor.) (1883)
HL	**prompto, pronto**	promptement	promptly, pronto (1862)
LLL	**PROPRIO**	propriétaire	proprietor (1878)
LL	**proto**	proviseur	lycée director
HL	**proxo**	proxénète	pimp (1977)
HL	**PRUSCO, *prussco***	prussien	Prussian (1886) CNRTL
LL	**RACHO**	rachitique	puny; skimpy (1976)
LL	*raido*	raide 'stiff'	tough, hard to do
LLL	**RAMOLLO**	ramolli 'softened'	senile (or senile person); flabby, limp (strong pejorative sense from ending in -o: Antoine, 2000) (1923)
LLL	**RAPIDO(S)**	rapidement	quickly (1928)
LLL	**ravito**	ravitaillement	supplies (dated) (1943) (analogical formation: K-S&D)
LLL	**RÉDHIBOS**	rédhibitoire	nauseating, unbearable
HL	**RÉGLO**	réglementaire	required by regulation (1917)
HL	**RÉGLO**	régulier	straight, on the level, legitimate (1878)
LLL	**RÉVISO**	révisionniste	revisionist (pejorative political term) (1969)
LLL	rhumago	rhumatisme	rheumatism (1950) CNRTL
LLL	rigolo	rigoler 'to have a laugh'	funny, bizarre (1980) CNRTL
LHL	RINGARDOS	ringard	tacky, out of fashion
LLL	**robico, *robigo***	robinet	faucet, tap (1957)
LLL	**ROMANIGO**	romanichel	gypsy (dated) (1883)
LLL	**romano**	romanichel	gypsy (often pejor.) (1928)
LL	rondo	rondement	nicely, in the round (1981)
LL	**ROTO**	rotative, rotativiste	(rotary) press, press operator (1951)
LLL	*rototo*	moteur rotif	airplane motor
HL	**rusco**	russe	Russian (1955)
LL	**SADO**	sadique	sadist (1981)
LLL	SALIGOT	salaud? < sale 'dirty'	swine (as metaphorically applied to people)
LLL	SECRÉTO	secrétariat	secretariat
HL	*serbo*	Serbe	Serbian
HL	**sergo(t)**	sergent	sergeant (1868)
LLL	**SOCIALO**	socialiste	socialist (1878)
LL	**socio**	socialiste	socialist (1906; renewed use, 1981)
LLL	**SPÉCIALO**	spécialiste	specialist
LL	STALO	stalinien	Stalinist
LLL	**subito(s)**	subitement	suddenly
LLL	**SYPHILO**	syphilis, syphilitique	syphilis, syphilitic (1907)
LL	TACO(T)	taxi	taxicab (analogical formation: K-S&D)

HL	*tardo*	tard	late
LL	**taro**	tarin	(large) nose (1916)
LLL	*tésigo*	tézigue	you (slang)
HL	TEXTO	textuellement	literally (1960)
HL	texto	texte	text
LL	tracos	trac	stage-fright
LL	**trado**	traduction	translation
LLL	TRANQUILLO(s)	tranquillement	calmly, unhurriedly (1980)
LLL	*TRAVELO*	travestie	person in drag (pejor., due to ending in -o: Antoine, 2000) (1970)
LL	TRINGLOT	train (see *artiflot*)	train-soldier
HL	turco	Turc	(dated) 'Algerian gunner': Algeria was under Turkish control until 1830 (1856)
LL	TYPHO	typhique	affected with typhoid
LLL	**VENTILO**	ventilateur	fan (1915) (analogical formation: K-S&D)
HL	VERJO	verni	varnished
HLL	*VERSIGO*	Versailles	Versailles
LL	*VÉTO*	vétérinaire	veterinary (dated) (1899)
LLL	VIROLO	virage	bend, curve in the road
HL	**vulgo(s)**	vulgaire	vulgar, common (pejor. meaning emphasized by ending in -o: Antoine, 2000) (dated) (1832)
LLL	ZIGOTO	(base unknown)	extravagant behaviour; person not to be taken seriously (1900)
LL	zozo	< Joseph	fool, clown (1894), weirdo (current usage)

Note:
[1] Kilani-Schoch & Dressler (1993) give *(sour)dingo* (presumably from *sourd* 'deaf'; glossed in RE-VERSO as 'deafhead').

French hypocoristics: Prosodic and segmental analysis

Prosodic structure	Template	Name	Short form	Name	Short form
L	Open monosyllable	*Dominique*	Do	*Joséphine*	Jo
		Florence	Flo		
[H]	Closed monosyllable	*Augustin*	Gus	*Michelle*	Mèche
		Christelle	Chris	*Nathalie*	Nat
		Christophe	Tophe	*Patrick*	Pat
		Dominique	Dom	*Philippe*	Phil
		Florence	Flor	*Sébastien*	Seb
		Fréderic	Fred	*Stéphanie*	Steph
		Grégory	Greg	*Thibault*	Tib
		Marguerite	Guitte		
	Closed monosyllable with harmony	*Benoit*	Bèbe [bɛb]	*Jacqueline*	Nine [nin]
		Eveline	Nine [nin]		
[LL]	Reduplicated disyllable	*André*	Dédé	*Huguette*	Gugu
		Angeline	Gigi	*Irénée*	Néné
		Anne	Nana	*Jacqueline*	Kiki
		Annie	Nini	*Josèphe*	Jojo
		Augustin	Tintin	*Julie*	Juju
		Béatrice	Bibi	*Laurent*	Lolo
		Bénédicte	Bibi	*Liliane*	Lili
		Brigitte	Bibi, Bribri	*Lionel*	Yoyo
		Carole	Coco	*Louis*	Loulou
		Catherine	Titi	*Lucienne*	Néné
		Cécile	Sissi	*Madeleine*	Nana
		Chantal	Chacha	*Marie*	Mimi
		Charles	Chacha	*Michelle*	Mimi

		Christelle	Kriki	Nicole	Nini
		Christiane	Nana	Odile	Didi
		Christine	Cricri, Kiki	Olivier	Yéyé
		Christophe	Kiki	Otto	Toto
		Claire	Kéké	Paulette	Popo
		Claude	Cloclo, Coco, Cloco	Pierre	Piépié, Pépé, Pipi
		Corinne	Coco	Rachid	Riri
		Daniel	Nini	Robert	Roro
		Dominique	Dodo, Dédé, Mimi, Nini	Roger	Roro, Jojo
		Edouard	Doudou	Romuald	Mumu
		Eveline	Vivi, Vévé	Roselyne	Lolo
		Félix	Féfé, Fifi	Simone	Momo
		Florence	Floflo, Fofo	Sophie	Sosso
		François	Soisoi, Sasa, Fanfa	Sylvie	Sissi
		Françoise	Fanfan	Théophile	Toto
		Frédéric	Fréfé, Riri	Thérèse	Zézé
		Geneviève	Gégé, Viévié, Vévé, Gigi	Thomas	Toto
		Georges	Jojo	Valérie	Vava, Vévé, Lili
		Gérard	Jaja	Xavier [gzavje]	Xaxa [Gzagza]
		Hughes	Gugu	Yves	Vivi
Consonant harmony		Agnès	Nani	Elisabeth	Babé
		Anne	Nane	Eulalie	Lalie
		Anne-Marie	Nani	Fabrice	Babi
		Annie	Nani	Henri-Roger	Riro

Continued

Continued

Prosodic structure	Template	Name	Short form	Name	Short form
		Arnaud	Nano	*Isabelle*	Babé
		Bernadette	Babé	*Karine*	Kaki
		Brice	Bibe	*Laure-Lise*	Loli
		Carole	Caco	*Marie-Emilie*	Mami
		Danielle	Nine	*Olivier*	Loli
	Vowel harmony	*Bénédicte*	Béné	*Jean-Marie*	Jimi
		Colette	Colo	*Magdalena*	Magda
		Corinne	Coro	*Marianne*	Maya
		Dominique	Mini	*Marie-Alice*	Mili
		Dorothée	Doro	*Nathalie*	Natha
		Emilie	Milie	*Patricia*	Pata
		Geneviève	Givi, Geuneu	*Raphaël*	Rapha
	No harmony	*Alfred*	Frédo	*Marc*	Marco
		Amélie	Mélie	*Marie-Alice*	Mali
		Antony	Tony	*Marie-Bernard*	Mabé
		Carole	Caro	*Marie-Claude*	Maclo, Maco, Miclo
		Catherine	Cathy	*Marie-Françoise*	Mifa
		Cécile	Céli	*Marie-José*	Majo, Mijo
		Christina	Tina	*Marie-Noël*	Mano
		Danielle	Dani	*Marie-Thérèse*	Maté
		Dominique	Domi, Doni	*Nathalie*	Thalie
		Elisabeth	Lisa, Elisa, Eli	*Nicolas*	Nico, Colas
		Eléonore	Eli, Leo	*Paul*	Paulo

		Elodie	Lodi	Pierre	Pierrot
		Emilie	Milo	Priscilla	Cilla
		Emmanuel(le)	Manu	Romuald	Romu
		Eugénie	Génie	Rosalie	Zalie
		Frédéric	Frédo	Sébastien	Bastien
		Gabrielle	Gabi	Stéphanie	Stépha, Phanie
		Isabelle	Zabé	Suzanne	Suzon
		Jacques	Jaquot	Thierry	Téri
		Jean	Jeannot	Valérie	Valé
		Jean-Michel	Jean-Mi	Véronique	Véro
		Laetitia	Titia /tisja/	Virginie	Ginie
		Madeleine	Mado	Yasmina	Mina
		Magdalena	Magda, Lena		
[LH]	Closed disyllable	Alphonsine	Phonsine	Honorine	Norine
		Antoinette	Toinette	Isabelle	Zabelle
		Bernadette	Nadette	Jacqueline	Kiline
		Dominique	Minique	Jean-Bernard	Jamber
		Elisabeth	Zabeth	Marie-Alice	Malice
		Emmanuelle	Manuelle	Marie-Carmen	Mamen
		Germinal	Minal	Sébastien	Sébas
		Henriette	Ri[y]ette	Suzanne	Suzette
[HH]	Closed first syllable	Almeyric	Ricric	Ernestine	Nestine
[LH]	Closed disyllable with partial reduplication	Adolphe	Dodolphe	Emilie	Mimile
		Alfred	Féfed	Ernest	Nénesse
		Almeyric	Riric	Hélène	Lélene
		Auguste	Guguste	Henriette	Yéyette
		Bernadette	Dédette, Nanette	Hildegarde	Gagarde
		Bernard	Nanard	Hubert	Béber
		Brigitte	Gigit	Isabelle	Babelle

Continued

Continued

Prosodic structure	Template	Name	Short form	Name	Short form
		Chantal	Tatal	*Marc*	Mamarc
		Charlotte	Tototte, Lelotte	*Marcel*	Cécel
		Christine	Kikine	*Marguerite*	Guiguitte
		Christophe	Totophe	*Odile*	Didile
		Claire	Kékerre	*Pascal*	Cacal
		Dominique	Mimique	*Paul*	Popol
		Elisabeth	Babette	*Victor*	Totor

Estonian short forms and hypocoristics

Bold face marks the truncated portion of likely base. Stress is marked only where non-initial.

A. Short forms

Selected	Base form and gloss	Comments (published sources)
äks	*action* /ˈæksjon/(in film)	
dots	*do'tsent* 'docent'	mid-20th C
eks	*ek'semplar* 'copy (N)'	
frits	*Fritz* 'German soldier'	pejorative term, World War II
jats(-u, -i), jäts	*džäss* 'jazz'	Short form likely derives from English orthography
jõmps	*jõmps*ikas 'kid, small child, kid'	
kamps	*kamps*un 'sweater'	
kats	*kats*e 'experiment'	
konts	*kons*pekt 'course notes'	< *conspectus*
küss	*küs*imus 'question'	
kuts(a, u)	kuts*ikas 'doggy'*	
läks	*läks* 'let's go', literally 'went'	Calque < Russia *pashli*, literally '(we/they) went', used colloquially to mean 'let's go, we're on our way'
lenks	< German **leng**stang *'steeringbar (on bicycle)'*	
luks	*luks*uslik 'luxurious'	
muss	*mus*i 'kiss'	
nips	*nips*akas preili 'cheeky girl'	
nuts	*nuts*ak 'a small amount, little heap'	
ports	*ports*jon 'portion'	(Kasik, 2015)
rats	*rats*ionaliseerimisettepanek 'austerity proposal'	
rets	*rets*idivist 'repeat offender'	
säuts	*säuts*uma 'tweet (social media)'	
sots	*sots*iaaldemokraat 'socialist'	(Kasik, 2015)
sots	*sots*iolingvistika 'sociolinguistics'	*Questionnaire*
spets	*spets*ialist 'specialist'	
vamps	*vam*mus 'doublet'	

Adapted	Base form and gloss	Sources and comments
amps 'bite (N)'	*ham*mustama 'to bite'	Note that onset /h/ is commonly elided.
antibiots	*antibi*ootikum 'antibiotic'	
burks	*bur*ger	*Questionnaire*
davaiks	*davai* 'sure, let's do it!'	*Questionnaire*

Continued

Continued

dolts	*dollar*	
Dorps	*Dorpati konverentsikeskus* 'Dorpat conference centre'	*Questionnaire* (reference to workplace)
emps	*ema,* **emm**e 'mother, mom'	*Questionnaire*
eurts	*euro*	*Questionnaire*
grämps	*gram'pa* (*grandpa*)	*Questionnaire*; cf. Eng. *gramps*
gränts	*granny*	*Questionnaire*; one student – modelled on *gramps*?
heiks, heips	< Finnish **hei** '*hey, hi*'	(Loog, 1991)
jamps	*jama* 'nonsense'	
jänks	*jänku* 'bunny'	*Questionnaire*
japs	*jaapanlane* 'Japanese'	
jäts	*jäätis* 'icecream'	*Questionnaire*
jops	*jope* 'jacket'	
jõuks	*jõusaal* 'weight room'	
kaaps	*kaabu* 'bowler hat'	outdated
karts	*garderoob* 'cloak room'	*Questionnaire*
kätš	*kähmlus* 'scuffle'	*Questionnaire*; ERKK
kaups	*Kaubamaja* 'name of department store'	
kemps	*kemmergu* 'toilet'< Baltic German *Kämmerchen*	
kilts, kilt(i)	*kilomeeter* 'kilometer'	(prt. sg.)
*kints(i)	*kino* '(let's go to the) movies'	
klatš 'gossip'	base unknown	older form < German?
kleeps	*kleebispilt* 'sticker'	(Tender, 1996; Kasik, 2015)
koks	*kokteil* 'cocktail'	*Questionnaire*
kops	*kopikas* 'coin of small value'	< Russian *kopek*
kots	*kodu* 'home'	(Tender, 1996)
kraaps 'leg-scrape'	*kraapima* 'to scrape'	outdated; cf. *kraapjalg*, lit. 'scrape-leg', in reference to a traditional German custom
krõps	*krõbe* 'crisp (British), potato chip (American)'	
liks	*liköör* 'liqueur'	(Tender, 1996)
limps(i)	*limonaad* 'lemonade'	
lokats	*lo'kaator* 'locator'	(Tender, 1994)
loks	*loogiline* 'logical'	(Tender, 1996)
loks	*logisev* 'rattling; something that rattles'	
lõuksi	*lõuga andma* 'to hit (someone) (on the jaw)'	*Questionnaire*
Lõunts	*Lõunakeskus* 'Southern Mall'	*Questionnaire*
mamps	*mamma* 'mama'	
mats	*Madis* (proper name) 'country bumpkin'	
mints	*minut* 'minute'	
*mintsi	*(läheme)* **minu** *poole* '(let's go) to my place' (illative singular)	(cf. *sintsi*)

---

* Included in the lyrics to the popular song, 'Sexy body': http://sasslantis.ee/lyrics-genialistid-seksikas_keha

Mokits	*Moskvitš* (a type of Russian car)	(Tender, 1994)
möks	*möga,* **mög**in *'goo, gunk'*	
mops	*mob*iil 'cell phone'	*Questionnaire*
mungats	'cloak'< munk 'monk'	(Tender, 1994)
muss	*muus*ika 'music'	
nalʲts	*nal*i 'joke'	Note retention of palatalized /lʲ/ from base form in CVCi. *Questionnaire*
narkots	*narkoot*ikum 'drugs'	
nats(a)	*nat*uke 'a little'	
noks	*nok*u 'penis'	*Questionnaire*
nups, nöps	*nupp,* **nöö**p *'button'*	
näps	*näp*its 'clip'	
näts	*när*imiskumm 'chewing gum'	Note that /r/ is deleted here.
õlts	*õl*u(t) 'beer (prt. sg.)'	*Questionnaire*
õps	*õp*etaja 'teacher'	
paks	< Russian **pok**a /paˈka/	(Tender, 1994)
palʲks	*pal*un 'please'	Jocular response to *tänks* *Questionnaire*
paps	*pap*a 'father, dad'	*Questionnaire*
pilks	*pil*jard 'billiard'	*Questionnaire*
pinks	*ping*pong	
pliks	*plik*a 'girl'	
ponks	*bonbon* 'candy' < French, via German	nasalized vowel >/Vŋ/
porks	*porg*and 'carrot'	*Questionnaire*
ramps, rams	*Raamatukogu* 'library'	In use at least since 1990s
reps-imine	'hazing' < *rebased* 'freshmen' (lit. 'foxes')	treated as a deverbal noun, with the template form /reps/ as the base
rups	*rub*la < Russian *rubl* 'ruble'	
sintsi	*(lähme)* **sin**u juurde '(let's go) to your place' (illative singular)	cf. *mintsi*
sõbrants	*sõbr*anna '(girl) friend'	
sõps	*sõb*er 'friend'	*Questionnaire*
sonks	*soeng* 'hair-do'	*Questionnaire*
stats	*stat*istika 'statistics'	*Questionnaire*
sumps	*(auto)* **sum**muti *'(car) muffler'*	
surts	*Suure Jaani* (name of town)	
sünks	*süng*e 'grim', meaning 'cool' (slang)	(Tender, 1996)
šoks	*šok*olaad 'chocolate'	*Questionnaire*
tänks	*tän*an '(I) thank you'	Jocular echo of English *thanks*; /k/ is not motivated by *tänan*. *Questionnaire*

Continued

Continued

telks	*telekas* 'television'	*Questionnaire*
tinks ja tonks	'this and that', base unknown	
tips	*tibu* 'chick' (i.e., 'girl')	
tots	*tohter* 'doctor'	(outdated)
tõuks	*tõukeratas* 'scooter'	*Questionnaire*
tšauks	*tšauki* < Ital. *ciao*	(Tender, 1994)
vants	*vanaisa* 'grandfather'	*Questionnaire*
vaps	*Eesti* **Vab**adussõjalaste Liidu liige 'member of Estonian War of Independence Soldiers' Society'	1930s Nazi sympathizers
veits	*veidi* 'a little'	
vets	*WC* [**veet**see] 'toilet'	

B. Hypocoristics

Aks	*Agu*	(Hussar & Faster, 2015)
Aiks	*Aiki*	(Hussar & Faster, 2015)
Anks	*Angela*	*Questionnaire*
Ants	*Andreas, Andres, Andrus*	Questionnaire
Ats	*Artur*	*Questionnaire*
Arts	*Arda*	*Questionnaire*
Birks	*Birgit*	(Hussar & Faster, 2015)
Eiks	*Eigo*	(Hussar & Faster, 2015)
Erts	*Eero*	*Questionnaire*
Ets	*Eduard, Edgar*	*Questionnaire*, H&F, 2015
Gets	*Getter*	
Greks	*Gregor*	(Hussar & Faster, 2015)
Grets	*Grethel*	(Hussar & Faster, 2015) *Questionnaire*
Ints	*Indrek*	(Hussar & Faster, 2015)
Inks	*Ingrid*	(Hussar & Faster, 2015)
Kalts	*Kalle*	*Questionnaire*
Kats	*Katri(i)n, Katrina, Kadi, Kadri, Kati*	*Questionnaire* (Hussar & Faster, 2015)
Käts	*Kätrin, Kädi, Kätlin*	*Questionnaire*
Kerts	*Kertu*	*Questionnaire*
Krips	*Kribu* (cat's name)	
Malts	*Mallor*	*Questionnaire*
Mäks	*Mägi*	
Maks	*Margus, Markus*	
Mats	*Madis*	*Questionnaire*
Marks	*Margus, Marko*	(Hussar & Faster, 2015)
Pets	*Peeter*	*Questionnaire*
Pirks	*Piret, Pirgit*	*Questionnaire*
Raits	*Raivo*	*Questionnaire*
Raks	*Raido*	(Hussar & Faster, 2015)
Riks	*Riho*	*Questionnaire*
Romps	*Romet*	*Questionnaire*
Ruts	*Rudolf*	(Hussar & Faster, 2015)
Sirts(u)	*Siret*	*Questionnaire*
Sol^jts	*Solveig*	*Questionnaire*
Tarmps, Tarts, Tarms	*Tarmo*	

Teps	*Teppo* (surname)	
Tints	*Tiina*	
Tiuks	*Tiia (Tiiu)*	*Questionnaire*
Toits, Toiks	*Toivo, Toivokas*	
Trints	*Triinu*	*Questionnaire*
Velts, Velks	*Velvo, Velvokas*	
Vlats	*Vladislav*	

English rhyming compounds

Recognizable real words (that contribute meaning to the compound) are in **bold face**. Readily identifiable loanwords and abbreviations are in *italics*. ǂ Included in Wheatley (1866); * included in Thun (1963) but not in Wheatley. (Of the forms included in Wheatley, all are also in Thun with the exception of *powwow* and *whipper-snapper*.)

Labial onset, word2	*Comments, sources*	*Non-labial onset, word2*	*Comments, sources*
airy-fairy		* abra-cadabra	[+ syl.]
ǂ argie-bargie	cf. argle-bargle 'to argue' (Wheatley)	**artsy-craftsy**	
artsy-fartsy		**bandstand**	
arsy-versy		**bed**stead	
bigwig		**bee's knees**	
bleedie-peedies	G. Swift (1983), *Waterland*, p. 301	* **blackjack**	
* boogie-woogie		**blame game**	
ǂ cawdy-mawdy		*boho*	
* *charivari*		**boob**tube	
chick flick		**brain drain**	
* **chock**-a-**block**	[+ linking V]	**busy** Lizzie	
cuddle-puddle¹	< Instagram comment, 10/18	ǂ **claptrap**	
culture vulture		* **cracker**jack	[- syl]
curly-wurly		**deadhead**	
ǂ cushle-mushle		* ding-a-ling	[+ linking V] (onomatopoeia only, Thun.)
cutsie-wootsie		**double-trouble**	
eager beaver		**downtown**	
easy-peasy		**dream team**	
fender-bender		**even**-Stephen	
flower power		**fair share**	
fly-by		**fat cat**	

funny bunny		‡ flibberty-gibbet	[– final V] *flibber-gibber*
funny money		flubdub	
* **fuzzy**wuzzy		fol-de-rol	
gangbang		fuddy-duddy	
gender-bender		**fun run**	
‡ hanky-panky		**gloomy-doom**y	R. Ford (1986), *The Sportswriter*, p. 124
hells-**bells**		**God squad**	
hifi		**good** should	R. Ford (1986), *The Sportswriter*, p. 258
‡ higgledy-piggledy		**grandstand**	
hillbilly		**gruesome twosome**	
‡ hocus-pocus	< *hoc est corpus meum*	hackysack	[+ linking V]
‡ hodge-podge		‡ **handy**-dandy	children's game
hoi poloi		*hari-kari*	< *harakiri*
* hokey-pokey		‡ harum-scarum	
‡ holus-bolus		* heebie-jeebies	
Holy Moley		‡ helter-skelter	
honeybunny	'pretty girl'	herky-jerky	
hotpot		* heyday	
‡ hubble-bubble		hibbity-jibbity	
‡ hubbub		hiddy-giddy	
‡ **huff**puff		**hippy-dippy**	
‡ huggermugger	F. Spufford (2016), *Golden Hill*, p. 46	‡ hobnob	
‡ hullaballoo	[+V changes] halloo-balloo	‡ hob(son)-job(son)	hob-job (Wheatley)
hunkum-bunkum		‡ hoity-toity	
‡ hurly-burly		* honky-tonk	[- final V]
huzz-buzz		* hootchie-kootchie	
illwill		**hot**shot	
* itsy-**bitsy**		**hotspot**	

Continued

Continued

Labial onset, word2	Comments, sources	Non-labial onset, word2	Comments, sources
ǂ kickie-whickie (kicksie-wicksie)		* hotsy-totsy	
ǂ loco-foco		hully-gully	R. Ford (1986), *The Sportswriter*, p. 255
Lodgie-Podgie	Logic	ǂ humdrum	
ǂ nambypamby		ǂ hurdy-gurdy	
ǂ niminy-piminy		ǂ **hurry**scurry	
* **nitwit**		* inkydinky	
* **palsie-walsie**		**I-spy**	
peely-wally	[+V change] H. Mantel, *New York Review*, 9/17	*jai alai*	[+ V]
ǂ pee**wee**		jeepers-creepers	
ǂ pell-mell		jiminy criminy	
		jet set	
* **phoney**-baloney		**killer**-diller	
* **piggy**-wiggy		*kowtow*	
ǂ pinkie-winkie		la-di-da	[+ syl]
poke-moke		*lit crit*	
* **pop**sie-wopsie		**local yokel**	
ǂ *powwow*		**loosey**-goosey	
prissy missy	Jespersen, 1961	* **lovey-dovey**	
ragbag		ǂ mack-lack	
rich bitch		May Day	distress call, from Fr. *(venez) m'aider*
ǂ roly-poly		*mojo*	
roola-boola	N. Williams (2014), *History of the Rain*, p. 20	*mukluk*	
rumpy-pumpy		ǂ mumbo-jumbo	
sci fi		nitty-gritty	
seabee		**no-go**	
silly-billy		**no-show**	

silly-milly	L. Gordon (2017), *Outsiders*, pp. 237f.	numbly-**crumbly**	R. Ford (1986), *The Sportswriter*, p. 235
simple-pimple		okey-dokey	
slang whang		**old gold**	
snailmail		**peepie**-creepie	
snuggle-buggle	R. Ford (1986), *The Sportswriter*, p. 108	pink-twink	
* **snuggly**-wuggly		**plain**-Jane	
stinky pinky		plug-**ugly**	[– syl]
‡ teen(s)y-ween(s)y		**poop scoop**	
teepee		**potshot**	
Tex-Mex		**power shower**	
‡ tit**bit**		**prime time**	
tootie **fruitie**	(BT foot > woot)	‡ **ragtag**	*tag-rag* in same sense (Wheatley)
* **tootsie**-wootsie		**ram**-jam	
toyboy		**ram**-stam	B. MacLaverty (2017), *Midwinter Break*
true blue		* razzle-dazzle	
‡ **tussie** mussie		* razzmatazz	[+ linking syllable]
whambam		**ready-steady**	
wi-fi		**real deal**	
		redhead	
		rinky-dink	[+ V]
		rom com	
		rooty-tooty	
		rub-a-dub	[+ linking V]
		rumble-**tumble**	
		rumdum	
		sky high	
		slapdash	< *slashdash*
		space race	
		speed-read	
		stalk-talk	A. Burns (2018), *Milkman*, p. 168
		stun gun	

Continued

Continued

Labial onset, word2	Comments, sources	Non-labial onset, word2	Comments, sources
		super-duper	
		tinkle-chink	R. Ford (1986), *The Sportswriter*, p. 235
		to-do	
		voodoo	
		* **walkie-talkie**	
		waylay	
		wheeler-**dealer**	
		ǂ whipper-snapper	
		wild child	
		ǂ **willy-nilly**	
		wingding	< *will-you, nill-you*
		zoot**suit**	

Note:

[1] Comment on a photo of a hog house with a 14' × 14' footprint, built to protect overwintering pigs before the cold Maine winter: 'We had 6 big ones in [a hog house] 8' × 8' ... piggy pile cuddle puddle.'

References

Ackerman, F., Blevins, J. P., & Malouf, R. (2009). Parts and wholes: Patterns of relatedness in complex morphological systems and why they matter. In J. P. Blevins & J. Blevins (eds.), *Analogy in Grammar: Form and Acquisition*, pp. 54–82. Oxford: Oxford University Press.

Ackerman, F. & Malouf, R. (2017). Implicative relations in word-based morphological systems. In A. Hippisley & G. Stump (eds.), *The Cambridge Handbook of Morphology*, pp. 297–328. Cambridge: Cambridge University Press.

Ackerman, F. & Malouf, R. (2018). Systemic organization in word-based morphology. Talk presented at 18th International Morphology Meeting, Budapest.

Aitchison, J. (1972). Mini-malapropisms. *British Journal of Disorders of Communication*, 7, 38–43.

Aitchison, J. & Chiat, S. (1981). Natural phonology or natural memory? The interaction between phonological processes and recall mechanisms. *Language and Speech, 24*, 311–326.

Aitchison, J. & Straf, M. (1981). Lexical storage and retrieval: A developing skill? In A. Cutler (ed.), *Slips of the Tongue and Language Production*, pp. 751–95. Amsterdam: Mouton (= *Linguistics*, 19, 751–95).

Akhtar, N., Dunham, F., & Dunham, P. J. (1991). Directive interactions and early vocabulary development: The role of joint attentional focus. *Journal of Child Language*, 18, 41–9.

Akinlabi, A. & Urua, E. E. (2002). Foot structure in the Ibibio verb. *Journal of African Languages and Linguistics*, 23, 119–60.

Altvater-Mackensen, N. & Grossmann, T. (2015). Learning to match auditory and visual speech cues: Social influences on acquisition of phonological categories. *Child Development*, 86, 362–78.

Anderson, S. (1985). *Phonology in the Twentieth Century: Theories of Rules and Theories of Representations*. Chicago: University of Chicago Press.

Andreassen, H. N. & Eychenne, J. (2013). The French foot revisited. *Language Sciences*, 39, 126–40.

Antoine, F. (2000). *Dictionnaire français-anglais des mots tronqués*. Louvain: Peeters.

Aoyama, K. (2001). *A Psycholinguistic Perspective on Finnish and Japanese Prosody: Perception, Production and Child Acquisition of Consonantal Quantity Distinctions*. Norwell: Kluwer Academic.

Aoyama, K. (2002). Quantity contrasts in Japanese and Finnish: Differences in adult production and acquisition. In Y. Shirai, H. Kobayashi, S. Miyata, K. Nakamura, T. Ogura, & H. Sirai (eds.), *Studies in Language Sciences (2): Papers from the Second Annual Conference of the Japanese Society for Language Sciences*, pp. 121–35. Tokyo: Kuroshio.

Arriaga, R., Fenson, L., Cronan, T., & Pethick, S. (1998). Scores on the MacArthur Communicative Development Inventory of children from low and middle-income families. *Applied Psycholinguistics*, 19, 209–23.

Aslin, R. N. & Newport, E. (2014). Distributional language learning: Mechanisms and models of category formation. *Language Learning*, 64, Suppl. 2, 86–105.

Asu, E. L., Lippus, P., Pajusalu, K., & Teras, P. (2016). *Eesti keele hääldus* [Estonian Pronunciation]. Tartu: Tartu University Press.

Atkinson, K., MacWhinney, B., & Stoel, C. (1970). An experiment in the recognition of babbling. *Papers and Reports on Child Language Development*, 1, 73–6. California: Stanford University.

Baese-Berk, M. M. & Samuel, A. G. (2016). Listeners beware: Speech production may be bad for learning speech sounds. *Journal of Memory and Language*, 89, 23–36.

Baia, M. F. A. (2013). Templates in phonological development: The case of Brazilian Portuguese. Unpublished PhD thesis. São Paulo: University of São Paulo.

Baia, M. F. A. & Correia, S. (2010). The initial prosodic template in Brazilian and European Portuguese: A methodological matter? In J. Costa, A. Castro, M. Lobo, & F. Pratas (eds.), *Language Acquisition and Development: Proceedings of GALA 2009*, vol. 1, pp. 13–27. Newcastle: Cambridge Scholars Publishing.

Baia, M. F. A. & Santos, R. S. (2011a). Reduplicated words in Brazilian Portuguese acquisition. *Papers in Psycholinguistics*, 1, 114–20.

Baia, M. F. A. & Santos, R. S. (2011b). Discrepancy between naturalistic and experimental studies: The case of the initial prosodic template in Brazilian Portuguese. In S. M. Alvord (ed.), *Selected Proceedings of the 5th Conference on Laboratory Approaches to Romance Phonology*, pp. 127–35. Somerville, MA: Cascadilla Proceedings Project.

Baird-Pharr, A., Ratner, N. B., & Rescorla, L. (2000). Syllable structure development of toddlers with expressive specific language impairment. *Applied Psycholinguistics*, 21, 429–49.

Barlow, M. & Kemmer, S. (eds.) (2000). *Usage Based Models of Language*. Stanford, CA: CSLI.

Barton, D. (1980). Phonemic perception in children. In G. Yeni-Komshian, J. Kavanagh, & C. A. Ferguson (eds.), *Child Phonology, vol. 2: Perception*, pp. 97–114. New York: Academic Press.

Bates, E. (1979). Intentions, conventions and symbols. In E. Bates, L. Benigni, I. Bretherton, L. Camaioni, & V. Volterra (eds.), *The Emergence of Symbols: Cognition and Communication in Infancy*, pp. 33–68. New York: Academic Press.

Bates, E., Benigni, L., Bretherton, I., Camaioni, L., & Volterra, V. (1979). *The Emergence of Symbols: Cognition and Communication in Infancy*. New York: Academic Press.

Bates, E. & Elman, J. (1996). Learning rediscovered. *Science*, 274, 1849–50.

Baudouin de Courtenay, J. (1871/1972). *A Baudouin de Courtenay Anthology: The Beginnings of Structural Linguistics*, ed. and trans. E. Stankiewicz. Bloomington: Indiana University Press.

Beckman, M. E. & Edwards, J. (2000a). Lexical frequency effects on young children's imitative productions. In M. B. Broe & J. B. Pierrehumbert (eds.), *Papers in Laboratory Phonology V: Acquisition and the Lexicon*, pp. 208–18. Cambridge: Cambridge University Press.

Beckman, M. E. & Edwards, J. (2000b). The ontogeny of phonological categories and the primacy of lexical learning in linguistic development. *Child Development*, 71, 240–9.

Beckman, M. E., Munson, B., & Edwards, J. (2007). The influence of vocabulary growth on developmental changes in types of phonological knowledge. In J. Cole & J. Hualde (eds.), *Phonology 9*, pp. 241–64. New York: Mouton de Gruyter.

Benczes, R. (2012). Just a load of hibber gibber? Making sense of English rhyming compounds. *Australian Journal of Linguistics*, 32, 299–326.

Benczes, R. (2019). *Rhyme over Reason: Phonological Motivation in English*. Cambridge: Cambridge University Press.

Bendjaballah, S. & Haiden M. (2003). Templatic architecture. *Recherches Linguistiques de Vincennes*, 32, 157–68.

Bendjaballah, S. & Haiden, M. (2013). The representational anomalies of floating markers: Light prepositions in Taqbaylit of Chemini. In T. Biberauer & I. Roberts (eds.), *Challenges to Linearization*, pp. 331–76. Berlin: De Gruyter.

Bendjaballah, S. & Reintges, C. H. (2009). Ancient Egyptian verbal reduplication: Typology, diachrony, and the morphology-syntax interface. *Morphology*, 19, 135–57.

Berent, I. (2013). The phonological mind. *Trends in Cognitive Science*, 17, 319–27.

Berent, I., Vaknin, V., & Marcus, G. F. (2007). Roots, stems, and the universality of lexical representations: Evidence from Hebrew. *Cognition*, 104, 254–86.

Berman, R. A. (1977). Natural phonological processes at the one-word stage. *Lingua*, 43, 1–21.

Bhaya Nair, R. (1991). Monosyllabic English or disyllabic Hindi? *Indian Linguistics*, 52, 51–90.

Blevins, J. (2004). *Evolutionary Phonology: The Emergence of Sound Patterns.* Cambridge: Cambridge University Press.

Blevins, J. P. (2006). Word-based morphology. *Journal of Linguistics*, 42, 531–73.

Blevins, J. P. (2007). Conjugation classes in Estonian. *Linguistica Uralica*, 43, 250–67.

Blevins, J. P. (2008). Declension classes in Estonian. *Linguistica Uralica*, 44, 241–67.

Blevins, J. P. (2016). *Word and Paradigm Morphology.* Oxford: Oxford University Press.

Bloom, L. (1973). *One Word at a Time.* The Hague: Mouton.

Bloomfield, L. (1933). *Language.* New York: Holt, Rinehart & Winston.

Bohm, L. A., Nelson, M. E., Driver, L. E., & Green, G. E. (2010). Babbling, vegetative function, and language development after cricotracheal resection in aphonic children. *The Laryngoscope*, 120, 2494–7.

Booth, D. (1835). *Analytical Dictionary of the English Language.* London.

Bosch, L., Figueras, M., Teixidó, M., & Ramon-Casas, M. (2013). Rapid gains in segmenting fluent speech when words match the rhythmic unit: Evidence from infants acquiring syllable-timed languages. *Frontiers in Psychology*, 4, 106.

Boudelaa, S. & Marslen-Wilson, W. (2004). Abstract morphemes and lexical representation: The CV-skeleton in Arabic. *Cognition*, 92, 271–303.

Boysson-Bardies, B. de, Hallé, P., Sagart, L., & Durand, C. (1989). A crosslinguistic investigation of vowel formants in babbling. *Journal of Child Language*, 16, 1–17.

Boysson-Bardies, B. de, Sagart, L., & Durand, C. (1984). Discernible differences in the babbling of infants according to target language. *Journal of Child Language*, 11, 1–15.

Boysson-Bardies, B. de & Vihman, M. M. (1991). Adaptation to language: Evidence from babbling and first words in four languages. *Language*, 67, 297–319.

Brent, M. R. & Siskind, J. M. (2001). The role of exposure to isolated words in early vocabulary development. *Cognition*, 81, B33–B44.

Brown, H. & Gaskell, M. G. (2014). The time-course of talker-specificity and lexical competition effects during word learning. *Language, Cognition and Neuroscience*, 29, 1163–79.

Brown, R. (1958). *Words and Things.* Glencoe, IL: Free Press.

Brown, R. (1973). *A First Language.* Cambridge, MA: Harvard University Press.

Bruderer, A. G., Danielson, D. K., Kandhadai, P., & Werker, J. F. (2015). Sensorimotor influences on speech perception in infancy. *Proceedings of the National Academy of Sciences of the United States of America*, 112, 13531–6.

Bush, C. N. et al. (1973). On specifying a system for transcribing consonants in child language: A working paper with examples from American English and Mexican Spanish. Stanford University: Department of Linguistics.

Bybee, J. (1985). *Morphology: A Study of the Relation between Meaning and Form.* Philadelphia: John Benjamins.

Bybee, J. (2001). *Phonology and Language Use.* Cambridge: Cambridge University Press.

Bybee, J. (2006). From usage to grammar: The mind's response to repetition. *Language*, 82, 711–33.

Bybee, J. (2010). *Language, Usage and Cognition.* Cambridge: Cambridge University Press.

Bybee, J. & Hopper, P. (eds.) (2001). *Frequency and the Emergence of Linguistic Structure.* Amsterdam: John Benjamins.

Campos, J. J., Anderson, D. I., Barbu-Roth, M. A., Hubbard, E. M., Hertenstein, M. J., & Witherington, D. (2000). Travel broadens the mind. *Infancy*, 1, 149–219.

Caratini, E. (2009). Vocalic and consonantal quantity in German: synchronic and diachronic perspectives. Unpublished PhD thesis. Nice University and Leipzig University.

Carpenter, M., Nagell, K., & Tomasello, M. (1998). Social cognition, joint attention, and communicative competence from 9 to 15 months of age. *Monographs of the Society for Research in Child Development*, 63.

Carson, P. C., Klee, T., Carson, D. K., & Hime, L. K. (2003). Phonological profiles of 2-year-olds with delayed language development: Predicting clinical outcomes at age 3. *American Journal of Speech-Language Pathology*, 12, 28–39.

Carvalho, Brendão de J. (2003). Templatic morphology in the Portuguese verb. In T. Meisenburg & M. Selig (eds.), *Nouveaux départs en phonologie: les conceptions sub- et suprasegmentales*, pp. 13–32. Tübingen: Narr.

Carvalho, Brendão de J. (2006). Markedness gradient in the Portuguese verb: How morphology and phonology interact. In I. Fónagy et al. (eds.), *Prosody and Syntax*, pp. 157–74. Amsterdam: John Benjamins.

Cazden, C. (1968). The acquisition of noun and verb inflections. *Child Development*, 39, 433–48.

Cherry, E. C. (1953). Some experiments on the recognition of speech, with one and two ears. *Journal of the Acoustic Society of America*, 25, 975–9.

Chomsky, N. (1964). Discussion. *Monographs of the Society for Research in Child Development*, 29, no. 1: The Acquisition of Language: Report of the Fourth Conference Sponsored by the Committee on Intellective Processes, pp. 35–42.

Chomsky, N. (1965). *Aspects of the Theory of Syntax.* Cambridge, MA: MIT Press.

Chomsky, N. (1984). Current issues in linguistic theory. In J. Fodor & J. Katz (eds.), *The Structure of Language: Readings in the Philosophy of Language.* Englewood Cliffs, NJ: Prentice-Hall.

Chomsky, N. & Halle, M. (1968). *The Sound Pattern of English.* New York: Harper & Row.

Choo, R. Q., Vihman, M. M., & Keren-Portnoy, T. (2019). The acquisition of lexical tones by Mandarin-English bilinguals: A longitudinal study. Paper presented at the International Bilingualism Symposium, 12. Edmonton, Alberta.

Coleman, J., Bethin, C. Y., & John, C. (1998). *Phonological Representations: Their Names, Forms and Powers.* Cambridge: Cambridge University Press.

Cooper, R. & Shallice, T. (2000). Contention scheduling and the control of routine activities. *Cognitive Neuropsychology*, 17, 297–338.

Correia, S. (2009). The acquisition of primary word stress in European Portuguese. Unpublished PhD thesis. University of Lisbon.

Croft, W. (2001). *Radical Construction Grammar: Syntactic Theory in Typological Perspective.* Oxford: Oxford University Press.

Curtin, S., Byers-Heinlein, K., & Werker, J. F. (2011). Bilingual beginnings as a lens for theory development: PRIMIR in focus. *Journal of Phonetics*, 39, 492–504.

Davis, B. L. & MacNeilage, P. F. (1990). Acquisition of correct vowel production: A quantitative case study. *Journal of Speech and Hearing Research*, 33, 16–27.

Davis, B. L. & MacNeilage, P. F. (1995). The articulatory basis of babbling. *Journal of Speech and Hearing Research*, 38, 1199–211.

Davis, B. L. & MacNeilage, P. F. (2000). An embodiment perspective on the acquisition of speech perception. *Phonetica*, 57, 229–41.

Davis, B. L., MacNeilage, P. F., & Matyear, C. L. (2002). Acquisition of serial complexity in speech production: A comparison of phonetic and phonological approaches to first word production. *Phonetica*, 59, 75–107.

Dawdy-Hesterberg, L. G. & Pierrehumbert, J. B. (2014). Learnability and generalisation of Arabic broken plural nouns. *Language, Cognition and Neuroscience*, 29, 1268–82.

Demuth, K. (1996). Alignment, stress, and parsing in early phonological words. In B. Bernhardt, J. Gilbert, & D. Ingram (eds.), *Proceedings of the UB International Conference on Phonological Acquisition*, pp. 113–25. Somerville: Cascadilla Press.

Demuth, K., Culbertson, J., & Alter, J. (2006). Word-minimality, epenthesis and coda licensing in the early acquisition of English. *Language and Speech*, 49, 137–74.

Demuth, K. & Johnson, M. (2003). Truncation to sub-minimal words in French. *Canadian Journal of Linguistics*, 48, 211–41.

DePaolis, R. A., Keren-Portnoy, T., & Vihman, M. M. (2016). Making sense of infant familiarity and novelty responses to words at lexical onset. *Frontiers in Psychology*, 7, 715.

DePaolis, R., Vihman, M. M., & Keren-Portnoy, T. (2011). Do production patterns influence the processing of speech in prelinguistic infants? *Infant Behavior and Development*, 34, 590–601.

DePaolis, R. A., Vihman, M. M., & Keren-Portnoy, T. (2014). When do infants begin recognizing familiar words in sentences? *Journal of Child Language*, 41, 226–39.

DePaolis, R., Vihman, M. M., & Nakai, S. (2013). The influence of babbling patterns on the processing of speech. *Infant Behavior and Development*, 36, 642–9.

Deuchar, M. (2005). Congruence and Welsh–English code-switching. *Bilingualism: Language and Cognition*, 8, 255–69.

Deuchar, M. & Quay, S. (2000). *Bilingual Acquisition: Theoretical Implications of a Case Study*. Oxford: Oxford University Press.

Deutsch, A. & Meir, A. (2011). The role of the root morpheme in mediating word production in Hebrew. *Language and Cognitive Processes*, 26, 716–44.

Dinnsen, D. A. (2008). A typology of opacity effects in acquisition. In D. A. Dinnsen & J. A. Gierut (eds.), *Optimality Theory, Phonological Acquisition and Disorders*, pp. 121–76. London: Equinox.

Doleschal, U. & Thornton, A. M. (eds.) (2000). *Extragrammatical and Marginal Morphology*. München: Lincom Europa.

Dumay, N. & Gaskell, M. G. (2012). Overnight lexical consolidation revealed by speech segmentation. *Cognition*, 123, 119–32.

Edelman, G. (1987). *Neural Darwinism: The Theory of Neuronal Group Selection*. New York: Basic Books.

Edelman, G. (1988). *Topobiology: An Introduction to Molecular Embryology*. New York: Basic Books.

Edelman, G. (1989). *The Remembered Present: A Biological Theory of Consciousness*. New York: Basic Books.

Edelman, G. (1992). *Bright Air, Brilliant Fire: On the Matter of the Mind*. New York: Basic Books.

Edwards, J., Beckman, M. E., & Munson, B. (2004). The interaction between vocabulary size and phonotactic probability effects on children's production accuracy and fluency in nonword repetition. *Journal of Speech, Language, and Hearing Research*, 47, 421–36.

Edwards, S., Fletcher, P., Garman, M., Hughes, A., Letts, C., & Sinka, I. (1997). *Reynell Developmental Language Scales III: The University of Reading Edition* (London: NFER-Nelson).

Eek, A. & Meister, E. (1997). Simple perception experiments on Estonian word prosody: Foot structure. *Papers from a Symposium* (pp. 71–99). Tallinn: Institute of Estonian Language.

Eek, A. & Meister, E. (2003). Foneetilisi katseid ja arutlusi kvantiteedi alalt (I): Häälikukestusi muutvad kontekstid ja välde [Phonetic experiments and discussions about quantity, I: Contexts that affect segmental duration and grade]. *Keel ja Kirjandus*, 46 (11), 815–37; (12), 904–18.

Eek, A. & Meister, E. (2004). Foneetilisi katseid ja arutlusi kvantiteedi alalt (II): Takt, silp ja välde [Foot, syllable and grade]. *Keel ja Kirjandus*, 47 (4) 251–71; (5), 336–57.

Ehala, M. (2003). Estonian quantity: Implications for moraic theory. In D. Nelson & S. Manninen (eds.), *Generative Approaches to Finnic and Saami Linguistics*, pp. 51–79. Stanford, CA: CSLI Publications.

Eimas, P. D., Siqueland, E. R., Jusczyk, P. W., & Vigorito, J. (1971). Speech perception in infants. *Science*, 171, 303–6.

Elbers, L. (1997). Output as input: A constructivist hypothesis in language acquisition. *Archives de Psychologie*, 65, 131–40.

Elbers, L. & Ton, J. (1985). Play pen monologues: The interplay of words and babble in the first words period. *Journal of Child Language*, 12, 551–65.

Ellis, N. C. (2002). Frequency effects in language processing: A review with implications for theories of implicit and explicit language acquisition. *Studies in Second Language Acquisition*, 24, 143–88.

Ellis, N. C. (2005). At the interface: Dynamic interactions of explicit and implicit language knowledge. *Studies in Second Language Acquisition*, 27, 305–52.

Elman, J., Bates, E. A., Johnson, M. H., Karmiloff-Smith, A., Parisi, D., & Plunkett, K. (1996). *Rethinking Innateness: A Connectionist Perspective on Development*. Cambridge, MA: MIT Press.

Elsen, H. (1991). *Erstspracherwerb: Der Erwerb des deutschen Lautsystems*. Wiesbaden: Deutscher Universitäts.

Elsen, H. (1996). Two routes to language. *First Language*, 16, 141–58.

Engstrand, O., Williams, K., & Lacerda, F. (2003). Does babbling sound native? Listener responses to vocalizations produced by Swedish and American 12- and 18-month-olds. *Phonetica*, 60, 17–44.

Engstrand, O., Williams, K., & Strømqvist, S. (1991). Acquisition of the Swedish tonal word accent contrast. *Proceedings of the 12th International Congress of Phonetic Sciences*, 1, 324–7.

Evans, N. & Levinson, S. C. (2009). The myth of language universals: Language diversity and its importance for cognitive science. *Behavioral and Brain Sciences*, 32, 429–48.

Fabb, N. (1988). English suffixation is constrained only by selectional restrictions. *Natural Language & Linguistic Theory*, 6, 527–39.

Fay, D. & Cutler, A. (1977). Malapropisms and the structure of the mental lexicon. *Linguistic Inquiry*, 8, 505–20.

Ferguson, C. A. (1963). Contrastive analysis and language development. *Georgetown University Monograph Series*, 21, 101–12.

Ferguson, C. A. & Farwell, C. B. (1975). Words and sounds in early language acquisition. *Language*, 51, 419–39. Reprinted in William S.-Y. Wang, *The Lexicon in Phonological Change*. The Hague: Mouton, 1977 and in Vihman & Keren-Portnoy (2013b).

Ferguson, C. A. & Garnica, O. K. (1975). Theories of phonological development. In E. H. Lenneberg and E. Lenneberg (eds.), *Foundations of Language Development*, pp. 153–80. New York: Academic Press.

Ferguson, C. A., Menn, L., & Stoel-Gammon, C. (eds.) (1992). *Phonological Development: Models, Research, Implications*. Timonium, MD: York Press.

Ferguson, C. A., Peizer, D. B., & Weeks, T. A. (1973). Model-and-replica phonological grammar of a child's first words. *Lingua*, 31, 35–65.

Ferguson, C. A. & Slobin, D. I. (1973). *Studies of Language Development*. New York: Holt, Rinehart & Winston.

Fernald, A., Swingley, D., & Pinto, J. P. (2001). When half a word is enough: Infants can recognize spoken words using partial phonetic information. *Child Development*, 72, 1003–15.

Fikkert, P. (1994). *On the Acquisition of Prosodic Structure*. Amsterdam: Holland Institute of Generative Linguistics.

Fikkert, P. & Levelt, C. (2008). How does place fall into place? The lexicon and emergent constraints in children's developing grammars. In P. Avery, E. Dresher, & K. Rice (eds.), *Contrast in Phonology: Theory, Perception, Acquisition*, pp. 231–70. Berlin: Mouton.

Firth, J. R. (1948). Sounds and prosodies. *Transactions of the Philological Society*, 47, 127–52. Reprinted in Palmer (1970).

Floccia, C., Keren-Portnoy, T., DePaolis, R., Duffy, H., Delle Luche, C., Durrant, S., White, L., Goslin, J., & Vihman, M. (2016). British English infants segment words only with exaggerated infant-directed speech stimuli. *Cognition*, 148, 1–9.

Fradin, B. & Kerleroux, F. (2009). L'identité lexémique. In B. Fradin, F. Kerleroux, & M. Plénat (eds.), *Aperçus de morphologie du français*. Vincennes: Presses Universitaires de Vincennes.

Francescato, G. (1968). On the role of the word in first language acquisition. *Lingua*, 21, 144–53.

Freitas, M. J. (1997). Aquisição da estrutura silábica do Português Europeu [The acquisition of syllable structure in European Portuguese]. Unpublished PhD thesis. University of Lisbon.

Frost, R., Forster, K. J., & Deutsch, A. (1997). What can we learn from the morphology of Hebrew? A masked-priming investigation of morphological representation. *Journal of Experimental Psychology: Learning, Memory, and Cognition*, 23, 829–56.

Fry, D. B. (1966). The development of the phonological system in the normal and the deaf child. In F. Smith & G. Miller (eds.), *The Genesis of Language: A Psycholinguistic Approach*, pp. 187–206. Cambridge, MA: MIT Press.

Garmann, N. G., Kristoffersen, K., & Simonsen, H. G. (2017). Phonological patterns (templates) in 5p deletion syndrome. *International Journal of Clinical Linguistics and Phonetics* (online first).

Gaskell, M. G. & Dumay, N. (2003). Lexical competition and the acquisition of novel words. *Cognition*, 89, 105–32.

Gerken, L.-A. & Aslin, R. N. (2005). Thirty years of research on infant speech perception: The legacy of Peter W. Jusczyk. *Language Learning and Development*, 1, 5–21.

Gleitman, L. R. & Wanner, E. (1982). Language acquisition: The state of the state of the art. In E. Wanner & L. R. Gleitman (eds.), *Language Acquisition: The State of the Art*, pp. 3–48. Cambridge: Cambridge University Press.

Goldinger, S. D. (1996). Words and voices: Episodic traces in spoken word identification and recognition memory. *Journal of Experimental Psychology: Learning, Memory, and Cognition*, 22, 1166–83.

Goldinger, S. D. (1998). Echoes of echoes? An episodic theory of lexical access. *Psychological Review*, 105, 251–79.

Goldsmith, J. A. (1976). An overview of autosegmental phonology. *Linguistic Analysis*, 2, 23–68.

Goldsmith, J. A. (1990). *Autosegmental and Metrical Phonology*. Oxford: Blackwell.

Goldstein, M. H., King, A. P., & West, M. J. (2003). Social feedback to infants' babbling facilitates rapid phonological learning. *Proceedings of the National Academy of Sciences of the United States of America*, 100, 8030–5.

Goldstein, M. H. & Schwade, J. A. (2008). Social interaction shapes babbling: Testing parallels between birdsong and speech. *Psychological Science*, 19, 515–23.

Good, J. (2011). The typology of templates. *Language and Linguistic Compass*, 5, 731–47.

Good, J. (2016). *The Linguistic Typology of Templates*. Cambridge: Cambridge University Press.

Gottlieb, G. (2014). *Synthesizing Nature–Nurture: Prenatal Roots of Instinctive Behavior*. New York: Psychology Press.

Gottlieb, G., Wahlsten, D., and Lickliter, R. (2006). Biology and human development. In W. Damon & R. M. Lerner (eds.-in-chief) & R. M. Lerner (vol. ed.), *Handbook of Child Psychology*, vol. 1, pp. 210–57. Hoboken, NJ: Wiley.

Granlund, S., Kołak, J., Vihman, V.-A., Engelmann, F., Ambridge, B., Pine, J., Theakston, A., & Lieven, E. (2019). Language-general and language-specific phenomena in the acquisition of inflectional noun morphology: A cross-linguistic elicited-production study of Polish, Finnish and Estonian. *Journal of Memory and Language*, 107, 169–94.

Grieser, D. & Kuhl, P. K. (1989). Categorization of speech by infants: Support for speech-sound prototypes. *Developmental Psychology*, 25, 577–88.

Gros-Louis, J., West, M. J., Goldstein, M. H., & King, A. P. (2006). Mothers provide differential feedback to infants' prelinguistic sounds. *International Journal of Behavioral Development*, 30, 509–16.

Grunwell, P. (1982). *Clinical Phonology*. London: Croom Helm.

Guellaï, B., Streri, A., & Yeung, H. H. (2014). The development of sensorimotor influences in the audiovisual speech domain: Some critical questions. *Frontiers in Psychology*, 5, 1–7.

Hale, M. & Reiss, C. (2008). *The Phonological Enterprise*. Oxford: Oxford University Press.

Hall, K. C., Hume, E., Jaeger, F. T., & Wedel, A. (2018). The role of predictability in shaping phonological patterns. *Linguistics Vanguard*, 4.

Hallé, P. & Boysson-Bardies, B. de (1994). Emergence of an early lexicon: Infants' recognition of words. *Infant Behavior and Development*, 17, 119–29.

Hallé, P. & Boysson-Bardies, B. de (1996). The format of representation of recognized words in infants' early receptive lexicon. *Infant Behavior and Development*, 19, 463–81.

Hallé, P. Boysson-Bardies, B. de, & Vihman, M. M. (1991). Beginnings of prosodic organization: Intonation and duration patterns of disyllables produced by Japanese and French infants. *Language and Speech*, 34, 299–318.

Hamilton, A., Plunkett, K., & Schafer, T. (2000). Infant vocabulary development assessed with a British CDI. *Journal of Child Language*, 27, 689–705.

Hannahs, S. J. (2013). *The Phonology of Welsh*. Oxford: Oxford University Press.

Harris, Z. (1944). Simultaneous components in phonology. *Language*, 20, 181–205. Reprinted in Joos (1957).

Harrison, S. P. (1973). Reduplication in Micronesian languages. *Oceanic Linguistics*, 12, 407–54.

Harrison, S. P. (1976). *Mokilese Reference Grammar*. Honolulu: University Press of Hawaii.

Hauser, M. D. (1996). *The Evolution of Communication*. Cambridge, MA: MIT Press.

Hay, J. B. & Baayen, R. H. (2005). Shifting paradigms: Gradient structure in morphology. *Trends in Cognitive Science*, 9, 342–8.

Heinemann, S. (1953). Les mots déformés et abrégés en -o dans l'argot, dans le langage populaire et dans la langue commune. In *Mélanges de linguistiqe et de littérature romanes offerts à Mario Roques*, vol. 2, pp. 151–63. Paris: Art et Science.

Henderson, L., Devine, K., Weighall, A., & Gaskell, G. (2015). When the daffodat flew to the intergalactic zoo: Off-line consolidation is critical for word learning from stories. *Developmental Psychology*, 51, 406–17.

Henderson, L. M., Weighall, A., Brown, H., & Gaskell, M. G. (2012). Consolidation of vocabulary is associated with sleep in children. *Developmental Science*, 15, 674–87.

Henderson, L., Weighall, A., Brown, H., & Gaskell, M. G. (2013). On-line lexical competition during spoken word recognition and word learning in children and adults. *Child Development*, 84, 1668–85.

Henderson, L., Weighall, A., & Gaskell, G. (2013). Learning new vocabulary in childhood: Effects of semantic training on lexical consolidation and integration. *Journal of Experimental Child Psychology*, 116, 572–92.

Hennoste, T. (2000). Allkeeled. – Eesti keele allkeeled [Language varieties. Varieties of Estonian]. In T. Hennoste (ed.), *Tartu Ülikooli eesti keele õppetooli toimetised, 16* [University of Tartu Department of Estonian Working Papers], pp. 9–53. Tartu: Tartu Ülikool.

Hickok, G. & Poeppel, D. (2004). Dorsal and ventral streams: A framework for understanding aspects of the functional anatomy of language. *Cognition*, 92, 67–99.

Hickok, G. & Poeppel, D. (2007). The cortical organization of speech processing. *Nature Reviews Neuroscience*, 8, 393–402.

Hintzman, D. L. (1986). 'Schema abstraction' in a multiple-trace memory model. *Psychological Review*, 93, 411–28.

Hladký, J. (1998). *Notes on Reduplicative Words in English*. Brno Studies in English 24. Brno: Brno University.

Houston, D. M. & Jusczyk, P. W. (2000). The role of talker-specific information in word segmentation by infants. *Journal of Experimental Psychology: Human Perception and Performance*, 26, 1570–82.

Houston, D. M. & Jusczyk, P. W. (2003). Infants' long-term memory for the sound patterns of words and voices. *Journal of Experimental Psychology: Human Perception and Performance*, 29, 1143–54.

Houston, D. M., Jusczyk, P. W., Kuijpers, C., Coolen, R., & Cutler, A. (2000). Cross-language word segmentation by 9-month-olds. *Psychonomic Bulletin & Review*, 7, 504–9.

Huebner, T. (1999). Obituary: Charles Albert Ferguson, July 6, 1921 – September 2, 1998. *Language in Society*, 28, 431–7.

Hussar, A. & Faster, M. (2015). Eestlaste hüüdnimedest [Estonian nicknames]. *Emakeele Seltsi aastaraamat*, 61, 110–34.

Hyman, L. M. (2010). Affixation by place of articulation: The case of Tiene. In J. Wohlgemuth & M. Cysouw (eds.), *Rara & Rarissima: Documenting the Fringes of Linguistic Diversity*, pp. 145–84. Berlin: De Gruyter Mouton.

Imada, T., Zhang, Y., Cheour, M., Taulu, S., Ahonen, A., & Kuhl, P. K. (2006). Infant speech perception activates Broca's area: A developmental magnetoencephalography study. *NeuroReport*, 17, 957–62.

Ingram, D. (1974a). Fronting in child phonology. *Journal of Child Language*, 1, 233–41.

Ingram, D. (1974b). Phonological rules in young children. *Journal of Child Language*, 1, 49–64.

Ingram, D. (1976). *Phonological Disability in Children*. New York: Elsevier Press.

Ingram, D. (2002). The measurement of whole-word productions. *Journal of Child Language*, 29, 713–33.

Inkelas, S. (2003). J's rhymes: A longitudinal case study of language play. *Journal of Child Language*, 30, 557–81.

Inkelas, S. (2014). *The Interplay of Phonology and Morphology*. Oxford: Oxford University Press.

Itô, J. (1990). Prosodic minimality in Japanese. In M. Ziokowski, M. Noske, & K. Deaton (eds.), *Papers from the 21st Regional Meeting of the Chicago Linguistics Society, 2: The Parasession on the Syllable in Phonetics and Phonology*, pp. 213–39. Chicago: Chicago Linguistics Society.

Itô, J. & Mester, A. (1992). Word layering and word binarity. In T. Honma, M. Okazaki, T. Tabata, & S. Tanaka (eds.), *A New Century of Phonology and Phonological Theory. A Festschrift for Professor Shosuke Haraguchi on the occasion of his sixtieth birthday*, pp. 26–65. Tokyo: Kaitakusha.

Jacoby, L. L. & Brooks, L. R. (1984). Nonanalytic cognition: Memory, perception and concept learning. In G. Bower (ed.), *The Psychology of Learning and Motivation*, 18, pp. 1–47. New York: Academic Press.

Jaeger, J. J. (2005). *Kids' Slips: What Young Children's Slips of the Tongue Reveal about Language Development*. Mahwah, NJ: Lawrence Erlbaum.

Jakobson, R. (1941/1968). *Child Language, Aphasia, and Phonological Universals*. The Hague: Mouton. English translation of *Kindersprache, Aphasie und allgemeine Lautgesetze*. Uppsala, 1941.

Jakobson, R. (1949). Les lois phoniques du langage enfantin et leur place dans la phonologie générale. In N. S. Trubetzkoy (ed.), *Principes de phonologie*. Translated into French by J. Cantineau. Paris: Editions Klincksieck.

Jakobson, R. & Waugh, L. (1979). *The Sound Shape of Language*. Bloomington: Indiana University Press.

Johnson, E. K. (2016). Constructing a proto-lexicon: An integrated view of infant language development. *Annual Review of Linguistics*, 2, 391–412.

Johnson, E. K. & Jusczyk, P. W. (2001). Word segmentation by 8-month-olds: When speech cues count more than statistics. *Journal of Memory and Language*, 44, 548–67.

Johnson, K. (1997). Speech perception without speaker normalization: An exemplar model. In K. Johnson & J. W. Mullennix (eds.), *Talker Variability in Speech Processing*, pp. 145–66. San Diego: Academic Press.

Johnson, K. (2006). Resonance in an exemplar-based lexicon: The emergence of social identity and phonology. *Journal of Phonetics*, 34, 485–99.

Johnson, K. A. (2007). Decisions and mechanisms in exemplar-based phonology. In M.-J. Solé, P. S. Beddor, & M. Ohala (eds.), *Experimental Approaches to Phonology*, pp. 25–40. Oxford: Oxford University Press.

Jones, D. M., Macken, W. J., & Nicolls, A. P. (2004). The phonological store of working memory. *Journal of Experimental Psychology: Learning, Memory and Cognition*, 30, 656–74.

Joos, M. (ed.) (1957). *Readings in Linguistics, I*. Washington, DC: American Council of Learned Societies.

Jusczyk, P. W. (1986). Toward a model of the development of speech perception. In J. S. Perkell & D. H. Klatt (eds.), *Invariance and Variability in Speech Processes*, pp. 1–19. Hillsdale, NJ: Lawrence Erlbaum.

Jusczyk, P. W. (1992). Developing phonological categories from the speech signal. In C. A. Ferguson, L. Menn, & C. Stoel-Gammon (eds.), *Phonological Development: Models, Research, Implications*, pp. 17–64. Timonium, MD: York Press.

Jusczyk, P. W. (1993). From general to language-specific capacities: The WRAPSA model of how speech perception develops. *Journal of Phonetics*, 21, 3–28.

Jusczyk, P. W. (1997). *The Discovery of Spoken Language*. Cambridge, MA: MIT Press.

Jusczyk, P. W. & Aslin, R. N. (1995). Infants' detection of the sound patterns of words in fluent speech. *Cognitive Psychology*, 29, 1–23.

Jusczyk, P. W., Cutler, A., & Redanz, N. J. (1993). Infants' preference for the predominant stress patterns of English words. *Child Development*, 64, 675–87.

Jusczyk, P. W., Friederici, A. D., Wessels, J., Svenkerud, V. Y., & Jusczyk, A. M. (1993). Infants' sensitivity to the sound patterns of native language words. *Journal of Memory and Language*, 32, 402–20.

Jusczyk, P. W., Hirsh-Pasek, K., Kemler Nelson, D. G., Kennedy, L., Woodward, A., & Piwoz, J. (1992). Perception of acoustic correlates of major phrasal units by young infants. *Cognitive Psychology*, 24, 252–93.

Jusczyk, P. W., Hohne, E. A., & Bauman, A. (1999). Infants' sensitivity to allophonic cues for word segmentation. *Perception and Psychophysics*, 62, 1465–76.

Jusczyk, P. W., Houston, D., & Newsome, M. (1999). The beginnings of word segmentation in English-learning infants. *Cognitive Psychology*, 39, 159–207.

Jusczyk, P. W. & Kemler Nelson, D. G. (1996). Syntactic units, prosody, and psychological reality during infancy. In J. L. Morgan & K. D. Demuth (eds.), *Signal to Syntax: Bootstrapping from Speech to Grammar in Early Acquisition*, pp. 389–408. Hillsdale, NJ: Lawrence Erlbaum.

Jusczyk, P. W., Luce, P. A., & Charles-Luce, J. (1994). Infants' sensitivity to phonotactic patterns in the native language. *Journal of Memory and Language*, 33, 630–45.

Kaalep, H.-J. (2012). Käänamissüsteemi seaduspärasused [Regularities in the Estonian declension system]. *Keel ja Kirjandus*, 6, 418–49.

Kager, R. (1999). *Optimality Theory*. Cambridge: Cambridge University Press.

Karmiloff-Smith, A. (1992). *Beyond Modularity*. Cambridge, MA: MIT Press.

Kasik, R. (2015). *Sõnamoodustus* [Word Formation]. Tartu: University of Tartu Press.

Kay-Raining Bird, E. & Chapman, R. (1998). Partial representation and phonological selectivity in the comprehension of 13- to 16-month olds. *First Language*, 18, 105–27.

Kehoe, M. (2013). *The Development of Prosody and Prosodic Structure*. New York: Nova Publishers.

Kehoe, M. (2015). Lexical-phonological interactions in bilingual children. *First Language*, 35, 93–125.

Kehoe, M. & Stoel-Gammon, C. (1997). The acquisition of prosodic structure: An investigation of current accounts of children's prosodic development. *Language*, 73, 113–44.

Kehoe, M. & Stoel-Gammon, C. (2001). Development of syllable structure in English-speaking children with particular reference to rhymes. *Journal of Child Language*, 28, 393–432.

Kemler Nelson, D. G., Hirsh-Pasek, K., Jusczyk, P. W., & Wright Cassidy, K. (1989). How the prosodic cues in motherese might assist language learning. *Journal of Child Language*, 16, 55–68.

Kent, R. D. (1992). The biology of phonological development. In C. A. Ferguson, L. Menn, & C. Stoel-Gammon (eds.), *Phonological Development: Models, Research, Implications*, pp. 65–89. Timonium, MD: York Press.

Keren-Portnoy, T., DePaolis, R. A., & Vihman, M. M. (in prep.). Dynamic interactions between production and perception in early word learning.

Keren-Portnoy, T., Majorano, M., & Vihman, M. M. (2009). From phonetics to phonology: The emergence of first words in Italian. *Journal of Child Language*, 36, 235–67.

Keren-Portnoy, T. & Segal, O. (2016). Phonological development in Israeli-Hebrew-learning infants and toddlers: Perception and perception. In R. Berman (ed.), *Acquisition and Development of Hebrew*, pp. 69–94. Trends in Language Acquisition Research, 19. Amsterdam: John Benjamins.

Keren-Portnoy, T., Vihman, M. M., DePaolis, R., Whitaker, C., & Williams, N. A. (2010). The role of vocal practice in constructing phonological working memory. *Journal of Speech, Language, and Hearing Research*, 53, 1280–93.

Keren-Portnoy, T., Vihman, M. M., & Lindop Fisher, R. (2019). Do infants learn from isolated words? An ecological study. *Language Learning and Development*, 15, 47–63.

Khattab, G. & Al-Tamimi, J. (2013). Early phonological patterns in Lebanese Arabic. In M. M. Vihman & T. Keren-Portnoy (eds.), *The Emergence of Phonology: Whole-Word Approaches and Cross-Linguistic Evidence*, pp. 374–414. Cambridge: Cambridge University Press.

Kidd, E., Kemp, N., Kashima, E. S., & Quinn, S. (2016). Language, culture, and group membership: An investigation into the social effects of colloquial Australian English. *Journal of Cross-Cultural Psychology*, 47, 713–33.

Kidd, E., Kemp, N., & Quinn, S. (2011). Did you have a *choccie bickie* this *arvo*? A quantitative look at Australian hypocoristics. *Language Sciences*, 33, 359–68.

Kilani-Schoch, M., & Dressler, W. U. (1993). *Prol-o, intell-o, gauch-o* et les autres: Propriétés formelles de deux opérations du français parlé. *Romanistisches Jahrbuch*, 43, 65–86.

Kiparsky, P. & Menn, L. (1977). On the acquisition of phonology. In J. Macnamara (ed.), *Language Learning and Thought*, pp. 47–78. New York: Academic Press.

Kisseberth, C. W. (1970). On the functional unity of phonological rules. *Linguistic Inquiry*, 1, 291–306.

Kjellmann, H. (1920). *Mots abrégés et tendances d'abréviation en français*. Uppsala: Lundequistska Bokhandeln.

Koerner, K. (ed.) (1995). *Mikolaj Kruszewski: Writings in General Linguistics*. Amsterdam Classics in Linguistics, 1800–1925. Amsterdam: John Benjamins.

Kõrgvee, K. (2001). Lapse sõnavara areng vanuses 1; 8-2; 1 [Development of a child's vocabulary at age 1; 8-2; 1]. Unpublished BA thesis, Tartu University.

Krull, D. (1997). Prepausal lengthening in Estonian: Evidence from conversational speech. In I. Lehiste & J. Ross (eds.), *Estonian Prosody: Papers from a Symposium*, pp. 136–48. Tallinn: Eesti Keele Instituut.

Kruszewski, M. (1883). Outline of linguistic science. In R. A. Orr (ed.), *Writings in General Linguistics*. Amsterdam Studies in the Theory and History of Linguistic Science. Series I: Amsterdam Classics in Linguistics, 1800–1925. Volume 11, pp. 34–178. Amsterdam: John Benjamins, 1996.

Kuhl, P. K. (1986). Reflections on infants' perception and representation of speech. In J. S. Perkell & D. H. Klatt (eds.), *Invariance and Variability in Speech Processes*, pp. 19–30. Hillsdale, NJ: Lawrence Erlbaum.

Kuhl, P. K. (1991). Human adults and human infants show a 'perceptual magnet effect' for the prototypes of speech categories, monkeys do not. *Perception & Psychophysics*, 50, 93–107.

Kuhl, P. K. & Miller, J. D. (1975). Speech perception by the chinchilla: Voiced–voiceless distinction in alveolar plosive consonants. *Science*, 190, 69–72.

Kuhl, P. K. & Miller, J. D. (1978). Speech perception by the chinchilla: Identification functions for synthetic VOT stimuli. *Journal of the Acoustical Society of America*, 63, 905–17.

Kuhl, P. K. & Padden, D. M. (1982). Enhanced discriminability at the phonetic boundaries for the voicing feature in macaques. *Perception & Psychophysics*, 32, 542–50.

Kunnari, S. (2000). *Characteristics of Early Lexical and Phonological Development in Children Acquiring Finnish*. Acta Universitatis Ouluensis B34, University of Oulu.

Kunnari, S. (2003). Consonant inventories: A longitudinal study of Finnish-speaking children. *Journal of Multilingual Communication Disorders*, 1, 124–31.

Labov, W. (1981). Resoloving the neogrammarian controversy. *Language*, 57, 267–309.

Lahrouchi, M. (2003). Manifestations gabaritiques dans la morphologie verbale du berbère (parler Chleuh d'Agadir). *Recherches linguistiques de Vincennes*, 32, 61–82.

Laing, C. E. & Bergelson, E. (2017). What did you say? Infants' early productions match caregiver input. Paper presented at Boston University Conference on Language Development.

Laing, C., E., Vihman, M. M., & Keren-Portnoy, T. (2017). How salient are onomatopoeia in the early input? A prosodic analysis of infant-directed speech. *Journal of Child Language*, 44, 1117–39.

Langacker, R. (1987). *Foundations of Cognitive Grammar, vol. 1: Theoretical Prerequisites*. Stanford, CA: Stanford University Press.

Leach, L. & Samuel, A. G. (2007). Lexical configuration and lexical engagement: When adults learn new words. *Cognitive Psychology*, 55, 306–53.

Lee, C.-C., Jhang, Y., Chen, L., Relyea, B., & Oller, D. K. (2017). Subtlety of ambient-language effects in babbling: A study of English- and Chinese-learning infants at 8, 10, and 12 months. *Language Learning and Development*, 13, 100–26.

Lehiste, I. (1960). Segmental and syllabic quantity in Estonian. *American Studies in Uralic Linguistics*, 1, 21–82.

Lehiste, I. (1970). Diphthongs vs. vowel sequences in Estonian. In *Proceedings of the Sixth International Congress of the Phonetic Sciences*, pp. 539–44. Munich.

Lehiste, I. (2003). Prosodic change in progress: From quantity language to accent language. In P. Fikkert & H. Jacobs (eds.), *Development in Prosodic Systems*, pp. 47–65. Berlin: Mouton de Gruyter.

Leonard, L. B., Schwartz, R. G., Morris, B., & Chapman, K. (1981). Factors affecting early lexical acquisition: Lexical orientation and phonological composition. *Child Development*, 52, 882–7.

Leopold, W. F. (1939). *Speech Development of a Bilingual Child, vol. 1: Vocabulary Growth in the First Two Years*. Evanston: Northwestern University Press.

Lewis, M. M. (1936). *Infant Speech: A Study of the Beginnings of Language*. New York: Harcourt, Brace. Reprint, New York: Arno Press, 1975.

Lewkowicz, D. J. & Hansen-Tift, A. M. (2012). Infants deploy selective attention to the mouth of a talking face when learning speech. *Proceedings of the National Academy of Sciences of the United States of America*, 109, 1431–6.

Lieven, E. & Behrens, H. (2012). Dense sampling. In E. Hoff (ed.), *Research Methods in Child Language: A Practical Guide*, pp. 226–39. Malden, MA: Blackwell.

Lindblom, B. & Zetterström, R. (eds.) (1986). *Precursors of Early Speech*. Basingstoke: Macmillan.

Lindsay, S. & Gaskell, M. G. (2013). Lexical integration of novel words without sleep. *Journal of Experimental Psychology: Learning, Memory & Cognition*, 39, 608–22.

Lippus, P., Asu, E. L., Teras, P., & Tuisk, T. (2013). Quantity-related variation of duration, pitch and vowel quality in spontaneous Estonian. *Journal of Phonetics*, 41, 17–28.

Lleó, C. (1990). Homonymy and reduplication: On the extended availability of two strategies in phonological acquisition. *Journal of Child Language*, 17, 267–78.

Locke, J. L. (1986). Speech perception and the emergent lexicon: An ethological approach. In P. Fletcher & M. Garman (eds.), *Language Acquisition: Studies in First Language Development*, pp. 240–50. Cambridge: Cambridge University Press.

Locke, J. (1993). *The Child's Path to Spoken Language*. Cambridge, MA: Harvard University Press.

Locke, J. L. & Pearson, D. (1992). Vocal learning and the emergence of phonological capacity: A neurobiological approach. In C. A. Ferguson, L. Menn, & C. Stoel-Gammon (eds.), *Phonological Development: Models, Research, Implications*, pp. 91–129. Timonium, MD: York Press.

Logan, G. D. (1988). Towards an instance theory of automatization. *Psychological Review*, 95, 492–527.

Loog, M. (1991). *Esimene eesti slängi sõnaraamat* [First Estonian Slang Dictionary]. Tallinn: Eesti Keele Instituut.

Lou, S.-S., Vihman, M. M., & Keren-Portnoy, T. (2018). Pitch differences in the babbling of Mandarin- and English-learning infants. Poster presented at the British Association of Academic Phoneticians, Kent.

McAllister Byun, T. & Tessier, A.-M. (2016). Motor influences on grammar in an emergentist model of phonology. *Language and Linguistics Compass*, 10, 431–52.

McAllister Byun, T., Inkelas, S., & Rose, Y. (2016). The A-map model: Articulatory reliability in child-specific phonology. *Language*, 92, 141–78.

McCarthy, J. (1979). Formal problems in Semitic phonology and morphology. Unpublished PhD thesis. Cambridge, MA, MIT.

McCarthy, J. (1981). A prosodic theory of nonconcatenative morphology. *Linguistic Inquiry*, 12, 373–418.

McCarthy, J. (1982). Prosodic templates, morphemic templates, and morphemic tiers. In H. van der Hulst & N. Smith (eds.), *The Structure of Phonological Representations, Part I*, pp. 191–223. Dordrecht: Foris Publications.

McCarthy, J. (2000). Faithfulness and prosodic circumscription. In J. Dekkers, V. van der Leeuw, & J. van de Weijer (eds.), *Optimality Theory: Phonology, Syntax and Acquisition*, pp. 151–89). New York: Oxford University Press.

McCarthy, J. J. & Prince, A. S. (1986). Prosodic morphology. Reprinted in J. Goldsmith (ed.), *Phonological Theory: The Essential Readings*, pp. 238–88. Malden, MA: Blackwell, 1999.

McCarthy, J. J. & Prince, A. S. (1990). Foot and word in prosodic morphology: The Arabic broken plural. *Natural Language and Linguistic Theory*, 8, 209–83.

McCarthy, J. J. & Prince, A. S. (1995). Prosodic morphology 1. In J. A. Goldsmith (ed.), *The Handbook of Phonological Theory*, pp. 318–66. Oxford: Blackwell.

McCarthy, J. J. & Prince, A. S. (1996). *Prosodic morphology 1986*. Rutgers University Center for Cognitive Science.

McClelland, J. & Elman, J. L. (1986). Interactive processes in speech perception: The TRACE model. In D. E. Rumelhart, J. L. McClelland, & the PDP Research Group (eds.), *Parallel Distributed Processing*, vol. 2, pp. 58–121. Cambridge, MA: MIT Press.

McClelland, J. L., McNaughton, B. L. & O'Reilly, R. C. (1995). Why there are complementary learning systems in the hippocampus and neocortex: Insights from the successes and failures of connectionist models of learning and memory. *Psychological Review*, 102, 419–517.

McCune, L. (1992). First words: A dynamic systems view. In C. A. Ferguson, L. Menn, & C. Stoel-Gammon (eds.), *Phonological Development: Models, Research, Implications*, pp. 313–36. Timonium, MD: York Press.

McCune, L. (1995). A normative study of representational play at the transition to language. *Developmental Psychology*, 31, 198–206.

McCune, L. (2008). *How Children Learn to Learn Language: Productive Skills in a Dynamic System*. Oxford: Oxford University Press.

McCune, L. & Vihman, M. M. (1987). Vocal motor schemes. *Papers and Reports on Child Language Development*, 26, 72–9.

McCune, L. & Vihman, M. M. (2001). Early phonetic and lexical development. *Journal of Speech, Language and Hearing Research*, 44, 670–84.

McGillion, M. M., Matthews, D., Herbert, J., Pine, J., Vihman, M. M., Keren-Portnoy, T., & DePaolis, R. A. (2017a). What paves the way to conventional language? The predictive value of babble, pointing and socioeconomic status. *Child Development*, 88, 156–66.

McGillion, M., Pine, J., Herbert, J., & Matthews, D. (2017b). A randomised controlled trial to test the effect of promoting caregiver contingent talk on language development in infants from diverse socioeconomic status backgrounds. *Journal of Child Psychology and Psychiatry*, 58, 1122–31.

Macken, M. A. (1978). Permitted complexity in phonological development: One child's acquisition of Spanish consonants. *Lingua*, 44, 219–53.

Macken, M. A. (1979). Developmental reorganization of phonology: A hierarchy of basic units of acquisition. *Lingua*, 49, 11–49. Reprinted in Vihman & Keren-Portnoy (2013b).

Macken, M. A. (1980). Aspects of the acquisition of stop systems: A cross-linguistic perspective. In G. Yeni-Komshian, J. F. Kavanagh, & C. A. Ferguson (eds.), *Child Phonology, vol. 1: Production*. New York: Academic Press.

Macken, M. A. (1992). Where's phonology? In C. A. Ferguson, L. Menn, & C. Stoel-Gammon (eds.), *Phonological Development: Models, Research, Implications*, pp. 249–69. Timonium, MD: York Press.

Macken, M. A. (1995). Phonological acquisition. In J. A. Goldsmith (ed.), *The Handbook of Phonological Theory*, pp. 671–96. Oxford: Blackwell.

Macken, M. A. & Ferguson, C. A. (1983). Cognitive aspects of phonological development. In K. E. Nelson (ed.), *Children's Language*, vol. 4, pp. 256–82. Hillsdale, NJ: Lawrence Erlbaum.

McMurray, B., Horst, J., & Samuelson, L. K. (2012). Word learning emerges from the interaction of online referent selection and slow associative learning. *Psychological Review*, 119, 831–77.

MacNeilage, P. F. (1979). Speech production. Report to the Ninth International Congress of Phonetic Sciences, Copenhagen.

MacNeilage, P. F. & Davis, B. L. (1990). Acquisition of speech production: Frames, then content. In M. Jeannerod (ed.), *Attention and Performance XIII: Motor Representation and Control*, pp. 453–76. Hillsdale, NJ: Lawrence Erlbaum.

MacNeilage, P. F. & Davis, B. L. (2001). Motor mechanisms in speech ontogeny: Phylogenetic, neurobiological and linguistic implications. *Current Opinion in Neurobiology*, 11, 696–700.

Macrae, T. (2017). Stimulus characteristics of single-word tests of children's speech sound production. *Language Speech and Hearing Services in the Schools*, 48, 219–33.

Majorano, M., Bastianello, T., Morelli, M., Lavelli, M., & Vihman, M. M. (2019). Vocal production and novel word learning in the first year. *Journal of Child Language*, 46, 606–16.

Majorano, M. & D'Odorico, L. (2011). The transition into ambient language: A longitudinal study of babbling and first word production of Italian children. *First Language*, 31, 47–66.

Majorano, M., Vihman, M. M., & DePaolis, R. A. (2014). The relationship between infants' production experience and their processing of speech. *Language Learning and Development*, 10, 179–204.

Malkiel, Y. (1967). Each word has a history of its own. *Glossa*, 1, 137–49.

Mareschal, D., Johnson, M. H., Sirois, S., Spratling, M., Thomas, M. S., & Westermann, G. (2007). *Neuroconstructivism: How the Brain Constructs Cognition*, vol. 1. Oxford: Oxford University Press.

Masapollo, M., Polka, L., & Ménard, L. (2016). When infants talk, infants listen: Pre-babbling infants prefer listening to speech with infant vocal properties. *Developmental Science*, 19, 318–28.

Masur, E. F., Flynn, V., & Eichorst, D. L. (2005). Maternal responsive and directive behaviours and utterances as predictors of children's lexical development. *Journal of Child Language*, 32, 63–91.

Mattiello, E. (2013). *Extra-Grammatical Morphology in English: Abbreviations, Blends, Reduplicatives, and Related Phenomena*. Berlin & New York: Mouton De Gruyter.

Mattys, S. L. & Jusczyk, P. W. (2001a). Phonotactic cues for segmentation of fluent speech by infants. *Cognition*, 78, 91–121.

Mattys, S. L. & Jusczyk, P. W. (2001b). Do infants segment words or recurring contiguous patterns? *Journal of Experimental Psychology: Human Perception and Performance*, 27, 644–55.

Mattys, S. L., Jusczyk, P. W., Luce, P. A., & Morgan, J. L. (1999). Phonotactic and prosodic effects on word segmentation in infants. *Cognitive Psychology*, 38, 465–94.

Maye, J., Werker, J. F., & Gerken, L. (2002). Infant sensitivity to distributional information can affect phonetic discrimination. *Cognition*, 82, B101–B111.

Mayor, J. & Plunkett, K. (2014). Infant word recognition: Insights from TRACE simulations. *Journal of Memory and Language*, 71, 89–123.

Mehler, J., Dupoux, E., Nazzi, T., & Dehaene-Lambertz, G. (1996). Coping with linguistic diversity: The infant's viewpoint. In J. Morgan & K. Demuth (eds.), *Signal to Syntax*, pp. 101–16. Mahwah, NJ: Lawrence Erlbaum.

Mehler, J., Jusczyk, P., Lambertz, G., Halsted, N., Bertoncini, J., & Amiel-Tison, C. (1988). A precursor of language acquisition in young infants. *Cognition*, 29, 143–78.

Menn, L. (1971). Phonotactic rules in beginning speech: A study in the development of English discourse. *Lingua*, 26, 225–51.

Menn, L. (1975). Counter-example to 'fronting' as a universal of child phonology. *Journal of Child Language*, 2, 293–6.

Menn, L. (1978). Phonological units in beginning speech. In A. Bell & J. B. Hooper (eds.), *Syllables and Segments*, pp. 157–71. Amsterdam: North-Holland.

Menn, L. (1983). Development of articulatory, phonetic, and phonological capabilities. In B. Butterworth (ed.), *Language Production*, vol. 2. London: Academic Press. Reprinted in Vihman & Keren-Portnoy (2013b).

Menn, L. & Matthei, E. (1992). The 'two-lexicon' account of child phonology. In C. A. Ferguson, L. Menn, & C. Stoel-Gammon (eds.), *Phonological Development: Models, Research, Implications*, pp. 211–47. Timonium, MD: York Press.

Menn, L., Schmidt, E., & Nicholas, B. (2009). Conspiracy and sabotage in the acquisition of phonology: Dense data undermine existing theories, provide scaffolding for a new one. *Language Sciences*, 31, 285–304.

Menn, L., Schmidt, E., & Nicholas, B. (2013). Challenges to theories, charges to a model: The Linked-Attractor model of phonological development. In M. M. Vihman & T. Keren-Portnoy (eds.), *The Emergence of Phonology: Whole-Word Approaches and Cross-Linguistic Evidence*, pp. 460–502. Cambridge: Cambridge University Press.

Menn, L. & Vihman, M. M. (2011). Features in child phonology: Inherent, emergent, or artefacts of analysis? In N. Clements & R. Ridouane (eds.), *Where Do Phonological Features Come From?*, pp. 261–301. Amsterdam: John Benjamins.

Menyuk, P. & Menn, L. (1979). Early strategies for the perception and production of words and sounds. In P. Fletcher & M. Garman (eds.), *Language Acquisition: Studies in First Language Development*, pp. 49–70. Cambridge: Cambridge University Press.

Menyuk, P., Menn, L. & Silber, R. (1986). Early strategies for the perception and production of words and sounds. In P. Fletcher & M. Garman (eds.), *Language Acquisition: Studies in First Language Development*, 2nd edn., pp. 198–222. Cambridge: Cambridge University Press.

Mersad, K., Goyet, L., & Nazzi, T. (2010). Cross-linguistic differences in early word form segmentation: A rhythmic-based account. *Journal of Portuguese Linguistics*, 9, 37–65.

Messum, P. & Howard, I. S. (2015). Creating the cognitive form of phonological units: The speech sound correspondence problem in infancy could be solved by mirrored vocal interactions rather than by imitation. *Journal of Phonetics*, 53, 125–40.

Mester, R. A. (1990). Patterns of truncation. *Linguistic Inquiry*, 21, 478–85.

Metsala, J. L. & Walley, A. C. (1998). Spoken vocabulary growth and the segmental restructuring of lexical representations: Precursors to phonemic awareness and early reading ability. In J. L. Metsala & L. C. Ehri (eds.), *Word Recognition in Beginning Literacy*, pp. 89–120. Mahwah, NJ: Lawrence Erlbaum.

Mirak, J. & Rescorla, L. (1998). Phonetic skills and vocabulary size in late talkers: Concurrent and predictive relationships. *Applied Psycholinguistics*, 19, 1–17.

Mok, P. P. K. & Lee, A. (2018). The acquisition of lexical tones by Cantonese-English bilingual children. *Journal of Child Language*, 45, 1357–76.

Monaghan, P., Arciuli, J., & Seva, N. (2016). Cross-linguistic evidence for probabilistic orthographic cues to lexical stress. In J. Thomson & L. Jarmulowicz (eds.), *Linguistic Rhythm and Literacy*, pp. 215–36. Amsterdam: John Benjamins.

Morgan, J. L. & Demuth, K. (eds.) (1996). *Signal to Syntax: Bootstrapping from Speech to Grammar in Early Acquisition*. Mahwah, NJ: Lawrence Erlbaum.

Morin, Y. (1972). The phonology of echo-words in French. *Language*, 48, 97–105.

Morrisette, M. L., Dinnsen, D. A., & Gierut, J. A. (2003). Markedness and context effects in the acquisition of place features. *Canadian Journal of Linguistics/La revue canadienne de linguistique*, 48, 329–55.

Moskowitz, B. A. (1970). The two-year-old stage in the acquisition of phonology. *Language*, 46, 426–41.

Munson, B., Edwards, J. & Beckman, M. E. (2012). Phonological representation in language acquisition: Climbing the ladder of abstraction. In A. C. Cohn, C. Fougeron, & M. K. Huffman (eds.), *The Oxford Handbook of Laboratory Phonology*, pp. 288–309. Oxford: Oxford University Press.

Myers, J., Jusczyk, P. W., Kemler Nelson, D. G., Charles-Luce, J., Woodward, A. L., & Hirsh-Pasek, K. (1996). Infants' sensitivity to word boundaries in fluent speech. *Journal of Child Language*, 23, 1–30.

Nazzi, T., Iakimova, G., Bertoncini, J., Frédonie, S., & Alcantara, C. (2006). Early segmentation of fluent speech by infants acquiring French. *Journal of Memory and Language*, 54, 283–99.

Nazzi, T., Mersad, K., Sundara, M., Iakimova, G., & Polka, L. (2014). Early word segmentation in infants acquiring Parisian French: Task-dependent and dialect-specific effects. *Journal of Child Language*, 41, 600–33.

Nespor, M. & Vogel, I. (1986). *Prosodic Phonology*. Dordrecht: Foris Publications.

Nevins, A. & Vaux, B. (2003). Metalinguistic, shmetalinguistic: The phonology of shm-reduplication. In D. W. Kaiser, J. E. Cihlar, A. L. Franklin, & I. Kimbara (eds.), *Proceedings of the Chicago Linguistic Society, 39–1: Main session*, pp. 702–22. Chicago: Chicago Linguistic Society.

Newman, P. (2000). *The Hausa Language: An Encyclopedic Reference Grammar*. New Haven, CT: York University Press.

Newman, R. (2005). The cocktail party effect in infants revisited: Listening to one's name in noise. *Developmental Psychology*, 41, 352–62.

Nichols, J. (2007). What, if anything, is typology? *Linguistic Typology*, 11, 231–8.

Norman, D. A. & Shallice, T. (1986). Attention to action: Willed and automatic control of behavior. In R. Davidson, G. Schwartz, & D. Shapiro (eds.), *Consciousness and Self-Regulation: Advances in Research and in Theory*, vol. 4, pp. 1–18. NY: Plenum Press.

Norris, D., McQueen, J. M., & Cutler, A. (2003). Perceptual learning in speech. *Cognitive Psychology*, 47, 204–38.

Oliveira Guimarães, M. L. D. (2008). Percurso de contução da fonologia pela criança: uma abordagem dinâmica [The course of phonological construction by the child]. Unpublished PhD thesis. Federal University of Minas Gerais.

Oliveira-Guimarães, D. (2013). Beyond early words: Word template development in Brazilian Portuguese. In M. M. Vihman & T. Keren-Portnoy (eds.), *The Emergence of Phonology: Whole-Word Approaches and Cross-Linguistic Evidence*, pp. 291–316. Cambridge: Cambridge University Press.

Oller, D. K. (1980). The emergence of the sounds of speech in infancy. In G. Yeni-Komshian, J. F. Kavanagh, & C. A. Ferguson (eds.), *Child Phonology*, vol. 1: *Production*, pp. 73–112. New York: Academic Press.

Oller, D. K. (2000). *The Emergence of the Speech Capacity*. Mahwah, NJ: Lawrence Erlbaum.

Oller, D. K., Wieman, L. A., Doyle, W. J., & Ross, C. (1976). Infant babbling and speech. *Journal of Child Language*, 3, 1–11.

Olmsted, D. (1966). A theory of the child's learning of phonology. *Language*, 42, 531–5. Reprinted in A. Bar-Adon & W. Leopold (eds.), *Child Language: A Book of Readings*. Englewood Cliffs, NJ: Prentice-Hall, 1971.

Ota, M. & Green, S. J. (2012). Input frequency and lexical variability in phonological development: A survival analysis of word-initial cluster production. *Journal of Child Language*, 39, 1–28.

Pacton, S., Jaco, A. A., Nys, M., Foulin, J. N., Treiman, R., & Peereman, R. (2018). Children benefit from morphological relatedness independently of orthographic relatedness when they learn to spell new words. *Journal of Experimental Child Psychology*, 171, 71–83.

Palmer, F. R. (ed.) (1970). *Prosodic Analysis*. London: Oxford University Press.

Pari (Põlma), M. (2016). Eesti vastupidavussportlaste släng [The slang of Estonian endurance sports participants]. Unpublished MA thesis. Tartu.

Parra, M., Hoff, E., & Core, C. (2011). Relations among language exposure, phonological memory, and language development in Spanish–English bilingually developing 2-year-olds. *Journal of Experimental Child Psychology*, 108, 113–25.

Pater, J. & Barlow, J. A. (2003). Constraint conflict in cluster reduction. *Journal of Child Language*, 30, 487–526.

Paul, R. & Jennings, P. (1992). Phonological behavior in toddlers with slow expressive language development. *Journal of Speech and Hearing Research*, 35, 99–107.

Payne, E., Post, B., Astruc, L., Prieto, P. & Vanrell, M. M. (2012). Measuring child rhythm. *Language and Speech, 55*, 203–229.

Pearson, B. Z. (2007). Social factors in childhood bilingualism in the United States. *Applied Psycholinguistics*, 28, 399–410.

Peters, A. M. & Menn, L. (1993). False starts and filler syllables: Ways to learn grammatical morphemes. *Language*, 69, 742–77.

Piaget, J. (1951). *Play, Dreams and Imitation in Childhood*, trans. C. Gattegno & F. M. Hodgson. London: Heinemann.

Pierrehumbert, J. (2003). Phonetic diversity, statistical learning, and acquisition of phonology. *Language and Speech*, 46, 115–54.

Pierrehumbert, J. (2016). Phonological representation: Beyond abstract vs. episodic. *Annual Review of Linguistics*, 2, 33–52.

Pierrehumbert, J. & Nair, R. (1995). Word games and syllable structure. *Language and Speech*, 38, 77–114.

Plénat, M. (1984). Toto, Fanfa, Totor et même Guiguitte sont des ANARs. In F. Dell, D. Hirst, & J.-R. Vergnaud (eds.), *Forme sonore du langage. Structure des représentations en phonologie*, pp. 161–81. Paris: Hermann.

Plénat, M. (1991). Le javanais: concurrence et haplologie. *Langages*, 101, 95–116.

Plénat, M. (1994). L''extramétricité' des voyelles initiales. In C. Lyche (ed.), *French Generative Phonology: Retrospective and Perspectives*, pp. 239–58. Salford: Association for French Language Studies.

Plénat, M. (1995). Une approche prosodique de la morphologie du verlan. *Lingua*, 95, 97–129.

Plénat, M. & Roche, M. (2003). Prosodic constraints on suffixation in French. In G. Booij, J. DeCesaris, A. Railli, & S. Scalise (eds.), *Topics in Morphology: Selected Papers from the Third Mediterranean Morphology Meeting*, pp. 285–99. Barcelona: IULA-Universitat Pompeu Fabra.

Pöchträger, M. A. (2006). The structure of length. Unpublished PhD thesis. University of Vienna.

Pöchträger, M. A. (2010). Does one size fit all? Talk presented at Workshop on Templates, Old-World Phonology Conference, Nice.

Polka, L. & Sundara, M. (2012). Word segmentation in monolingual infants acquiring Canadian English and Canadian French: Native language, cross-dialect, and cross-language comparisons. *Infancy*, 17, 198–232.

Preston, J. & Edwards, M. L. (2010). Phonological awareness and types of sound errors in preschoolers with speech sound disorders. *Journal of Speech, Language, and Hearing Research*, 53, 44–60.

Priestly, T. M. S. (1977). One idiosyncratic strategy in the aquisition of phonology. *Journal of Child Language*, 4, 45–66. Reprinted in Vihman & Keren-Portnoy (2013b).

Prieto, P. & Esteve-Gilbert, N. (2018). *Prosodic Development in First Language Acquisition*. Trends in Language Acquisition Research (TiLAR) 23. Amsterdam: John Benjamins.

Prigogine, I. & Stengers, I. (1984). *Order Out of Chaos: Man's New Dialogue with Nature*. New York: Bantam.

Prince, A. (1980). A metrical theory for Estonian quantity. *Linguistic Inquiry*, 11, 511–62.

Prince, A. S. & Smolensky, P. (2004 [1993]). *Optimality Theory: Constraint Interaction in Generative Grammar*. Cambridge, MA: Blackwell.

Pufahl, A. & Samuel, A. G. (2014). How lexical is the lexicon? Evidence for integrated auditory memory representations. *Cognitive Psychology*, 70, 1–30.

Queller, K. (1988). Review of N. Waterson, *Prosodic Phonology*. *Journal of Child Language*, 15, 463–7.

Ramus, F., Nespor, M., & Mehler, J. (1999). Correlates of linguistic rhythm in the speech signal. *Cognition*, 73, 265–92.

Rapp, D. N. & Samuel, A. G. (2002). A reason to rhyme: Phonological and semantic influences on lexical access. *Journal of Experimental Psychology: Learning, Memory, and Cognition*, 28, 564–71.

Reber, A. S. (1967). Implicit learning of artificial grammars. *Journal of Verbal Learning and Verbal Behavior*, 6, 855–63.

Reber, A. S. (1993). *Implicit Learning and Tacit Knowledge*. New York: Oxford University Press.

Redford, M. A. (2015). Unifying speech and language in a developmentally sensitive model of production. *Journal of Phonetics*, 53, 141–52.

Renner, L. (2017). The magic of matching: Speech production and perception in language acquisition. Unpublished PhD thesis. Stockholm University.

Rescorla, L. & Ratner, N. B. (1996). Phonetic profiles of toddlers with Specific Expressive Language Impairment (SLI-E). *Journal of Speech, Language, and Hearing Research*, 39, 153–65.

Robins, R. H. (1957). Aspects of prosodic analysis. *Proceedings of the University of Durham Philosophical Society, I, Series B (Arts)*, 1, 1–12. Reprinted in Palmer (1970).

Rollins, P. (2003). Caregiver contingent comments and subsequent vocabulary comprehension. *Applied Psycholinguistics*, 24, 221–34.

Ronneberger-Sibold, E. (1996). Preferred sound shapes of new roots: On some phonotactic and prosodic properties of shortenings in German and French. In B. Hurch & R. A. Rhodes (eds.), *Natural Phonology: The State of the Art*, pp. 261–92. Berlin: Mouton de Gruyter.

Rose, Y. (2018). Phonological categories and their manifestation in child phonology. In M. Hickman, E. Veneziano, & H. Jisa (eds.), *Sources of Variation in First Language Acquisition: Languages, Contexts, and Learners*. Trends in Language Acquisition Research (TiLAR). Amsterdam: John Benjamins.

Saffran, J. (2014). Sounds and meanings working together: Word learning as a collaborative effort. *Language Learning*, 64, Suppl. 2, 106–20.

Saffran, J. R., Aslin, R. N., & Newport, E. L. (1996). Statistical learning by 8-month-old infants. *Science*, 274, 1926–8.

Saffran, J. R., Newport, E. L., Aslin, R. N., Tunick, R. A., & Barrueco, S. (1997). Incidental language learning: Listening (and learning) out of the corner of your ear. *Psychological Science*, 8, 101–5.

Sagna, S., Brown, D., Vihman, M. M., & Vihman, V.-A. (2018). Acquisition of noun class prefixes and agreement in an Atlantic language: A naturalistic study of the acquisition of Eegimaa. Poster presented at Child Language Seminar, Reading.

Santos, R. S. (2007). A aquisição prosódica do português brasileiro de 1 a 3 anos: padrões de palavra e processos de sândi externo [On the acquisition of prosody in Brasilian Portuguese from 1 to 3 years: Word patterns and the processes of external sandhi]. Unpublished PhD thesis. University of São Paolo.

Saussure, F. de (1959). *Course in General Linguistics*, trans. W. Baskin. New York: Philosophical Library. First edition, 1915, ed. C. Bally & A. Sechehaye, in collaboration with A. Reidlinger.

Savinainen-Makkonen, T. (2000a). Learning long words: A typological perspective. *Language and Speech*, 43, 205–25.

Savinainen-Makkonen, T. (2000b). Word initial consonant omissions: A developmental process in children learning Finnish. *First Language*, 20, 161–85.

Savinainen-Makkonen, T. (2001). *Suomalainen lapsi fonologiaa omaksumassa* [Finnish Children Acquiring Phonology]. Publications of the Department of Phonetics, University of Helsinki, 42.

Savinainen-Makkonen, T. (2007). Geminate template: A model for first Finnish words. *First Language*, 27, 347–59. Reprinted in Vihman & Keren-Portnoy (2013b).

Scarborough, H. (1990). Index of productive syntax. *Applied Psycholinguistics*, 11, 1–12.

Scheer, T. (2003). The key to Czech vowel length: Templates. In P. Kosta, J. Blaszczak, J. Frasek, L. Geist, & M. Zygis (eds.), *Investigations into Formal Slavic Linguistics*, pp. 97–118. Frankfurt am Main: Peter Lang.

Scheer, T. (2004). Le corpus heuristique: un outil qui montre mais ne démontre pas. *Corpus*, 3, 153–92.

Scheer, T. (2011). Aspects of the development of generative phonology. In B. Botma, N. C. Kula, & K. Nasukawa (eds.), *The Continuum Companion to Phonology*, pp. 397–446. New York: Continuum.

Scheer, T. (2016). Variable shape templates and the position of Czech in templatic phonology. *Linguistica Brunensia*, 64, 89–107.

Schiering, R., Bickel, B., & Hildebrandt, K. A. (2010). The prosodic word is not universal, but emergent. *Journal of Linguistics*, 46, 657–709.

Schluter, K. (2013). Hearing words without structure: Subliminal speech priming and the organization of the Moroccan Arabic lexicon. Unpublished PhD thesis. University of Arizona.

Schwartz, R. G. (1988). Phonological factors in early acquisition. In M. D. Smith & J. L. Locke (eds.), *The Emergent Lexicon: The Child's Development of a Linguistic Vocabulary*, pp. 185–222. New York: Academic Press.

Schwartz, R. G. & Leonard, L. B. (1982). Do children pick and choose? An examination of phonological selection and avoidance in early lexical acquisition. *Journal of Child Language*, 9, 411–18.

Scullen, M. E. (1997). *French Prosodic Morphology: A Unified Account*. Bloomington: Indiana University Linguistics Club.

Segal, O., Keren-Portnoy, T., & Vihman, M. M. (in revision). Untrained infant word form recognition: Robust effects of accentual pattern. *Journal of Child Language*.

Ségéral, P. & Scheer, T. (1998). A generalized theory of Ablaut: The case of Modern German strong verbs. In *Models of Inflection*, pp. 28–59. Tübingen: Max Niemeyer.

Seidl, A. & Johnson, E. (2006). Infant word segmentation revisited: Edge alignment facilitates target extraction. *Developmental Science*, 9, 565–73.

Selkirk, E. (1980). The role of prosodic categories in English word stress. *Linguistic Inquiry*, 11, 563–605.

Selkirk, E. (1996). The prosodic structure of function words. In J. Morgan & K. Demuth (eds.), *Signal to Syntax*, pp. 187–213. Mahwah, NJ: Lawrence Erlbaum.

Shimron, J. (2003). *Language Processing and Acquisition in Languages of Semitic, Root-Based, Morphology*. Amsterdam: John Benjamins.

Shook, A. & Marian, V. (2013). The bilingual language interaction network for comprehension of speech. *Bilingualism: Language and Cognition*, 16, 304–24.

Shriberg, L. D., Austin, D., Lewis, B. A., McSweeny, J. L.,& Wilson, D. L. (1997). The Percentage of Consonants Correct (PCC) metric: Extensions and reliability data. *Journal of Speech, Language, and Hearing Research*, 40, 708–22.

Simpson, J. (2006). Hypocoristics in Australian English. In B. Kortmann & E. W. Schneider (eds.), *A Handbook of Varieties of English*, vol. 2: *Morphology and Syntax*, pp. 643–56. Berlin: Mouton de Gruyter.

Singh, R. (2005). Reduplication in Modern Hindi and the theory of reduplication. In B. Hurch (ed.), *Studies on Reduplication*, pp. 263–82. Berlin: Mouton de Gruyter.

Smith, N. V. (1973). *The Acquisition of Phonology: A Case Study*. Cambridge: Cambridge University Press.

Smith, N. V. (2010). *Acquiring Phonology: A Cross-Generational Case-Study*. Cambridge: Cambridge University Press.

Snow, C. E. & Ferguson, C. A. (eds.) (1977). *Talking to Children: Language Input and Acquisition*. Cambridge: Cambridge University Press.

Sosa, A. V. & Stoel-Gammon, C. (2006). Patterns of intra-word phonological variability in the second year of life. *Journal of Child Language*, 33, 31–50.

Sóskuthy, M. (2012). Morphology in the extreme: Echo-pairs in Hungarian. In F. Kiefer & Z. Bánréti (eds.), *Twenty Years of Theoretical Linguistics in Budapest*, pp. 123–44. Budapest: Tinta.

Sóskuthy, M. & Hay, J. (2017). Changing word usage predicts changing word durations in New Zealand English. *Cognition*, 156, 298–313.

Southern, M. R. V. (2005). *Contagious Couplings: Transmission of Expressives in Yiddish Echo Phrases*. Westport, CT: Praeger.

Sowers-Wills, S. (2017). Using schema theory to support a whole-word approach to phonological acquisition. *Cognitive Linguistics*, 28, 155–91.

Spradling, L. (2016). OMG the word-final alveopalatals are cray-cray prev(alent): The morphophonology of totes constructions in English. *University of Pennsylvania Working Papers*, 22: *Proceedings of the 39th Annual Penn Linguistics Conference*, 275–84.

Stark, R. E. (1980). Stages of speech development in the first year of life. In G. Yeni-Komshian, J. F. Kavanagh, & C. A. Ferguson (eds.), *Child Phonology*, vol. 1: *Production*, pp. 73–92. New York: Academic Press.

Stoel-Gammon, C. (1989). Prespeech and early speech development of two late talkers. *First Language*, 9, 207–23.

Stoel-Gammon, C. (1992). Prelinguistic vocal development: Measurement and predictions. In C. A. Ferguson, L. Menn, & C. Stoel-Gammon (eds.), *Phonological Development: Models, Research, Implications*, pp. 439–56. Timonium, MD: York Press.

Stoel-Gammon, C. (2011). Relationships between lexical and phonological development in young children. *Journal of Child Language*, 38, 1–34.

Stoel-Gammon, C. & Cooper, J. A. (1984). Patterns of early lexical and phonological development. *Journal of Child Language*, 11, 247–71.

Storkel, H. (2001). Learning new words: Phonotactic probability in language development. *Journal of Speech, Language, and Hearing Research*, 44, 1321–37.

Storkel, H. L. (2004). The emerging lexicon of children with phonological delays: Phonotactic constraints and probability in acquisition. *Journal of Speech, Language, and Hearing Research*, 47, 1194–212.

Studdert-Kennedy, M. (1983). Foreword to J. L. Locke, *Phonological Acquisition and Change*, pp. ix–xii. New York: Academic Press.

Studdert-Kennedy, M. (1986). Sources of variability in early speech development. In J. S. Perkell & D. H. Klatt (eds.), *Invariance and Variability in Speech Processes*, pp. 58–76. Hillsdale, NJ: Lawrence Erlbaum.

Suomi, K. & Ylitalo, R. (2004). On durational correlates of word stress in Finnish. *Journal of Phonetics*, 32, 35–63.

Swingley, D. (2005). Eleven-month-olds' knowledge of how familiar words sound. *Developmental Science*, 8, 432–43.

Swingley, D. (2007). Lexical exposure and word-form encoding in 1.5-year-olds. *Developmental Psychology*, 43, 454–64.

Swingley, D. (2009). Contributions of infant word learning to language development. *Philosophical Transactions of the Royal Society, B*, 364, 3617–32.

Swingley, D. (2017). The infant's developmental path in phonological acquisition. *British Journal of Psychology*, 108, 28–30.

Szreder, M. (2013). The acquisition of consonant clusters in Polish: A case study. In M. M. Vihman & T. Keren-Portnoy (eds.), *The Emergence of Phonology: Whole-Word Approaches and Cross-Linguistic Evidence*, pp. 343–61. Cambridge: Cambridge University Press.

Szreder-Ptasinska, M. (2012). Child phonology as a dynamic system. Unpublished PhD thesis. University of York.

Taelman, H. (2004). *Syllable Omissions and Additions in Dutch Child Language: An Inquiry into the Function of Rhythm and the Link with Innate Grammar*. Antwerp: University of Antwerp.

Tamminen, J. & Gaskell, M. G. (2013). Novel word integration in the mental lexicon: Evidence from unmasked and masked semantic priming. *Quarterly Journal of Experimental Psychology*, 66, 1001–25.

Tauli, V. (1968). On quantity and stress in Estonian. *Congressus Secundus Internationalis Fenno-Ugristarum*. Societas Fenno-Ugrica, Helsinki.

Tender, T. (1994). Eesti slang: olemus ja uurimislugu [Estonian slang: Description and research review]. *Keel ja Kirjandus*, 5, 291–9; 6, 346–56.

Tender, T. (1996). Some fragments about the Estonian slang: Its essence and research. In M. Kõiva (ed.), *Contemporary Folklore: Changing World View and Tradition*, pp. 339–46. Tartu: Institute of Estonian Language and Estonian Museum of Literature.

Tessier, A.-M. (2015). *Phonological Acquisition: Child Language and Constraint-Based Grammar*. Basingstoke: Palgrave Macmillan.

Tessier, A.-M. (2019). U-shaped development in error-driven child phonology. *Wiley Interdisciplinary Reviews: Cognitive Science*, e1505.

Thelen, E. (1981). Rhythmical behavior in infancy. *Developmental Psychology*, 17, 237–57.

Thelen, E. (1991). Motor aspects of emergent speech: A dynamic approach. In N. Krasnegor, D. Rumbaugh, & M. Studdert-Kennedy (eds.), *Biological and Behavioral Determinants of Language Development*, pp. 339–65. Hillsdale, NJ: Lawrence Erlbaum.

Thelen, E., Corbetta, D., & Spencer, P. (1996). The development of reaching during the first year: The role of movement speed. *Journal of Experimental Psychology: Human Perception and Performance*, 22, 1059–76.

Thelen, E. & Smith, L. B. (1994). *A Dynamic Systems Approach to the Development of Cognition and Action*. Cambridge, MA: MIT Press.

Thevenin, D. M., Eilers, R. E., Oller, D. K., & Lavoie, L. (1985). Where's the drift in babbling drift? A cross-linguistic study. *Applied Psycholinguistics*, 6, 3–15.

Thiessen, E. D. & Saffran, J. R. (2003). When cues collide: Use of stress and statistical cues to word boundaries by 7- and 9-month-old infants. *Developmental Psychology*, 39, 706–16.

Thun, N. (1963). Reduplicative words in English: A study of formations of the types tick-tick, hurly-burly and shilly-shally. Unpublished PhD thesis. Uppsala University.

Tomasello, M. & Farrar, M .J. (1986). Joint attention and early language. *Child Development*, 57, 1454–63.

Treiman, R. (1983). The structure of spoken syllables: Evidence from novel word games. *Cognition*, 15, 49–74.

Trubetzkoy, N. S. (1949). *Principes de phonologie*, trans. J. Cantineau. Paris: Editions Klincksieck.

Ussishkin, A. (2005). A fixed prosodic theory of nonconcatenative templatic morphology. *Natural Language and Linguistic Theory*, 23, 169–218.

Ussishkin, A., Dawson, C. R., Wedel, A., & Schluter, K. (2015). Auditory masked priming in Maltese spoken word recognition. *Language, Cognition and Neuroscience*, 30, 1096–115.

Varela, F., Thompson, E., & Rosch, E. (1991). *The Embodied Mind*. Cambridge, MA: MIT Press.

Velleman, S. L. (1994). The interaction of phonetics and phonology in developmental verbal dyspraxia: Two case studies. *Clinics in Communication Disorders*, 4, 67–78.

Velleman, S. L. (2016). *Speech Sound Disorders in Children*. Baltimore, MD: Wolters Kluwer Health.

Velleman, S. L. & Vihman, M. M. (2002). Whole-word phonology and templates. *Language, Speech & Hearing Services in Schools*, 33, 9–23.

Veneziano, E. (1981). Early language and nonverbal representation: A reassessment. *Journal of Child Language*, 8, 541–63.

Veneziano, E. & Sinclair, H. (2000). The changing status of 'filler syllables' on the way to grammatical morphemes. *Journal of Child Language*, 27, 461–500.

Vihman, E. (1974). Estonian quantity re-viewed. *Foundations of Language*, 11, 415–32.

Vihman, M. M. (1976). From pre-speech to speech: On early phonology. *Papers and Reports on Child Language Development*, 12, 230–43.

Vihman, M. M. (1981). Phonology and the development of the lexicon: Evidence from children's errors. *Journal of Child Language*, 8, 239–64.

Vihman, M. M. (1982). The acquisition of morphology by a bilingual child: A whole-word approach. *Applied Psycholinguistics*, 3, 141–60.

Vihman, M. M. (1991). Ontogeny of phonetic gestures: Speech production. In I. G. Mattingly & M. Studdert-Kennedy (eds.), *Modularity and the Motor Theory of Speech Perception*, pp. 69–84. Mahwah, NJ: Lawrence Erlbaum.

Vihman, M. M. (1993). Variable paths to early word production. *Journal of Phonetics*, 21, 61–82.

Vihman, M. M. (1996). *Phonological Development: The Origins of Language in the Child*. Oxford: Basil Blackwell.

Vihman, M. M. (2000). Prosodic development: A cross-linguistic analysis of the first word period. End of award report, Economic and Social Research Council Award R000237087, January.

Vihman, M. M. (2002). Getting started without a system: From phonetics to phonology in bilingual development. *International Journal of Bilingualism*, 6, 239–54.

Vihman, M. M. (2003). Later phonological development. In J. E. Bernthal & N. W. Bankson (eds.), *Articulation and Phonological Disorders*, 5th edn., pp. 105–38. Englewood Cliffs, NJ: Prentice-Hall.

Vihman, M. M. (2010). Phonological templates in early words: A cross-linguistic study. In C. Fougeron, B. Kühnert, M. D'Imperio, & N. Vallée (eds.), *Laboratory Phonology 10*, pp. 261–84. New York: Mouton de Gruyter.

Vihman, M. M. (2014). *Phonological Development: The First Two Years*, 2nd edn. Malden, MA: Wiley-Blackwell.

Vihman, M. M. (2015). Perception and production in phonological development. In B. MacWhinney & W. O'Grady (eds.), *Handbook of Language Emergence*, pp. 437–57. Malden, MA: Wiley-Blackwell.

Vihman, M. M. (2016). Prosodic structures and templates in bilingual phonological development. *Bilingualism: Language and Cognition*, 19, 69–88.

Vihman, M. M. (2017). Learning words and learning sounds: Advances in language development. *British Journal of Psychology*, 108, 1–27.

Vihman, M. M. (2018). First word learning. In S.-A. Rueschemeyer & G. Gaskell (eds.), *The Oxford Handbook of Psycholinguistics*, 2nd edn, pp. 714–35. Oxford: Oxford University Press.

Vihman, M. M. & Boysson-Bardies, B. de (1994). The nature and origins of ambient language influence on infant vocal production and early words. *Phonetica*, 51, 159–69.

Vihman, M. M. & Croft, W. (2007). Phonological development: Toward a 'radical' templatic phonology. *Linguistics*, 45, 683–725. Reprinted in Vihman & Keren-Portnoy (2013b).

Vihman, M. M., DePaolis, R. A., & Davis, B. L. (1998). Is there a 'trochaic bias' in early word learning? Evidence from English and French. *Child Development*, 69, 933–47.

Vihman, M. M., DePaolis, R. A., & Keren-Portnoy, T. (2009). A dynamic systems approach to babbling and words. In E. Bavin (ed.), *The Cambridge Handbook of Child Language*, pp. 163–82. Cambridge: Cambridge University Press.

Vihman, M. M., DePaolis, R. A., & Keren-Portnoy, T. (2014). The role of production in infant word learning. *Language Learning*, 64, Suppl. 2, 121–40.

Vihman, M. M., DePaolis, R. A. & Keren-Portnoy, T. (2016). A dynamic systems approach to babbling and words. In E. L. Bavin & L. R. Naigles (eds.), *The Cambridge Handbook of Child Language*, 2nd edn., pp. 207–29. Cambridge: Cambridge University Press.

Vihman, M. M., Ferguson, C. A., & Elbert, M. (1986). Phonological development from babbling to speech: Common tendencies and individual differences. *Applied Psycholinguistics*, 7, 3–40.

Vihman, M. M. & Greenlee, M. (1987). Individual differences in phonological development: Ages one and three years. *Journal of Speech and Hearing Research*, 30, 503–21.

Vihman, M. M. & Hochberg, J. G. (1986). Velars and final consonants in early words. In J. A. Fishman et al. (eds.), *The Fergusonian Impact, 1: From Phonology to Society*. Berlin: Mouton de Gruyter.

Vihman, M. M., Kay, E., Boysson-Bardies, B. de, Durand, C., & Sundberg, U. (1994). External sources of individual differences? A cross-linguistic analysis of the phonetics of mothers' speech to one-year-old children. *Developmental Psychology*, 30, 652–63.

Vihman, M. M. & Keren-Portnoy, T. (2013a). Introduction. In M. M. Vihman & T. Keren-Portnoy (eds.), *The Emergence of Phonology: Whole-Word Approaches and Cross-Linguistic Evidence*, pp. 1–14. Cambridge: Cambridge University Press.

Vihman, M. M. & Keren-Portnoy, T. (eds.) (2013b). *The Emergence of Phonology: Whole-Word Approaches and Cross-Linguistic Evidence*. Cambridge: Cambridge University Press.

Vihman, M. M., Keren-Portnoy, T., Whitaker, C., Bidgood, A., & McGillion, M. (2013). Late talking toddlers: Relating early phonological development to later language advance. *York Papers in Linguistics*, 2, 47–68.

Vihman, M. M. & Kunnari, S. (2006). The sources of phonological knowledge: A cross-linguistic perspective. *Recherches Linguistiques de Vincennes*, 35, 133–64.

Vihman, M. M. & McCune L. (1994). When is a word a word? *Journal of Child Language*, 21, 517–42.

Vihman, M. M., Macken, M. A., Miller, R., Simmons, H., & Miller, J. (1985). From babbling to speech: A reassessment of the continuity issue. *Language*, 61, 395–443.

Vihman, M. M. & Majorano, M. (2017). The role of geminates in infants' early words and word-form recognition. *Journal of Child Language*, 44, 158–84.

Vihman, M. M. & Miller, R. (1988). Words and babble at the threshold of lexical acquisition. In M. D. Smith & J. L. Locke (eds.), *The Emergent Lexicon: The Child's Development of a Linguistic Vocabulary*, pp. 151–83. New York: Academic Press.

Vihman, M. M., Nakai, S., & DePaolis, R. A. (2006). Getting the rhythm right: A cross-linguistic study of segmental duration in babbling and first words. In L. Goldstein, D. Whalen, & C. Best (eds.), *Laboratory Phonology 8*, pp. 341–66. New York: Mouton de Gruyter.

Vihman, M. M., Nakai, S., DePaolis, R. A., & Hallé, P. (2004). The role of accentual pattern in early lexical representation. *Journal of Memory and Language*, 50, 336–53.

Vihman, M. M., Thierry, G., Lum, J., Keren-Portnoy, T., & Martin, P. (2007). Onset of word form recognition in English, Welsh and English–Welsh bilingual infants. *Applied Psycholinguistics*, 28, 475–93.

Vihman, M. M. & Velleman, S. (1989). Phonological reorganization: A case study. *Language and Speech*, 32, 149–70.

Vihman, M. M. & Velleman, S. L. (2000). Phonetics and the origins of phonology. In N. Burton-Roberts, P. Carr, & G. Docherty (eds.), *Phonological Knowledge: Its Nature and Status*, pp. 305–39. Oxford: Oxford University Press.

Vihman, M. M., Velleman, S. L., & McCune, L. (1994). How abstract is child phonology? Towards an integration of linguistic and psychological approaches. In M. Yavas (ed.), *First and Second Language Phonology*, pp. 9–94. San Diego: Singular Publishing.

Vihman, M. M. & Vihman, V.-A. (2011). From first words to segments: A case study in phonological development. In I. Arnon & E. V. Clark (eds.), *Experience, Variation, and Generalization: Learning a First Language*. Trends in Language Acquisition Research 7, pp. 109–33. Amsterdam: John Benjamins.

Vihman, V.-A. & Vihman, M. M. (2017). 'Lähme mintsi!' Ühest produktiivsest morfofonoloogisest mallist ['Let's go to my place!' On a productive morphophonological template]. *Muutuva keele päev* [Dynamic Language Day]. Workshop, University of Tallinn, November.

Viks, Ü. (1992). *Morphological Dictionary of Estonian: Introduction and Grammar*. Tallinn: Keel ja Kirjanduse Instituut.

Vitevitch, M. S. (1997). The neighborhood characteristics of malapropisms. *Language and Speech*, 40, 211–28.

Vitevich, M. S. & Luce, P. A. (1998). Probabilistic phonotactics and neighborhood activation in spoken word recognition. *Journal of Memory and Language*, 40, 374–408.

Wade, T. & Möbius, B. (2010). Detailed phonetic memory for multi-word and part-word sequences. *Journal of Lab Phonology*, 1, 283–94.

Waterson, N. (1971). Child phonology: A prosodic view. *Journal of Linguistics*, 7, 179–211. Reprinted in Vihman & Keren-Portnoy (2013b).

Waterson, N. (1987). *Prosodic Phonology: The Theory and its Application to Language Acquisition and Speech Processing*. Newcastle upon Tyne: Grevatt & Grevatt.

Wauquier S. (2014). Templates and representations in phonology: From Semitic to child language. In S. Benjaballah, N. Faust, M. Lahrouchi, & N. Lapitelli (eds.), *The Form of Structure, the Structure of Form: Essays in honor of Jean Lowenstamm*, pp. 219–34. Université Paris: Diderot.

Wauquier, S. & Yamaguchi, N. (2013). Templates in French. In M. M. Vihman & T. Keren-Portnoy (eds.), *The Emergence of Phonology: Whole-Word Approaches and Cross-Linguistic Evidence*, pp. 317–42. Cambridge: Cambridge University Press.

Wedel, A., Jackson, S., & Kaplan, A. (2013). Functional load and the lexicon: Evidence that syntactic category and frequency relationships in minimal lemma pairs predict the loss of phoneme contrasts in language change. *Language and Speech*, 56, 395–417.

Weeda, D. (1992). Word truncation in prosodic morphology. Unpublished PhD thesis. University of Texas, Austin.

Werker, J. F. & Curtin, S. (2005). PRIMIR: A developmental framework of infant speech processing. *Language, Learning and Development*, 1, 197–234.

Wheatley, H. B. (1866). *A Dictionary of Reduplicated Words in the English Language* (Appendix to the *Transactions of the Philological Society* for 1865). London: Asher & Co.

Wheeldon, L. (2003). Inhibitory form priming of spoken word production. *Language and Cognitive Processes*, 18, 81–109.

Williams, J. R. (1993). *A Paradigm Lost: The Linguistic Theory of Mikolaj Kruszewski*. Amsterdam: John Benjamins.

Wood, N. & Cowan, N. (1995). The cocktail party phenomenon revisited. *Journal of Experimental Psychology: Learning, Memory, and Cognition*, 21, 255–60.

Woodward, A. L. (2009). Infants' grasp of others' intentions. *Current Directions in Psychological Science*, 18, 53–7.

Yeni-Komshian, G. H., Kavanagh, J. F., & Ferguson, C. A. (eds.) (1980). *Child Phonology*, vol. 1: *Production*; vol. 2: *Perception*. New York: Academic Press.

Yeung, H. & Werker, J. F. (2013). Lip movements affect infants' audiovisual speech perception. *Psychological Science*, 24, 603–12.

Yip, M. (1992). Reduplication with fixed melodic material. *Proceedings of the New England Linguistic Society*, 22, 459–76. Amherst: GLSA.

Zanobini, M., Viterbori, P., & Saraceno, F. (2012). Phonology and language development in Italian children: An analysis of production and accuracy. *Journal of Speech, Language and Hearing Research*, 55, 16–31.

Zwicky, A. M. (1978–9). Classical malapropisms. *Language Sciences*, 1, 339–48.

Author index

Subject index